Pro Hibernate and MongoDB

Anghel Leonard

Apress·

Pro Hibernate and MongoDB

ISBN-13 (pbk): 978-1-4302-5794-3

ISBN-13 (electronic): 978-1-4302-5795-0

President and Publisher: Paul Manning
Lead Editor: Steve Anglin
Technical Reviewer: Manuel Jordan
Editorial Board: Steve Anglin, Ewan Buckingham, Gary Cornell, Louise Corrigan, Morgan Ertel,
    Jonathan Gennick, Jonathan Hassell, Robert Hutchinson, Michelle Lowman, James Markham,
    Matthew Moodie, Jeff Olson, Jeffrey Pepper, Douglas Pundick, Ben Renow-Clarke, Dominic Shakeshaft,
    Gwenan Spearing, Matt Wade, Tom Welsh
Coordinating Editor: Kevin Shea
Copy Editor: Sharon Terdeman
Compositor: SPi Global
Indexer: SPi Global
Artist: SPi Global
Cover Designer: Anna Ishchenko

Distributed to the book trade worldwide by Springer Science+Business Media New York, 233 Spring Street, 6th Floor, New York, NY 10013. Phone 1-800-SPRINGER, fax (201) 348-4505, e-mail orders-ny@springer-sbm.com, or visit www.springeronline.com.

For information on translations, please e-mail rights@apress.com, or visit www.apress.com.

Apress and friends of ED books may be purchased in bulk for academic, corporate, or promotional use. eBook versions and licenses are also available for most titles. For more information, reference our Special Bulk Sales–eBook Licensing web page at www.apress.com/bulk-sales.

Any source code or other supplementary materials referenced by the author in this text is available to readers at www.apress.com. For detailed information about how to locate your book's source code, go to www.apress.com/source-code/.

This book is dedicated to Rafael Nadal.
Of course, it is also dedicated to my parents and my wife.
Love you all, each and every one.

—Anghel Leonard

Contents at a Glance

Contents

About the Author

Anghel Leonard is a senior Java developer with more than 12 years of experience in Java SE, Java EE, and related frameworks. He has written and published more than 50 articles about Java technologies and more than 500 tips and tricks for JavaBoutique, O'Reilly, DevX, Developer and InformIT. In addition, he wrote two books about XML and Java (one for beginners and one for advanced developers) for Albastra, a Romanian publisher; three books for Packt: JBoss Tools 3 Developer Guide, JSF 2.0 Cookbook, and JSF 2.0 Cookbook LITE; and two books for Apress: Pro Java 7 NIO 2, and Pro Hibernate and MongoDB. Currently, he's developing web applications using the latest Java technologies (EJB 3.0, CDI, Spring, JSF, Struts, Hibernate, and so on). For the past two years, he has focused on developing rich Internet applications for geographic information systems.

About the Technical Reviewer

Manuel Jordan Elera is an autodidactic developer and researcher who enjoys learning new technologies for his own experiments and for creating new integrations.

Manuel won the 2010 Springy Award—Community Champion. In his little free time, he reads the Bible and composes music on his guitar. Manuel is a senior member, known as dr_pompeii, of the Spring Community Forums.

Manuel has served as a technical reviewer for the following books (all published by Apress):

- Pro SpringSource dm Server (2009)
- Spring Enterprise Recipes (2009)
- Spring Recipes (Second Edition) (2010)
- Pro Spring Integration (2011)
- Pro Spring Batch (2011)
- Pro Spring 3 (2012)
- Pro Spring MVC: With Web Flow (2012)
- Pro Spring Security (2013)

You can read his blog and contact him at http://manueljordan.wordpress.com/. You can also follow his Twitter account, @dr_pompeii.

Acknowledgments

Thank you, God, because without you nothing is possible. Thank you to the Apress team for trusting in me to write this book and for the hard work you put into this project. Special thanks to Steve Anglin, Manuel Jordan, Kevin Shea, Sharon Terdeman, and Tom Welsh.

—Anghel Leonard

Introduction

This book covers all the important aspects of developing Hibernate OGM-MongoDB applications. It provides clear instructions for getting the most out of the Hibernate OGM-MongoDB duo and offers many examples of integrating Hibernate OGM by means of both the Hibernate Native API and the Java Persistence API. You will learn how to develop desktop, web, and enterprise applications for the most popular web and enterprise servers, such as Tomcat, JBoss AS, and Glassfish AS. You'll see how to take advantage of Hibernate OGM-MongoDB together with many common technologies, such as JSF, Spring, Seam, EJB, and more. Finally, you'll learn how to migrate to the cloud—MongoHQ, MongoLab, and OpenShift.

Who This Book Is For

This book is for experienced Java developers who are interested in exploring Hibernate solutions for NoSQL databases. For the opening chapters (Chapters 1–3), it's enough to be familiar with the main aspects of the ORM paradigm, the Hibernate Native API, and JPA. The book provides brief overviews of these concepts. Starting with Chapter 4, you should have some knowledge about developing web applications (using NetBeans or Eclipse) deployed under the Tomcat, JBoss AS, or GlassFish AS servers. Moreover, you need to be familiar with the Java technologies and frameworks that are commonly used in web applications, such as servlets, EJB, JSF, JSP, Seam, Spring, and so on.

How This Book Is Structured

Here's the main focus of each chapter:

Chapter 1: Getting Started with Hibernate OGM

This chapter provides a brief introduction to the Hibernate OGM world. In the first part of the chapter, I discuss the Hibernate OGM architecture, its current features, and what we can expect in terms of future support. I then offer several alternatives for downloading, installing, and configuring Hibernate OGM and MongoDB.

Chapter 2: Hibernate OGM and MongoDB

In this chapter, I define more clearly the relationship between Hibernate OGM and MongoDB by focusing on how Hibernate OGM works with MongoDB. You learn how data is stored, how primary keys and associations are mapped, and how to deal with transactions and queries.

Chapter 3: Bootstrapping Hibernate OGM

This chapter shows how Hibernate OGM can be bootstrapped by means of the Hibernate Native API and JPA.

Chapter 4: Hibernate OGM at Work

This is one of the most important chapters. You learn how to integrate Hibernate OGM and MongoDB in the most common web and enterprise Java applications deployed on different servers. Here is the entire list of applications:

- Java SE and Mongo DB—a "Hello world" example
- Hibernate OGM (via Hibernate Native API) in a non-JTA environment (JDBC Transactions, Tomcat 7)
- Hibernate OGM (via Hibernate Native API) in a standalone JTA environment (JBoss JTA, Tomcat 7)
- Hibernate OGM (via Hibernate Native API) in a built-in JTA environment (no EJB, GlassFish 3)
- Hibernate OGM (via Hibernate Native API) in a built-in JTA environment (EJB/BMT, GlassFish 3)
- Hibernate OGM (via Hibernate Native API) in a built-in JTA environment (EJB/CMT, GlassFish 3)
- Hibernate OGM (via JPA) in a built-in JTA environment (GlassFish AS 3)
- Hibernate OGM (via JPA) in a built-in JTA environment (JBoss AS 7)
- Hibernate OGM (via JPA) in a built-in JTA environment (JBoss AS 7 and Seam application)
- Hibernate OGM (via JPA) in a built-in JTA environment (GlassFish and Spring application)
- Hibernate OGM (via JPA) JPA/JTA in a standalone JTA environment (Tomcat)
- Hibernate OGM in a non- JTA environment (RESOURCE_LOCAL, Apache Tomcat 7)

Chapter 5: Hibernate OGM and JPA 2.0 Annotations

Mapping Java entities in Hibernate OGM can be divided into supported and non-supported annotations. In this chapter, I show the supported annotations, as well as how much of each annotation is supported.

Chapter 6: Hibernate OGM Querying MongoDB

This chapter explores the querying capabilities of Hibernate OGM. I start with a MongoDB native query and progress to complex queries written with Hibernate Search and Apache Lucene.

Chapter 7: MongoDB e-Commerce Database Model

At this point in the book, you will have acquired suffcient expertise to develop a real application that involves Hibernate OGM and MongoDB. An e-commerce web site is a good start and an interesting study case, so in this chapter I adapt a classic SQL database model to the Hibernate OGM and MongoDB style. I also examine aspects of e-commerce database architecture.

Chapter 8: MongoDB e-Commerce Database Querying

After you develop a MongoDB e-commerce database model, it's time to sketch and implement the main e-commerce-specific queries. In this chapter, I use Hibernate Search and Apache Lucene to write such queries. The result is a complete e-commerce application named RafaEShop.

Chapter 9: Migrate MongoDB Database to Cloud

In this chapter, you learn how to migrate the MongoDB e-commerce database developed in Chapter 7 into two clouds: MongoHQ and MongoLab.

Chapter 10: Migrating RafaEShop Application on OpenShift

This final chapter is a detailed guide for migrating the e-commerce RafaEShop application to the OpenShift cloud on two enterprise servers: JBoss AS and GlassFish AS.

Downloading the Code

The code for the examples shown in this book is available on the Apress web site, `www.apress.com`. You'll find the link on the book's information page under the Source Code/Downloads tab. This tab is located underneath the Related Titles section of the page.

Contacting the Author

Should you have any questions or comments—or even spot a mistake you think I should know about—you can contact me at `leoprivacy@yahoo.com`.

CHAPTER 1

■ ■ ■

Getting Started with Hibernate OGM

Chances are, you're familiar with Hibernate ORM, a powerful, robust tool for converting data between relational databases (RDBMS) and object-oriented programming languages. As an object-relational mapping (ORM) framework, Hibernate ORM works with SQL stores. In recent years, however, developers have become interested in NoSQL databases, which are optimized for storing and retrieving enormous quantities of data. NoSQL databases tend to be non-relational, open-source, horizontally scalable, distributed, and schema-free.

There are a number of ways to describe NoSQL stores, but they are generally classified by data model, particularly the following:

- Document stores (Mongo DB, RavenDB, CouchDB and more)

- Wide column stores (Hypertable, Cassandra, HBase and more)

- Key value/tuple stores (DynamoDB, LevelDB, Redis, Ryak and more)

- Graph databases (Neo4J, GraphBase, InfoGrid and more)

These are also common:

- Multimodel databases (OrientDB, ArangoDB and more)

- Object databases (db4o, Versant and more)

- Grid and cloud databases (GigaSpaces, Infinispan and more)

- XML databases (eXist, Sedna and more)

Clearly, NoSQL stores are complex and very diverse. Some have significant user bases, while others are barely known. And each has its own strong points and weaknesses. You could even say that NoSQL is such a keenly disputed topic that programmers talk about it more than they actually use it.

That's likely to change, however, with the recent release of the Hibernate OGM (Object Grid Mapper) project, which offers a complete Java Persistence API (JPA) engine for storing data in NoSQL stores. This project gives a real boost to Java developers looking to exploit NoSQL stores, since it provides a common interface—the well-known JPA programming model—as a front end to various NoSQL approaches. Hibernate OGM is based on the Hibernate ORM Core engine, reuses the Java Persistence Query Language (JP-QL) as an interface for querying stored data, and already provides support for three NoSQL stores: MongoDB, Ehcache, and Infinispan, and Apache Cassandra should see support in the future. Despite the youth of the project, the aims of the Hibernate OGM team guarantee it has huge potential in the future—and a lot of work to accomplish.

Features and Expectations

As this book is written, the latest Hibernate OGM distribution is 4.0.0 Beta2, which already successfully provides a common interface for different NoSQL approaches; rapid scaling of a data store up or down; independence from the underlying store technology; and Hibernate Search. Here's what Hibernate OGM supports so far:

- Storing data in document stores (MongoDB)

- storing data in key/value stores (Infinispan's data grid and Ehcache)

- Create, Read, Update and Delete (CRUD) operations for JPA entities

- Polymorphic entities (support for superclasses, subclasses, and so forth)

- Embeddable objects (for example, embeddable classes, annotated in JPA with @Embeddable; collections of instances of embeddable classes, annotated in JPA with @ElementCollection)

- Basic types (such as numbers, String, URL, Date, enums)

- Associations (@ManyToOne, @OneToOne, @OneToMany and @ManyToMany)

- Bidirectional associations

- Collections (Set, List, Map, etc)

- Hibernate Search's full-text queries

- JPA and native Hibernate ORM API (Hibernate OGM can be bootstrapped via JPA or via Hibernate Session, as I'll show you in Chapter 3.)

In the future, Hibernate OGM will support:

- Other key/value pair systems

- Other NoSQL engines

- Declarative denormalization

- Complex JP-QL queries, including to-many joins and aggregation

- Fronting existing JPA applications

■ **Note**   Denormalization is a database technique for speeding up the read process. The idea is to reduce the number of joins in queries as much as possible; joins slow read performance because data must be picked up from multiple tables without disrupting their associations. While normalization promotes splitting related data into multiple associated tables, denormalization encourages adding a small number of redundancies to limit joins. Even if some data gets duplicated, performance generally improves.

Hibernate OGM Architecture

Because Hibernate OGM uses the existing Hibernate ORM modules as much as possible, the OGM architecture essentially extends the ORM architecture by plugging different components in and out. Hibernate ORM converts and persists data between relational databases and object-oriented programming languages using a set of interfaces and classes. These include the JDBC layer, used for connecting to databases and sending queries, and the Persisters and Loaders interfaces, responsible for persisting and loading entities and collections, as shown in Figure 1-1.

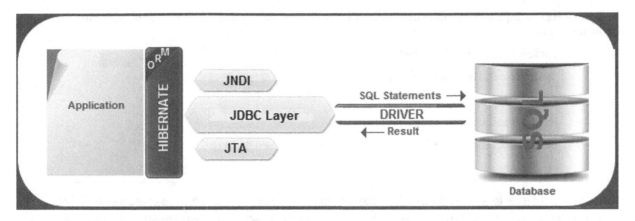

Figure 1-1. *Hibernate ORM Architecture*

Hibernate OGM is meant to accomplish the same goals, but using NoSQL stores. Thus, Hibernate OGM doesn't need the JDBC layer anymore and instead comes with two new elements: a *datastore provider* and a *datastore dialect*, as shown in Figure 1-2. Both of these act as adaptors between Hibernate OGM Core and the NoSQL store. (A *datastore* is an adaptor that connects the core mapping engine with the specific NoSQL technology.)

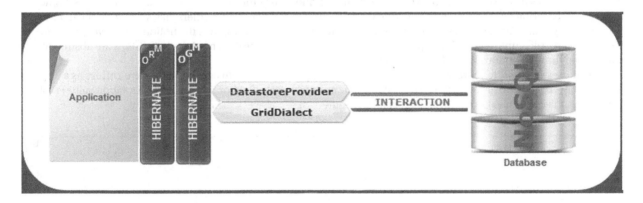

Figure 1-2. *Hibernate OGM datastore provider and datastore dialect*

The datastore provider is responsible for managing connections to NoSQL stores, while the datastore dialect manages communications with NoSQL storage engines. Practically, these notions are materialized in two interfaces, org.hibernate.ogm.datastore.spi.DatastoreProvider and org.hibernate.ogm.dialect.GridDialect. The DatastoreProvider interface is responsible for starting, maintaining, and stopping a store connection, while the GridDialect interface deals with data persistence in NoSQL stores. Moreover, the Persisters and Loaders interfaces were rewritten to support NoSQL store features.

Currently there are four implementations of DatastoreProvider:

- EhcacheDatastoreProvider (for NoSQL Encache)

- InfinispanDatastoreProvider (for NoSQL Infinispan)

- MongoDBDatastoreProvider (for NoSQL MongoDB)

- MapDatastoreProvider (for testing purposes)

There are five implementations of GridDialect for abstracting Hibernate OGM from a particular grid implementation:

- EhcacheDialect (for EhCache)

- InfinispanDialect (for Infinispan)

- MongoDBDialect (for MongoDB)

- HashMapDialect (for testing)

- GridDialectLogger (for logging calls performed on the real dialect)

■ **Note** If you decide to write a new datastore, you have to implement a DatastoreProvider and a GridDialect. Find more details about this at https://community.jboss.org/wiki/HowToWriteADatastoreInHibernateOGM.

Persisting Data

Through the modified Loaders and Persisters interfaces, Hibernate OGM is capable of saving data to NoSQL stores. Before doing so, however, OGM needs to represent and store the data internally. For this purpose, Hibernate OGM retains as much as it can of the relational database concepts, and adapts these notions according to its needs. Some concepts, like storing entities, follow the relational model fairly completely, while others, like storing associations, do so partially. Data, therefore, is stored as basic types (entities are stored as tuples); the notions of *primary key* and *foreign key* are still employed; and the application data model and the store data model relationships are abstractly maintained through notions like *table* and *column*.

OGM uses the *tuple* to represent the basic unit of data. Tuples are meant to conceptually store entities as a Map<String, Object>. The key is the column name (the entity property/field or the @Column annotation value) and the value is the column value as a primitive type (see Figure 1-3).

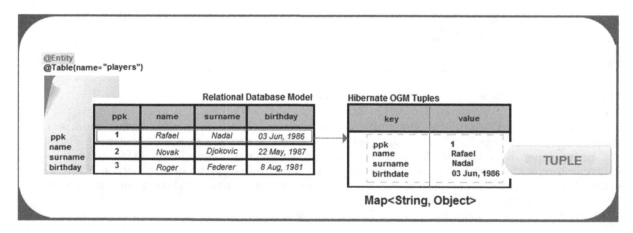

Figure 1-3. *The Hibernate OGM tuple*

Each tuple, representing an entity instance, is stored in a specific key. An entity instance is identified with a specific key lookup composed of the table name, the primary key column name(s), and the primary key column value(s). See Figure 1-4.

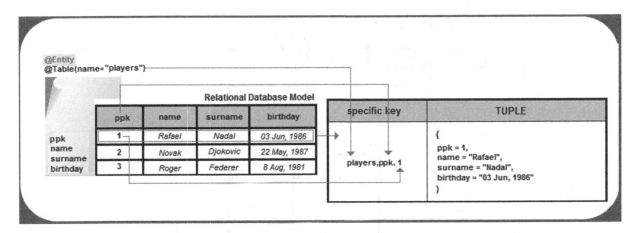

Figure 1-4. *Hibernate OGM storing an entity instance*

▪ **Note**   Java collections are represented as a list of tuples. The specific key is composed of the name of the table containing the collection, and column names and column values representing the foreign key.

Figure 1-5 shows the relational database model of a many-to-many association.

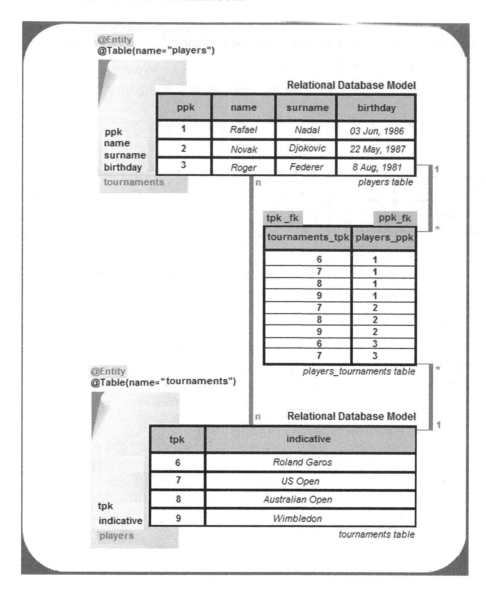

Figure 1-5. *Relational database model of a many-to-many association*

Associations in Hibernate OGM, in contrast, are stored as sets of tuples of type `Map<String, Object>`. For example, for a many-to-many association, each tuple stores a pair of foreign keys. Hibernate OGM stores the information necessary to navigate from an entity to its associations in a specific key composed of the table name and the column name(s) and value(s) representing the foreign key to the entity we come from. This `@ManyToMany` association is stored internally by Hibernate OGM as shown in Figure 1-6. (You can see the association tuples starting with row 8.) This approach fosters reachable data via key lookups, but it has disadvantages: that data may be redundant since the information has to be stored for both sides of the association.

key	value
players, ppk, 1	{ppk=1, name="Rafael", surname="Nadal", birthday="03 Jun, 1986"}
players, ppk, 2	{ppk=2, name="Novak", surname="Djokovic", birthday="22 May, 1987"}
players, ppk, 3	{ppk=3, name="Roger", surname="Federer", birthday="8 Aug, 1981"}
tournaments, tpk, 6	{tpk=6, indicative="Roland Garos"}
tournaments, tpk, 7	{tpk=7, indicative="US Open"}
tournaments, tpk, 8	{tpk=8, indicative="Australian Open"}
tournaments, tpk, 9	{tpk=9, indicative="Wimbledon"}
players_tournaments, ppk_fk , 1	{{ppk_fk =1, tpk_fk =6}, {ppk_fk=1, tpk_fk=7}, {ppk_fk =1, tpk _fk =8}, {ppk_fk=1, tpk _fk =9}}
players_tournaments, ppk_fk , 2	{{ppk_fk =2, tpk_fk =7}, {ppk_fk =2, tpk_fk =8}, {ppk _fk =2, tpk_fk =9}}
players_tournaments, ppk_fk , 3	{{ppk_fk =3, tpk_fk =6}, {ppk_fk =3, tpk_fk =7}}
players_tournaments, tpk_fk , 6	{{ppk_fk=1, tpk_fk=6}, {ppk_fk=3, tpk_fk=6}}
players_tournaments, tpk_fk , 7	{{ppk_fk=1, tpk_fk=7}, {ppk_fk=2, tpk _fk=7}, {ppk_fk=3, tpk_fk=7}}
players_tournaments, tpk_fk , 8	{{ppk_fk=1, tpk_fk =8}, {ppk_fk =2, tpk_fk =8}}
players_tournaments, tpk_fk , 9	{{ppk_fk=1, tpk_fk =9}, {ppk_fk =2, tpk_fk =9}}

Figure 1-6. Hibernate OGM data grid of a many-to-many relationship

Hibernate OGM stores JPA entities as tuples instead of serializable blobs. This is much closer to the relational model. There are a few disadvantages in serializing entities:

- Entities that are in associations with other entities must be also be stored, very possibly resulting in a big graph.

- It's hard to guarantee object identity or even consistency among duplicated objects.

- It's hard to add or remove a property or include a superclass and deal with deserialization issues.

■ **Note**   Hibernate OGM stores seeds (when identifiers requires seeds) in the value whose key is composed of the table name and the column name and column value representing the segment.

Obviously, this representation is not common to all NoSQL stores. It's different, for instance, for MongoDB, which is a document-oriented store. In such cases, `GridDialect` is used, and its main task consists of converting this representation into the expected representation for the NoSQL store. For MongoDB, the `MongoDBDialect` converts it into MongoDB documents.

■ **Note**   Since NoSQL stores are not aware of the *schema* notion, Hibernate OGM tuples are not tied to schemas.

Querying Data

Of course, Hibernate OGM needs to offer a powerful querying data engine and, at the time of this writing, this is implemented in a number of different ways depending on the nature of the query and the NoSQL querying support.

CRUD operations are the responsibility of the Hibernate ORM engine and they follow a straightforward process. Independently of JPA or the Hibernate Native API, Hibernate ORM delegates persistence and load queries to the OGM engine, which delegates CRUD operations to `DatastoreProvider/GridDialect`, which interacts with the NoSQL store. Figure 1-7 depicts this process.

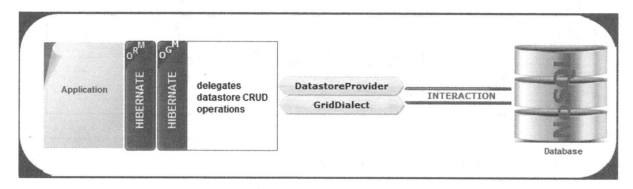

Figure 1-7. *Hibernate OGM and CRUD operations*

Because Hibernate OGM wants to offer the entire JPA, it needs to support JP-QL queries. This implies a sophisticated query engine (QE) that should be sensitive to the particular NoSQL store querying capabilities and to JP-QL query complexity. The most optimistic instance is NoSQL with query capabilities and simple JP-QL queries. In this case, the query is delegated to the NoSQL-specific query translator, and the results are managed by Hibernate OGM to compose the specific objects (see Figure 1-8).

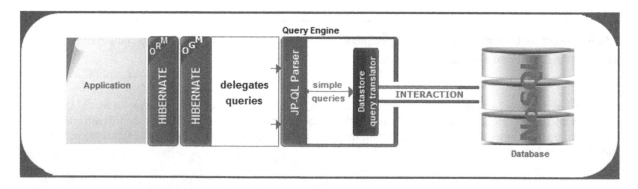

Figure 1-8. *Hibernate OGM and JP-QL simple queries (NoSQL with query support)*

A less optimistic case arises when a NoSQL store does not support the current query. In this case, the JBoss Teiid data virtualization system intervenes to split the JP-QL query into simple queries that can be executed by the data store. (See `www.jboss.org/teiid` for more information). Teiid also processes the results to obtain the final query result, as Figure 1-9 shows.

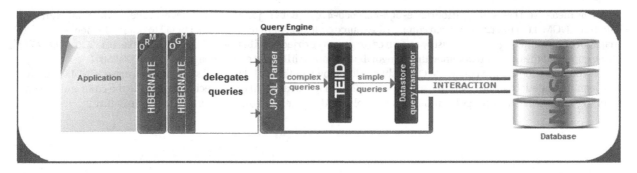

Figure 1-9. *Hibernate OGM and JP-QL complex queries*

The worst case is a NoSQL store that has little or no query support. Since this is a hard case, it requires heavy artillery, like Hibernate Search, an enterprise full-text search tool based on Hibernate Core and Apache Lucene. Basically, the Hibernate Search Indexing Engine receives events from the Hibernate ORM Core and keeps the entity indexing process up to date, while the JP-QL Query Parser delegates query translation to the Hibernate Search Query Engine (for simple queries) or to Teiid (for intermediate to complex queries), and executes them using Lucene indexes (see Figure 1-10). In addition, Hibernate Search provides clustering support and an object-oriented abstraction that includes a query domain-specific language (DSL).

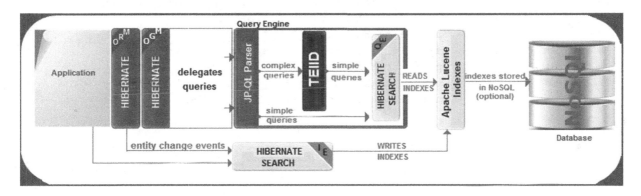

Figure 1-10. *Hibernate OGM and JP-QL queries (little or no NoSQL support)*

Get the Hibernate OGM Distribution

At the time of writing, the Hibernate OGM distribution was 4.0.0.Beta2. The best way to get it with full documentation, sources, and dependencies is to access `www.hibernate.org/subprojects/ogm.html` and download the corresponding ZIP/TGZ archive.

Unfortunately, this isn't as simple as it might seem. Since the focus of this book is Hibernate OGM and MongoDB, you'll want to locate the JARs dedicated to "connecting" OGM with MongoDB: `hibernate-ogm-mongodb-x.jar` and `mongo-java-driver-x.jar`. (MongoDB has client support for most programming languages; this is the MongoDB Java driver developed by MongoDB team and used by Hibernate OGM to interact with MongoDB). In Hibernate OGM version 4.0.0.Beta1, you'll find these JARs in the `\hibernate-ogm-4.0.0.Beta1\dist\lib\mongodb` folder: `hibernate-ogm-mongodb-4.0.0.Beta1.jar` and `mongo-java-driver-2.8.0.jar`. In Hibernate OGM version 4.0.0.Beta2, the `\mongodb` folder is missing, so the new JARs are not bundled out of the box.

This means you can still use hibernate-ogm-mongodb-4.0.0.Beta1.jar and mongo-java-driver-2.8.0.jar with Hibernate OGM 4.0.0.Beta2, or you can compile the source code of Hibernate OGM 4.0.0.Beta2 to obtain the newest snapshots. For compiling the code, visit www.sourceforge.net/projects/hibernate/files/hibernate-ogm/4.0.0.Beta2/. I have compiled the code and obtained the MongoDB JAR, named hibernate-ogm-mongodb-4.0.0-SNAPSHOT.

If you take a look at the Hibernate OGM change log shown in Figure 1-11, you'll see that Hibernate OGM 4.0.0.Beta2 has been upgraded to support MongoDB Java Driver 2.9.x. This means that if you decide to compile the code and use the resulting snapshot of the MongoDB profile, you can also add a 2.9.x MongoDB Java driver, instead of 2.8.x.

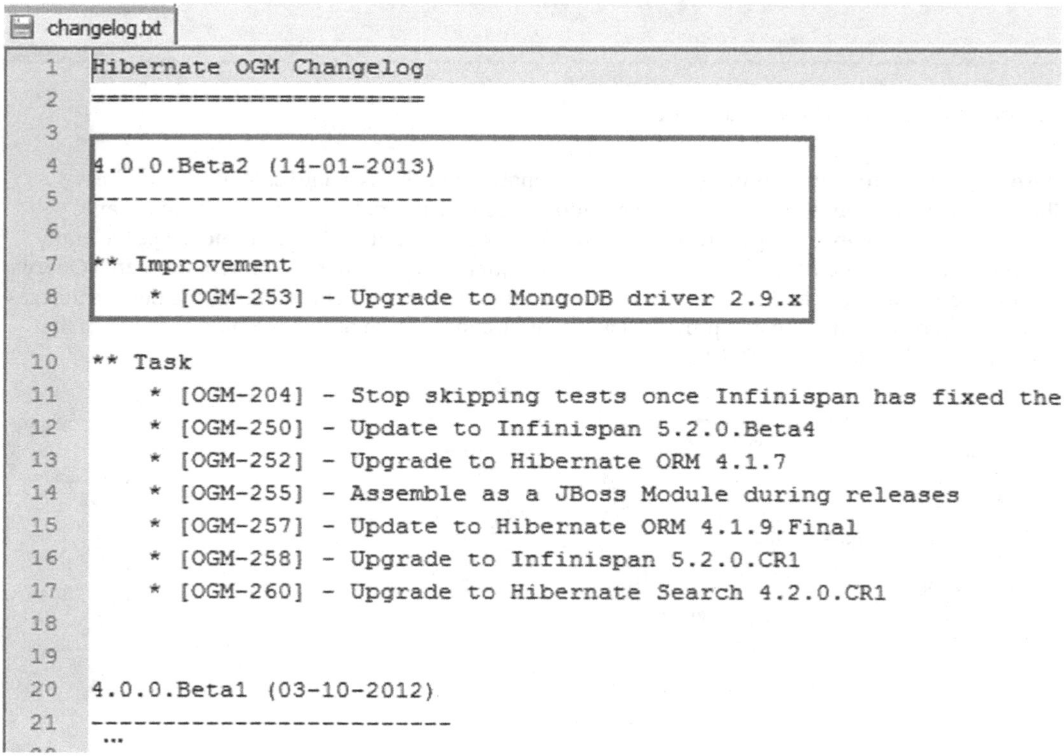

```
changelog.txt

1   Hibernate OGM Changelog
2   ========================
3
4   4.0.0.Beta2 (14-01-2013)
5   ------------------------
6
7   ** Improvement
8       * [OGM-253] - Upgrade to MongoDB driver 2.9.x
9
10  ** Task
11      * [OGM-204] - Stop skipping tests once Infinispan has fixed the
12      * [OGM-250] - Update to Infinispan 5.2.0.Beta4
13      * [OGM-252] - Upgrade to Hibernate ORM 4.1.7
14      * [OGM-255] - Assemble as a JBoss Module during releases
15      * [OGM-257] - Update to Hibernate ORM 4.1.9.Final
16      * [OGM-258] - Upgrade to Infinispan 5.2.0.CR1
17      * [OGM-260] - Upgrade to Hibernate Search 4.2.0.CR1
18
19
20  4.0.0.Beta1 (03-10-2012)
21  ------------------------
        ...
```

Figure 1-11. *Hibernate OGM change log*

For this book, I chose to use the Hibernate OGM 4.0.0.Beta2 with Hibernate OGM for MongoDB 4.0.0.Beta1.

Getting Hibernate OGM from the Maven Central Repository

You can also download Hibernate OGM from the Maven Central Repository (www.search.maven.org/). Search for "hibernate ogm," which will return what you see in Figure 1-12.

≡ The Central Repository

```
hibernate ogm
```
SEARCH

New: App Scan   Advanced Search | API Guide | Help

Search Results

< 1 > displaying 1 to 6 of 6

GroupId	ArtifactId	Latest Version	Updated	Download
org.hibernate.ogm	hibernate-ogm-parent	4.0.0.Beta2 all (4)	14-Jan-2013	pom tests.jar
org.hibernate.ogm	hibernate-ogm-modules	4.0.0.Beta2	14-Jan-2013	pom jbossas-71-dist.zip tests.jar
org.hibernate.ogm	hibernate-ogm-infinispan	4.0.0.Beta2 all (2)	14-Jan-2013	pom jar javadoc.jar sources.jar tests.jar
org.hibernate.ogm	hibernate-ogm-ehcache	4.0.0.Beta2 all (2)	14-Jan-2013	pom jar javadoc.jar sources.jar tests.jar
org.hibernate.ogm	hibernate-ogm-core	4.0.0.Beta2 all (4)	14-Jan-2013	pom jar javadoc.jar sources.jar tests.jar
org.hibernate.ogm	hibernate-ogm-mongodb	4.0.0.Beta1	02-Oct-2012	pom jar javadoc.jar sources.jar tests.jar

Figure 1-12. *Hibernate OGM distribution listed in Maven Central Repository*

As you can see, it's very easy to dowload the Hibernate OGM core and profiles, including the MongoDB profile. You can download the JARs or the POMs (Project Object Model) files.

Getting Hibernate OGM from the Maven Command Line

Hibernate OGM is also available from the Apache Maven command line. Obviously, Maven must be installed and configured on your computer. First, you have to modify your `settings.xml` document, which is stored in the Maven local repository `.m2` folder (the default location). For Unix/Mac OS X users, this folder should be `~/.m2`; for Windows users, it's `C:\Documents and Settings\{your username}\.m2` or `C:\Users\{your username}\.m2`. If the `settings.xml` file doesn't already exist, you should create it in this folder, as shown in Listing 1-1. (If you already have this file, just modify its contents accordingly.)

■ **Note** If it seems too complicated to create or modify `settings.xml` since it's so verbose, you can simply use `<repository>` and `<dependency>` tags in your `pom.xml`.

Listing 1-1. Settings.xml

```xml
<?xml version="1.0" encoding="UTF-8"?>

<settings xmlns="http://maven.apache.org/SETTINGS/1.0.0"
xmlns:xsi="http://www.w3.org/2001/XMLSchema-instance"
         xsi:schemaLocation="http://maven.apache.org/SETTINGS/1.0.0
                              http://maven.apache.org/xsd/settings-1.0.0.xsd">
<!-- jboss.org config start -->
<profiles>
   <profile>
     <id>jboss-public-repository</id>
     <repositories>
       <repository>
         <id>jboss-public-repository-group</id>
         <name>JBoss Public Maven Repository Group</name>
```

```xml
          <url>https://repository.jboss.org/nexus/content/groups/public-jboss/</url>
          <layout>default</layout>
          <releases>
            <enabled>true</enabled>
            <updatePolicy>never</updatePolicy>
          </releases>
          <snapshots>
            <enabled>true</enabled>
            <updatePolicy>never</updatePolicy>
          </snapshots>
        </repository>
      </repositories>
      <pluginRepositories>
        <pluginRepository>
          <id>jboss-public-repository-group</id>
          <name>JBoss Public Maven Repository Group</name>
          <url>https://repository.jboss.org/nexus/content/groups/public-jboss/</url>
          <layout>default</layout>
          <releases>
            <enabled>true</enabled>
            <updatePolicy>never</updatePolicy>
          </releases>
          <snapshots>
            <enabled>true</enabled>
            <updatePolicy>never</updatePolicy>
          </snapshots>
        </pluginRepository>
      </pluginRepositories>
    </profile>
    <profile>
      <id>jboss-deprecated-repository</id>
      <repositories>
        <repository>
          <id>jboss-deprecated-repository</id>
          <name>JBoss Deprecated Maven Repository</name>
          <url>https://repository.jboss.org/nexus/content/repositories/deprecated/</url>
          <layout>default</layout>
          <releases>
            <enabled>true</enabled>
            <updatePolicy>never</updatePolicy>
          </releases>
          <snapshots>
            <enabled>false</enabled>
            <updatePolicy>never</updatePolicy>
          </snapshots>
        </repository>
      </repositories>
    </profile>
    <!-- jboss.org config end -->
  </profiles>
```

```
<!-- jboss.org config start -->
<activeProfiles>
  <activeProfile>jboss-public-repository</activeProfile>
</activeProfiles>
<!-- jboss.org config end -->
</settings>
```

■ **Note**   You can modify the default location of the Maven local repository by adding into settings.xml the tag localRepository, like this: `<localRepository>new_repository_path</localRepository>`.

Next, you need to create a pom.xml file. Obviously, this file's content depends on what you want to obtain from the Hibernate OGM repository. For example, the pom.xml in Listing 1-2 will download the Hibernate OGM Core distribution (including dependencies) and store it locally in D:/Hibernate_OGM (you can also use the default ./m2 folder, but this makes it much clearer and easier to navigate).

Listing 1-2. Pom.xml

```
<project xmlns="http://maven.apache.org/POM/4.0.0"
         xmlns:xsi="http://www.w3.org/2001/XMLSchema-instance"
         xsi:schemaLocation="http://maven.apache.org/POM/4.0.0
http://maven.apache.org/xsd/maven-4.0.0.xsd">
    <modelVersion>4.0.0</modelVersion>
    <groupId>maven.hibernate.ogm</groupId>
    <artifactId>Maven_HOGM</artifactId>
    <version>1.0-SNAPSHOT</version>
    <packaging>pom</packaging>
    <name>Maven_HOGM</name>
    <dependencies>
        <dependency>
            <groupId>org.hibernate.ogm</groupId>
            <artifactId>hibernate-ogm-core</artifactId>
            <version>4.0.0.Beta2</version>
        </dependency>
    </dependencies>
    <build>
        <directory>D:/Hibernate_OGM</directory>
        <defaultGoal>dependency:copy-dependencies</defaultGoal>
    </build>
</project>
```

The final step consists of executing the Maven mvn command. To do so, open a command prompt, navigate to the folder containing the pom.xml file, and run the mvn command (see Figure 1-13). After a few seconds, you should find the Hibernate OGM binary (including dependencies) in the path specified in the pom.xml file.

Figure 1-13. *Running the mvn command*

Adding MongoDB Artifacts

Now you know how to obtain the Hibernate OGM 4.0.0.Beta2 Core (and dependencies), but without any NoSQL data store artifacts. Currently, you can add artifacts for the following NoSQL stores: Ehcache, Infinispan, and MongoDB. Since our focus is Hibernate OGM and MongoDB, you'll need to add MongoDB artifacts by placing the following dependency into the pom.xml file:

```
...
<dependency>
    <groupId>org.hibernate.ogm</groupId>
    <artifactId>hibernate-ogm-mongodb</artifactId>
    <version>4.0.0.Beta1</version>
</dependency>
...
```

> ■ **Note** For Infinispan, just replace the artifact id with `hibernate-ogm-infinispan`, and for Ehcache with `hibernate-ogm-ehcache`.

Now, running the mvn command again will add two more JARs, hibernate-ogm-mongodb-4.0.0.Beta1.jar and mongo-java-driver-2.8.0.jar, as shown in Figure 1-14. The MongoDB drivers are also available for download as JARs at www.mongodb.org/display/DOCS/Drivers address.

Figure 1-14. Running the mvn command after adding MongoDB artifacts

Getting a Hibernate OGM Distribution Using the NetBeans IDE

If you're a NetBeans fan, it's much simpler to use Maven from a NetBeans Maven project. This section describes the main steps in creating such a project to obtain the Hibernate OGM distribution as a NetBeans Library ready to be used in other projects. Launch NetBeans (I tested on NetBeans 7.2.1) and follow these steps:

1. From the File menu, select the New Project option. In the New Project wizard, select Maven in the Categories list and POM Project in the Projects list, as shown in Figure 1-15.

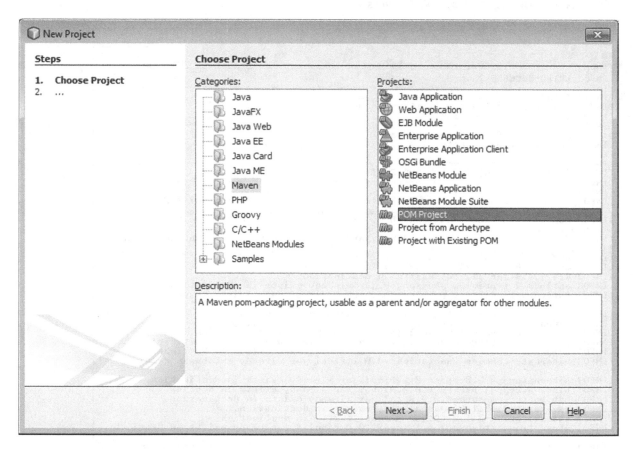

Figure 1-15. *Creating a POM project with NetBeans 7*

■ **Note** If Maven isn't available in your NetBeans distribution, you can install it by following the tutorial about third-party plug-in installations at http://wiki.netbeans.org/InstallingAPlugin.

---

2. Type the project name (Maven_HOGM), select the project location (D:\Apress\apps\ NetBeans), type the group id (maven.hibernate.ogm) and the version (1.0-SNAPSHOT) and click Finish as shown in Figure 1-16. (Note that I've used example names and locations here. Feel free to choose your own.) The empty project will be created and listed under the Projects panel.

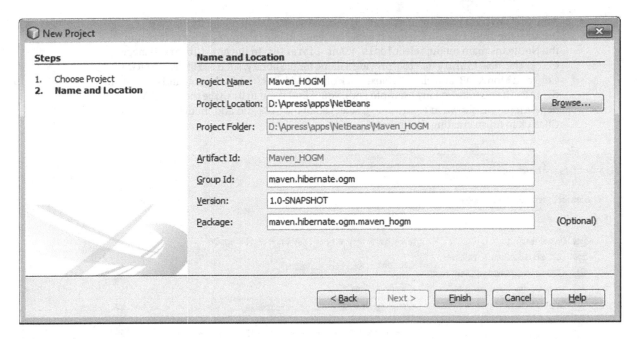

Figure 1-16. *Setting the project name and location*

3. Expand the Maven_HOGM | Project Files node and locate pom.xml and settings.xml.
   If settings.xml isn't listed, right-click on the Project Files node, select Create settings.xml
   (as shown in Figure 1-17), and fill the file with the appropriate content.

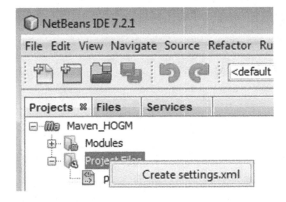

Figure 1-17. *Creating the settings.xml file from NetBeans 7*

4. Edit pom.xml according to your needs. At this point, both files should be ready to be
   processed by Maven.

5. Right-click on the Maven-HOGM node and select Clean and Build. Wait until the task ends
   successfully, then expand the Maven_OGM | Dependencies node to see the downloaded JARs.

6. Now you can create a NetBeans library. (I recommend that you create this library because the applications developed with NetBeans, in later chapters, refer to it.) From the NetBeans main menu, select Tools | Ant Libraries. In the Ant Library Manager, click the New Library button, provide a name for the library, such as Hibernate OGM Core and MongoDB, and click OK. Next, click on the Add JAR/Folder button and navigate to the JARs (if you followed my example path, you'll find them in D:\Hibernate_OGM\ dependency, as shown in Figure 1-18). Select all of the JARs and add them to this library. Click OK to finish creating the library.

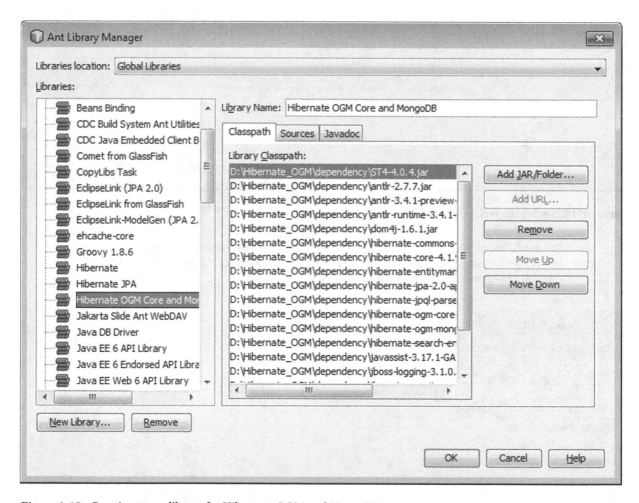

Figure 1-18. *Creating a user library for Hibernate OGM and MongoDB*

Now you can easily integrate the Hibernate OGM/MongoDB distribution into any of your NetBeans projects by adding Hibernate OGM Core/Hibernate OGM Core and MongoDB library into your project libraries.

The complete application is available in the Apress repository. It's a NetBeans project named Maven_HOGM.

Getting the Hibernate OGM Distribution Using the Eclipse IDE

If you're an Eclipse fan, it's much simpler to use Maven from an Eclipse Maven project. This section describes the main steps for creating such a project to obtain the Hibernate OGM distribution as an Eclipse library ready to be used in other projects. So launch Eclipse (we tested on Eclipse JUNO) and follow these steps:

1. From the File menu, select New | Other. In the New wizard, expand the Maven node and select Maven Project as shown in Figure 1-19. Click Next.

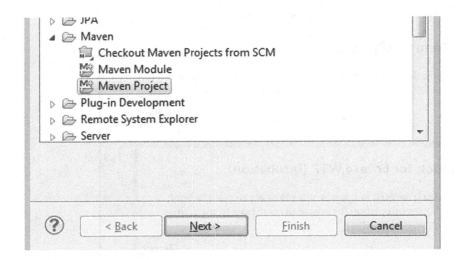

Figure 1-19. *Creating a new Maven project with Eclipse JUNO*

If Maven isn't available in your Eclipse distribution, you can either download a standalone Maven distribution and install it from Window | Preferences | Maven | Installations, or you can install Maven for Eclipse from the Eclipse Marketplace, which you'll find on the Help menu. Once you locate Maven in the Marketplace, follow the wizard to complete the installation (see Figure 1-20).

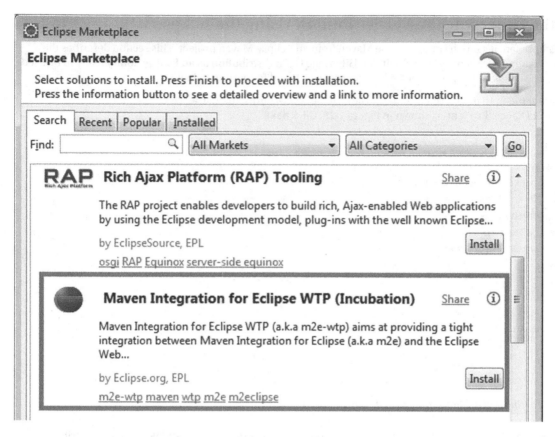

Figure 1-20. *Creating a new Maven project with Eclipse JUNO*

2. Check the box labeled `Create a simple project (skip archetype selection)`. You can choose the default workspace and click `Next`.

3. Type the group id (`maven.hibernate.ogm`) and artifact id (`Maven_HOGM`). Click he `Finish` button and wait until the project has been successfully created and is listed in the `Package Explorer` panel.

4. Manually update or create the `settings.xml` file in the maven local repository.

5. Locate `pom.xml` in the `Maven_HOGM` project and double-click it.

6. Next, in the editor, switch to the `pom.xml` tab where you'll see a `pom.xml` skeleton. Add to it the missing parts from your `pom.xml` and save the project (see Figure 1-21).

```
M Maven_HOGM/pom.xml ⊠                                                                    ⊟ ☐
  ⊝ <project xmlns="http://maven.apache.org/POM/4.0.0" xmlns:xsi="http://www.w3.org/2001/XMLSchema-instance" xs ▲
     <modelVersion>4.0.0</modelVersion>
     <groupId>maven.hibernate.ogm</groupId>
     <version>0.0.1-SNAPSHOT</version>
  ⊝  <dependencies>
  ⊝     <dependency>
           <groupId>org.hibernate.ogm</groupId>
           <artifactId>hibernate-ogm-core</artifactId>
           <version>4.0.0.Beta2</version>
        </dependency>
  ⊝     <dependency>
           <groupId>org.hibernate.ogm</groupId>
           <artifactId>hibernate-ogm-mongodb</artifactId>
           <version>4.0.0.Beta1</version>
        </dependency>
     </dependencies>
  ⊝  <build>
        <directory>D:/Hibernate_OGM</directory>
        <defaultGoal>dependency:copy-dependencies</defaultGoal>
     </build>
     <artifactId>Maven_HOGM</artifactId>
  </project>
  ◄                            ⫶⫶⫶                                    ►
Overview │ Dependencies │ Dependency Hierarchy │ Effective POM │ pom.xml
```

Figure 1-21. *Editing pom.xml file in Eclipse JUNO*

7.   In the Package Explorer panel, right-click the project name and select Run As | Maven build. When the process ends successfully, you should see the Hibernate OGM distribution (including dependencies) under the path defined by the <directory> tag in pom.xml.

8.   Select Preferences in the Window menu. In the tree on the left, expand the Java | Build Path node and select User Libraries.

9.   Click the New button to create a new library. Type a name for the new library, such as Hibernate OGM Core and MongoDB, and click the OK.

10.   Click the Add External JARs button and navigate to the folder where the Hibernate OGM distribution was downloaded. Select all of the JARs and add them to the library. Click OK.

Now you can easily integrate Hibernate OGM/MongoDB distribution into any of your Eclipse projects by adding Hibernate OGM Core/Hibernate OGM Core and MongoDB library into your project build path.

■ **Note**   If you'd prefer to create the entire project with Maven, just add the Hibernate OGM dependencies accordingly. All you have to do is add the corresponding <repository> and <dependency> tags.

The complete application is available in the Apress repository. It's an Eclipse project named Maven_HOGM.

Obtain the MongoDB Distribution

When this book was written, the recommended MongoDB distribution was version 2.2.2 (I chose this version because is "preferred" by Hibernate OGM and OpenShift). You can easily download it from the official web site at http://www.mongodb.org/. You'll find the installation steps at http://docs.mongodb.org/manual/installation/.

The examples in this book were developed and tested under the 64-bit versions of Windows 7 and 8, for which the installation is straightforward.

After downloading and installing the MongoDB distribution, you're ready to see if the MongoDB server starts and responds to commands. Open a command prompt, navigate to the {MONGODB_HOME}/bin folder and type mongod --dbpath ../ command to start the server (the --dbpath option indicates the location of the /data/db folder you manually created in the {MONGODB_HOME} folder, following installation guide). If there are no errors, open another command prompt, navigate to the same folder, and type mongo. If you see something similar to what's shown in Figure 1-22, MongoDB was successfully installed.

```
D:\mongodb\bin>mongo
MongoDB shell version: 2.2.2
connecting to: test
>
```

Figure 1-22. *Checking MongoDB server availability*

To test more thoroughly, try the commands from the Getting Started tutorial at http://docs.mongodb.org/manual/tutorial/getting-started/. You can easily shut down the MongoDB server by pressing CTRL-C.

Summary

In this introductory chapter we took the first steps toward understanding and using Hibernate OGM. We looked at Hibernate OGM concepts, features and aims, as well as giving a brief overview of the Hibernate OGM architecture. (It's important to know how things are managed internally if you want to understand the next chapter).

You then saw how to obtain the Hibernate OGM distribution as a ZIP/TGZ, as a command-line Maven project, and as a NetBeans/Eclipse Maven based project. Finally, you learned how to install a MongoDB distribution and how to add the corresponding JARs to the Hibernate OGM distribution.

■ ■ ■

CHAPTER 2

Hibernate OGM and MongoDB

By now, you should have some idea of the general scope and architecture of Hibernate OGM. In Chapter 1, I discussed how Hibernate OGM works with generic NoSQL stores, and I spoke about its general focus and how you represent, persist, and query data. In addition, you learned how to obtain a Hibernate OGM distribution, and you've installed a MongoDB NoSQL store and performed a simple command-line test to verify that the MongoDB server responds correctly.

In this chapter, I'll define more clearly the relationship between Hibernate OGM and MongoDB. Instead of generic possibilities, I'll focus on how Hibernate OGM works with the MongoDB store, and you'll see how much of MongoDB can be "swallowed" by Hibernate OGM and some MongoDB drawbacks that force Hibernate OGM to work overtime to manage them.

Configuring MongoDB-Hibernate OGM Properties

Hibernate OGM becomes aware of MongoDB when you provide a bundle of configuration properties. If you've worked before with Hibernate ORM, you're already familiar with these kinds of properties. In particular, there are three ways of setting these properties, as you'll see in the next chapters:

- declarative, through the `hibernate.cfg.xml` configuration file

- programmatically, through Hibernate native APIs

- declarative, through the `persistence.xml` configuration file in JPA context

---

■ **Note**　Remember, we're using Hibernate OGM 4.0.0.Beta.2 with Hibernate OGM for MongoDB 4.0.0.Beta1 and the Java driver for MongoDB 2.8.0.

Let's take look at the properties that enable Hibernate OGM to work with MongoDB.

`hibernate.ogm.datastore.provider`

As you know from Chapter 1, Hibernate OGM currently supports several NoSQL stores, including MongoDB. This property value is how you let Hibernate OGM know which NoSQL store you want to use. For MongoDB, the value of this property must be set to `mongodb`.

`hibernate.ogm.mongodb.host`

Next, Hibernate OGM needs to locate the MongoDB server instance. First, it must locate the hostname, which is represented by the IP address of the machine that hosts the MongoDB instance. By default, the value of this property is 127.0.0.1, which equivalent to localhost, and it can be set through the MongoDB driver as well:

```
Mongo mongo = new Mongo("127.0.0.1");
Mongo mongo = new Mongo(new ServerAddress( "127.0.0.1"));
```

hibernate.ogm.mongodb.port

And what is a hostname without a port? By default, the MongoDB instance runs on port number 27017, but you can use any other MongoDB port as long as you specify it as the value of this property. If you are using the MongoDB driver directly, the port is typically set like this:

```
Mongo mongo = new Mongo("127.0.0.1", 27017);
Mongo mongo = new Mongo( new ServerAddress("127.0.0.1", 27017));
```

hibernate.ogm.mongodb.database

Now Hibernate OGM can locate MongoDB through its host and port. You also have to specify the database to connect to. If you indicate a database name that doesn't exist, a new database with that name will be automatically created (there's no default value for this property). You can also connect using the MongoDB driver, like this:

```
DB db = mongo.getDB("database_name");
Mongo db = new Mongo( new DBAddress( "127.0.0.1", 27017, "database_name" ));
```

hibernate.ogm.mongodb.username
hibernate.ogm.mongodb.password

These two properties represent authentication credentials. They have no default values and usually appear together to authenticate a user against the MongoDB server (though if you set the password without setting the username, Hibernate OGM will ignore the hibernate.ogm.mongodb.password property). You can also use the MongoDB driver to set authentication credentials, like so:

```
boolean auth = db.authenticate("username", "password".toCharArray());
```

hibernate.ogm.mongodb.safe

Note that this property is a little tricky. MongoDB isn't adept at transactions; it doesn't do rollback and can't guarantee that the inserted data is, in fact, in the database since the driver doesn't wait for the write operation to be applied before returning. Behind the great speed advantage—resulting from the fact that the driver performs a write behind to the MongoDB server—lurks a dangerous trap that can lose data.

The MongoDB team knew of this drawback, so it developed a new feature called *Write Concerns* to tell MongoDB how important a piece of data is. This is also used to indicate the initial state of the data, the default write, (WriteConcern.NORMAL).

MongoDB defines several levels of data importance, but Hibernate OGM lets you switch between the default write and write safe write concerns.

With write safe, the driver doesn't return immediately; it waits for the write operation to succeed before returning. Obviously, this can have serious consequences for performance. You can set this value using the hibernate.ogm. mongodb.safe property. By default, the value of this property is true, which means write safe is active, but you can set it to false if loss of writes is not a major concern for your case.

Here's how to use the MongoDB driver directly to set write safe:

```
DB db = mongo.getDB("database_name");
DBCollection dbCollection = db.getCollection("collection_name");
dbCollection.setWriteConcern(WriteConcern.SAFE);
dbCollection.insert(piece_of_data);
//or, shortly
dbCollection.insert(piece_of_data, WriteConcern.SAFE);
```

■ **Note**   Currently, Hibernate OGM only lets you enable the write safe MongoDB write concern (WriteConcern.SAFE). Strategies like Write FSYNC_SAFE (WriteConcern.FSYNC_SAFE), Write JOURNAL_SAFE (WriteConcern.JOURNAL_SAFE), and Write Majority (WriteConcern.MAJORITY) are thus controllable only through MongoDB driver.

```
hibernate.ogm.mongodb.connection_timeout
```

MongoDB supports a few timeout options for different kinds of time-consuming operations. Currently, Hibernate OGM exposes through this property the MongoDB option connectTimeout (see com.mongodb.MongoOptions). This is expressed in milliseconds and represents the timeout used by the driver when the connection to the MongoDB instance is initiated. By default, Hibernate OGM sets it to 5000 milliseconds to override the driver default of 0 (which means no timeout). You can set this property as follows:

```
mongo.getMongoOptions().connectTimeout=n_miliseconds;
```

```
hibernate.ogm.mongodb.associations.store
```

This property defines the way Hibernate OGM stores information relating to associations. The accepted values are: IN_ENTITY, COLLECTION, and GLOBAL_COLLECTION. I'll discuss these three strategies a little later in this chapter.

```
hibernate.ogm.datastore.grid_dialect
```

This is an optional property that's usually ignored because the datastore provider chooses the best grid dialect automatically. But if you want to override the recommended value, you have to specify the fully qualified class name of the GridDialect implementation. For MongoDB, the correct value is org.hibernate.ogm.dialect.mongodb. MongoDBDialect.

This is the set of properties that Hibernate OGM uses for configuring a connection to MongoDB server. At this point, you have access to the essential settings for creating decent communications with the MongoDB server. In future OGM releases, we can hope to be able to access many more settings for the MongoDB driver.

Data Storing Representation

As you know, the relational data model is useless in terms of MongoDB, which is a document-based database system; all records (data) in MongoDB are documents. But, even so, MongoDB has to keep a conceptual correspondence between relational terms and its own notions. Therefore, instead of *tables*, MongoDB uses *collections* and instead of *records*, it uses *documents* (collections contain documents). MongoDB documents are BSON (Binary JSON—binary-encoded serialization of JSON-like documents) objects and have the following structure:

```
{
    field1: value1,
    field2: value2,
    field3: value3,
    ...
    fieldN: valueN
}
```

Storing Entities

OK, but we are still storing and retrieving Java entities, right? Yes, the answer is definitely yes! If Hibernate ORM provides complete support for transforming Java entities into relational tables, Hibernate OGM provides complete support for transforming Java entities into MongoDB collections. Each entity represents a MongoDB collection; each entity instance represents a MongoDB document; and each entity property will be translated into a document field (see Figure 2-1).

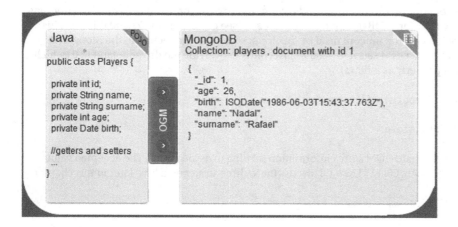

Figure 2-1. *Storing a Java object in a MongoDB document*

The Hibernate OGM team worked hard to store data as naturally as possible for MongoDB so that third-party applications can exploit this data without Hibernate OGM assistance. For example, let's suppose we have a POJO class like the one in Listing 2-1. (I'm sure you've stored tons of Java objects like this into relational databases, so I'm providing no details about this simple class.)

Listing 2-1. A POJO Class

```
import java.util.Date;

public class Players {

    private int id;
    private String name;
    private String surname;
    private int age;
    private Date birth;
```

```java
    public int getId() {
        return id;
    }

    public void setId(int id) {
        this.id = id;
    }

    public String getName() {
        return name;
    }

    public void setName(String name) {
        this.name = name;
    }

    public String getSurname() {
        return surname;
    }

    public void setSurname(String surname) {
        this.surname = surname;
    }

    public int getAge() {
        return age;
    }

    public void setAge(int age) {
        this.age = age;
    }

    public Date getBirth() {
        return birth;
    }

    public void setBirth(Date birth) {
        this.birth = birth;
    }
}
```

Now, suppose an instance of this POJO is stored into the MongoDB players collection using Hibernate OGM, like this:

```
{
        "_id": 1,
        "age": 26,
        "birth": ISODate("1986-06-03T15:43:37.763Z"),
        "name": "Nadal",
        "surname": "Rafael"
}
```

This is exactly what you obtain if you manually store via the MongoDB shell with the following command:

```
>db.players.insert(
                {
                        _id: 1,
                        age: 26,
                        birth: new ISODate("1986-06-03T15:43:37.763Z"),
                        name: "Nadal",
                        surname: "Rafael"
                }
                    )
```

Practically, there's no difference in the result. You can't tell if the document was generated by Hibernate OGM or inserted through the MongoDB shell. That's great! Moreover, Hibernate OGM knows how to transform this result back into an instance of the POJO. That's even greater! And you won't feel any programmatic discomfort, since Hibernate OGM doesn't require you write any underlying MongoDB code. That's the greatest!

Storing Primary Keys

A MongoDB document or collection has a very flexible structure. It supports simple objects: the embedding of objects and arrays within other objects and arrays; different kinds of documents in the same collection; and more, but it also contains a document field especially reserved for storing primary keys. This field is named _id and its value can be any information as long as it's unique. If you don't set _id to anything, the value will be set automatically to "MongoDB Id Object".

Hibernate OGM recognizes these specifications when storing identifiers into a MongoDB database; it lets you use identifiers of any Java type, even composite identifiers, and it always stores them into the reserved _id field.

Figure 2-2 shows some identifiers of different Java types and how they look in MongoDB.

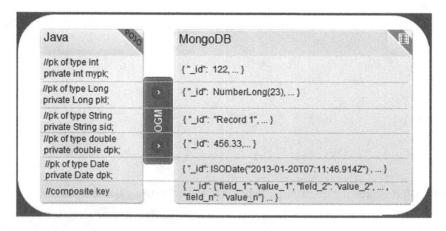

Figure 2-2. *Correspondence between Java-style primary keys and MongoDB identifiers*

Storing Associations

Probably the most powerful feature of relational databases relies on associations. Any database of any meaningful capability take advantages of associations: one-to-one, one-to-many, many-to-one, and many-to-many. In the relational model, associations require storing additional information, known as *navigation information for associations*.

For example, in a bidirectional many-to-many association, the relational model usually uses three tables, two tables for data and an additional table, known as a *junction table*. The junction table holds a composite key that consists of the two foreign key fields that refer to the primary keys of both data tables (see Figure 2-3). Note that the same pair of foreign keys can only occur once.

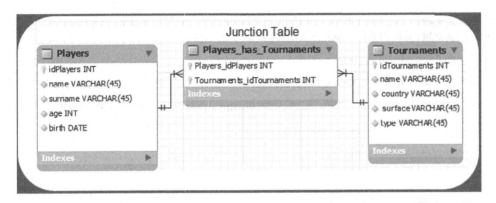

Figure 2-3. *A bidirectional many-to-many association, shown in a relational model representation*

In a MongoDB many-to-many association, you store the junction table as a document. Hibernate OGM provides three solutions to accomplish this: IN_ENTITY, COLLECTION, and GLOBAL_COLLECTION. To better understand these strategies, let's improvise a simple scenario—two relational tables (Players and Tournaments) populated respectively with three players, two tournaments, and a many-to-many association as shown in Figure 2-4. (The first and second players, P1 and P2, participate in both tournaments, T1 and T2, and the third player (P3) participates only in the second tournament, T2. Or, from the other side of the association, the first tournament, T1, includes the first and second players, P1 and P2, and the second tournament, T2, includes the first, second, and third players, P1, P2, and P3.)

Players Table						Players_has_Tournaments Table							
					n	Players_idPlayers	Tournaments_idTournaments					n	Tournaments Table
P1	idPlayers	name	surname	age	birth	1	1	type	surface	country	name	idTournaments	T1
	1	Nadal	Rafael	26	3.6.1986	1	2	Grand Slam	grass	United Kingdom, London	Wimbledon	1	
						2	1						
P2	idPlayers	name	surname	age	birth	2	2	type	surface	country	name	idTournaments	T2
	2	Ferrer	David	30	2.4.1982	3	2	Grand Slam	hard	U.S.A, New York	US Open	2	
P3	idPlayers	name	surname	age	birth	Junction Table							
	3	Federer	Roger	31	8.8.1981								

Figure 2-4. *A bidirectional many-to-many association in a relational model representation—test case*

Now, let's look at the Hibernate OGM strategies for storing associations, using this test case. We want to observe how the junction table is stored in MongoDB based on the selected strategy. We'll begin with the default strategy, IN_ENTITY, and continue with GLOBAL_COLLECTION, and finally COLLECTION.

In JPA terms, the main ways to represent this relational model are: the Players entity defines a primary key field named idPlayers and is the owner of the association; the Tournaments entity defines a primary key named idTournaments and is the non-owner side of the association—it contains the mappedBy element. Moreover, the Players entity defines a Java collection of Tournaments, named tournaments, and the Tournaments entity defines a Java collection of Players, named players.

IN_ENTITY

The default strategy for storing navigation information for associations is named IN_ENTITY. In this case, Hibernate OGM stores the primary key of the other side of the association (the foreign key) into:

- a field if the mapping concerns a single object.

- an embedded collection if the mapping concerns a collection.

Running the relational scenario for MongoDB using the IN_ENTITY strategy reveals the results shown in Figure 2-5 and Figure 2-6.

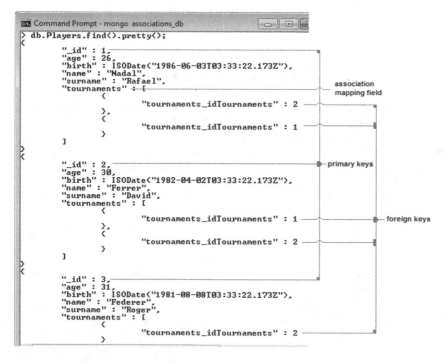

Figure 2-5. *Hibernate OGM-IN_ENTITY strategy result (Players collection)*

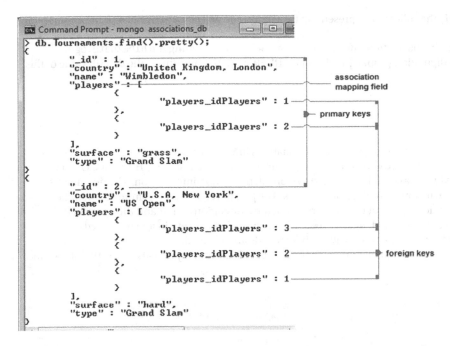

Figure 2-6. *Hibernate OGM-IN_ENTITY strategy result (tournaments collection)*

Figure 2-5 shows the MongoDB Players collection corresponding to the Players relational table; as you can see, each collection's document contains part of the association as an embedded collection. (The Players collection contains the part of the junction table that references the Tournaments collection.)

■ **Note**   The simplest way to explore a MongoDB collection from the shell is to call the find method, which returns all documents from the specified collection. In addition, calling the pretty method results in the output being nicely formatted. When a collection contains more documents than fit in a shell window, you need to type the it command, which supports document pagination.

The Players collection shows three main documents with the _id set as 1, 2, and 3, and each document encapsulates the corresponding foreign keys in a field named like the Java collection declared by the owner side (tournaments). Each document in the embedded collection contains a foreign key value stored in a field whose name is composed of the Java collection name declared by the owner side (tournaments) concatenated with an underscore and the non-owner side primary key field name (idTournaments).

The Tournaments collection, which corresponds to the Tournaments relational table, is like a reflection of the Players collection—the Players primary keys become Tournaments foreign keys (the Tournaments collection contains the part of the junction table that references the Players collection). Figure 2-6 shows the contents of the Tournaments collections.

The Tournaments collection includes two main documents with the _id set as 1 and 2. Each one encapsulates the corresponding foreign keys in a field named like the Java collection declared by the non-owner side (players). Each document of the embedded collection contains a foreign key value stored in a field whose name is composed of the Java collection name declared by non-owner side (players) concatenated with an underscore and the owner side primary key field name (idPlayers).

In the unidirectional case, only the collection representing the owner side will contain navigation information for the association.

You can use this strategy of storing navigation information for associations by setting the `hibernate.ogm.mongodb.associations.store` configuration property to the value `IN_ENTITY`. Actually, this is the default value of this property.

GLOBAL_COLLECTION

When you don't want to store the navigation information for associations into an entity's collections, you can choose the `GLOBAL_COLLECTION` strategy (or `COLLECTION`, as you'll see in the next section). In this case, Hibernate OGM creates an extra collection named `Associations`, especially designed to store all navigation information. The documents of this collection have a particular structure composed of two parts. The first part contains a composite identifier, `_id`, made up of two fields whose values represent the primary key of the association owner and the name of the association table; the second part contains a field, named `rows`, which stores foreign keys in an embedded collection. For bidirectional associations, another document is created where the ids are reversed.

Running our relational scenario for MongoDB and the `GLOBAL_COLLECTION` strategy reveals the results shown in Figure 2-7 and Figure 2-8.

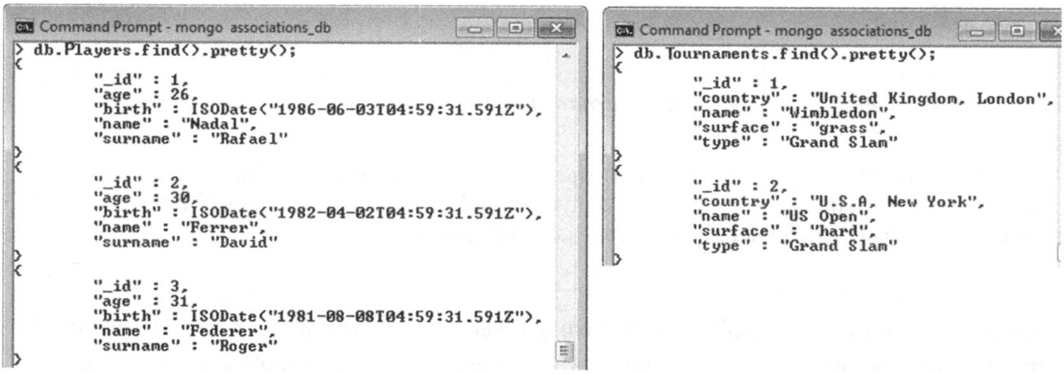

Figure 2-7. *Hibernate OGM-GLOBAL_COLLECTION strategy result (Players and Tournaments collections)*

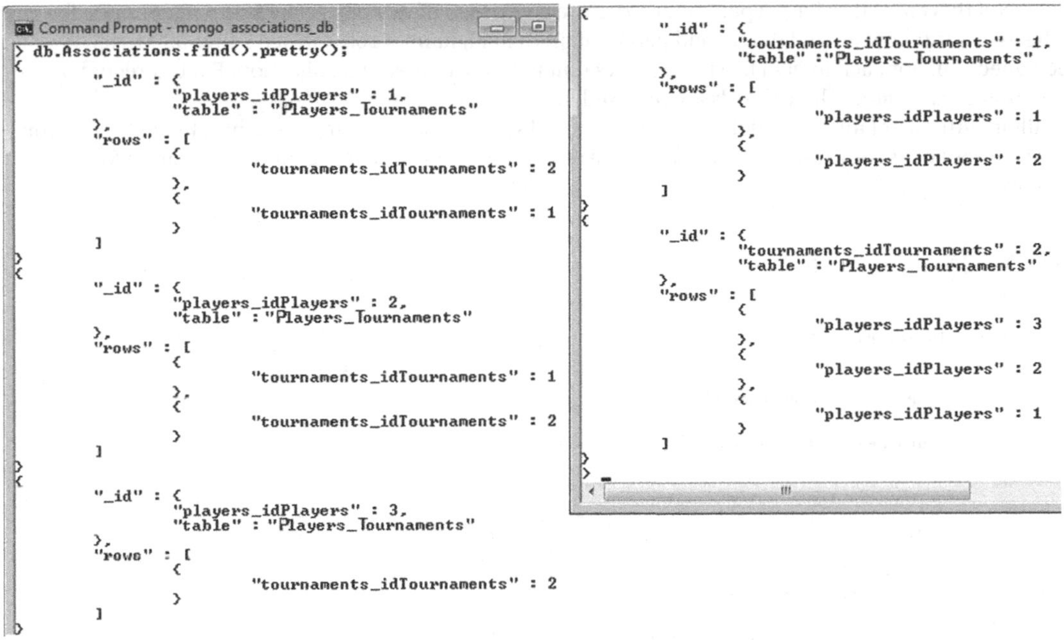

Figure 2-8. *Hibernate OGM-GLOBAL_COLLECTION strategy result (Associatins collection)*

In Figure 2-7, you can see that the Players and Tournaments collections contain only pure information, no navigation information.

The extra, unique collection that contains the navigation association is named Associations and is listed in Figure 2-8.

This is a bidirectional association. The owner side (Players) is mapped on the left side of Figure 2-8 and the non-owner side (Tournaments) is mapped on the right side of Figure 2-8. In a unidirectional association, only the owner side exists.

Now, focus on the nested document under the first _id field (Figure 2-8, left side). The first field name, players_idPlayers, is composed from the corresponding Java collection name defined in the non-owner side (players), or, for unidirectional associations, the collection name representing the owner side (Players) concatenated with an underscore and the name of the field representing the primary key of the owner side (idPlayers). The second field name is table; its value is composed of the collection name representing the the owner side concatenated with an underscore and the collection name representing the non-owner side (Players_Tournaments). The rows nested collection contains one document per foreign key. Each foreign key is stored in a field whose name is composed of the corresponding Java collection name defined in the owner side (tournaments) concatenated with an underscore and the primary key field name of the non-owner side (idTournaments). As a consequence of bidirectionality, things get reversed, as shown on the right side of Figure 2-8.

You can use this strategy for storing navigation information for associations by setting the hibernate.ogm. mongodb.associations.store configuration property to the value GLOBAL_COLLECTION.

COLLECTION

If GLOBAL_COLLECTION stores all the navigation information in one global collection, the COLLECTION strategy is less global and creates one MongoDB collection per association. For example, in our scenario, there will be one extra collection named associations_Players_Tournaments. In this strategy, each collection is prefixed with the word associations followed by the name of the association table. Using this convention makes it easy to differentiate the associations collections from the other collections.

The documents of this collection have a particular structure composed of two parts. The first part contains the primary key of the association owner and the second part contains a field, named rows, which stores all foreign keys in an embedded collection. For each foreign key there's a document in the embedded collection. For bidirectional cases, another document is created where the ids are reversed.

If you're familiar with the relational model this strategy should seem closer to your experience. In Figure 2-9, you can see the partial content of associations_Players_Tournaments collection—the navigation information for the owner side (Players).

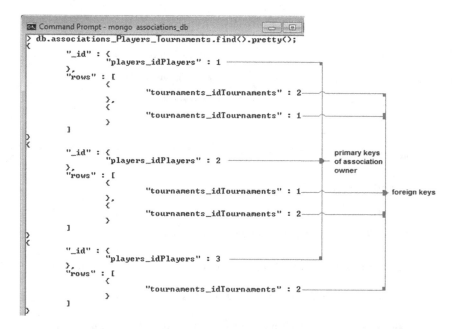

Figure 2-9. *Hibernate OGM-COLLECTION strategy result (associations_Players_Tournaments collection)*

You can easily see that the collection structure is the same as in the GLOBAL_COLLECTION case. The only difference is that the _id field no longer contains the association table name in a field named table, which is logical since the association table name is a part of the collection name (associations_Players_Tournaments).

You can use this strategy of storing navigation information for associations by setting the hibernate.ogm. mongodb.associations.store configuration property to the value COLLECTION.

■ **Note** Based on this example, you can easily intuit how the associations are represented in one-to-one, one-to-many, and many-to-one cases. Keep in mind that collections and field names can be altered by JPA annotations, like @Column, @Table, @JoinTable and so on. The example I presented doesn't use such annotations.

From the JPA perspective, when a bidirectional association doesn't define the owning side (using the mappedBy element), Hibernate OGM considers each side to be an individual association. In other words, you'll obtain two associations instead of one in such cases. For example, the COLLECTION strategy will produce two collections for storing two associations.

Now, it's up to you to decide which strategy better meets your needs.

Managing Transactions

Before switching from a relational model system to a NoSQL platform like Mongo DB, it's important to understand the differences between them, and the advantages and drawbacks of each in the context of your application needs. Knowing only that MongoDB doesn't support SQL, while relational models don't support collections and documents, can lead to serious problems in application implementation. This is actually the fundamental difference between the two, but there are many others, including the amount of space consumed and the time necessary to perform statements, caching, indexing, and, probably the most painful, managing transactions.

Many pioneer projects with MongoDB fail miserably when the developers realize that data transactional integrity is a must, because MongoDB doesn't support transactions. MongoDB follows this directive: "*write operations are atomic on the level of a single document: no single write operation can atomically affect more than one document or more than one collection.*" It also provides the two-phase commit mechanism for simulating transactions over multiple documents. You'll find more details at `www.docs.mongodb.org/manual/tutorial/perform-two-phase-commits/`. But both mechanisms omit the most powerful feature of transactional systems—the rollback operation.

Thus, if you need transactions, using MongoDB can be a delicate or even inappropriate choice. MongoDB is not an alternative to SQL as a "fashion" choice and should be used only if it satisfies your application needs better than an RDBMS. You should choose MongoDB when your database model doesn't imply transactions or when you can shape your database model not to need transactions.

Hibernate OGM can't provide the rollback facility, but it does diminish the transactions issue by querying all changes before applying them during flush. For this, OGM recommends using transaction demarcations to trigger the flush operation on commit.

Managing Queries

Hibernate OGM provides three solutions for executing queries against a MongoDB database:

- Partial JP-QL support
- Hibernate Search
- Native MongoDB queries

Each of these will be discussed and demonstrated in Chapter 6.

Summary

Though this is a short chapter, it contains plenty of information. I presented the rules that govern the relationship between Hibernate OGM and MongoDB. You saw how to configure MongoDB from Hibernate OGM and how data can be persisted in MongoDB according to the OGM implementation. In addition, I described the MongoDB view of transactions and finished with a quick enumeration of the query mechanism supported by Hibernate OGM.

CHAPTER 3

■ ■ ■

Bootstrapping Hibernate OGM

Since Hibernate OGM acts as a JPA implementation for NoSQL data stores, it's obvious we can bootstrap it through JPA. Moreover, it can be bootstrapped through the Hibernate Native APIs as well. No matter which way you choose to bootstrap Hibernate OGM, it's strongly recommended you use it in a Java Transaction API (JTA) environment, even if you're not using Java EE.

Before getting into the actual bootstrapping process, let's take a brief look at these specifications. You'll want to keep the main features of these technologies in mind over the course of the next sections and chapters. Of course, if you're already a guru, you can skip ahead.

Brief Overview of JPA

The Java Persistence API aims to provide support for operations that store, update, and map data from relational databases to Java objects and vice versa. You could say that JPA is the perfect tool for developers who have decided to work directly with objects rather than with SQL statements (the ORM paradigm).

■ **Note** Object-relational mapping is a programming technique that provides a virtual object layer between relational databases and object-oriented programming languages. Programming languages read from and write to relational databases through this layer. Instead of writing SQL statements to interact with your database, you use objects. Moreover, the code is much cleaner and easier to read, since it is not "plumbed" with SQL statements. As this book is written, the JPA specification has several implementations or *persistence providers.* Some are popular, tested, and stable (EclipseLink, Hibernate and Apache OpenJPA), while others may be less common but have very high benchmark performances (BatooJPA). EclipseLink is the reference implementation of JPA and it works, as every JPA implementation should, in both Java EE environments and standalone Java applications.

JPA is easy to use, thanks to *persistence metadata* that defines the relationships between Java objects and database tables. You are probably familiar with persistence metadata as JDK 5.0 annotations or XDoclet-style annotations at the language level, which are type safe and checked at compile time. It could be said that JPA annotations are actually plain JDK 5.0 annotations. Some hide complex tasks. One such annotation is javax.persistence.Entity (@Entity annotation), which is used to mark a POJO Java class that should be persisted in a database—each class annotated with @Entity is stored into a table and each table row is an entity class instance. Entities must define primary keys (a simple or complex primary key, explicitly specified or auto-generated if the @GeneratedValue annotation is present). Entities must not be final and must define a constructor with no arguments. The table name can reflect the class name or it can be explicitly provided through @Table annotation, like @Table(name="*my_table_name*").

An entity class defines a set of fields and each field defaults to a table's column that has the same name as the field; you can alter this using the @Column annotation, such as @Column(name="*my_column_name*"). JPA can access fields through *getter* and *setter* methods. Fields annotated with @Transient won't be persisted while the other fields are persisted by default.

Entity classes are where you define relationships between and among classes (tables). Classes can have one-to-one (@OneToOne), one-to-many (@OneToMany), many-to-one (@ManyToOne), and many-to-many (@ManyToMany) relationships with other classes. When two classes store references to each other, the relationship is *bidirectional* and you must specify the owning side of the relationship in the other class with the element mappedBy. When the reference is only from one class to another and not vice versa, the relationship is *unidirectional* and the mappedBy element isn't necessary.

Once you have the entities that reflect the database tables, you need an *entity manager* (an interface between the application and the *persistence context,* what the Hibernate documentation describes as a "set of entity instances in which for any persistent entity identity there is a unique entity instance," or, more succinctly, all the entities of one entity manager capable of providing methods for storing, retrieving, merging, and finding objects in the database. In practice, this is the javax.persistence.EntityManager, which is automatically provided in Java EE environments, such GlassFish or JBoss. If you're in a non-Java EE environment, such as Tomcat or Java SE, you have to manage the EntityManager lifecycle on your own.

The set of entities (usually logically related) that can be managed by a given EntityManager instance is defined as a *persistence unit,* each of which has a unique name and resides in an XML document named persistence.xml. Persistence.xml is a standard configuration file for JPA. It contains the JPA provider, the JTA or non-JTA data source, the database connection information, such as driver, user, password, DDL generation, and more. (In a Java SE application, this file is usually saved in the source directory in a folder named META-INF, while in a web application it's typically stored in the /src/conf folder, but, depending on application architecture, it can be located in other places). A persistence.xml file may contain multiple persistence units; based on the one your application uses, the server will know against which database to execute queries. In other words, through a persistence unit the EntityManagerFactory, used by the application to obtain an application-managed entity manager, is configured for a set of entities. You can look at this as a portable way to instantiate an EntityManagerFactory in JPA.

Figure 3-1 shows the relationships among the main components of the JPA architecture.

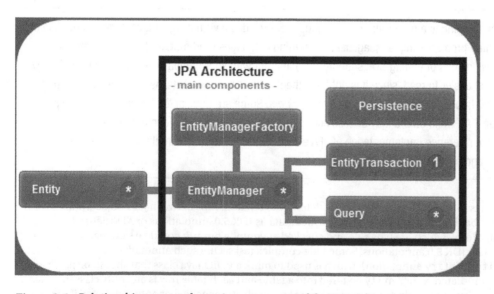

Figure 3-1. Relationships among the main components of the JPA architecture

Well, that was pretty quick. Now let's take a look at JTA.

Brief Overview of JTA

The Java Transaction API (JTA) enables distributed transactions. Basically, a transaction consists of a set of *tasks* (for example, SQL statements) that must be processed as an inseparable unit. This is an atomic operation and, in fact, the rule of "one task for all and all tasks for one" is a transaction's overriding principle. Transactions are characterized by ACID properties, as follows:

- *Atomicity* requires that if any of the tasks fail then the transaction fails and it is *rolled back*. If all tasks are successfully executed, the transaction is *committed*. In other words, a transaction is an all-or-nothing proposition.

- *Consistency* ensures that any committed transaction will leave the database in a valid state (written data must be valid according to all defined rules).

- *Isolation* means that your transaction is yours and yours alone; no other transaction can touch it because the database uses a locking mechanism to protect the transaction until it ends, successfully or otherwise. There are four levels of isolation:

  - *Read Uncommitted:* your transaction can read the uncommitted data of other transactions (never recommended in a multi-threaded environment).

  - *Read Committed:* your transaction can never read uncommitted data of other transactions.

  - *Repeatable:* your transaction will get the same data on multiple reads of the same rows until it ends.

  - *Serializable:* this level of isolation guarantees that everything you touch (all tables) remains unchanged during a transaction. It's the strictest isolation level and, with the most overhead, it causes the most performance bottlenecks.

- *Durability* guarantees that any committed transactions are safe, after system crashes.

These concepts are very important since transactions typically modify shared resources. Generally, there are two ways of managing transactions:

- Container Managed Transactions (CMT) use deployment descriptors or annotations (transaction attributes). In this case, the container is responsible for starting, committing, and rolling back a transaction. This is the *declarative* technique of demarcating transactions. In EJB containers, you can explicitly indicate a container-managed transaction using the annotation @TransactionManagement, like this:

  `@TransactionManagement(TransactionManagementType.CONTAINER)`

- Moreover, you can tell the EJB container how to handle the transaction via the @TransactionAttribute annotation, which supports six values: REQUIRED (default), REQUIRES_NEW, SUPPORTS, MANDATORY, NOT_SUPPORTED, NEVER. For example, you can set MANDATORY like this:

  `@TransactionAttribute(TransactionAttributeType.MANDATORY)`

- Bean Managed Transactions (BMT) require you to explicitly (programmatically) start, commit, and roll back transactions. This is the *programmatic* technique of demarcating transactions. In EJB containers, you can explicitly indicate a bean-managed transaction via the annotation @TransactionManagement, like this:

  `@TransactionManagement(TransactionManagementType.BEAN)`

And there are two types of transactions:

- *local* transactions access and update data on a single networked resource (one database).

- *distributed* transactions access and update data on two or more networked resources (multiple databases).

Programmatically speaking, JTA is a high-level API for accessing transactions based on three main interfaces:

- `UserTransaction`: The javax.transaction.UserTransaction interface allows developers to control transaction boundaries programmatically. To demarcate a JTA transaction, you invoke the begin, commit, and rollback methods of this interface.

- `TransactionManager`: The javax.transaction.TransactionManager allows the application server to control transaction boundaries.

- `XAResource`: The javax.transaction.xa.XAResource is a Java mapping of the standard XA interface based on the X/Open CAE Specification. You can find more details about XA at www.en.wikipedia.org/wiki/X/Open_XA and about XAResource and at www.docs.oracle.com/javaee/6/api/javax/transaction/xa/XAResource.html.

And that was a quick look at JTA.

MongoDB and Transactions

MongoDB does not support transactions, and this might seem like a limitation that cancels any potential benefit. MongoDB supports atomicity only when the changes affect a single document or multiple subdocuments of a single document. When changes (such as write operations) affect multiple documents, they are *not* applied atomically, which may lead to inconsistent data, other operations that interleave, and so on. Obviously, since the changes to multiple documents are not atomic, rollback is not applicable.

MongoDB does better with regard to consistency and durability. MongoDB write operations can be made consistent across connections. Moreover, MongoDB supports near-real-time replication, so it's possible to ensure an operation has been replicated before returning.

Hibernate OGM mitigates MongoDB's lack of support for transactions by queuing all changes before applying them during flush time. Even though MongoDB doesn't support transactions, Hibernate OGM recommends using transaction demarcations to trigger the flush operation transparently (on commit). But, as the official documentation indicates, rollback is not an option. Therefore, the applications developed in this book will use JTA, as Hibernate OGM recommends.

■ **Note**   Based on the limitations I've noted, it's easy to conclude that MongoDB can't meet our application's needs. But, let's consider why we might jump to that conclusion. Are we too addicted to complex database schema designs, with many joins and tables that require transactions, and queries that are hard to write and manage? It's far from my aim to debate such questions here, but maybe you'll take a little time to think about them and find the correct answers for your applications.

Brief Overview of Hibernate Native API

Applications that use the Hibernate API directly are known as native Hibernate applications. Developing a native Hibernate application consists of a few straightforward steps in which you:

- define persistence classes

- specify properties and mapping documents

- load these into the application's configuration

- based on this configuration, create a session factory

- obtain (open) sessions from the session factory

- execute queries and transactions

The starting point and core of the Native API is the org.hibernate.cfg.Configuration class, which uses the properties and mapping documents (.properties, .cfg.xml and hbm.xml files) to create org.hibernate.SessionFactory, a thread-safe object that's instantiated once and provides a factory for obtaining sessions (org.hibernate.Session). Session instances are used to execute transactions (JTA) and/or queries.

Figure 3-2 represents the Hibernate Native API architecture.

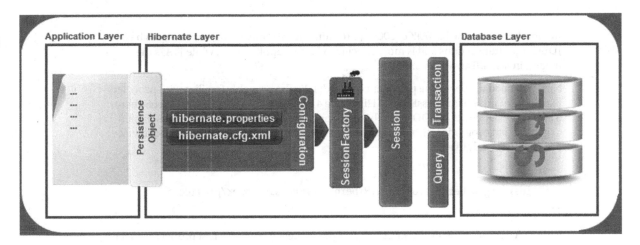

Figure 3-2. *Hibernate Native API architecture*

Bootstrapping Hibernate OGM Using JPA

Bootstrapping Hibernate OGM using JPA is the simplest case, since Hibernate OGM acts as a persistence provider. As noted earlier, the persistence provider is specified in the persistence.xml file within a persistence unit. The contents of persistence.xml may differ depending on how certain variables are defined, such as environment (Java EE, Java SE); JTA or non-JTA; database-specific requirements; server configurations; and so on. I tried to write a persistence.xml file for Hibernate OGM that contains the minimum mandatory settings.

1. The first step is to write a persistence.xml skeleton, which (in a Java SE/EE application) generally looks like this:

   ```xml
   <?xml version="1.0" encoding="UTF-8"?>
   <persistence version="2.0" xmlns="http://java.sun.com/xml/ns/persistence"
   xmlns:xsi="http://www.w3.org/2001/XMLSchema-instance"
   xsi:schemaLocation="http://java.sun.com/xml/ns/persistence
   http://java.sun.com/xml/ns/persistence/persistence_2_0.xsd">
   ...
   </persistence>
   ```

   This file is typically saved in the source directory in a folder named META-INF, though in a web application it's usually saved in the /src/conf folder.

Next, you add a persistence unit; you can name it whatever you want. JPA implementations can either manage transactions themselves through RESOURCE_LOCAL, or have them managed by the application server's JTA implementation. You use the transaction-type attribute to specify whether the entity managers provided by the entity manager factory for the persistence unit should be JTA or resource-local. Here I'll indicate the transaction type as JTA, because we want to use a JTA entity manager. (Whatever the server environment, Hibernate OGM recommends using JTA).

```
<persistence-unit name="{PU_NAME}" transaction-type="JTA">
</persistence-unit>
...
```

Remember to not use RESOURCE_LOCAL (a resource-local entity manager) as it uses basic JDBC-level transactions and is more specific to Java SE applications, while JTA is the default in Java EE environments.

2. Now you need to specify the persistence provider. You're probably familiar with providers like EclipseLink 2.0 for GlassFish v3, Hibernate 4 for JBoss AS 7, OpenJPA for WebSphere 6 and 7, and OpenJPA/KODO for WebLogic. For Hibernate OGM, the provider is named org.hibernate.ogm.jpa.HibernateOgmPersistence and it can be explicitly added into persistence.xml, like so:

```
...
<provider>org.hibernate.ogm.jpa.HibernateOgmPersistence</provider>
...
```

3. Now we've come to the properties section of persistence.xml. The first property to set is the JTA platform using hibernate.transaction.jta.platform. This property can have the following values (these classes belong to Hibernate core; they are the transaction managers as deployed on different application servers):

    - JBoss Application Server 7 (www.jboss.org/as7)[1]
      org.hibernate.service.jta.platform.internal.JBossAppServerJtaPlatform

    - Bitronix JTA Transaction Manager (www.docs.codehaus.org/display/BTM/Home)
      org.hibernate.service.jta.platform.internal.BitronixJtaPlatform

    - Borland Enterprise Server 6.0 (www.techpubs.borland.com/am/bes/v6/)
      org.hibernate.service.jta.platform.internal.BorlandEnterpriseServerJtaPlatform

    - JBoss Transactions (standalone JTA transaction manager known to work with
      org.jboss.jbossts:jbossjta:4.9.0.GA; not for use with Jboss AS 7)
      (www.jboss.org/jbosstm)
      org.hibernate.service.jta.platform.internal.JBossStandAloneJtaPlatform

    - JOnAS OSGi Enterprise Server (OW2) (www.jonas.ow2.org/xwiki/bin/view/Main/)
      org.hibernate.service.jta.platform.internal.JOnASJtaPlatform

---

[1]In April 2013 Red Hat, Inc. announced that the next generation of JBoss Application Server would be known as Wildfly. See http://gb.redhat.com/about/news/press-archive/2013/4/red-hat-reveals-plans-for-its-next-generation-java-application-server-project.

- Java Open Transaction Manager (JOTM), a standalone transaction manager (www.jotm.objectweb.org/)
  org.hibernate.service.jta.platform.internal.JOTMJtaPlatform

- JRun 4 Application Server (www.adobe.com/products/jrun/)
  org.hibernate.service.jta.platform.internal.JRun4JtaPlatform

- NoJtaPlatform class, a no-op version for use when no JTA has been configured (www.docs.jboss.org/hibernate/orm/4.0/javadocs/org/hibernate/service/jta/platform/internal/NoJtaPlatform.html)
  org.hibernate.service.jta.platform.internal.NoJtaPlatform

- Oracle Application Server 10g (OC4J)
  (www.oracle.com/technetwork/middleware/ias/index-099846.html)
  org.hibernate.service.jta.platform.internal.OC4JJtaPlatform

- Caucho Resin Application Server (www.caucho.com/)
  org.hibernate.service.jta.platform.internal.ResinJtaPlatform

- Sun ONE Application Server 7 (This transaction manager also works with GlassFish v3 Application Server) (www.docs.oracle.com/cd/E19957-01/817-2180-10/pt_chap1.html)
  org.hibernate.service.jta.platform.internal.SunOneJtaPlatform

- Weblogic Application Server (www.oracle.com/us/products/middleware/cloud-app-foundation/weblogic/overview/index.html)
  org.hibernate.service.jta.platform.internal.WeblogicJtaPlatform

- WebSphere Application Server version 6
  (www-01.ibm.com/software/webservers/appserv/was/)
  org.hibernate.service.jta.platform.internal.WebSphereExtendedJtaPlatform

- WebSphere Application Server versions 4, 5.0 and 5.1
  (www-01.ibm.com/software/webservers/appserv/was/)
  org.hibernate.service.jta.platform.internal.WebSphereJtaPlatform

- Transaction Manager Lookup Bridge, a bridge to legacy (and deprecated)
  org.hibernate.transaction.TransactionManagerLookup implementations
  (www.docs.jboss.org/hibernate/orm/4.0/javadocs/org/hibernate/service/jta/platform/internal/TransactionManagerLookupBridge.html)
  org.hibernate.service.jta.platform.internal.TransactionManagerLookupBridge

- Orion Application Server - it seems that this server does not exist any more
  org.hibernate.service.jta.platform.internal.OrionJtaPlatform

---

■ **Note** Keep in mind that these values were valid when this book was written. They were available in Hibernate 4.1, but it's quite possible they will change in the future. You can check the list in the *Hibernate Developer Guide*, at www.docs.jboss.org/hibernate/orm/4.1/devguide/en-US/html_single/.

Here's an example of setting the JTA platform for Caucho Resin:

```
...
<property name="hibernate.transaction.jta.platform"
        value="org.hibernate.service.jta.platform.internal.ResinJtaPlatform"/>
...
```

The next five properties configure which NoSQL data store to use and how to connect to it. For example, you can connect to an out-of-the-box MongoDB distribution by setting the data store provider, grid dialect (optional), database, host and port, like this:

```
...
<property name="hibernate.ogm.datastore.provider" value="mongodb"/>
<property name="hibernate.ogm.datastore.grid_dialect"
            value="org.hibernate.ogm.dialect.mongodb.MongoDBDialect"/>
<property name="hibernate.ogm.mongodb.database" value="test"/>
<property name="hibernate.ogm.mongodb.host" value="127.0.0.1"/>
<property name="hibernate.ogm.mongodb.port" value="27017"/>
...
```

That's it! Now we can glue the pieces together and provide a generic persistence.xml for out-of-the-box MongoDB, as shown in Listing 3-1. In the next chapter we'll adapt this file to fit into different environments.

Listing 3-1. A Generic persistence.xml File

```
<?xml version="1.0" encoding="UTF-8"?>
<persistence version="2.0" xmlns="http://java.sun.com/xml/ns/persistence"
                           xmlns:xsi="http://www.w3.org/2001/XMLSchema-instance"
xsi:schemaLocation="http://java.sun.com/xml/ns/persistence
http://java.sun.com/xml/ns/persistence/persistence_2_0.xsd">
  <persistence-unit name="{PU_NAME}" transaction-type="JTA">
    <provider>org.hibernate.ogm.jpa.HibernateOgmPersistence</provider>
    <properties>
      <property name="hibernate.transaction.jta.platform"
                value="{JTA_PLATFORM}"/>
      <property name="hibernate.ogm.datastore.provider" value="mongodb"/>
      <property name="hibernate.ogm.datastore.grid_dialect"
                value="org.hibernate.ogm.dialect.mongodb.MongoDBDialect"/>
      <property name="hibernate.ogm.mongodb.database" value="test"/>
      <property name="hibernate.ogm.mongodb.host" value="127.0.0.1"/>
      <property name="hibernate.ogm.mongodb.port" value="27017"/>
    </properties>
  </persistence-unit>
</persistence>
```

Bootstrap Hibernate OGM Using Hibernate Native API

Earlier, you saw that a native API application can be developed by following a few straightforward steps. Three of these steps—loading properties and mapping files into the application; creating a global thread-safe SessionFactory for the current configuration; and obtaining Sessions (single-threaded units of work) through SessionFactory—are usually implemented in the well-known HibernateUtil class. (You can write this class, but you also can find it on Internet in different "shapes.") Invariably, in this class, you'll have some lines of code similar to this (for Hibernate 3):

```
private static final SessionFactory sessionFactory;
...
sessionFactory = new Configuration().configure().buildSessionFactory();
...
```

Look at the second line, which builds the SessionFactory through an instance of the org.hibernate.cfg. Configuration class. Actually, this is the entry point to setting Hibernate OGM to work with Native API, because instead of using the org.hibernate.cfg.Configuration class, which is specific to Hibernate ORM, you need to use the org.hibernate.ogm.cfg.OgmConfiguration class. Therefore, that second line will become:

```
...
sessionFactory = new OgmConfiguration().configure().buildSessionFactory();
...
```

Starting with Hibernate 4, this code will present a warning about the deprecated method buildSessionFactory(). In this case, the javadoc recommends using the form buildSessionFactory(ServiceRegistry serviceRegistry). So if you are using Hibernate 4 (recommended), replace the previous code with this:

```
private static final SessionFactory sessionFactory;
private static final ServiceRegistry serviceRegistry;
...
OgmConfiguration cfgogm = new OgmConfiguration();
cfgogm.configure();
serviceRegistry = new ServiceRegistryBuilder().
applySettings(cfgogm.getProperties()).buildServiceRegistry();
sessionFactory = cfgogm.buildSessionFactory(serviceRegistry);
...
```

This approach (using either Hibernate 3 or 4) requires a hibernate.cfg.xml file that contains specific configurations. For Hibernate OGM, the file needs to contain the correct transaction strategy and the correct transaction manager lookup strategy. You have to specify a factory class for Transaction instances by setting the Hibernate configuration property hibernate.transaction.factory_class. The accepted values are:

- org.hibernate.transaction.JDBCTransactionFactory—this is the default value and it delegates to database (JDBC) transactions.

- org.hibernate.transaction.JTATransactionFactory —with this, bean-managed transactions are used, which means you must manually demarcate transaction boundaries.

- org.hibernate.transaction.CMTTransactionFactory—this value delegates to container-managed JTA transactions.

Programmatically, you can achieve this setting like this:

```
...
OgmConfiguration cfgogm = new OgmConfiguration();
...
cfgogm.setProperty(Environment.TRANSACTION_STRATEGY,
"{TRANSACTION_STRATEGY}");
...
```

Next, you have to specify the JTA platform by setting the property named hibernate.transaction.jta.platform. The value of this property must consist of the fully qualified class name of the lookup implementation. The acceptable values were listed earlier in the "*Bootstrap Hibernate OGM Using JPA*" section.

Programmatically, you can achieve this setting like this:

```
...
OgmConfiguration cfgogm = new OgmConfiguration();
...
cfgogm.setProperty(Environment.JTA_PLATFORM,"{JTA_PLATFORM}");
...
```

Finally, you need configure which NoSQL data store you want to use and how to connect to it.

For an out-of-the-box MongoDB distribution, you need to set the data store provider, grid dialect (optional), database, host and port, like this:

```
...
<property name="hibernate.ogm.datastore.provider">mongodb</property>
<property name="hibernate.ogm.mongodb.database">test</property>
<property name="hibernate.ogm.datastore.grid_dialect">
               org.hibernate.ogm.dialect.mongodb.MongoDBDialect</property>
<property name="hibernate.ogm.mongodb.host">127.0.0.1</property>
<property name="hibernate.ogm.mongodb.port">27017</property>
...
```

Programmatically, you can achieve these settings with the code in Listing 3-2.

Listing 3-2. Configuring MongoDB as the Data Store

```
...
OgmConfiguration cfgogm = new OgmConfiguration();
...
cfgogm.setProperty("hibernate.ogm.datastore.provider","mongodb");
cfgogm.setProperty("hibernate.ogm.mongodb.database","test");
cfgogm.setProperty("hibernate.ogm.datastore.grid_dialect ","
                    org.hibernate.ogm.dialect.mongodb.MongoDBDialect");
cfgogm.setProperty("hibernate.ogm.mongodb.host","127.0.0.1");
cfgogm.setProperty("hibernate.ogm.mongodb.port","27017");
...
```

Therefore, if you are using non-programmatically settings then the `hibernate.cfg.xml` may look like this:

```
<?xml version="1.0" encoding="UTF-8"?>
<!DOCTYPE hibernate-configuration PUBLIC "-//Hibernate/Hibernate Configuration DTD 3.0//EN"
"http://www.hibernate.org/dtd/hibernate-configuration-3.0.dtd">
<hibernate-configuration>
  <session-factory>
    <property name="hibernate.transaction.factory_class">
      {TRANSACTION_STRATEGY}
    </property>
    <property name="hibernate.transaction.jta.platform">
      {JTA_PLATFORM}
    </property>
    <property name="hibernate.ogm.datastore.provider">mongodb</property>
    <property name="hibernate.ogm.mongodb.database">test</property>
    <property name="hibernate.ogm.datastore.grid_dialect">
      org.hibernate.ogm.dialect.mongodb.MongoDBDialect</property>
```

```
    <property name="hibernate.ogm.mongodb.host">127.0.0.1</property>
    <property name="hibernate.ogm.mongodb.port">27017</property>
    <mapping resource="..."/>
    ...
  </session-factory>
</hibernate-configuration>
```

Listing 3-3 shows the HibernateUtil class that uses this configuration file.

Listing 3-3. HibernateUtil

```
import java.util.logging.Level;
import java.util.logging.Logger;
import org.hibernate.SessionFactory;
import org.hibernate.ogm.cfg.OgmConfiguration;
import org.hibernate.service.ServiceRegistry;
import org.hibernate.service.ServiceRegistryBuilder;

/**
 * HibernateUtil class (based on hibernate.cfg.xml)
 *
 */
public class HibernateUtil {

    private static final Logger log = Logger.getLogger(HibernateUtil.class.getName());
    private static final SessionFactory sessionFactory;
    private static final ServiceRegistry serviceRegistry;

    static {
        try {
            // create a new instance of OmgConfiguration
            OgmConfiguration cfgogm = new OgmConfiguration();

            //process configuration and mapping files
            cfgogm.configure();
            // create the SessionFactory
            serviceRegistry = new ServiceRegistryBuilder().
                applySettings(cfgogm.getProperties()).buildServiceRegistry();
            sessionFactory = cfgogm.buildSessionFactory(serviceRegistry);
        } catch (Throwable ex) {
            log.log(Level.SEVERE,
                    "Initial SessionFactory creation failed !", ex);
            throw new ExceptionInInitializerError(ex);
        }
    }

    public static SessionFactory getSessionFactory() {
        return sessionFactory;
    }
}
```

If you're using programmatic settings, you don't need a `hibernate.cfg.xml` file and your `HibernateUtil` will look like what's shown in Listing 3-4.

Listing 3-4. A HibernateUtil Class That Doesn't Need Hibernate.cfg.xml

```java
import java.util.logging.Level;
import java.util.logging.Logger;
import org.hibernate.SessionFactory;
import org.hibernate.cfg.Environment;
import org.hibernate.ogm.cfg.OgmConfiguration;
import org.hibernate.service.ServiceRegistry;
import org.hibernate.service.ServiceRegistryBuilder;

/**
 * HibernateUtil class (no need of hibernate.cfg.xml)
 *
 */
public class HibernateUtil {

    private static final Logger log = Logger.getLogger(HibernateUtil.class.getName());
    private static final SessionFactory sessionFactory;
    private static final ServiceRegistry serviceRegistry;

    static {
        try {
            // create a new instance of OmgConfiguration
            OgmConfiguration cfgogm = new OgmConfiguration();

            // enable transaction strategy
            cfgogm.setProperty(Environment.TRANSACTION_STRATEGY,
                                            "{TRANSACTION_STRATEGY}");
            // specify JTA platform
            cfgogm.setProperty(Environment.JTA_PLATFORM, "{JTA_PLATFORM}");

            //configure MongoDB connection   -
            cfgogm.setProperty("hibernate.ogm.datastore.provider", "mongodb");
            cfgogm.setProperty("hibernate.ogm.datastore.grid_dialect",
              "org.hibernate.ogm.dialect.mongodb.MongoDBDialect");
            cfgogm.setProperty("hibernate.ogm.mongodb.database", "test");
            cfgogm.setProperty("hibernate.ogm.mongodb.host", "127.0.0.1");
            cfgogm.setProperty("hibernate.ogm.mongodb.port", "27017");

            //add our annotated class
            cfgogm.addAnnotatedClass(*.class);

            // create the SessionFactory
            serviceRegistry = new ServiceRegistryBuilder().
                applySettings(cfgogm.getProperties()).buildServiceRegistry();
            sessionFactory = cfgogm.buildSessionFactory(serviceRegistry);
```

```
        } catch (Throwable ex) {
            log.log(Level.SEVERE,
                "Initial SessionFactory creation failed !", ex);
            throw new ExceptionInInitializerError(ex);
        }
    }

    public static SessionFactory getSessionFactory() {
        return sessionFactory;
    }
}
```

Now, the Hibernate Native API presented in Figure 3-2 can be redrawn as in Figure 3-3.

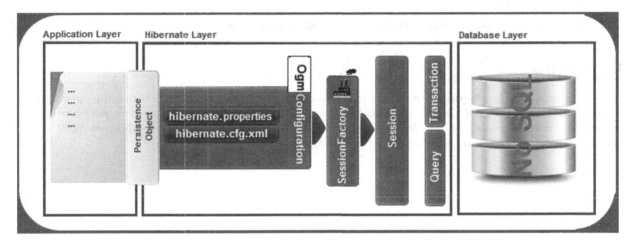

Figure 3-3. *Hibernate Native API architecture in Hibernate OGM*

■ **Note** Setting up Infinispan with the default configuration (org/hibernate/ogm/datastore/infinispan/
default-config.xml) can be accomplished by specifying the value of the hibernate.ogm.datastore.provider
property as infinispan. And you can set up Ehcache with the default configuration (org/hibernate/ogm/datastore/
ehcache/default-ehcache.xml) by setting the same property to Ehcache. For these two NoSQL products, Hibernate
OGM also supports a specific property for indicating an XML configuration file. For Infinispan, this property is called
hibernate.ogm.infinispan.configuration_resourcename and for Ehcache it's hibernate.ogm.ehcache.configuration_
resourcename. For Infinispan and Ehcache, therefore, you don't need to set dialect, database, port and host.

Hibernate OGM Obsolete Configuration Options

With the advent of Hibernate OGM, a set of options from Hibernate ORM are no longer available. Therefore, in accordance with the Hibernate OGM specification, the following options should not be used in OGM environments:

- `hibernate.dialect`
- `hibernate.connection.*` and in particular `hibernate.connection.provider_class`
- `hibernate.show_sql` and `hibernate.format_sql`
- `hibernate.default_schema` and `hibernate.default_catalog`
- `hibernate.use_sql_comments`
- `hibernate.jdbc.*`
- `hibernate.hbm2ddl.auto` and `hibernate.hbm2ddl.import_file`

Summary

After a brief look at the Java Persistence API (JPA), Java Transaction API (JTA), and Hibernate Native API, you saw how to bootstrap Hibernate OGM using JPA and Hibernate Native API. You learned how to write a generic persistence. xml and how to implement a HibernateUtil class for Hibernate OGM. Finally, you saw the list of Hibernate ORM configuration properties that are no longer available in Hibernate OGM.

CHAPTER 4

■ ■ ■

Hibernate OGM at Work

So far, you've learned that Hibernate OGM can be used via Java Persistence APIs or Hibernate Native APIs. Moreover, you understand the principles for accomplishing Hibernate OGM bootstrapping and you've looked at some relevant code snippets. Obviously, jumping from those code snippets to real applications requires more than copying and pasting, since you have to deal with the integration process and each environment's specific features and settings.

Trying to give an example that exactly matches each individual programmer's needs would be hopelessly overambitious, but what I can do is to provide a series of examples that use Hibernate OGM. In this chapter, I'll show you some out-of-the-box Hibernate OGM applications deployable on Java EE 6 servers (such as JBoss and GlassFish) and on Web servers (such as Tomcat), using frameworks like Seam and Spring and specifications like EJB. In addition to the kernel technologies that interact directly with Hibernate OGM, we'll use some development tools, IDEs like NetBeans and Eclipse, as well as Maven, JBoss Forge, Ant and so on, which help us build the applications with a minimum of effort. Consider these tools as my choice and not a must. You can use any other tools that yield the same results.

The entire set of applications share some simple business logic that stores a random integer in a MongoDB collection—we'll call this integer a lucky number. As you'll see, the stored integer is not even solicited from the user; it's randomly generated when the user presses a button (each press generates and stores a new integer). The point of this trivial business logic is to keep the application code as simple as possible and focus on Hibernate OGM integration into the context. What we're really concerned with is successfully binding Hibernate OGM to an application context and setting up interaction with MongoDB. In later chapters, we'll have plenty of time to discuss advanced setting for MongoDB, storage principles, JP-QL, Hibernate Search, and so on.

General Prerequisites

Before we start, make sure you've correctly installed MongoDB (as you saw in the Chapter 1) and that you have the Hibernate OGM JARs available, including the JARs needed for MongoDB support (locally or through Maven artifacts). The rest of the tools, such as application servers, frameworks, IDEs and so on, can be installed separately according to your needs; you probably won't be interested in all of the following examples. In any case, for testing the complete suite of applications from this chapter, you'll need the following:

- Java EE 6
- JDK 1.7
- GlassFish AS 3 (bundled with NetBeans 7.2.1 or 7.3)
- JBoss AS 7 (should be installed separately)
- Apache Tomcat 7 (bundled with NetBeans 7.2.1 or 7.3)
- NetBeans 7.2.1 or 7.3 (recommended with GlassFish AS 3 and Tomcat 7)

- Eclipse JUNO (JBoss AS 7 can be configured under this Eclipse distribution through JBoss AS Tools)

- MongoDB 2.2.2 (you should have this installed from Chapter 1)

- Hibernate OGM 4.0.0.Beta2 (from Chapter 1, you should have a NetBeans and Eclipse library named Hibernate OGM Core and MongoDB)

- MongoDB Java Driver 2.8.0 (this is present in Hibernate OGM Core and MongoDB library)

- JBoss JTA 4.16.4 Final

- Forge 1.0.5 or 1.3.1 (standalone or running as an Eclipse plug-in)

- Spring 3.3.1 (bundled with NetBeans 7.2.1 or 7.3)

Moreover, before you start, you may find it helpful to know that:

- Each application presented in this chapter can be downloaded from the Apress repository. Each application includes a small paragraph that describes the application name and the technical conditions under which it was tested. In other words, there's no need for you to reconstruct each application as you read this book, unless you want to.

- The examples show you how to integrate MongoDB and Hibernate OGM in different kinds of applications that involve several technologies. As you know, such applications need many additional files—XML configuration files, XHTML pages, servlets, managed beans, controllers and so on. I tried to keep the code as clean as possible to make it easier to understand how to integrate MongoDB and Hibernate OGM, so I've skipped the "spaghetti" code that isn't relevant. Furthermore, I don't try to teach you how to create a servlet, a session bean, or an XHTML page, or how to write a web.xml file. I assume you already know how, probably with NetBeans, Eclipse or another IDE. Don't expect to see a step-by-step NetBeans or Eclipse tutorial.

■ **Note**   For the applications developed as Apache Maven projects, don't forget to edit `settings.xml` as you saw in Chapter 1. Or, if you think that `settings.xml` is too verbose, you can simply use `<repository>` tags in your `pom.xml`. Keep in mind, though, that missing repositories will cause errors.

Java SE and MongoDB—the Hello World Example

We'll start our series of applications with an exception: the first application won't involve Hibernate OGM. This application is actually just a quick test to make sure that the MongoDB server is running and responds to a connection attempt. Consider this our Hello World application for Java-MongoDB novices. You can skip it if you think it's a waste of your time. Otherwise, let's go!

This is the simplest Java SE/MongoDB example ever—it simply stores a random number into a MongoDB collection.

Prerequisites

- MongoDB 2.2.2

- MongoDB Java driver 2.8.0 (mongo-java-driver-2.8.0.jar)

- JDK 1.7

- NetBeans 7.2.1 (or Eclipse JUNO)

Developing

After launching NetBeans, create a new project consisting of a simple Maven Java application and name it HelloWorld. In the New Java Application wizard, type HelloWorld for the Artifact Id, and hello.world.mongodb for the Group Id and Package. Once you see the project listed in the Projects window, edit the pom.xml file (which must be under the Project Files node). In the pom.xml file, add the MongoDB Java driver, version 2.8.0, by pasting in the following code:

```
<dependencies>
   <dependency>
      <groupId>org.mongodb</groupId>
      <artifactId>mongo-java-driver</artifactId>
      <version>2.8.0</version>
</dependency>
..
<dependencies>
```

Now save the project and the driver JAR will be listed under the Dependencies node.

■ **Note**   If you're not a Maven fan, create a simple Java application and download the MongoDB Java driver 2.8.0 from GitHub, https://github.com/mongodb/mongo-java-driver/downloads. Obviously, in this case, you have to add it manually to the Libraries node.

Now the necessary libraries are available. Next, edit the application's main class. If you didn't rename it, it's listed as App.java in the Source Packages node of the hello.world.mongodb.helloworld package. Under the main method, insert the following code, step by step:

1. Connect to the MongoDB store at localhost (127.0.0.1) on default port, 270127

   ```
   Mongo mongo = new Mongo("127.0.0.1", 27017);
   ```

2. Create a MongoDB database named helloworld_db. Most likely this database will be automatically created by MongoDB since it doesn't exist.

   ```
   DB db = mongo.getDB("helloworld_db");
   ```

3. Create a MongoDB collection named helloworld. This collection will probably be created automatically in the helloworld_db database by MongoDB since it doesn't exist.

   ```
   DBCollection dbCollection = db.getCollection("helloworld");
   ```

4. Create a document for storing a key/value pair. The key is just text and the value is the generated number.

   ```
   BasicDBObject basicDBObject = new BasicDBObject();
   basicDBObject.put("Lucky number", new Random().nextInt(1000));
   ```

53

5. Save the pair to the helloworld collection:

```
dbCollection.insert(basicDBObject);
```

Done!

Now, put those five steps together. Listing 4-1 shows the result.

Listing 4-1. The Hello World Example

```java
package hello.world.mongodb.helloworld;

import com.mongodb.BasicDBObject;
import com.mongodb.DB;
import com.mongodb.DBCollection;
import com.mongodb.Mongo;
import com.mongodb.MongoException;
import java.net.UnknownHostException;
import java.util.Random;

/**
 * Hello world!
 *
 */
public class App {

    public static void main(String[] args) {
        try {
            // connect to the MongoDB store
            Mongo mongo = new Mongo("127.0.0.1", 27017);

            // get the MongoDB database, helloworld_db
            DB db = mongo.getDB("helloworld_db");

            //get the MongoDB collection named helloworld
            DBCollection dbCollection = db.getCollection("helloworld");

            // create a document for storing a key/value pair
            BasicDBObject basicDBObject = new BasicDBObject();
            basicDBObject.put("Lucky number", new Random().nextInt(1000));

            // save the pair into helloworld collection
            dbCollection.insert(basicDBObject);

            System.out.println("MongoDB has stored the lucky number!");

        } catch (UnknownHostException e) {
            System.err.println("ERROR: " + e.getMessage());
        } catch (MongoException e) {
            System.err.println("ERROR: " + e.getMessage());
        }
    }
}
```

Testing

Start the MongoDB server as in Chapter 1. Next, since you are in NetBeans (or Eclipse), there's a Run button that does the magic. Run the application and if you get the message "*MongoDB has stored the lucky number!*", everything worked perfectly.

Open a command prompt and type the commands shown in Figure 4-1 to see the results of your work.

```
D:\mongodb\bin>mongo helloworld_db
MongoDB shell version: 2.2.2
connecting to: helloworld_db
> show collections
helloworld
system.indexes
> db.helloworld.find();
{ "_id" : ObjectId("50ee7a9f01650fd45122b728"), "Lucky number" : 493 }
{ "_id" : ObjectId("50ee7cd10165f47be8309032"), "Lucky number" : 643 }
{ "_id" : ObjectId("50ee7cd30165bfb73940ed38"), "Lucky number" : 180 }
{ "_id" : ObjectId("50ee7cd401652e8c0924c492"), "Lucky number" : 660 }
> _
```

Figure 4-1. *Checking the "helloworld" collection content*

If you don't obtain similar results, there's a problem that must be fixed before creating the next application.

The complete Hello World application is available in the Apress repository and, of course, is named HelloWorld. It comes as a NetBeans project and was tested under JDK 1.7 and MongoDB 2.2.2.

Hibernate OGM via Hibernate Native API

Once you've checked that MongoDB is ready to serve your applications, it's time to move on to Hibernate OGM. In this section, we'll develop a series of applications that involve Hibernate OGM using the Hibernate Native API. Here are the applications we'll develop:

- Hibernate OGM in a non-JTA environment (JDBC Transactions, Apache Tomcat 7)
- Hibernate OGM in a standalone JTA environment (JBoss JTA, Apache Tomcat 7)
- Hibernate OGM in a built-in JTA environment (no EJB, GlassFish AS 3)
- Hibernate OGM in a built-in JTA environment (EJB 3/BMT, GlassFish AS 3)
- Hibernate OGM in a built-in JTA environment (EJB 3/CMT, GlassFish AS 3)

Hibernate OGM in a Non-JTA Environment (JDBC Transactions, Apache Tomcat 7)

This application will bootstrap Hibernate OGM via Hibernate Native API in a non-JTA environment. Instead of JTA, we'll use the old-style JDBC transactions. Actually, instead of calling the JDBC API directly!, we'll use Hibernate's Transaction API and the built-in *session-per-request* functionality. The application will be deployable under an Apache Tomcat 7 web container.

■ **Note**   When Hibernate OGM is used in a non-JTA environment, the rollback feature is not guaranteed. This is why the Hibernate OGM team doesn't recommend this environment for the Hibernate OGM 4.0.0.Beta2 release, but there are hopes that this situation will become more favorable in the next releases. Since we are using MongoDB, which does not support transactions, this is a less concern for us.

Prerequisites

- MongoDB 2.2.2
- Hibernate OGM 4.0.0.Beta2
- JDK 1.7
- NetBeans 7.2.1 (or Eclipse JUNO)
- Apache Tomcat 7

Developing

After launching NetBeans, create a new project consisting of an empty Maven web application and name it HOGMviaHNAPI_JDBC_Tomcat7. In the New Web Application wizard, type hogm.hnapi for the Group Id and Package fields. Don't forget to select the Apache Tomcat 7 web server for deployment of this application. Once you see the project listed in Projects window, edit the pom.xml file (which must be under the Project Files node). In the pom.xml file, add the Hibernate OGM distribution (including MongoDB support) by pasting in the following dependencies:

```
<dependencies>
    <dependency>
        <groupId>org.hibernate.ogm</groupId>
        <artifactId>hibernate-ogm-core</artifactId>
        <version>4.0.0.Beta2</version>
    </dependency>
    <dependency>
        <groupId>org.hibernate.ogm</groupId>
        <artifactId>hibernate-ogm-mongodb</artifactId>
        <version>4.0.0.Beta1</version>
    </dependency>
...
<dependencies>
```

Now save the project and the MongoDB Java driver JAR will be listed under the Dependencies node.

Coding the Application

Now we're ready to add some code. We start with a simple POJO class, which has the ability to represent objects in the database. As you can see in Listing 4-2, the class contains a single field (apart from primary key field), named luckynumber and the well-known getter and setter methods.

Listing 4-2. The LuckyNumberPojo Class

```
package hogm.hnapi.pojo;

public class LuckyNumberPojo {

    private String id;
    private int luckynumber;
```

```java
    public String getId() {
        return id;
    }

    public void setId(String id) {
        this.id = id;
    }

    public int getLuckynumber() {
        return luckynumber;
    }

    public void setLuckynumber(int luckynumber) {
        this.luckynumber = luckynumber;
    }
}
```

Most applications that use Hibernate require a special class named HibernateUtil, a helper class that provides access to the SessionFactory everywhere in the code. There are many versions available for Hibernate ORM on the Internet, like the one from the CaveatEmptor demo. For Hibernate OGM, we can develop a HibernateUtil based on the simplest of the versions for Hibernate ORM, which usually looks like what's shown in Listing 4-3. You're probably familiar with it and have used it many times in Hibernate 3.

Listing 4-3. A Basic HibernateUtil Class for Hibernate ORM

```java
import org.hibernate.SessionFactory;
import org.hibernate.cfg.Configuration;

public class HibernateUtil {

    private static final SessionFactory sessionFactory;

    static {
        try {
            sessionFactory = new
                          Configuration().configure().buildSessionFactory();
        } catch (Throwable ex) {
            System.err.println("Initial SessionFactory creation failed." + ex);
            throw new ExceptionInInitializerError(ex);
        }
    }

    public static SessionFactory getSessionFactory() {
        return sessionFactory;
    }
}
```

Now, developing a HibernateUtil for Hibernate OGM is a task based on two main modifications of this source. First, instead of creating a new instance of the Configuration class, we need to instantiate the OgmConfiguration class, which is used to configure the Hibernate OGM environment. And second, starting with Hibernate 4, the session factory has to be obtained through a service registry passed to the buildSessionFactory method. With these in mind, the code can be easily transformed into a HibernateUtil for Hibernate OGM, as shown in Listing 4-4.

Listing 4-4. A HibernateUtil Class for Hibernate OGM

```java
package hogm.hnapi.util.with.hibernate.cfg;

import java.util.logging.Level;
import java.util.logging.Logger;
import org.hibernate.SessionFactory;
import org.hibernate.ogm.cfg.OgmConfiguration;
import org.hibernate.service.ServiceRegistry;
import org.hibernate.service.ServiceRegistryBuilder;

public class HibernateUtil {

    private static final Logger log =
            Logger.getLogger(HibernateUtil.class.getName());
    private static final SessionFactory sessionFactory;
    private static final ServiceRegistry serviceRegistry;

    static {
        try {
            // create a new instance of OmgConfiguration
            OgmConfiguration cfgogm = new OgmConfiguration();

            // process configuration and mapping files
            cfgogm.configure();
            // create the SessionFactory
            serviceRegistry = new ServiceRegistryBuilder().
             applySettings(cfgogm.getProperties()).buildServiceRegistry();
            sessionFactory = cfgogm.buildSessionFactory(serviceRegistry);
        } catch (Throwable ex) {
            log.log(Level.SEVERE,
                    "Initial SessionFactory creation failed !", ex);
            throw new ExceptionInInitializerError(ex);
        }
    }

    public static SessionFactory getSessionFactory() {
        return sessionFactory;
    }
}
```

To get a valid session factory from this HibernateUtil, we need to build the Hibernate configuration file (hibernate.cfg.xml) and the corresponding mapping files (*.hbm.xml). As you know, the hibernate.cfg.xml file contains the main information for adjusting the Hibernate environment and database connection. Since we're in a non-JTA environment and are following the well-known Hibernate *thread-bound* strategy (Hibernate binds the current session to the current Java thread), we start by setting two properties that are mandatory for accessing this strategy:

```xml
<property name="hibernate.transaction.factory_class">
          org.hibernate.transaction.JDBCTransactionFactory
</property>
<property name="hibernate.current_session_context_class">
          thread
</property>
```

The next five properties are the top priority for us since they represent the MongoDB configuration, so we specify the datastore provider, dialect, the name of the database to connect to, the MongoDB server host, and the port (we'll use the localhost and the MongoDB server's default port of 27017):

```
<property name="hibernate.ogm.datastore.provider">mongodb</property>
<property name="hibernate.ogm.datastore.grid_dialect">
        org.hibernate.ogm.dialect.mongodb.MongoDBDialect</property>
<property name="hibernate.ogm.mongodb.database">tomcat_db</property>
<property name="hibernate.ogm.mongodb.host">127.0.0.1</property>
<property name="hibernate.ogm.mongodb.port">27017</property>
```

Finally, we add the mapping resource, which, in this case, is represented by the single class, LuckyNumberPojo. Add this final line:

```
<mapping resource="/LuckyNumberPojo.hbm.xml"/>
```

to the end of hibernate.cfg.xml to get the code shown in Listing 4-5.

Listing 4-5. A Hibernate Configuration File

```
<?xml version="1.0" encoding="UTF-8"?>
<!DOCTYPE hibernate-configuration PUBLIC "-//Hibernate/Hibernate Configuration DTD 3.0//EN"
"http://www.hibernate.org/dtd/hibernate-configuration-3.0.dtd">
<hibernate-configuration>
  <session-factory>
    <property name="hibernate.transaction.factory_class">
            org.hibernate.transaction.JDBCTransactionFactory</property>
    <property name="hibernate.current_session_context_class">thread</property>
    <property name="hibernate.ogm.datastore.provider">mongodb</property>
    <property name="hibernate.ogm.datastore.grid_dialect">
            org.hibernate.ogm.dialect.mongodb.MongoDBDialect</property>
    <property name="hibernate.ogm.mongodb.database">tomcat_db</property>
    <property name="hibernate.ogm.mongodb.host">127.0.0.1</property>
    <property name="hibernate.ogm.mongodb.port">27017</property>
    <mapping resource="/LuckyNumberPojo.hbm.xml"/>
  </session-factory>
</hibernate-configuration>
```

The file hibernate.cfg.xml must reside in the root of the classpath when the web app is started. In a Maven project, like this one, it should be saved in the src/main/resources directory (in NetBeans, this directory can be found in the Other Sources node). In a non-Maven application, save the file in the WEB-INF/classes directory.

Writing LuckyNumberPojo.hbm.xml is our next goal. Since we have an ordinary POJO, the task is simple. First, we describe the primary key field and the generator as UUID2. (This generates an IETF RFC 4122-compliant (variant 2) 128-bit UUID. More details are available at www.ietf.org/rfc/rfc4122.txt.) Then we describe the luckynumber field. The result is shown in Listing 4-6.

Listing 4-6. LuckyNumberPojo.hbm.xml

```
<?xml version="1.0" encoding="UTF-8"?>
<!DOCTYPE hibernate-mapping PUBLIC "-//Hibernate/Hibernate Mapping DTD 3.0//EN"
"http://www.hibernate.org/dtd/hibernate-mapping-3.0.dtd">
```

```
<hibernate-mapping>
    <class name="hogm.hnapi.pojo.LuckyNumberPojo" table="jdbc">
        <id name="id" type="string">
            <column name="id" />
            <generator class="uuid2" />
        </id>
        <property name="luckynumber" type="int">
            <column name="luckynumber"/>
        </property>
    </class>
</hibernate-mapping>
```

This file should go in the same folder as `hibernate.cfg.xml`.

The assignment `table="jdbc"` creates a collection named `jdbc` in MongoDB. If you want to create a collection named *XXX*.`jdbc`, you can add `catalog="`*XXX*`"`, like this:

```
<class name="hogm.hnapi.pojo.LuckyNumberPojo" table="jdbc" catalog="XXX">
```

Finally, we've reached the point where we can add some business logic. We'll write a DAO class that persists the lucky numbers into the database. Such a class would typically contain, at the least, methods for all the CRUD operations. However, all we need is a method for the persist operation. Actually, there are two implementations of persist, one per opening session strategy. As you know, Hibernate provides both the `getCurrentSession` and `openSession` methods for obtaining the current session. Calling `getCurrentSession` returns the "current" session bound by Hibernate behind the scenes to the transaction scope, or opens a new session when `getCurrentSession` is called for the first time. The session is available everywhere in the code as long as the transaction runs, and it is automatically closed and flushed when the transaction ends. If you want to flush and close the session explicitly, you have to use the `openSession` method. Listing 4-7 shows our DAO class with two `persist` methods, one for `getCurrentSession` and one for `openSession`. Both use declarative demarcation of transactions boundaries, using `org.hibernate.Session` methods such as `beginTransaction` and `commit`.

Listing 4-7. The DAO Class with Two `persist` Methods

```
package hogm.hnapi.dao;

import hogm.hnapi.pojo.LuckyNumberPojo;
import java.util.logging.Level;
import java.util.logging.Logger;
import org.hibernate.Session;

public class LuckyNumberDAO {

    private static final Logger log = Logger.getLogger(LuckyNumberDAO.class.getName());

    /**
     * Insert data (use getCurrentSession and POJO)
     *
     * @param transientInstance
     * @throws Exception
     */
```

```java
public void persist_cs_with_cfg(LuckyNumberPojo transientInstance) throws java.lang.Exception {

    log.log(Level.INFO, "Persisting LuckyNumberPojo instance ...");
    Session session = hogm.hnapi.util.with.hibernate.cfg.HibernateUtil.
                                getSessionFactory().getCurrentSession();
    try {
        session.beginTransaction();
        session.persist(transientInstance);
        session.getTransaction().commit();

        log.log(Level.INFO, "Persist successful...");
    } catch (RuntimeException re) {
        session.getTransaction().rollback();
        log.log(Level.SEVERE, "Persist failed...", re);
        throw re;
    }
}

/**
 * Insert data (use openSession and POJO)
 *
 * @param transientInstance
 * @throws Exception
 */
public void persist_os_with_cfg(LuckyNumberPojo transientInstance) throws java.lang.Exception {

    log.log(Level.INFO, "Persisting LuckyNumberPojo instance ...");
    Session session = hogm.hnapi.util.with.hibernate.cfg.HibernateUtil.
                                getSessionFactory().openSession();

    try {
        session.beginTransaction();
        session.persist(transientInstance);
        session.flush(); // flush happens automatically anyway
        session.getTransaction().commit();

        log.log(Level.INFO, "Persist successful...");
    } catch (RuntimeException re) {
        session.getTransaction().rollback();
        log.log(Level.SEVERE, "Persist failed...", re);
        throw re;
    } finally {
        session.close();
    }
}
}
```

■ **Note** Though it's not listed here, the source code for this application (available in the Apress repository) also demonstrates using an entity instead of a POJO, and replacing `hibernate.cfg.xml` with programmatic configuration in the `HibernateUtil` class.

We're almost done! A simple user interface and a servlet are all we have left to implement. When the user presses a button in the interface, an empty form is submitted to the servlet, which calls our DAO class (either persist_cs_with_cfg or persist_os_with_cfg) to store the generated lucky number into the database. The main snippet of code from the servlet is shown in Listing 4-8.

Listing 4-8. The Lucky Number Servlet

```
package hogm.hnapi.servlet;
...
@WebServlet(name = "LuckyNumberServlet", urlPatterns = {"/LuckyNumberServlet"})
public class LuckyNumberServlet extends HttpServlet {
  ...
 protected void processRequest(HttpServletRequest request, HttpServletResponse
 response) throws ServletException, IOException, Exception {
    ...
    LuckyNumberDAO luckyNumberDAO = new LuckyNumberDAO();
    LuckyNumberPojo luckyNumberPojo = new LuckyNumberPojo();
    luckyNumberPojo.setLuckynumber(new Random().nextInt(1000000));

    luckyNumberDAO.persist_cs_with_cfg(luckyNumberPojo);
    // luckyNumberDAO.persist_os_with_cfg(luckyNumberPojo);
    ...
  }
}
```

And the HTML form that's submitted to this servlet is also extremely simple. The code goes on the index.jsp page, which, in a NetBeans project, is listed under the Web Pages node of the project).

```
...
<form action="./LuckyNumberServlet" method="POST">
    <input type="submit" value="Generate Lucky Number">
</form>
...
Done!
```

Testing

Start the MongoDB server as you saw in Chapter 1. Next, since you're in a NetBeans/Tomcat (or Eclipse/Tomcat) environment, just save the project and click the Run (or Run on Server in Eclipse) button to start Tomcat and deploy and run the application. If the application starts successfully, you'll see in the browser something like what's shown in Figure 4-2.

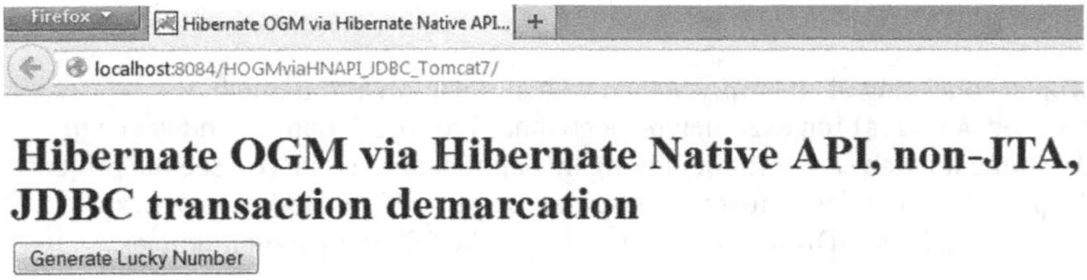

Hibernate OGM via Hibernate Native API, non-JTA, JDBC transaction demarcation

Generate Lucky Number

Figure 4-2. *Running the HOGMviaHNAPI_JDBC_Tomcat7 application*

Press the Generate Lucky Number button a few times to persist some lucky numbers into the MongoDB database (tomcat_db) collection (jdbc). Open a command prompt and type the commands shown in Figure 4-3 to see the results of your work. This lets you monitor Tomcat log messages in case anything unwanted happens.

```
D:\mongodb\bin>mongo tomcat_db
MongoDB shell version: 2.2.2
connecting to: tomcat_db
> show collections
jdbc
system.indexes
> db.jdbc.find();
{ "_id" : "073c17b9-3759-4584-b675-a6c40a3aab15", "luckynumber" : 397159 }
{ "_id" : "bf6e4623-24a4-4e78-9fd4-8b925e1140ad", "luckynumber" : 111416 }
{ "_id" : "f78c45a3-86db-4f1f-a818-640adb066656", "luckynumber" : 680446 }
```

Figure 4-3. *Checking the "jdbc" collection content*

The complete source code for this application, which is called HOGMviaHNAPI_JDBC_Tomcat7, is available in the Apress repository. It comes as a NetBeans project and it was tested under Tomcat 7. (I used the Tomcat bundled with NetBeans 7.2.1.)

Hibernate OGM in a Standalone JTA Environment (JBoss JTA, Apache Tomcat 7)

Our next application will bootstrap Hibernate OGM via the Hibernate Native API in a standalone JTA environment. As you'll see, Hibernate works in any environment that uses JTA and, in fact, can automatically bind the current session to the current JTA transaction. Since Tomcat is not a J2EE environment, it does not provide an automatic JTA transaction manager, so we have to choose a standalone implementation of JTA. There are several open source implementations, such as JOTM, Bitronix JTA, and Atomikos, but I prefer the JBoss JTA. It's part of the well-known JBoss TS (Arjuna Transaction Service) that comes with a very robust implementation of JTA and JTS APIs.

Now let's see what the prerequisites for this application are.

Prerequisites

- MongoDB 2.2.2
- Hibernate OGM 4.0.0.Beta2
- JBoss JTA 4.16.4 Final
- JDK 1.7
- NetBeans 7.2.1 (or Eclipse JUNO)
- Apache Tomcat 7

Developing

Launch NetBeans and create a new project consisting of an empty Maven web application and name it HOGMviaHNAPI_JTA_Tomcat7. In the New Web Application wizard, type hogm.hnapi for the Group Id and Package fields. Don't forget to select the Apache Tomcat 7 web server for deploying this application. Once you see the project listed in the Projects window, edit the pom.xml file (which must be under the Project Files node). In pom.xml, add the Hibernate OGM distribution (including MongoDB support) by pasting in the following dependencies.

```
<dependencies>
    <dependency>
        <groupId>org.hibernate.ogm</groupId>
        <artifactId>hibernate-ogm-core</artifactId>
        <version>4.0.0.Beta2</version>
    </dependency>
    <dependency>
        <groupId>org.hibernate.ogm</groupId>
        <artifactId>hibernate-ogm-mongodb</artifactId>
        <version>4.0.0.Beta1</version>
    </dependency>
...
<dependencies>
```

Now save the project and the driver JAR will be listed under the Dependencies node.

We still need to add JARs for JBoss JTA in the application classpath, so now add this dependency:

```
<dependencies>
    <dependency>
        <groupId>org.jboss.jbossts</groupId>
        <artifactId>jbossjta</artifactId>
        <version>4.16.4.Final</version>
    </dependency>
...
<dependencies>
```

Coding the Application

We have all the necessary artifacts now so it's time to start developing the application. First we'll create a basic entity class that can represent objects in the database. The class will contain just a single field (apart from the primary key), which is named luckynumber. You should be familiar with these kind of entities, which are, technically speaking, just annotated POJOs. (For more details, refer back to Chapter 2.) Listing 4-9 shows the LuckyNumberEntity class.

Listing 4-9. The LuckyNumberEntity Class

```
package hogm.hnapi.pojo;

import java.io.Serializable;
import javax.persistence.Column;
import javax.persistence.Entity;
import javax.persistence.GeneratedValue;
import javax.persistence.Id;
import javax.persistence.Table;
import org.hibernate.annotations.GenericGenerator;
```

```
@Entity
@Table(name="jta")
public class LuckyNumberEntity implements Serializable {

    private static final long serialVersionUID = 1L;
    @Id
    @GeneratedValue(generator = "uuid")
    @GenericGenerator(name="uuid", strategy="uuid2")
    private String id;

    @Column(name="luckynumber", nullable=false)
    private int luckynumber;

    public String getId() {
        return id;
    }

    public void setId(String id) {
        this.id = id;
    }

    public int getLuckynumber() {
        return luckynumber;
    }

    public void setLuckynumber(int luckynumber) {
        this.luckynumber = luckynumber;
    }
}
```

In the previous application, we used a simple POJO, and we developed a HibernateUtil class especially designed to obtain a session factory anywhere in the code based on hibernate.cfg.xml and mapping files. In this application, we'll take another approach—we'll use an entity (a POJO extended with JDK 5 annotations) and a HibernateUtil that provides a session factory configured programmatically. In other words, no hibernate.cfg.xml and no mapping files.

There are several configuration properties specific to our application. First of all, we tell Hibernate we want to use manual transaction demarcation by setting the hibernate.transaction.factory_class to org.hibernate.transaction.JTATransactionFactory and hibernate.current_session_context_class to jta. Programmatically speaking, these properties are mapped as constant values in the org.hibernate.cfg.Environment class:

```
...
// create a new instance of OmgConfiguration
OgmConfiguration cfgogm = new OgmConfiguration();

cfgogm.setProperty(Environment.TRANSACTION_STRATEGY,
                        "org.hibernate.transaction.JTATransactionFactory");
cfgogm.setProperty(Environment.CURRENT_SESSION_CONTEXT_CLASS, "jta");
...
```

Next, we specify the JTA platform, JBoss JTA. To do so, we add the following:

```
cfgogm.setProperty(Environment.JTA_PLATFORM,
"org.hibernate.service.jta.platform.internal.JBossStandAloneJtaPlatform");
```

Notice that we set the JBoss JTA standalone distribution, not the one used by the JBoss AS.

According to the JBoss TS documentation, in order to select the local JBoss JTA implementation, you need to specify two properties, com.arjuna.ats.jta.jtaTMImplementation and com.arjuna.ats.jta.jtaUTImplementation. Since these properties aren't part of Hibernate environment, they don't have correlates in the Environment class. You can specify them like this:

```
cfgogm.setProperty("com.arjuna.ats.jta.jtaTMImplementation",
"com.arjuna.ats.internal.jta.transaction.arjunacore.TransactionManagerImple");
cfgogm.setProperty("com.arjuna.ats.jta.jtaUTImplementation",
"com.arjuna.ats.internal.jta.transaction.arjunacore.UserTransactionImple");
```

Next, we configure the MongoDB connection: the datastore provider, the dialect, the name of the database to connect to, the host and the port (we will use the localhost and the default MongoDB server port of 27017):

```
cfgogm.setProperty("hibernate.ogm.datastore.provider", "mongodb");
cfgogm.setProperty("hibernate.ogm.datastore.grid_dialect",
                   "org.hibernate.ogm.dialect.mongodb.MongoDBDialect");
cfgogm.setProperty("hibernate.ogm.mongodb.database", "tomcat_db");
cfgogm.setProperty("hibernate.ogm.mongodb.host", "127.0.0.1");
cfgogm.setProperty("hibernate.ogm.mongodb.port", "27017");
```

Finally, we add our entity into the equation, dropping the LuckyNumberEntity.hbm.xml mapping file:

```
cfgogm.addAnnotatedClass(hogm.hnapi.pojo.LuckyNumberEntity.class);
```

Now add all of these configuration properties into the HibernateUtil class specific to the OGM distribution to get the code shown in Listing 4-10. Note that I discussed this class in more detail in the previous application.

Listing 4-10. Another HibernateUtil Class

```
package hogm.hnapi.util.without.hibernate.cfg;

import java.util.logging.Level;
import java.util.logging.Logger;
import org.hibernate.SessionFactory;
import org.hibernate.cfg.Environment;
import org.hibernate.ogm.cfg.OgmConfiguration;
import org.hibernate.service.ServiceRegistry;
import org.hibernate.service.ServiceRegistryBuilder;

public class HibernateUtil {

    private static final Logger log = Logger.getLogger(HibernateUtil.class.getName());
    private static final SessionFactory sessionFactory;
    private static final ServiceRegistry serviceRegistry;
```

```java
static {
    try {
        // create a new instance of OmgConfiguration
        OgmConfiguration cfgogm = new OgmConfiguration();

        // enable JTA strategy
        cfgogm.setProperty(Environment.TRANSACTION_STRATEGY,
                                    "org.hibernate.transaction.JTATransactionFactory");
        cfgogm.setProperty(Environment.CURRENT_SESSION_CONTEXT_CLASS, "jta");

        // specify JTA platform
        cfgogm.setProperty(Environment.JTA_PLATFORM,
                    "org.hibernate.service.jta.platform.internal.JBossStandAloneJtaPlatform");

        // in order to select the local JBoss JTA implementation it is necessary to specify
        these properties
        cfgogm.setProperty("com.arjuna.ats.jta.jtaTMImplementation",
                    "com.arjuna.ats.internal.jta.transaction.arjunacore.TransactionManagerImple");
        cfgogm.setProperty("com.arjuna.ats.jta.jtaUTImplementation",
                    "com.arjuna.ats.internal.jta.transaction.arjunacore.UserTransactionImple");

        //configure MongoDB connection
        cfgogm.setProperty("hibernate.ogm.datastore.provider", "mongodb");
        cfgogm.setProperty("hibernate.ogm.datastore.grid_dialect",
                    "org.hibernate.ogm.dialect.mongodb.MongoDBDialect");
        //you can ignore this setting
        cfgogm.setProperty("hibernate.ogm.mongodb.database", "tomcat_db");
        cfgogm.setProperty("hibernate.ogm.mongodb.host", "127.0.0.1");
        cfgogm.setProperty("hibernate.ogm.mongodb.port", "27017");

        //add our annotated class
        cfgogm.addAnnotatedClass(hogm.hnapi.pojo.LuckyNumberEntity.class);

        // create the SessionFactory
        serviceRegistry = new ServiceRegistryBuilder().applySettings(cfgogm.getProperties()).
                                    buildServiceRegistry();
        sessionFactory = cfgogm.buildSessionFactory(serviceRegistry);
    } catch (Throwable ex) {
        log.log(Level.SEVERE, "Initial SessionFactory creation failed !", ex);
        throw new ExceptionInInitializerError(ex);
    }
}

public static SessionFactory getSessionFactory() {
    return sessionFactory;
}
}
```

Well, so far we have the entity and the session factory provider. The next part is very interesting, because we start developing the DAO class. This means using JBoss JTA to demarcate transactions, and for this we focus on two JBoss JTA classes:

- `com.arjuna.ats.jta.UserTransaction`—This class automatically associates newly created transactions with the invoking thread, and exposes methods like `begin`, `commit`, and `rollback` for controlling the transaction boundaries. It also provides a static method named `userTransaction` that returns a `javax.transaction.UserTransaction` representing user transactions:

  `javax.transaction.UserTransaction tx = com.arjuna.ats.jta.UserTransaction.userTransaction();`

- `com.arjuna.ats.jta.TransactionManager`—This is an interface that allows the application server to control transaction boundaries. It also provides methods like `begin`, `commit`, and `rollback`, but it's especially designed for application servers that can initialize the transaction manager and call it to demarcate transactions for you. You can obtain the `javax.transaction.TransactionManager` through `transactionManager` method, like so:

`javax.transaction.TransactionManager tx = com.arjuna.ats.jta.TransactionManager.transactionManager();`

If you prefer the Hibernate `getCurrentSession` approach for getting current `Session`, you can implement a DAO method of persisting lucky numbers into the database using JBoss JTA, as shown in Listing 4-11.

Listing 4-11. The LuckyNumberDAO Class - getCurrentSession Approach

```
package hogm.hnapi.dao;
...
public class LuckyNumberDAO {
...
 private static final Logger log =
   Logger.getLogger(LuckyNumberDAO.class.getName());
...
 public void persist_cs_without_cfg(LuckyNumberEntity transientInstance) throws
 java.lang.Exception {

        log.log(Level.INFO, "Persisting LuckyNumberEntity instance ...");

        // javax.transaction.TransactionManager tx =
                            com.arjuna.ats.jta.TransactionManager.transactionManager();
        javax.transaction.UserTransaction tx = com.arjuna.ats.jta.UserTransaction.userTransaction();

        try {
            tx.begin();
            hogm.hnapi.util.without.hibernate.cfg.HibernateUtil.getSessionFactory().
                                            getCurrentSession().persist(transientInstance);
            tx.commit();

            log.log(Level.INFO, "Persist successful...");
        } catch (RuntimeException re) {
```

```
                tx.rollback();
                log.log(Level.SEVERE, "Persist failed...", re);
                throw re;
            }
        }
    }
}
```

But, if you want to control the session flush and close by yourself, choose the Hibernate openSession approach, which can be interwoven with JBoss JTA in almost the same manner, as in Listing 4-12.

Listing 4-12. The LuckyNumberDAO Class - openSession Approach

```
package hogm.hnapi.dao;
...
public class LuckyNumberDAO {
 ...
 private static final Logger log =
   Logger.getLogger(LuckyNumberDAO.class.getName());
 ...
 public void persist_os_without_cfg(LuckyNumberEntity transientInstance) throws
 java.lang.Exception {

        log.log(Level.INFO, "Persisting LuckyNumberEntity instance ...");

        // javax.transaction.TransactionManager tx =
                            com.arjuna.ats.jta.TransactionManager.transactionManager();
        javax.transaction.UserTransaction tx = com.arjuna.ats.jta.UserTransaction.userTransaction();
        Session session = hogm.hnapi.util.without.hibernate.cfg.HibernateUtil.
                            getSessionFactory().openSession();

        try {
            tx.begin();
            session.persist(transientInstance);
            session.flush();
            tx.commit();

            log.log(Level.INFO, "Persist successful...");
        } catch (RuntimeException re) {
            tx.rollback();
            log.log(Level.SEVERE, "Persist failed...", re);
            throw re;
        } finally {
            session.close();
        }
    }
}
```

The application is almost finished. Its main parts are available and we just need to add a servlet to call the DAO methods, as well as a simple user interface to submit an empty form to this servlet. The main snippet of code from LuckyNumberServlet is shown in Listing 4-13.

Listing 4-13. A Snippet from LuckyNumberServlet

```
package hogm.hnapi.servlet;
...
@WebServlet(name = "LuckyNumberServlet", urlPatterns = {"/LuckyNumberServlet"})
public class LuckyNumberServlet extends HttpServlet {
...

 protected void processRequest(HttpServletRequest request, HttpServletResponse
 response) throws ServletException, IOException, Exception {
  ...
  LuckyNumberDAO luckyNumberDAO = new LuckyNumberDAO();
  LuckyNumberEntity luckyNumberEntity = new LuckyNumberEntity();
  luckyNumberEntity.setLuckynumber(new Random().nextInt(1000000));

  luckyNumberDAO.persist_cs_without_cfg(luckyNumberEntity);
  // luckyNumberDAO.persist_os_without_cfg(luckyNumberEntity);
  ...
 }
}
```

And here's the form that interacts with this servlet (in index.jsp):

```
...
<form action="./LuckyNumberServlet" method="POST">
   <input type="submit" value="Generate Lucky Number">
</form>
...
```

Done!

Testing

Begin by starting the MongoDB server as in Chapter 1. Next, since you're in a NetBeans/Tomcat (or Eclipse/Tomcat) environment, just save the project and click the Run (or Run on Server in Eclipse) button to start Tomcat and deploy and run the application. If the application successfully starts, you'll see in your browser something similar to what's shown in Figure 4-4.

Figure 4-4. *Running the HOGMviaHNAPI_JTA_Tomcat7 application*

Press the Generate Lucky Number button a few times for persisting some lucky numbers into the MongoDB database (tomcat_db) collection (jta). Open a command prompt and type the commands shown in Figure 4-5 to see the result of your work. As before, you can monitor Tomcat log messages to see if anything unwanted happens.

```
D:\mongodb\bin>mongo tomcat_db
MongoDB shell version: 2.2.2
connecting to: tomcat_db
> show collections
jdbc
jta
system.indexes
> db.jta.find();
{ "_id" : "f6aaf0e5-55e8-4fe6-8356-18d2593442ca", "luckynumber" : 220718 }
{ "_id" : "3e0a51d6-6295-42e2-b5d8-56263dfd4a79", "luckynumber" : 791213 }
{ "_id" : "da84ad35-a028-4ce3-9d36-dfe903ea7de2", "luckynumber" : 77994 }
```

Figure 4-5. *Checking the jta collection content*

The complete source code for this application, called HOGMviaHNAPI_JTA_Tomcat7, is available in the Apress repository. It comes as a NetBeans project and it was tested under Tomcat 7 (I used the Tomcat bundled to NetBeans 7.2.1).

Hibernate OGM in a Built-in JTA Environment (no EJB, GlassFish AS 3)

In the previous example, we developed an application based on a standalone JTA environment. We can reuse most of the code to write the same kind of application, but based this time on a built-in JTA environment provider, like GlassFish v3 AS. As you probably know, this is a fully compatible J2EE application server that automatically handles (through a JTA TransactionManager) the transaction lifecycle for each data source. In other words, we will develop the same application as in the last section, but instead of using and configuring JBoss JTA, we will use the JTA transaction manager provided by the container. Notice that we are still manually demarcating transaction boundaries; this is not a container managed transaction (CMT) strategy.

Prerequisites

- MongoDB 2.2.2

- Hibernate OGM 4.0.0.Beta2

- JDK 1.7

- NetBeans 7.2.1 (or Eclipse JUNO)

- GlassFish 3.1.2.2

Developing

After launching NetBeans, create a new project consisting of an empty Maven web application and name it HOGMviaHNAPI_JTA_GlassFish3. In the New Web Application wizard, type hogm.hnapi for the Group Id and Package fields, and select GlassFish web server for deploying this application. Now, just follow the scenario from the preceding section. We'll make some small but important modifications.

Coding the Application

After adding Hibernate OGM/Mongo DB JARs (using Maven as in the previous example), create the same LuckyNumberEntity entity. Continue by writing the HibernateUtil class shown in Listing 4-14.

Listing 4-14. A Modified HibernateUtil Class

```
package hogm.hnapi.util.without.hibernate.cfg;

import java.util.logging.Level;
import java.util.logging.Logger;
import org.hibernate.SessionFactory;
import org.hibernate.cfg.Environment;
import org.hibernate.ogm.cfg.OgmConfiguration;
import org.hibernate.service.ServiceRegistry;
import org.hibernate.service.ServiceRegistryBuilder;

public class HibernateUtil {

    private static final Logger log = Logger.getLogger(HibernateUtil.class.getName());
    private static final SessionFactory sessionFactory;
    private static final ServiceRegistry serviceRegistry;

    static {
        try {
            // create a new instance of OmgConfiguration
            OgmConfiguration cfgogm = new OgmConfiguration();

            // enable JTA strategy
            cfgogm.setProperty(Environment.TRANSACTION_STRATEGY,
                        "org.hibernate.transaction.JTATransactionFactory");
            cfgogm.setProperty(Environment.CURRENT_SESSION_CONTEXT_CLASS, "jta");

            // specify JTA platform
            cfgogm.setProperty(Environment.JTA_PLATFORM,
                        "org.hibernate.service.jta.platform.internal.SunOneJtaPlatform");

            //configure MongoDB connection
            cfgogm.setProperty("hibernate.ogm.datastore.provider", "mongodb");
            cfgogm.setProperty("hibernate.ogm.datastore.grid_dialect",
                        "org.hibernate.ogm.dialect.mongodb.MongoDBDialect");
            //you can ignore this setting
            cfgogm.setProperty("hibernate.ogm.mongodb.database", "glassfish_db");
            cfgogm.setProperty("hibernate.ogm.mongodb.host", "127.0.0.1");
            cfgogm.setProperty("hibernate.ogm.mongodb.port", "27017");

            //add our annotated class
            cfgogm.addAnnotatedClass(hogm.hnapi.pojo.LuckyNumberEntity.class);

            // create the SessionFactory
            serviceRegistry = new ServiceRegistryBuilder().applySettings(cfgogm.getProperties()).
                                    buildServiceRegistry();
```

```
            sessionFactory = cfgogm.buildSessionFactory(serviceRegistry);
        } catch (Throwable ex) {
            log.log(Level.SEVERE, "Initial SessionFactory creation failed !", ex);
            throw new ExceptionInInitializerError(ex);
        }
    }

    public static SessionFactory getSessionFactory() {
        return sessionFactory;
    }
}
```

As you can see, the relevant code is shown in bold:

```
cfgogm.setProperty(Environment.JTA_PLATFORM,
            "org.hibernate.service.jta.platform.internal.SunOneJtaPlatform");
```

This code tells Hibernate the JTA platform to be used. Obviously, we want to use the built-in JTA platform, which, for GlassFish v3 AS is org.hibernate.service.jta.platform.internal.SunOneJtaPlatform. No library or JAR is needed; everything is provided by the container. You can easily modify this property (hibernate.transaction.jta.platform) for other supported containers (the JTA built-in platform) by checking the list of available JTA platforms in Chapter 2. For example, if you deploy this application under JBoss 7 AS, the built-in JTA platform is org.hibernate.service.jta.platform.internal.JBossAppServerJtaPlatform; don't confuse this JTA with the standalone JBoss JTA platform.

If you decide to use hibernate.cfg.xml, add the JTA platform, like this:

```
<property name="hibernate.transaction.jta.platform">
                org.hibernate.service.jta.platform.internal.SunOneJtaPlatform</property>
```

Now let's develop the DAO class. If you followed the earlier applications, you know we are focusing only on persisting objects into a database in Hibernate sessions obtained using the getCurrentSession or openSession methods. As you know, Hibernate can automatically bind the current session to the current JTA transaction, but for this we need to take control of the transaction itself and add the corresponding demarcation boundaries. To accomplish this task in a J2EE environment, we can simply take advantage of the standard JNDI subcontext java:comp/UserTransaction. The javax.transaction.UserTransaction should be available in java:comp/UserTransaction, following the J2EE specification:

```
UserTransaction tx = (UserTransaction) new InitialContext().lookup("java:comp/UserTransaction");
```

Now, for the getCurrentSession approach, we can call the begin, commit, and rollback methods shown in Listing 4-15.

Listing 4-15. The getCurrentSession Approach

```
package hogm.hnapi.dao;
...
public class LuckyNumberDAO {
...
private static final Logger log =
   Logger.getLogger(LuckyNumberDAO.class.getName());
 ...
```

```
public void persist_cs_without_cfg(LuckyNumberEntity transientInstance) throws
java.lang.Exception {

        log.log(Level.INFO, "Persisting LuckyNumberEntity instance ...");

        UserTransaction tx = (UserTransaction) new
                        InitialContext().lookup("java:comp/UserTransaction");

        try {
            tx.begin();
            hogm.hnapi.util.without.hibernate.cfg.HibernateUtil.getSessionFactory().
                                            getCurrentSession().persist(transientInstance);
            tx.commit();

            log.log(Level.INFO, "Persist successful...");
        } catch (RuntimeException re) {
            tx.rollback();
            log.log(Level.SEVERE, "Persist failed...", re);
            throw re;
        }
    }
}
```

Or, if you prefer openSession, use the approach in Listing 4-16.

Listing 4-16. *The openSession Approach*

```
package hogm.hnapi.dao;
...
public class LuckyNumberDAO {
...
private static final Logger log =
   Logger.getLogger(LuckyNumberDAO.class.getName());
 ...
 public void persist_os_without_cfg(LuckyNumberEntity transientInstance) throws
 java.lang.Exception {

        log.log(Level.INFO, "Persisting LuckyNumberEntity instance ...");

        UserTransaction tx = (UserTransaction) new InitialContext().lookup("java:comp/UserTransaction");
        Session session = hogm.hnapi.util.without.hibernate.cfg.HibernateUtil.
                                                getSessionFactory().openSession();

        try {
            tx.begin();
            session.persist(transientInstance);
            session.flush();
            tx.commit();

            log.log(Level.INFO, "Persist successful...");
        } catch (RuntimeException re) {
```

```
                tx.rollback();
                log.log(Level.SEVERE, "Persist failed...", re);
                throw re;
            } finally {
                session.close();
            }
        }
    }
}
```

Now the entire Hibernate OGM mechanism is set. All that remains is to add a simple user interface that submits an "empty" form to a basic JSF bean (replace this with a servlet if you aren't a JSF fan) that communicates with the DAO class. Listing 4-17 shows the code that interacts with the DAO class.

Listing 4-17. The TestManagedBean Class

```
package hogm.hnapi.jsf;
...
public class TestManagedBean {
...
public void persistAction() throws Exception {
    ...
    LuckyNumberDAO luckyNumberDAO = new LuckyNumberDAO();
    LuckyNumberEntity luckyNumberEntity = new LuckyNumberEntity();
    luckyNumberEntity.setLuckynumber(new Random().nextInt(1000000));

    luckyNumberDAO.persist_cs_without_cfg(luckyNumberEntity);
    // luckyNumberDAO.persist_os_without_cfg(luckyNumberEntity);
    ...
}
}
```

And here's code for the user form, which goes on the index.xhtml page:

```
...
<h:form>
    <h:commandButton action="#{bean.persistAction()}" value="Generate Lucky Number"/>
</h:form>
...
```

That's it!

Testing

Now start the MongoDB server as you saw in Chapter 1. Next, since you're in a NetBeans/GlassFish (or Eclipse/GlassFish) environment, just save the project and click the Run (or Run on Server in Eclipse) button to start GlassFish and deploy and run the application. If the application successfully starts, you'll see in your browser something similar to what's shown in Figure 4-6.

Hibernate OGM via Hibernate Native API, JTA environment, built-in JTA platform

Generate Lucky Number

Figure 4-6. *Running the HOGMviaHNAPI_JTA_GlassFish3 application*

Press the Generate Lucky Number button a few times to persist some lucky numbers into the MongoDB database (glassfish_db) collection (jta). Open a command prompt and type the commands from Figure 4-7 to see the results of your work. You can also monitor GlassFish log messages in case anything unwanted happens.

```
D:\mongodb\bin>mongo glassfish_db
MongoDB shell version: 2.2.2
connecting to: glassfish_db
> show collections
jta
system.indexes
> db.jta.find();
{ "_id" : "3f2a1a6e-ce1d-422c-ac30-80cba443f73a", "luckynumber" : 355161 }
{ "_id" : "0df3eaf7-8f9c-4cdd-9498-4c0d2072da0e", "luckynumber" : 369579 }
```

Figure 4-7. *Checking the jta collection content*

The complete source code for this application is named HOGMviaHNAPI_JTA_GlassFish3 and is available in the Apress repository. It comes as a NetBeans project and was tested it under GlassFish 3 (I used the GlassFish bundled with NetBeans 7.2.1).

Hibernate OGM in a Built-in JTA Environment (EJB 3/BMT, GlassFish AS 3)

In the previous example, we developed an application based on the GlassFish 3 built-in JTA environment. You saw how to obtain the current transaction via lookup in the JNDI subcontext java:comp/UserTransaction and manually demarcate transaction boundaries in a plain DAO class. Now we're going to develop the same kind of application, but this time we'll use an EJB component annotated as a bean managed transaction (BMT).

Prerequisites

- MongoDB 2.2.2
- Hibernate OGM 4.0.0.Beta1
- JDK 1.7
- NetBeans 7.2.1 (or Eclipse JUNO)
- GlassFish 3.1.2.2

Developing

After launching NetBeans, create a new project consisting of an empty Maven web application and name it HOGMviaHNAPI_JTA_EJB_BMT_GlassFish3. In the New Web Application wizard, type hogm.hnapi for the Group Id and Package fields. Don't forget to select the GlassFish web server for deployment of this application. Notice that even if we're going to add an EJB component, we won't be creating an enterprise application to separate the web module from the EJB module. We prefer a web application because we want to have the ability to call web components from the EJB component.

Coding the Application

After adding Hibernate OGM/Mongo DB JARs (using Maven as in previous examples) create the well-known LuckyNumberEntity entity (this time use @Table(name="bmt"), or the POJO version, LuckyNumberPojo, if you want to use hibernate.cfg.xml). Continue by writing the HibernateUtil class, enabling the JTA strategy and adding the GlassFish 3 built-in JTA platform:

```
OgmConfiguration cfgogm = new OgmConfiguration();
...
cfgogm.setProperty(Environment.TRANSACTION_STRATEGY,
                            "org.hibernate.transaction.JTATransactionFactory");
cfgogm.setProperty(Environment.CURRENT_SESSION_CONTEXT_CLASS, "jta");
cfgogm.setProperty(Environment.JTA_PLATFORM,
                            "org.hibernate.service.jta.platform.internal.SunOneJtaPlatform");
```

Or, if you prefer using the hibernate.cfg.xml file, add it there (in this case, don't forget to write the LuckyNumberPojo.hbm.xml and specify table="bmt"):

```
<property name="hibernate.transaction.factory_class">
                            org.hibernate.transaction.JTATransactionFactory</property>
<property name="hibernate.current_session_context_class">jta</property>
<property name="hibernate.transaction.jta.platform">
                            org.hibernate.service.jta.platform.internal.SunOneJtaPlatform</property>
```

Next, add a stateless bean (an EJB component) named BMTBean; there's no need to create an interface for it. Since code inside EJB methods is executed in a transaction by default, we have to modify this by adding the @TransactionManagement statement, as in the following:

```
package hogm.hnapi.ejb;
...
@Stateless
@TransactionManagement(TransactionManagementType.BEAN)
public class BMTBean {
...
```

You can find more details about this annotation in Chapter 2.

Now we have control over transaction boundaries. All we need is the UserTransaction that can be obtained using the @Resource annotation, like this:

```
@Resource
private UserTransaction userTransaction;
```

> ■ **Note**   You can also obtain the `UserTransaction` through `EJBContext`, via JNDI lookup or even through a CDI
> injection mechanism (`@Inject UserTransaction`). It's always a good idea to consult the official documentation of the
> J2EE implementation before choosing your approach.

Now, we can easily call the `UserTransaction.begin`, `commit` and `setRollbackOnly` methods to control the
transactions with the MongoDB database via Hibernate OGM sessions obtained from `getCurrentSession` or
`openSession`. (If it sounds like MongoDB supports transactions, it doesn't. Remember, we're using this approach
because the OGM documentation recommends using transaction demarcations, even with MongoDB.) For example,
we can store a lucky number, as shown in Listing 4-18. Note that the code contains both cases—using entity and POJO.

Listing 4-18. Two Ways to Store a Lucky Number - the BMT Approach

```
package hogm.hnapi.ejb;

import hogm.hnapi.pojo.LuckyNumberEntity;
import hogm.hnapi.pojo.LuckyNumberPojo;
import java.util.Random;
import javax.annotation.Resource;
import javax.ejb.Stateless;
import javax.ejb.TransactionManagement;
import javax.ejb.TransactionManagementType;
import javax.inject.Named;
import javax.transaction.SystemException;
import javax.transaction.UserTransaction;
import org.jboss.logging.Logger;

@Stateless
@Named("bean")
@TransactionManagement(TransactionManagementType.BEAN)
public class BMTBean {

    @Resource
    private UserTransaction userTransaction;
    private static final Logger log = Logger.getLogger(BMTBean.class.getName());

    public void persistAction() {

        log.info("Persisting LuckyNumberEntity instance ...");

        LuckyNumberEntity luckyNumberEntity = new LuckyNumberEntity();
        luckyNumberEntity.setLuckynumber(new Random().nextInt(1000000));
        LuckyNumberPojo luckyNumberPojo = new LuckyNumberPojo();
        luckyNumberPojo.setLuckynumber(new Random().nextInt(1000000));

        try {
            // Start the transaction
            userTransaction.begin();
```

```
          hogm.hnapi.util.without.hibernate.cfg.HibernateUtil.getSessionFactory().
                                    getCurrentSession().persist(luckyNumberEntity);
          hogm.hnapi.util.with.hibernate.cfg.HibernateUtil.getSessionFactory().
                                    getCurrentSession().persist(luckyNumberPojo);

          //persist here through openSession method

          // Commit the transaction
          userTransaction.commit();
      } catch (Exception ex) {
          try {
              //Rollback the transaction
              userTransaction.setRollbackOnly();
          } catch (IllegalStateException ex1) {
              log.log(Logger.Level.ERROR, ex1, ex1);
          } catch (SystemException ex1) {
              log.log(Logger.Level.ERROR, ex1, ex1);
          }
      }
      log.info("Persist successful ...");
   }
}
```

To run this application, we choose to activate the JSF framework and CDI support (by adding the corresponding beans.xml in the /WEB-INF folder). We have annotated the EJB component with @Named("bean")—as shown in the code—and we call it from the application start page using a simple JSF form, like this (index.xhtml):

```
...
<h:form>
   <h:commandButton action="#{bean.persistAction()}"
                    value="Generate Lucky Number"/>
</h:form>
...
```

Testing

Start the MongoDB server as you saw in Chapter 1. Next, since you're in a NetBeans/GlassFish (or Eclipse/GlassFish) environment, save the project and click the Run (or Run on Server in Eclipse) button to start GlassFish and deploy and run the application. If the application successfully starts, you'll see in your browser something like what's shown in Figure 4-8.

Hibernate OGM via Hibernate Native API, JTA environment, EJB/BMT (Bean Managed Transaction)

Generate Lucky Number

Figure 4-8. *Running the HOGMviaHNAPI_JTA_EJB_BMT_GlassFish3 application*

Press the Generate Lucky Number button a few times to persist some lucky numbers to the MongoDB database (glassfish_db) collection, (bmt). For each press, two new documents are inserted, one for enitity and one for POJO. Open a command prompt and type the commands from Figure 4-9 to see the results of your work. You can also monitor GlassFish log messages in case anything unwanted happens.

```
D:\mongodb\bin>mongo glassfish_db
MongoDB shell version: 2.2.2
connecting to: glassfish_db
> show collections
bmt
jta
system.indexes
> db.bmt.find();
{ "_id" : "21215aa0-2f96-4a59-ad00-331b0e2a78a2", "luckynumber" : 734490 }
{ "_id" : "296c81ab-2f5d-4c88-862f-691db2b2cebd", "luckynumber" : 279245 }
```

Figure 4-9. *Checking the bmt collection content*

The complete source code for this application is available in the Apress repository and is named HOGMviaHNAPI_JTA_EJB_BMT_GlassFish3. It comes as a NetBeans project and it was tested under GlassFish 3 (I used the GlassFish bundled to NetBeans 7.2.1).

Hibernate OGM in a Built-in JTA Environment (EJB 3/CMT, GlassFish AS 3)

In the previous example we developed an application based on the GlassFish 3 built-in JTA environment and a bean managed transaction (BMT). We can easily transform this application into a container managed transaction (CMT) by applying a few essential changes. I could just tell you to "check the previous example and modify this, modify that . . .", but if you're not interested in the previous application, you probably wouldn't find that too appealing. So I'll try to provide as much information as possible here and ask you to copy from the previous application only the parts that have been repeated several times in this chapter.

Prerequisites

- MongoDB 2.2.2

- Hibernate OGM 4.0.0.Beta1

- JDK 1.7

- NetBeans 7.2.1 (or Eclipse JUNO)

- GlassFish 3.1.2.2

Developing

After launching NetBeans, create a new project consisting of an empty Maven web application and name it HOGMviaHNAPI_JTA_EJB_CMT_GlassFish3. In the New Web Application wizard, type hogm.hnapi for the Group Id and Package fields. Don't forget to select the GlassFish web server for deploying this application. Note that even though we're adding an EJB component, we won't create an enterprise application to separate the web module from the EJB module. We prefer a web application because we want to have the ability to call web components from the EJB component.

Coding the Application

After adding Hibernate OGM/MongoDB JARs (using Maven as in previous examples), create the well-known `LuckyNumberEntity` entity (this time use `@Table(name="cmt")`, or the POJO version, `LuckyNumberPojo`, if you want to use `hibernate.cfg.xml`). Continue by writing the `HibernateUtil` class, enabling the CMT strategy and adding the GlassFish 3 built-in JTA platform:

```
OgmConfiguration cfgogm = new OgmConfiguration();
 ...
cfgogm.setProperty(Environment.TRANSACTION_STRATEGY,
                            "org.hibernate.transaction.CMTTransactionFactory");
cfgogm.setProperty(Environment.JTA_PLATFORM,
                            "org.hibernate.service.jta.platform.internal.SunOneJtaPlatform");
```

Or, if you prefer using the `hibernate.cfg.xml` file, add it there (in this case, don't forget to write the `LuckyNumberPojo.hbm.xml` and specify `table="cmt"`):

```
<property name="hibernate.transaction.factory_class">
                            org.hibernate.transaction.CMTTransactionFactory</property>
<property name="hibernate.transaction.jta.platform">
                            org.hibernate.service.jta.platform.internal.SunOneJtaPlatform</property>
```

Add a stateless bean (an EJB component) named `CMTBean` (no need to create an interface for it). Since the code in the EJB methods is executed in a transaction by default, we don't need to interfere. However, just for fun, we can manually provide the annotations that are already default—`@TransactionManagement` and `@TransactionAttribute`. More details about this annotation can be found in Chapter 2.

Now we can easily take advantage of the CMT strategy and use Hibernate OGM sessions obtained from the `getCurrentSession` or `openSession` methods to store lucky numbers in the MongoDB database, as shown in Listing 4-19. Note that the code contains both cases—using entity and POJO.

Listing 4-19. Two Ways to Store a Lucky Number—the CMT Approach

```
package hogm.hnapi.ejb;

import hogm.hnapi.pojo.LuckyNumberEntity;   //entity case
import hogm.hnapi.pojo.LuckyNumberPojo;     //POJO case
import java.util.Random;
import javax.ejb.Stateless;
import javax.ejb.TransactionAttribute;
import javax.ejb.TransactionAttributeType;
import javax.ejb.TransactionManagement;
import javax.ejb.TransactionManagementType;
import javax.inject.Named;
import org.jboss.logging.Logger;

@Stateless
@Named("bean")
@TransactionManagement(TransactionManagementType.CONTAINER) //this is the default
public class CMTBean {

    private static final Logger log = Logger.getLogger(CMTBean.class.getName());
```

```
@TransactionAttribute(TransactionAttributeType.REQUIRED) //this is the default
public void persistAction() {

    log.info("Persisting LuckyNumberEntity instance ...");

    LuckyNumberEntity luckyNumberEntity = new LuckyNumberEntity();
    luckyNumberEntity.setLuckynumber(new Random().nextInt(1000000));
    LuckyNumberPojo luckyNumberPojo = new LuckyNumberPojo();
    luckyNumberPojo.setLuckynumber(new Random().nextInt(1000000));

    hogm.hnapi.util.without.hibernate.cfg.HibernateUtil.getSessionFactory().
                                   getCurrentSession().persist(luckyNumberEntity);
    hogm.hnapi.util.with.hibernate.cfg.HibernateUtil.getSessionFactory().
                                   getCurrentSession().persist(luckyNumberPojo);
    //persist here through openSession method
    log.info("Persist successful ...");
    }
}
```

To run this application, we'll activate the JSF framework and CDI support (by adding the corresponding beans.xml in the /WEB-INF folder). We have annotated the EJB component with @Named("bean")—as shown in the code—and we call it from the application start page using a simple JSF form, like this (index.xhtml):

```
...
<h:form>
    <h:commandButton action="#{bean.persistAction()}"
                     value="Generate Lucky Number"/>
</h:form>
...
```

Testing

Start the MongoDB server as in Chapter 1. Next, since you're in a NetBeans/GlassFish (or Eclipse/GlassFish) environment, just save the project and click the Run (or Run on Server in Eclipse) button to start GlassFish and deploy and run the application. If the application successfully starts, you'll see in the browser something similar to what's shown in Figure 4-10.

Figure 4-10. *Running the HOGMviaHNAPI_JTA_EJB_CMT_GlassFish3 application*

Press the Generate Lucky Number button a few times to persist some lucky numbers into the MongoDB database (glassfish_db) collection (cmt). For each press, two new documents are inserted, one for the enitity and one for the POJO. Open a command prompt and type the commands from Figure 4-11 to see the results of your work. You can monitor GlassFish log messages in case anything unwanted happens.

```
D:\mongodb\bin>mongo glassfish_db
MongoDB shell version: 2.2.2
connecting to: glassfish_db
> show collections
bmt
cmt
jta
system.indexes
> db.cmt.find();
{ "_id" : "2cd10497-7281-4281-a647-e43b5b6dd218", "luckynumber" : 666129 }
{ "_id" : "d66693f5-f68d-4efa-95e7-907d198a8fb4", "luckynumber" : 585125 }
```

Figure 4-11. *Checking the "cmt" collection content*

The complete source code for this application is named HOGMviaHNAPI_JTA_EJB_CMT_GlassFish3 and is available in the Apress repository. It comes as a NetBeans project and was tested under GlassFish 3 (I used the GlassFish bundled to NetBeans 7.2.1).

Hibernate OGM via the Java Persistence API (JPA 2.0)

Hibernate OGM can also be bootstrapped via JPA. This is very useful since it doesn't involve any knowledge of Hibernate ORM and doesn't require any code related to Hibernate. Practically, if you've used JPA before (no matter which implementation), it should be a piece of cake to configure Hibernate OGM as your JPA provider.

In this section you'll see a set of applications that will exploit Hibernate OGM as a JPA provider under different architectures and technologies. You will see how it works in a:

- built-in JTA environment (EJB 3, GlassFish AS 3)

- built-in JTA environment (EJB 3, JBoss AS 7)

- standalone JTA environment (Apache Tomcat 7)

- built-in JTA environment (JBoss AS 7 and Seam 3 application)

- built-in JTA environment (GlassFish 3 and Spring 3 application)

- non-JTA environment (RESOURCE_LOCAL, Apache Tomcat 7)

Hibernate OGM in a Built-in JTA Environment (EJB 3, GlassFish AS 3)

We start with an enterprise application (known as EAR—Enterprise Archive) deployed on GlassFish AS. This is one of the classic heavy applications in the Java world that's used quite often and usually involves several technologies, like JPA, JSF, Struts, EJB, Hibernate, Spring and so on. Web technologies go into one module (the WAR module) and EJB components in another (the EJB module). The WAR module has access to the EJB module, but not vice versa. From a programmer's perspective, the core of JPA consists of an XML file, named persistence.xml, which goes in the EJB module as a configuration file. So, let's see how this file looks for Hibernate OGM acting as a JPA provider.

Prerequisites

- MongoDB 2.2.2

- Hibernate OGM 4.0.0.Beta2

- JDK 1.7

- NetBeans 7.2.1 (or Eclipse JUNO)

- GlassFish 3.1.2.2

Developing

After launching NetBeans, create a new project consisting of an empty Maven enterprise application and name it HOGMviaJPA_EE_GlassFish. In the New Enterprise Application wizard, type hogm for the Group Id and Package fields, and select the GlassFish application server for deploying this application. Once you see the project in the Projects window, you can edit the pom.xml file in the HOGMviaJPA_EE_GlassFish-ear project module (it has to be under Project Files node). In the pom.xml, add the Hibernate OGM distribution (including MongoDB support) by pasting in the following dependencies:

```
<dependencies>
    <dependency>
        <groupId>org.hibernate.ogm</groupId>
        <artifactId>hibernate-ogm-core</artifactId>
        <version>4.0.0.Beta2</version>
    </dependency>
    <dependency>
        <groupId>org.hibernate.ogm</groupId>
        <artifactId>hibernate-ogm-mongodb</artifactId>
        <version>4.0.0.Beta1</version>
    </dependency>
...
<dependencies>
```

Now save the project and the MongoDB Java driver JAR will be listed under the Dependencies node.

Coding the Application

Now, we have all the needed artifacts, so we're ready to add some code. First, in the HOGMviaJPA_EE_GlassFish-ejb module, we develop a basic entity class that has the ability to represent objects in the database. It contains a single field (apart from the primary key field) named luckynumber. (You should be familiar with these kind of entities, which are, technically speaking, just annotated POJOs. You can find more details in Chapter 2.) Listing 4-20 shows the code for the LuckyNumberEntity class.

Listing 4-20. The LuckyNumberEntity Class

```
package hogm.jpa.entities;

import java.io.Serializable;
import javax.persistence.Column;
import javax.persistence.Entity;
import javax.persistence.GeneratedValue;
import javax.persistence.GenerationType;
import javax.persistence.Id;
import javax.persistence.Table;

@Entity
@Table(name = "jpa")
public class LuckyNumberEntity implements Serializable {

    private static final long serialVersionUID = 1L;
    @Id
```

```
    @GeneratedValue(strategy = GenerationType.AUTO)
    private Long id;
    @Column(name = "luckynumber", nullable = false)
    private int luckynumber;

    public Long getId() {
        return id;
    }

    public void setId(Long id) {
        this.id = id;
    }

    public int getLuckynumber() {
        return luckynumber;
    }

    public void setLuckynumber(int luckynumber) {
        this.luckynumber = luckynumber;
    }
}
```

Let's continue with the main point of our interest, integrating Hibernate OGM as a JPA provider. You can start by creating a `persistence.xml` skeleton using the NetBeans wizard. This will provide an "empty" persistence unit for the GlassFish default data source (which is most convenient, since we don't actually need it) or no data source. From the Hibernate OGM perspective, this data source is not needed and never used, but depending on the situation you may need to specify an existing data source as it's a JPA requirement. (According to the JPA 1.0/2.0 specification, *"A transaction-type of JTA assumes that a JTA data source will be provided—either as specified by the jta-data-source element or provided by the container."*) To be certain, you'll have to test it yourself. As far as I can tell, there's no need to specify a data source; leave that field empty in the NetBeans wizard and you'll obtain a `persistence.xml` skeleton without a data source involved—no `<jta-data-source>` tag. If you get related errors on this, then add the default data source in GlassFish, like this:

```
...
<!-- out of the box data source for GlassFish v3-->
<jta-data-source>jdbc/sample</jta-data-source>
...
```

We also rename the persistence unit to `HOGM_JPA_GLASSFISH_PU` and indicate the transaction type as `JTA`. This is recommended. Remember that we have two possible values: `RESOURCE_LOCAL` indicates that transactions will be managed by the JPA provider implementation, and `JTA` indicates that transactions will be managed by the application server (GlassFish in this case). Finally, we specify the list of entities managed by this persistence unit.

In addition, we are adding Hibernate OGM as the JPA provider. This is very easy and fast, since all it requires is adding the `<provider>` tag, like this:

```
...
<provider>org.hibernate.ogm.jpa.HibernateOgmPersistence</provider>
...
```

By default, NetBeans will auto-detect entities and will add into persistence.xml the tag `<exclude-unlisted-classes>`, which defaults to false—all entity beans in the archive managed by this persistence unit. You can leave it that way, or delete this tag and add the entity class explicitly:

```
...
<class>hogm.jpa.entites.LuckyNumberEntity</class>
...
```

Since we're in a JTA environment, the JTA platform should be automatically detected and used without our intervention. But, to be sure, you can set the `hibernate.transaction.jta.platform` property accordingly:

```
...
<property name="hibernate.transaction.jta.platform"
value="org.hibernate.service.jta.platform.internal.SunOneJtaPlatform"/>
...
```

We're almost done. We just need to configure the MongoDB connection (the provider, dialect (optional), database name, host, and port). Once we've done that, we have the entire persistence.xml file, as shown in Listing 4-21.

Listing 4-21. persistence.xml

```xml
<?xml version="1.0" encoding="UTF-8"?>
<persistence version="2.0" xmlns="http://java.sun.com/xml/ns/persistence"
xmlns:xsi="http://www.w3.org/2001/XMLSchema-instance"
xsi:schemaLocation="http://java.sun.com/xml/ns/persistence
http://java.sun.com/xml/ns/persistence/persistence_2_0.xsd">

<persistence-unit name="HOGM_JPA_GLASSFISH_PU" transaction-type="JTA">
    <provider>org.hibernate.ogm.jpa.HibernateOgmPersistence</provider>
    <class>hogm.jpa.entities.LuckyNumberEntity</class>
    <properties>
      <property name="hibernate.transaction.jta.platform"
                   value="org.hibernate.service.jta.platform.internal.SunOneJtaPlatform"/>
      <property name="hibernate.ogm.datastore.provider" value="mongodb"/>
      <property name="hibernate.ogm.datastore.grid_dialect"
                   value="org.hibernate.ogm.dialect.mongodb.MongoDBDialect"/>
      <property name="hibernate.ogm.mongodb.database" value="glassfish_db"/>
      <property name="hibernate.ogm.mongodb.host" value="127.0.0.1"/>
      <property name="hibernate.ogm.mongodb.port" value="27017"/>
    </properties>
  </persistence-unit>
</persistence>
```

Hibernate OGM is now ready to serve our application as the JPA provider.

This is an enterprise application, so an EJB component (transactional by default) is perfect for exploiting the brand-new entity manager provided by OGM. The CMTBean implements the business logic for storing lucky numbers into a MongoDB database (no need for a local or remote interface), as shown in Listing 4-22.

Listing 4-22. The CMTBean Class

```
package hogm.jpa.ejb;

import hogm.jpa.entities.LuckyNumberEntity;
import java.util.Random;
import javax.ejb.Stateless;
import javax.inject.Named;
import javax.persistence.EntityManager;
import javax.persistence.PersistenceContext;

@Stateless
@Named("bean")
public class CMTBean {

    @PersistenceContext(unitName = "HOGM_JPA_GLASSFISH_PU")
    private EntityManager em;

    public void persistAction() {
        LuckyNumberEntity luckyNumberEntity = new LuckyNumberEntity();
        luckyNumberEntity.setLuckynumber(new Random().nextInt(1000000));

        em.persist(luckyNumberEntity);
    }
}
```

Finally, we need some glue code to obtain a functional application. As you see, the EJB component was annotated with @Named, which means you need to activate CDI support by adding the beans.xml file. NetBeans will do that for you if you push the right buttons, but you can also add it manually. In a Maven project, in the *-ejb module, beans.xml should be placed in the src/main/resources folder (under the Other Resource node). And in the *-war module, beans.xml should be placed in the /WEB-INF folder (under the Web Pages node). Add beans.xml in both places.

Calling the EJB through CDI can be done from a JSF form—you need to activate the JSF framework:

```
...
<h:form>
    <h:commandButton action="#{bean.persistAction()}" value="Generate Lucky Number"/>
</h:form>
...
```

And it's done!

Testing

Start the MongoDB server as you saw in Chapter 1. Next, since you are in a NetBeans/GlassFish (or Eclipse/GlassFish) environment, just save the project and select the HOGMviaJPA_EE_GlassFish-ear node. Click the Run (or Run on Server in Eclipse) button to start Glassfish and to deploy and run the application. If the application successfully starts, you'll see in your browser something like what's shown in Figure 4-12.

Figure 4-12. *Running the HOGMviaJPA_EE_GlassFish application*

Press the `Generate Lucky Number` button a few times to persist some lucky numbers into the MongoDB database (`glassfish_db`) collection (`jpa`). Open a command prompt and type the commands from Figure 4-13 to see the result of your work. You can monitor GlassFish log messages in case anything unwanted happens.

```
D:\mongodb\bin>mongo glassfish_db
MongoDB shell version: 2.2.2
connecting to: glassfish_db
> show collections
bmt
cmt
hibernate_sequences
jpa
jta
system.indexes
> db.jpa.find();
{ "_id" : NumberLong(1), "luckynumber" : 263118 }
{ "_id" : NumberLong(2), "luckynumber" : 502571 }
```

Figure 4-13. *Checking jpa collection content*

■ **Note**   Ignore the `hibernate_sequences` collection, since is not relevant for the moment. You'll learn how and why it appears in Chapter 5.

The complete source code for this application is named `HOGMviaJPA_EE_GlassFish` and is available in the Apress repository. It comes as a NetBeans project and was tested under GlassFish 3 (I used the GlassFish bundled to NetBeans 7.2.1).

Hibernate OGM in a Built-in JTA Environment (EJB 3, JBoss AS 7)

In this section you'll see how to run the application developed in the preceding section, but using JBoss AS rather than GlassFish AS. Unfortunately, it won't work as is under the JBoss application server, so you need to adjust a few things at application server level and add several modifications in the `persistence.xml` file.

Prerequisites

- MongoDB 2.2.2
- Hibernate OGM 4.0.0.Beta2
- JDK 1.7
- Eclipse JUNO
- JBoss AS 7.1

Developing

There's an unwritten rule that GlassFish fans prefer the NetBeans IDE and JBoss AS fans like to work with the Eclipse IDE. Obviously, this is not mandatory. After all, we're talking about enterprise applications that are independent of IDEs and should work under any certified EE application server. Still, chances are good that you agree with this association, and that's why we'll develop the JBoss AS applications using the Eclipse IDE. So, after launching Eclipse, create a new project consisting of an empty `Enterprise Application Project` named `HOGMviaJPA_EE_JbossAS`. Select EAR version 6.0 and JBoss AS 7.1 with the default configuration of target runtime. Add the Web and EJB modules, named `HOGMviaJPA_EE_JBossAS-web` and `HOGMviaJPA_EE_JBossAS-ejb`.

■ **Note** I used the Eclipse JUNO distribution and added JBoss AS 7.1 via the JBoss AS Tools plug-in, because this application server isn't available by default in JUNO (the link I used was `www.download.jboss.org/jbosstools/updates/development/indigo/`). Feel free to use any other Eclipse distribution, as long as it's bound to JBoss AS 7.1.

For now, we'll leave this application as is and switch our attention to the JBoss AS 7 modules because we need to configure the Hibernate OGM JARs as a module inside the application server. Without this module, we won't be able to successfully deploy a Hibernate OGM-contained application.

First, locate three JARs: `hibernate-ogm-core-4.0.0.Beta2.jar`, `hibernate-ogm-mongodb-4.0.0.Beta1.jar` and `mongo-java-driver-2.8.0.jar`. Next, browse the `{JBOSSAS_HOME}`/modules/org/hibernate path and create a new folder named ogm. Copy the three JARs to this new folder, and also add to this folder the module.xml file shown in Listing 4-23.

Listing 4-23. module.xml

```xml
<module xmlns="urn:jboss:module:1.1" name="org.hibernate" slot="ogm">
    <resources>
        <resource-root path="hibernate-ogm-mongodb-4.0.0.Beta1.jar"/>
        <resource-root path="hibernate-ogm-core-4.0.0.Beta2.jar"/>
         <resource-root path="mongo-java-driver-2.8.0.jar"/>
    </resources>

    <dependencies>
        <module name="org.jboss.as.jpa.hibernate" slot="4"/>
        <module name="org.hibernate" slot="main" export="true" />
        <module name="javax.api"/>
        <module name="javax.persistence.api"/>
        <module name="javax.transaction.api"/>
        <module name="javax.validation.api"/>
        <module name="org.infinispan"/>
        <module name="org.javassist"/>
```

```
            <module name="org.jboss.logging"/>
    </dependencies>
</module>
```

Save the file. We have to do one more thing here—add Hibernate 4.1.9 in place of 4.0.1 in the module. First, locate the following JARs: `hibernate-core-4.1.9.Final.jar` and `hibernate-entitymanager-4.1.9.Final.jar` and then browse the `{JBOSSAS_HOME}`/modules/org/hibernate/main path. Now, replace the old JARs with these ones, or just add these. Edit the `module.xml` file in the same folder and replace the old references accordingly:

```xml
<module xmlns="urn:jboss:module:1.1" name="org.hibernate">
    <resources>
        <resource-root path="hibernate-core-4.1.9.Final.jar"/>
        <resource-root path="hibernate-entitymanager-4.1.9.Final.jar"/>
        <resource-root path="hibernate-commons-annotations-4.0.1.Final.jar"/>
        <resource-root path="hibernate-infinispan-4.0.1.Final.jar"/>
        <!-- Insert resources here -->
    </resources>
...
```

Done! We finished everything necessary for preparing JBoss AS 7.1 for Hibernate OGM applications.

Coding the Application

Now, we can switch back to application development and, more specifically, to the `persistence.xml` file, which must undergo some significant modification, as you'll see in the next paragraphs. To add this file, you can use the Eclipse IDE wizard, like this:

- In `Project Explorer`, locate the `HOGMviaJPA_EE_JBossAS-ejb` module. Right-click on it and select `Properties` from the context menu. Navigate to `Project Facets` in the `Properties` window and locate the JPA facet. Select it and you should see something like what's shown in Figure 4-14.

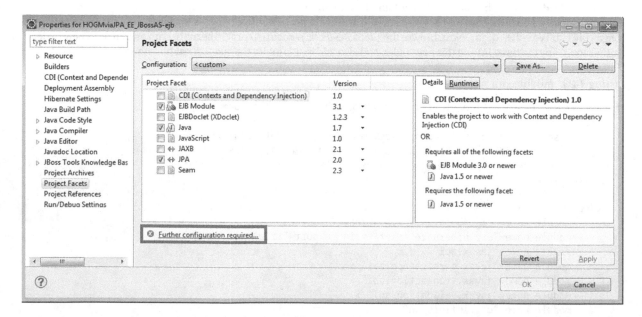

Figure 4-14. *Adding the JPA facet*

- We are especially interested in the bottom text, "Further configuration required..." (or it might say "Further configuration available..."). Click on that text to open the Modify Faceted Project window. We have to choose the JPA implementation, which is Hibernate OGM. Select Generic 2.0 as the Platform and User Library as the Type in the JPA Implementation section.

- Next, we have to specify the Hibernate OGM and MongoDB libraries. If you followed along in the Chapter 1 section "Getting Hibernate OGM Distribution Using the Eclipse IDE," you should have the Hibernate OGM Core and MongoDB library. Select it and click OK, as shown in Figure 4-15. If you don't have this library, create it now. Click Apply and OK to return to the main application screen.

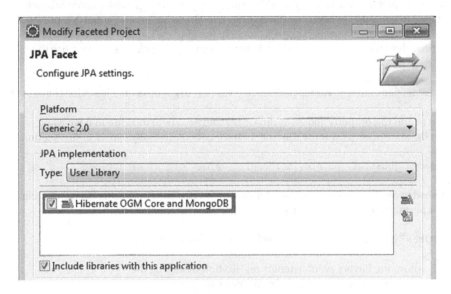

Figure 4-15. *Select the JPA implementation*

Now you should see an empty persistence.xml leaf under the HOGMviaJPA_FF_JBossAS-ejb | JPA Content node. Open this file in the editor and let's add what we need:

- Rename the persistence unit to HOGM_JPA_JBOSSAS_PU and set the transaction type as JTA:

```
<persistence-unit name="HOGM_JPA_JBOSSAS_PU" transaction-type="JTA">
```

- Specify the JPA provider as Hibernate OGM using the <provider> tag:

```
<provider>org.hibernate.ogm.jpa.HibernateOgmPersistence</provider>
```

- Add the entities that can be managed by the EntityManager instance defined by the persistence unit (in our case, a single entity named LuckyNumberEntity :

```
<class>hogm.jpa.entities.LuckyNumberEntity</class>
```

- Optionally, indicate the JTA platform. Normally, this is auto-detected in an EE environment. Notice that for JBoss AS 7, the correct value is:

```
org.hibernate.service.jta.platform.internal.JBossAppServerJtaPlatform
```

It's not the value used for JBoss JTA standalone.

```
<property name="hibernate.transaction.jta.platform"
              value="org.hibernate.service.jta.platform.internal.JBossAppServerJtaPlatform"/>
```

- By default, JPA applications will use Hibernate integration classes that are configured in the JBoss AS 7 integration adapter module, unless you add the property jboss.as.jpa.adapterModule set to another value to your persistence.xml properties list. The value of this property represents the name of the Hibernate integration classes that help the application server to work with the persistence provider. In our case, we need the Hibernate integration classes 4, so we use the following setting:

```
<property name="jboss.as.jpa.adapterModule" value="org.jboss.as.jpa.hibernate:4"/>
```

- We also need to add the property jboss.as.jpa.providerModule to indicate that we want Hibernate OGM to be used. This is the module we have added manually earlier in this section:

```
<property name="jboss.as.jpa.providerModule" value="org.hibernate:ogm"/>
```

- Further, we need to disable class transformers for the persistence unit (by default, class enhancing or rewriting is permitted). For this, set the jboss.as.jpa.classtransformer to false:

```
<property name="jboss.as.jpa.classtransformer" value="false"/>
```

- Next, turn off automatic Envers event listeners registration by setting the hibernate.listeners.envers.autoRegister property to false:

```
<property name="hibernate.listeners.envers.autoRegister" value="false"/>
```

- Finally, configure the MongoDB connection (provider, dialect (optional), database name, host, and port). Once you've done that, the entire persistence.xml file is available, shown in Listing 4-24.

Listing 4-24. persistence.xml

```xml
<?xml version="1.0" encoding="UTF-8"?>
<persistence version="2.0" xmlns="http://java.sun.com/xml/ns/persistence"
xmlns:xsi="http://www.w3.org/2001/XMLSchema-instance"
xsi:schemaLocation="http://java.sun.com/xml/ns/persistence
http://java.sun.com/xml/ns/persistence/persistence_2_0.xsd">

 <persistence-unit name="HOGM_JPA_JBOSSAS_PU" transaction-type="JTA">
   <provider>org.hibernate.ogm.jpa.HibernateOgmPersistence</provider>
   <class>hogm.jpa.entities.LuckyNumberEntity</class>
   <properties>
      <property name="hibernate.transaction.jta.platform"
                   value="org.hibernate.service.jta.platform.internal.JBossAppServerJtaPlatform"/>
      <property name="jboss.as.jpa.adapterModule" value="org.jboss.as.jpa.hibernate:4"/>
```

```
        <property name="jboss.as.jpa.providerModule" value="org.hibernate:ogm"/>
        <property name="jboss.as.jpa.classtransformer" value="false"/>
        <property name="hibernate.listeners.envers.autoRegister" value="false"/>
        <property name="hibernate.ogm.datastore.provider" value="mongodb"/>
        <property name="hibernate.ogm.datastore.grid_dialect"
                    value="org.hibernate.ogm.dialect.mongodb.MongoDBDialect"/>
        <property name="hibernate.ogm.mongodb.database" value="jbossas_db"/>
        <property name="hibernate.ogm.mongodb.host" value="127.0.0.1"/>
        <property name="hibernate.ogm.mongodb.port" value="27017"/>
    </properties>
  </persistence-unit>
</persistence>
```

Regarding the fact that there is no data source specified, remember, as I pointed out earlier, Hibernate OGM doesn't need a data source. However, in some cases a data source must be specified to conform to JPA specification. For JBoss AS 7.1, the simplest way to provide a data source (in case you get related errors, which I didn't) is to add the out-of-the-box data source, like this:

```
...
<!-- out of the box data source for GlassFish v3-->
<jta-data-source> java:jboss/datasources/ExampleDS</jta-data-source>
...
```

At this point, I can say that we are respecting every single JBoss AS 7 requirement for running Hibernate OGM applications.

Next, you have to add the application code (the LuckyNumberEntity entity, the CMTBean EJB component (don't forget to change the unit name to HOGM_JPA_JBOSSAS_PU), and the index.xhtml web page) discussed in the previous example, and to add the CDI and JSF settings (which can be selected from the Project Facets wizard). When you're done, you should be able to deploy and run the application without any unpleasant events. To do this, I used JBoss AS Tools for Eclipse JUNO, but you can do it however you like.

Testing

Start the MongoDB server as in Chapter 1. Next, since you're in an Eclipse/JBoss AS (or NetBeans/JBoss AS) environment, just save the project and select Run on Server (or Run, in NetBeans) to deploy and run the application. If the application successfully starts, you'll see in the browser something similar to what's shown in Figure 4-16.

Hibernate OGM via Java Persistence API, J2EE application under JBoss AS 7

[Generate Lucky Number]

Figure 4-16. *Running the HOGMviaJPA_EE_JBossAS Application*

Press the Generate Lucky Number button a few times to persist some lucky numbers into the MongoDB database (jbossas_db) collection (jpa). Open a command prompt and type the commands from Figure 4-17 to see the results of your work. You can monitor JBoss AS log messages in case anything unwanted happens.

```
D:\mongodb\bin>mongo jbossas_db
MongoDB shell version: 2.2.2
connecting to: jbossas_db
> show collections
hibernate_sequences
jpa
system.indexes
> db.jpa.find();
{ "_id" : NumberLong(1), "luckynumber" : 970881 }
{ "_id" : NumberLong(2), "luckynumber" : 947110 }
{ "_id" : NumberLong(3), "luckynumber" : 304506 }
```

Figure 4-17. *Checking jpa collection content*

■ **Note**   You will see how and why the hibernate_sequences collection appears in Chapter 5.

The complete source code for this application is named HOGMviaJPA_EE_JBossAS and is available in the Apress repository. It comes as an Eclipse project and it was tested under JBoss AS 7.1.

Hibernate OGM in a Standalone JTA environment (Apache Tomcat 7)

Earlier in this chapter we created a Hibernate OGM via Hibernate Native API that was deployed in a standalone JTA environment with a Tomcat 7 web server. In this section, we will replace the Hibernate Native API part with the Java Persistence API. Instead of Hibernate Session, we'll use an EntityManager.

Prerequisites

- MongoDB 2.2.2
- Hibernate OGM 4.0.0.Beta1
- JDK 1.7
- NetBeans 7.2.1 (or Eclipse JUNO)
- Apache Tomcat 7

Developing

After launching NetBeans, create a new project consisting of an empty Maven web application and name it HOGMviaJPAJTA_Tomcat7. In the New Web Application wizard, type hogm.hnapi for the Group Id and Package fields and select Apache Tomcat 7 web server for deploying this application. When you see the project in the Projects window, edit the pom.xml file (which must be under the Project Files node). In the pom.xml file, add the Hibernate OGM (including MongoDB support) and JBoss JTA (JTA standalone from JBoss) distributions by pasting in the following dependencies:

```
<dependencies>
  <dependency>
    <groupId>org.hibernate.ogm</groupId>
```

```
          <artifactId>hibernate-ogm-core</artifactId>
          <version>4.0.0.Beta2</version>
      </dependency>
      <dependency>
          <groupId>org.hibernate.ogm</groupId>
          <artifactId>hibernate-ogm-mongodb</artifactId>
          <version>4.0.0.Beta1</version>
      </dependency>
      <dependency>
          <groupId>org.jboss.jbossts</groupId>
          <artifactId>jbossjta</artifactId>
          <version>4.16.4.Final</version>
      </dependency>
...
<dependencies>
```

Now save the project and the driver JAR will be listed under the Dependencies node.

Coding the Application

Now add the well-known entity named LuckyNumberEntity. You can find this in the previous examples; it's a simple POJO annotated with @Entity, @Table(name="jpa"), with a primary key field, named id, of type String and generated using a UUID2 generator, and an int field named luckynumber.

Next, we'll write the persistence.xml file. In a Maven project, place this file in the Other Sources/src/main/resources/META-INF folder and start by naming the persistence unit as HOGM_JPA_JTA_TOMCAT_PU and the transaction type as JTA:

```
<persistence-unit name="HOGM_JPA_JTA_TOMCAT_PU" transaction-type="JTA">
...
```

Set Hibernate OGM as the JPA provider by adding the <provider> tag:

```
<provider>org.hibernate.ogm.jpa.HibernateOgmPersistence</provider>
```

Add the entity class in this persistence unit using the <class> attribute:

```
<class>hogm.hnapi.entities.LuckyNumberEntity</class>
```

Next, we need to specify the JTA platform—JBoss JTA. Do this by adding the following:

```
<property name="hibernate.transaction.jta.platform"
            value="org.hibernate.service.jta.platform.internal.JBossStandAloneJtaPlatform"/>
```

Notice that we specified the JBoss JTA standalone distribution, not the one used by the JBoss AS.

The JBoss TS documentation indicates that, in order to select the local JBoss JTA implementation, you have to specify two properties: com.arjuna.ats.jta.jtaTMImplementation and com.arjuna.ats.jta.jtaUTImplementation. We can specify them like this:

```
<property name="com.arjuna.ats.jta.jtaTMImplementation"
            value="com.arjuna.ats.internal.jta.transaction.arjunacore.TransactionManagerImple"/>
<property name="com.arjuna.ats.jta.jtaUTImplementation"
            value="com.arjuna.ats.internal.jta.transaction.arjunacore.UserTransactionImple"/>
```

Now we'll configure the MongoDB connection using the datastore provider, the dialect, the name of the database to connect to, and the host and port (we will use the localhost and the default MongoDB server port, 27017). Putting everything together, we get the persistence.xml file shown in Listing 4-25.

Listing 4-25. Persistence.xml

```xml
<?xml version="1.0" encoding="UTF-8"?>
<persistence version="2.0" xmlns="http://java.sun.com/xml/ns/persistence"
xmlns:xsi="http://www.w3.org/2001/XMLSchema-instance"
xsi:schemaLocation="http://java.sun.com/xml/ns/persistence
http://java.sun.com/xml/ns/persistence/persistence_2_0.xsd">
    <persistence-unit name="HOGM_JPA_JTA_TOMCAT_PU" transaction-type="JTA">
        <provider>org.hibernate.ogm.jpa.HibernateOgmPersistence</provider>
        <class>hogm.hnapi.entities.LuckyNumberEntity</class>
        <properties>
            <property name="hibernate.transaction.jta.platform"
                    value="org.hibernate.service.jta.platform.internal.
JBossStandAloneJtaPlatform"/>
            <property name="com.arjuna.ats.jta.jtaTMImplementation"
                    value="com.arjuna.ats.internal.jta.transaction.arjunacore.
TransactionManagerImple"/>
            <property name="com.arjuna.ats.jta.jtaUTImplementation"
                    value="com.arjuna.ats.internal.jta.transaction.arjunacore.
UserTransactionImple"/>
            <property name="hibernate.ogm.datastore.provider" value="mongodb"/>
            <property name="hibernate.ogm.datastore.grid_dialect"
                    value="org.hibernate.ogm.dialect.mongodb.MongoDBDialect"/>
            <property name="hibernate.ogm.mongodb.database" value="tomcat_db"/>
            <property name="hibernate.ogm.mongodb.host" value="127.0.0.1"/>
            <property name="hibernate.ogm.mongodb.port" value="27017"/>
        </properties>
    </persistence-unit>
</persistence>
```

At this point, we have one entity and the corresponding persistence unit, so it's time to add a DAO class for storing lucky numbers into the MongoDB database. First, based on this persistence unit (HOGM_JPA_JTA_TOMCAT_PU), we need to obtain an entity manager factory, and an entity manager from this factory, like so:

```java
private static final EntityManagerFactory emf =
                        Persistence.createEntityManagerFactory("HOGM_JPA_JTA_TOMCAT_PU");
private final EntityManager em = emf.createEntityManager();
```

Now the entity manager is ready to join a transaction and execute statements against the MongoDB database (in our case, persist statements), but for this we need to obtain the user transaction for setting the transaction boundaries. We've done this before in a previous application, but in case you don't remember, it can be done in at least two ways:

- using the static method transactionManager:

```java
javax.transaction.TransactionManager tx = com.arjuna.ats.jta.TransactionManager.transactionManager();
```

- using the static method userTransaction:

  ```
  javax.transaction.UserTransaction tx = com.arjuna.ats.jta.UserTransaction.userTransaction();
  ```

■ **Note** The TransactionManager interface allows the application server to control transaction boundaries on behalf of the application being managed, while the UserTransaction interface allows applications to control transaction boundaries. Obviously, when the application controls transaction boundaries, you can use both of these, but when you allow the application server to control transaction boundaries, you must use TransactionManager.

Now, you can demarcate a persist statement with the begin, commit, and rollback methods for controlling the transaction flow. After a transaction begins (when the begin method is called), the entity manager must join it by calling the joinTransaction method, like this:

```
...
tx.begin();
em.joinTransaction();
em.persist(transientInstance);
tx.commit();
...
```

Supply the code for clearing and closing the entity manager, a few messages for monitoring the application flow, and you'll get the DAO class shown in Listing 4-26.

Listing 4-26. The LuckyNumberDAO Class

```java
package hogm.hnapi.dao;

import hogm.hnapi.entities.LuckyNumberEntity;
import java.util.logging.Level;
import java.util.logging.Logger;
import javax.persistence.EntityManager;
import javax.persistence.EntityManagerFactory;
import javax.persistence.Persistence;

public class LuckyNumberDAO {

    private static final Logger log = Logger.getLogger(LuckyNumberDAO.class.getName());
    private static final EntityManagerFactory emf =
                            Persistence.createEntityManagerFactory("HOGM_JPA_JTA_TOMCAT_PU");
    private final EntityManager em = emf.createEntityManager();

    public void persistAction(LuckyNumberEntity transientInstance) throws java.lang.Exception {

        log.log(Level.INFO, "Persisting LuckyNumberEntity instance ...");

        javax.transaction.TransactionManager tx =
                            com.arjuna.ats.jta.TransactionManager.transactionManager();
        // javax.transaction.UserTransaction tx = com.arjuna.ats.jta.UserTransaction.userTransaction();
```

```
        try {
            tx.begin();
            em.joinTransaction();
            em.persist(transientInstance);
            tx.commit();

            log.log(Level.INFO, "Persist successful ...");
        } catch (Exception re) {
            tx.rollback();

            log.log(Level.SEVERE, "Persist failed ...", re);
            throw re;
        }  finally {
            if (em != null) {
                em.clear();
                em.close();
            }
        }
    }
  }
}
```

The important part is done! We just have to add a simple servlet for working with the DAO class, like this:

```
package hogm.hnapi.servlet;
...
@WebServlet(name = "LuckyNumberServlet", urlPatterns = {"/LuckyNumberServlet"})

public class LuckyNumberServlet extends HttpServlet {
...
protected void processRequest(HttpServletRequest request, HttpServletResponse response) throws
ServletException, IOException, Exception {
  ...
  LuckyNumberDAO luckyNumberDAO = new LuckyNumberDAO();
  LuckyNumberEntity luckyNumberEntity = new LuckyNumberEntity();
  luckyNumberEntity.setLuckynumber(new Random().nextInt(1000000));

  luckyNumberDAO.persistAction(luckyNumberEntity);
  ...
  }
}
```

And a trivial JSP page (index.jsp) that sends empty requests to our servlet:

```
...
<form action="./LuckyNumberServlet" method="POST">
   <input type="submit" value="Generate Lucky Number">
</form>
...
```

Done!

Testing

Start the MongoDB server as in Chapter 1. Next, since you're in a NetBeans/Tomcat (or Eclipse/Tomcat) environment, just save the project and click the Run (or Run on Server in Eclipse) button to start Tomcat and deploy and run the application. If the application starts successfully, you'll see in your browser something similar to what's shown in Figure 4-18.

Figure 4-18. *Running the HOGMviaJPAJTA_Tomcat7 application*

Press the Generate Lucky Number button a few times to persist some lucky numbers into the MongoDB database (tomcat_db) collection (jpa). Open a command prompt and type the commands from Figure 4-19 to see the results of your work. You can monitor Tomcat log messages in case anything unwanted happens.

```
D:\mongodb\bin>mongo tomcat_db
MongoDB shell version: 2.2.2
connecting to: tomcat_db
> show collections
jdbc
jpa
jta
system.indexes
> db.jpa.find();
{ "_id" : "0b227225-204a-4b5a-827c-0ee73fad4bc4", "luckynumber" : 689160 }
{ "_id" : "85a2f260-b157-4725-9006-298798987536", "luckynumber" : 496694 }
```

Figure 4-19. *Checking jpa collection content*

The complete source code for this application is named HOGMviaJPAJTA_Tomcat7 and is available in the Apress repository. It comes as a NetBeans project and was tested under GlassFish AS 3.

Hibernate OGM in a Built-in JTA Environment (JBoss AS 7 and Seam 3 Application)

I saved for the end of this chapter two applications that involve Seam and Spring, two powerful and popular J2EE frameworks. As a Seam fan, I've seen Seam become a mature and robust framework, transforming in version 3 into *"a collection of modules and developer tooling tailored for Java EE 6 application development, with CDI as the central piece."*

Thanks to the modular framework structure and the CDI injection mechanism, you can create Seam 3 applications that involve only the modules you need. In the next application, we use a single Seam 3 module called Seam Persistence (this is the module closest to our subject), which *"brings transactions and persistence to managed beans, provides a simplified transaction API, and hooks transaction propagation events to the CDI event bus."* Among the many features of Seam Persistence, two stand out:

- Seam Managed Persistence Context—This is a built-in Seam component capable of managing entity managers (EntityManagers for JPA; it will work even in an SE environment because the Seam Persistence extensions will bootstrap the EntityManagerFactory) and sessions (Sessions for Hibernate). Moreover, it provides stability and robustness both outside and inside an EE container.

- Declarative transactions—Seam has upgraded the EJB 3 well-known @TransactionAttribute to provide declarative transactions for plain beans and, even cooler, this works outside the EE container where EJBs are totally unknown.

If you add to these two features simplicity of configuration and integration, you realize Seam Persistence really rocks! So, let's write an application that uses Seam 3 (the Seam Persistence module) and Hibernate OGM as JPA.

Prerequisites

- MongoDB 2.2.2
- Hibernate OGM 4.0.0.Beta2
- JDK 1.7
- Eclipse JUNO
- Forge 1.0.5 or 1.1.3
- JBoss AS 7

Developing

Our first concern was how to start a Seam Persistence project, because there are several possibilities. For example, you can add the Seam Persistence distribution through Maven artifacts:

```
<dependencies>
 <dependency>
    <groupId>org.jboss.seam.persistence</groupId>
    <artifactId>seam-persistence-api</artifactId>
    <version>${seam.persistence.version}</version>
</dependency>
<dependency>
    <groupId>org.jboss.seam.persistence</groupId>
    <artifactId>seam-persistence-impl</artifactId>
    <version>${seam.persistence.version}</version>
</dependency>
<dependency>
    <groupId>org.jboss.seam.solder</groupId>
    <artifactId>seam-solder</artifactId>
    <version>${seam.solder.version}</version>
</dependency>
```

```
<dependency>
   <groupId>org.jboss.seam.xml</groupId>
   <artifactId>seam-xml-config</artifactId>
   <version>${seam.xml.version}</version>
 </dependency>
 ...
</dependencies>
```

Or, even better, you could use JBoss Tools for Eclipse or Seam Forge Tools for Eclipse (actually Seam Forge Tools is now available as a sub-tool of JBoss Tools). However, for our needs the decision was clear: We'll use the Seam Forge Tools plug-in (www.forge.jboss.org/) for Eclipse JUNO. You may well already have it installed in your Eclipse distribution, or outside Eclipse, and have used it many times, but if you're new to Forge and you want to install it quickly, go to the Help|Install New Software window, add the JBoss Tools repository (http://download.jboss.org/jbosstools/updates/development/indigo/) or select it from the list), expand the Abridged JBoss Tools 3.3 node, and select Forge Tools (see Figure 4-20).

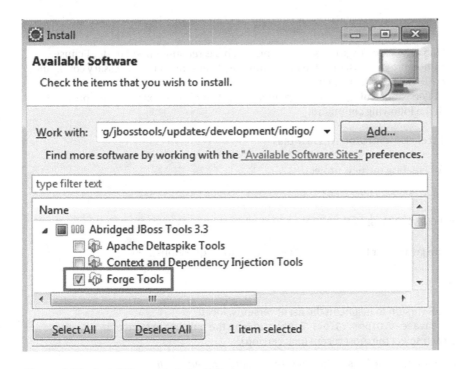

Figure 4-20. *Install Forge Tools for Eclipse*

Follow the steps in the wizard to install it and then restart the IDE. Now, from the Window | Show View window, you can activate the Forge | Forge Console. Initially Forge is not running, but it can be started by pressing the little green triangle on the Forge bar (Figure 4-21).

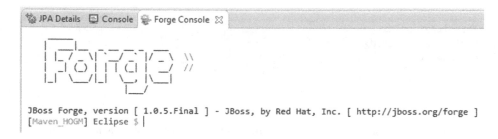

JBoss Forge, version [1.0.5.Final] - JBoss, by Red Hat, Inc. [http://jboss.org/forge]
[Maven_HOGM] Eclipse $ |

Figure 4-21. *Forge Console in Eclipse*

The big advantage of using Forge is that you don't need to read tons of tutorials, since it's just a shell for tooling and automation at the command line. There are no complicated wizards, settings, XMLs configurations, or anything, just a sheaf of commands that generate entire projects, including Seam and EE, in seconds.

Coding the Application

I'm going to assume that you're looking at a Seam Forge console right now. (This is recommended under Eclipse, because it lets you see the project creation progress after each typed command.) Let's insert the necessary commands for generating a new Seam 3 project with the Seam Persistence module.

First we need to install the Seam Persistence plug-in for Forge outside the project context (if it's not present). This can be easily accomplished with the following command:

```
forge install-plugin seam-persistence --version 3.1.0.Final
```

Now we can insert commands for creating the new project:

- Create a new project named HOGMviaJPA_SEAM3:

  ```
  new-project --named HOGMviaJPA_SEAM3
  ```

- Add to the new project the JavaServer Faces scaffold (answer yes to all questions):

  ```
  scaffold setup
  ```

- Select which JBoss Java EE version to install. In the list of versions, locate
  org.jboss.spec:jboss-javaee-6.0:pom::3.0.1.Final and type the number in front of it
  (if this is not available, then select the most recent final version).

- After a bunch of success messages, you'll see the question "*Create scaffold in which sub-directory of web-root?*". Type main.

- Install the Seam Persistence module:

  ```
  seam-persistence setup
  ```

- You'll be asked to indicate which version to install. Locate the
  org.jboss.seam.persistence:seam-persistence:::3.1.0.Final version and type the
  number in front of it (if this is not available, select the most recent final version).

- Install the Seam Managed Persistence Context:

  ```
  seam-persistence install-managed-persistence-context
  ```

- You'll be prompted to specify the package and class name for the Persistence Context Producer. Just press the Enter key for each question to accept the default suggestions.

- Activate declarative transactions support by typing:

  ```
  seam-persistence enable-declarative-tx
  ```

- Generate an entity class—the LuckyNumberEntity class (accept the suggested package name by pressing the Enter key):

  ```
  entity --named LuckyNumberEntity
  ```

- Add the field luckynumber to the entity by typing:

  ```
  field int --named luckynumber
  ```

- Done! We have all the components we need, so we're ready to build our project. Type:

  ```
  build
  ```

If the build ends successfully, you've done a great job and the project should be visible under Project Explorer tab in the Eclipse IDE. Don't worry about the red "x" that marks the project as having errors—this happens because the persistence.xml file is empty. (And even if you don't have that red "x," you still need to populate persistence.xml with the correct settings.)

Let's get rid of this annoying error using an Eclipse IDE wizard. In Project Explorer, locate the HOGMviaJPA_SEAM3 project node and right-click on it and select Properties from the context menu. Now, follow the instructions from the "*Coding the Application*" part of the "*Hibernate OGM in a Built-in JTA Environment (EJB 3, JBoss AS 7)*" section of this chapter to get the persistence.xml content shown in Listing 4-27.

Listing 4-27. persistence.xml

```
<?xml version="1.0" encoding="UTF-8" standalone="no"?>
<persistence xmlns="http://java.sun.com/xml/ns/persistence"
xmlns:xsi="http://www.w3.org/2001/XMLSchema-instance" version="2.0"
xsi:schemaLocation="http://java.sun.com/xml/ns/persistence
http://java.sun.com/xml/ns/persistence/persistence_2_0.xsd">
 <persistence-unit name="HOGM_JPA_SEAM3_PU" transaction-type="JTA">

   <provider>org.hibernate.ogm.jpa.HibernateOgmPersistence</provider>
   <class>com.example.HOGMviaJPA_SEAM3.model.LuckyNumberEntity</class>
   <properties>
      <property name="hibernate.transaction.jta.platform"
                    value="org.hibernate.service.jta.platform.internal.JBossAppServerJtaPlatform"/>
      <property name="jboss.as.jpa.adapterModule" value="org.jboss.as.jpa.hibernate:4"/>
      <property name="jboss.as.jpa.providerModule" value="org.hibernate:ogm"/>
      <property name="jboss.as.jpa.classtransformer" value="false"/>
      <property name="hibernate.listeners.envers.autoRegister" value="false"/>
      <property name="hibernate.ogm.datastore.provider" value="mongodb"/>
```

```
        <property name="hibernate.ogm.datastore.grid_dialect"
                       value="org.hibernate.ogm.dialect.mongodb.MongoDBDialect"/>
        <property name="hibernate.ogm.mongodb.database" value="jbossas_db"/>
        <property name="hibernate.ogm.mongodb.host" value="127.0.0.1"/>
        <property name="hibernate.ogm.mongodb.port" value="27017"/>
    </properties>
 </persistence-unit>
</persistence>
```

■ **Note** Before you save and build, edit the `LuckyNumberEntity` by adding a line that says `@Table(name="seam")`.

Save and build the project with the Forge build command and the error will disappear.

Now we need to add the business logic for persisting lucky numbers into the MongoDB database, and I think an EJB component is exactly what we need because we can make good use of its CDI features. First, create a new package named `com.example.HOGMviaJPA_SEAM3.view` under Java sources (`src/main/java`), with an empty stateless bean inside named `CMTBean`. If you create the stateless bean from the Eclipse wizard, select the Session Bean (EJB 3.x) leaf, under the EJB node.

Now we're going to use the Seam Managed Persistence Context. If you're not familiar with it, you might think it leads to a mass of spaghetti code to glue it into our EJB component. But keep in mind that all we need to do is to use the CDI `@Inject` annotation to obtain a Seam managed `EntityManager`:

```
@Inject @Forge EntityManager em;
```

The `@Forge` represents a CDI qualifier (both the Seam Managed Persistence Context factory class and the qualifier class were generated by Seam Forge and placed in the package `com.example.HOGMviaJPA_SEAM3`, under the Java sources `src/main/java`).

■ **Note** We didn't use the declarative transaction feature (even though we installed it) because we're in an EE environment and EJBs are by default transactional.

That single line of code does all the work of injecting and managing our entity manager. Next, we'll use the most common approach for giving life to the persisting process:

```
...
public void persistAction() {
    LuckyNumberEntity luckyNumberEntity = new LuckyNumberEntity();
    luckyNumberEntity.setLuckynumber(new Random().nextInt(1000000));
    em.persist(luckyNumberEntity);
  }
...
```

Finally, we annotate our EJB component with @Named to make it visible in a simple JSF form. Listing 4-28 shows the complete EJB code.

Listing 4-28. The Complete EJB Code

```java
package com.example.HOGMviaJPA_SEAM3.view;

import java.io.Serializable;
import java.util.Random;
import javax.ejb.Stateful;
import javax.enterprise.context.RequestScoped;
import javax.inject.Inject;
import javax.inject.Named;
import javax.persistence.EntityManager;

import com.example.HOGMviaJPA_SEAM3.Forge;
import com.example.HOGMviaJPA_SEAM3.model.LuckyNumberEntity;

@Named("bean")
@Stateful
@RequestScoped
public class CMTBean implements Serializable
{
    private static final long serialVersionUID = 1L;

    @Inject @Forge EntityManager em;

  public void persistAction() {
      LuckyNumberEntity luckyNumberEntity = new LuckyNumberEntity();
      luckyNumberEntity.setLuckynumber(new Random().nextInt(1000000));
      em.persist(luckyNumberEntity);
  }
}
```

Calling the persistAction method with a LuckyNumberEntity instance can be easily accomplished by adding a few modifications to the index.xhtml file generated by Seam Forge under src/main/webapp/main/index.xhtml. The first modification involves using the Taglib directives for importing the JSF tag library; use XML syntax for this (see the bold code):

```xml
<ui:composition xmlns="http://www.w3.org/1999/xhtml"
        xmlns:ui="http://java.sun.com/jsf/facelets"
        template="/resources/scaffold/pageTemplate.xhtml"
        xmlns:h="http://java.sun.com/jsf/html">
...
```

Second, slip the next form into the code somewhere—I paste it in the <ui:define> tag. Since this is just an example, I kept the generated design:

```xml
...
<ui:define name="subheader">
<h:form>
   <h:commandButton action="#{bean.persistAction()}" value="Generate Lucky Number"/>
</h:form>
</ui:define>
...
```

Finally, specify the application start page. Edit the `web.xml` file (under `src/main/webapp/WEB-INF` folder) and add this code at the end:

```
...
<welcome-file-list>
    <welcome-file>faces/main/index.xhtml</welcome-file>
</welcome-file-list>
...
```

Save and build the project again (use the Forge Console) and that's it!

Testing

Start the MongoDB server as in Chapter 1. Next, since you're in an Eclipse/JBoss AS (or NetBeans/JBoss AS) environment, just save the project and click the Run on Server (or Run in NetBeans) button to start JBoss AS and deploy and run the application. If the application successfully starts, you'll see in your browser something like what's shown in Figure 4-22.

Figure 4-22. *Running the HOGMviaJPA_SEAM3 application*

Press the Generate Lucky Number button a few times to persist some lucky numbers into the MongoDB database (`jbossas_db`) collection (`seam`). Open a command prompt and type the commands from Figure 4-23 to see the results of your work. You can monitor JBoss AS log messages in case anything unwanted happens.

```
D:\mongodb\bin>mongo jbossas_db
MongoDB shell version: 2.2.2
connecting to: jbossas_db
> show collections
hibernate_sequences
jpa
seam
system.indexes
> db.seam.find();
{ "_id" : NumberLong(1), "luckynumber" : 266538, "version" : 0 }
{ "_id" : NumberLong(2), "luckynumber" : 579707, "version" : 0 }
{ "_id" : NumberLong(3), "luckynumber" : 912420, "version" : 0 }
```

Figure 4-23. *Checking the seam collection content*

The complete source code for this application is is named HOGMviaJPA_SEAM3 and it's available in the Apress repository. It comes as an Eclipse project and was tested under JBoss AS 7.

Hibernate OGM in a Built-in JTA Environment (GlassFish 3 and Spring 3 Application)

One of the best open source Java enterprise frameworks on the market, with millions of fans, is Spring, especially distribution 3. In this section, we will develop an application that integrates Spring 3 and Hibernate OGM via JPA. Since you're reading this section, you're probably a Spring fan and the application may look pretty simple to you. Keep in mind that the point here is showing you how to add Hibernate OGM into this equation. So, let's persist some lucky numbers using Spring and Hibernate OGM.

Prerequisites

- MongoDB 2.2.2
- Hibernate OGM 4.0.0.Beta2
- JDK 1.7
- NetBeans IDE 7.2.1 (or Eclipse JUNO)
- Spring 3.1.1
- GlassFish 3.1.2.2

Developing

After launching NetBeans, create a new project consisting of an empty Web Application (notice that we won't use Maven for this application) and name it HOGMviaJPA_Spring3. Select GlassFish AS for deploying this application and add the Spring Web MVC framework from the NetBeans wizard.

Once you have the project under Projects window, you need to provide a few more JARs aside from the Spring 3.1.1 JARs that were automatically added by NetBeans. Begin with the Hibernate OGM/MongoDB JARs, which should be available in the Hibernate OGM Core and MongoDB user library created in Chapter 1. Continue with two JARs you can download from the Internet: asm-3.1.jar (http://asm.ow2.org/) and aopalliance.jar (http://aopalliance.sourceforge.net/).

Now you have all the necessary JARs and we can start coding.

Coding the Application

We'll start by developing the entity class and the persistence.xml. The entity class that feeds our MongoDB database with lucky numbers code, shown in Listing 4-29, is pretty straightforward.

Listing 4-29. The Entity Class

```
package hogm.spring;

import java.io.Serializable;
import javax.persistence.Column;
import javax.persistence.Entity;
import javax.persistence.GeneratedValue;
```

```java
import javax.persistence.GenerationType;
import javax.persistence.Id;
import javax.persistence.Table;

@Entity
@Table(name = "spring")
public class LuckyNumberEntity implements Serializable {

    private static final long serialVersionUID = 1L;
    @Id
    @GeneratedValue(strategy = GenerationType.AUTO)
    private Long id;
    @Column(name = "luckynumber", nullable = false)
    private int luckynumber;

    public LuckyNumberEntity() {
    }

    public int getLuckynumber() {
        return luckynumber;
    }

    public void setLuckynumber(int luckynumber) {
        this.luckynumber = luckynumber;
    }

    public Long getId() {
        return id;
    }

    public void setId(Long id) {
        this.id = id;
    }
}
```

Add an empty persistence.xml. The persistence.xml contains a single persistence unit, HOGMviaJPA_SPRING3_PU and a transaction type defined as JTA:

```xml
<persistence-unit name="HOGMviaJPA_SPRING3_PU" transaction-type="JTA">
...
```

Next, specify Hibernate OGM as the JPA provider by adding the <provider> tag:

```xml
<provider>org.hibernate.ogm.jpa.HibernateOgmPersistence</provider>
```

Add the entity class in Listing 4-28 to this persistence unit using the <class> attribute:

```xml
<class>hogm.spring.LuckyNumberEntity</class>
```

Specify the JTA platform using the `hibernate.transaction.jta.platform` property. The value of this property can be found in the list in Chapter 2. For GlassFish AS, use:

```
...
<property name="hibernate.transaction.jta.platform" value="org.hibernate.service.jta.platform.
internal.SunOneJtaPlatform"/>
...
```

We're almost done; we just need to configure the MongoDB connection (provider, dialect (optional), database name, host, and port). Once we've done that, we have the entire `persistence.xml` file as shown in Listing 4-30.

Listing 4-30. persistence.xml

```xml
<?xml version="1.0" encoding="UTF-8"?>
<persistence version="2.0" xmlns="http://java.sun.com/xml/ns/persistence"
xmlns:xsi="http://www.w3.org/2001/XMLSchema-instance"
xsi:schemaLocation="http://java.sun.com/xml/ns/persistence
http://java.sun.com/xml/ns/persistence/persistence_2_0.xsd">

 <persistence-unit name="HOGMviaJPA_SPRING3_PU" transaction-type="JTA">
    <provider>org.hibernate.ogm.jpa.HibernateOgmPersistence</provider>
    <class>hogm.spring.LuckyNumberEntity</class>
    <properties>
      <property name="hibernate.transaction.jta.platform"
                    value="org.hibernate.service.jta.platform.internal.SunOneJtaPlatform"/>
      <property name="hibernate.ogm.datastore.provider" value="mongodb"/>
      <property name="hibernate.ogm.datastore.grid_dialect"
                    value="org.hibernate.ogm.dialect.mongodb.MongoDBDialect"/>
      <property name="hibernate.ogm.mongodb.database" value="glassfish_db"/>
      <property name="hibernate.ogm.mongodb.host" value="127.0.0.1"/>
      <property name="hibernate.ogm.mongodb.port" value="27017"/>
    </properties>
  </persistence-unit>
</persistence>
```

Now, we're ready to add some DAO business logic to take advantage of the JPA settings. For this, we can write a simple Spring component (annotating the class with @Component) that injects an `EntityManager` and implements a transactional `persist` method, like the following:

```java
package hogm.spring;

import javax.persistence.EntityManager;
import javax.persistence.PersistenceContext;
import org.springframework.stereotype.Component;
import org.springframework.transaction.annotation.Transactional;

@Component
public class LuckyNumberDAO {

    @PersistenceContext
    private EntityManager em;
```

```
    @Transactional
    public void persist(LuckyNumberEntity luckyNumberEntity) {
        em.persist(luckyNumberEntity);
    }
}
```

Notice that we used the @Transactional annotation, since we want Spring to wrap that method in a transaction.

To create a classical Spring application, we need a Spring controller (annotating the class with @Controller) capable of receiving HTTP requests from multiple users and able to participate in an MVC workflow. Our controller will receive HTTP GET requests for its users and, for each request, will generate a new lucky number that becomes a parameter passed to the DAO persist method. For this, we use the @Autowired annotation that lets the container automatically wire beans—in our case, the LuckyNumberDAO bean shown in Listing 4-31.

Listing 4-31. The LuckyNumberDAO Bean

```
package hogm.spring;

import java.util.Random;
import org.springframework.beans.factory.annotation.Autowired;
import org.springframework.stereotype.Controller;
import org.springframework.ui.ModelMap;
import org.springframework.web.bind.annotation.RequestMapping;
import org.springframework.web.bind.annotation.RequestMethod;

@Controller
public class LuckyNumberController {

    @Autowired
    private LuckyNumberDAO luckyNumberDao;

    @RequestMapping(value = "/", method = RequestMethod.GET)
    public String index(ModelMap map) {
        LuckyNumberEntity luckyNumberEntity = new LuckyNumberEntity();
        luckyNumberEntity.setLuckynumber(new Random().nextInt(1000000));

        luckyNumberDao.persist(luckyNumberEntity);

        return "index";
    }
}
```

The user can fire HTTP GET requests using the Spring form we added to the WEB-INF/jsp/index.jsp page. We use the Taglib directives to import the Spring tag library:

```
<%@ taglib prefix="form" uri="http://www.springframework.org/tags/form" %>
...
<form:form method="GET" commandName="/">
   <input type="submit" value="Generate Lucky Number" />
</form:form>
...
```

Almost done. Two more XML configuration files and we'll be ready to run the application. The well-known dispatcher-servlet.xml, shown in Listing 4-32, needs to contain several settings, for example to enable the Spring MVC @Controller programming model and to define the entity manager factory (notice that we indicate our Hibernate OGM persistence unit name) and the Spring JTA transaction manager (it should be placed in the WEB-INF folder).

Listing 4-32. dispatcher-servlet.xml

```xml
<?xml version="1.0" encoding="UTF-8"?>
<beans xmlns="http://www.springframework.org/schema/beans"
       xmlns:xsi="http://www.w3.org/2001/XMLSchema-instance"
       xmlns:p="http://www.springframework.org/schema/p"
       xmlns:mvc="http://www.springframework.org/schema/mvc"
       xmlns:tx="http://www.springframework.org/schema/tx"
       xmlns:context="http://www.springframework.org/schema/context"
       xsi:schemaLocation="http://www.springframework.org/schema/beans
        http://www.springframework.org/schema/beans/spring-beans-3.0.xsd
        http://www.springframework.org/schema/tx
        http://www.springframework.org/schema/tx/spring-tx-3.0.xsd
        http://www.springframework.org/schema/context
        http://www.springframework.org/schema/context/spring-context-3.0.xsd
        http://www.springframework.org/schema/mvc
        http://www.springframework.org/schema/mvc/spring-mvc-3.0.xsd">

    <context:component-scan base-package="hogm.spring" />
    <context:annotation-config/>
    <mvc:annotation-driven />
    <tx:annotation-driven transaction-manager="txManager" />

    <bean id="jspViewResolver"
            class="org.springframework.web.servlet.view.InternalResourceViewResolver">
            <property name="viewClass"
                    value="org.springframework.web.servlet.view.JstlView" />
            <property name="prefix" value="/WEB-INF/jsp/" />
            <property name="suffix" value=".jsp" />
    </bean>

    <bean id="entityManagerFactory"
            class="org.springframework.orm.jpa.LocalEntityManagerFactoryBean">
            <property name="persistenceUnitName" value="HOGMviaJPA_SPRING3_PU"/>
    </bean>

    <bean id="txManager" class="org.springframework.transaction.jta.JtaTransactionManager">
    </bean>
</beans>
```

Finally, the generated web.xml should be adjusted accordingly, as shown in Listing 4-33. It should be placed in the WEB-INF folder.

Listing 4-33. web.xml

```xml
<?xml version="1.0" encoding="UTF-8"?>
<web-app    version="3.0"
    xmlns="http://java.sun.com/xml/ns/javaee"
    xmlns:xsi="http://www.w3.org/2001/XMLSchema-instance"
    xsi:schemaLocation="http://java.sun.com/xml/ns/javaee
    http://java.sun.com/xml/ns/javaee/web-app_3_0.xsd">
    <context-param>
        <param-name>contextConfigLocation</param-name>
        <param-value>/WEB-INF/dispatcher-servlet.xml</param-value>
    </context-param>
    <listener>
        <listener-class>org.springframework.web.context.ContextLoaderListener</listener-class>
    </listener>
    <servlet>
        <servlet-name>dispatcher</servlet-name>
        <servlet-class>org.springframework.web.servlet.DispatcherServlet</servlet-class>
        <load-on-startup>2</load-on-startup>
    </servlet>
    <servlet-mapping>
        <servlet-name>dispatcher</servlet-name>
        <url-pattern>/</url-pattern>
    </servlet-mapping>
    <session-config>
        <session-timeout>
            30
        </session-timeout>
    </session-config>
    <welcome-file-list>
        <welcome-file>/</welcome-file>
    </welcome-file-list>
</web-app>
```

Done!

■ **Note**   Spring also supports NoSQL datastores, like MongoDB, without Hibernate OGM. For more details, visit
www.springsource.org/spring-data/mongodb.

Testing

Start the MongoDB server as you saw in Chapter 1. Next, since you're in a NetBeans/GlassFish (or Eclipse/GlassFish)
environment, just save the project and click the Run (or Run on Server in Eclipse) button to start GlassFish and
deploy and run the application. If the application successfully starts, you'll see in the browser something like what's
shown in Figure 4-24.

Hibernate OGM via Java Persistence API, Spring 3

Generate Lucky Number

Figure 4-24. Running HOGMviaJPA_SPRING3 application

Press the Generate Lucky Number button a few times to persist some lucky numbers into the MongoDB database (glassfish_db) collection (spring). Open a command prompt and type the commands from Figure 4-25 to see the result of your work. You can monitor GlassFish log messages in case anything unwanted happens.

```
D:\mongodb\bin>mongo glassfish_db
MongoDB shell version: 2.2.2
connecting to: glassfish_db
> show collections
bmt
cmt
hibernate_sequences
jpa
jta
spring
system.indexes
> db.spring.find();
{ "_id" : NumberLong(1), "luckynumber" : 580963 }
{ "_id" : NumberLong(2), "luckynumber" : 206341 }
```

Figure 4-25. Checking the spring collection content

The complete source code for this application is named HOGMviaJPA_SPRING3 and is available in the Apress repository. It comes as a NetBeans project and it was tested under GlassFish AS 3.

Hibernate OGM in a non-JTA Environment (RESOURCE_LOCAL, Apache Tomcat 7)

In this section we'll develop a Hibernate OGM application that will run in a not-recommended condition and environment—this is why we saved it for last. The basic idea is that we will use a transaction of type RESOURCE_LOCAL in an non-EE environment (in a Tomcat web container). In other words, we will have the JPA provider implementation manage transactions in a non-JTA container (it doesn't provide a JTA implementation and so it obviously doesn't offer automatic transaction management).

Hibernate OGM documentation doesn't recommend using OGM outside a JTA environment (built-in or standalone). But, the fact that it's not recommended doesn't mean it doesn't work (especially for MongoDB which doesn't support transactions). Thus we can try it and draw some conclusions.

Prerequisites

- MongoDB 2.2.2

- Hibernate OGM 4.0.0.Beta2

- JDK 1.7

113

- NetBeans 7.2.1 (or Eclipse JUNO)

- Apache Tomcat 7

Developing

After launching NetBeans, create a new project consisting of an empty Maven web application and name it HOGMviaJPA_RESOURCELOCAL_Tomcat7. In the New Web Application wizard, type hogm.hnapi for the Group Id and Package fields and select the Tomcat application server for deploying this application. Once you see the project listed in the Projects window, you need to edit the pom.xml file (it has to be under Project Files node). In the pom.xml file, add the Hibernate OGM distribution (including MongoDB support) by pasting in the well-known dependencies.

Coding the Application

We start by developing the entity class and the persistence.xml. The entity class (LuckyNumberEntity) that feeds our MongoDB databases with lucky numbers code is pretty straightforward and we've used it in almost all of the preceding examples. We can therefore skip the listing here (just remember to use @Table(name="jpa_rl")). Next, we focus on persistence.xml, which goes in the Other Sources/src/main/resources/META-INF) folder. As you can see in Listing 4-34, it has no JTA platform specified, no special settings, just the transaction-type set as RESOURCE_LOCAL and the MongoDB connection settings.

Listing 4-34. persistence.xml

```xml
<?xml version="1.0" encoding="UTF-8"?>
<persistence version="2.0" xmlns="http://java.sun.com/xml/ns/persistence"
xmlns:xsi="http://www.w3.org/2001/XMLSchema-instance"
xsi:schemaLocation="http://java.sun.com/xml/ns/persistence
http://java.sun.com/xml/ns/persistence/persistence_2_0.xsd">
    <persistence-unit name="HOGM_JPA_RESOURCE_LOCAL_PU" transaction-
                            type="RESOURCE_LOCAL">
        <provider>org.hibernate.ogm.jpa.HibernateOgmPersistence</provider>
        <class>hogm.hnapi.entities.LuckyNumberEntity</class>
        <properties>
            <property name="hibernate.ogm.datastore.provider" value="mongodb"/>
            <property name="hibernate.ogm.datastore.grid_dialect"
                        value="org.hibernate.ogm.dialect.mongodb.MongoDBDialect"/>
            <property name="hibernate.ogm.mongodb.database" value="tomcat_db"/>
            <property name="hibernate.ogm.mongodb.host" value="127.0.0.1"/>
            <property name="hibernate.ogm.mongodb.port" value="27017"/>
        </properties>
    </persistence-unit>
</persistence>
```

Now we develop the DAO class responsible for persisting the lucky numbers in the MongoDB database, as shown in Listing 4-35. As you can see, we need some plumbing code since we're using the transaction mechanism provided by the JPA provider, which in our case is Hibernate OGM. The transaction methods begin, commit, and rollback are provided through the EntityManager.

Listing 4-35. The LuckyNumberDAO Class

```
package hogm.hnapi.dao;

import hogm.hnapi.entities.LuckyNumberEntity;
import java.util.logging.Level;
import java.util.logging.Logger;
import javax.persistence.EntityManager;
import javax.persistence.EntityManagerFactory;
import javax.persistence.Persistence;

public class LuckyNumberDAO {

    private static final Logger log = Logger.getLogger(LuckyNumberDAO.class.getName());
    private static EntityManagerFactory emf = Persistence.createEntityManagerFactory
("HOGM_JPA_RESOURCE_LOCAL_PU");
    private EntityManager em = emf.createEntityManager();

    public void persistAction(LuckyNumberEntity transientInstance) throws java.lang.Exception {

        log.log(Level.INFO, "Persisting LuckyNumberEntity instance ...");

        try {
            em.getTransaction().begin();
            em.persist(transientInstance);
            em.getTransaction().commit();

            log.log(Level.INFO, "Persist successful...");
        } catch (Exception re) {
            em.getTransaction().rollback();

            log.log(Level.SEVERE, "Persist failed...", re);
            throw re;
        } finally {
            if (em != null) {
                em.clear();
                em.close();
            }
        }
    }
}
```

Now suppose we have the piece of code that "connects" the user with the DAO class (a servlet and a simple XHTML page) and we run the application and see an error, like this:

```
Caused by: java.lang.ClassNotFoundException: Could not load requested class :
com.arjuna.ats.jta.TransactionManager
```

This error contains two hints for us: First, the JPA provider doesn't find any JTA implementation (normal, since we are in a non-JTA environment) and second, the JPA provider is looking, by default, for a JBoss JTA implementation. Therefore, we need to add JBoss JTA JARs, and we have to add the corresponding Maven artifacts in the pom.xml file:

```
<dependency>
    <groupId>org.jboss.jbossts</groupId>
    <artifactId>jbossjta</artifactId>
    <version>4.16.4.Final</version>
</dependency>
```

Now, run the application again and everything should work fine (don't forget the web page and the servlet—you can copy them from previous projects, or simply download the application from the Apress repository).

Testing

Start the MongoDB server as you saw in Chapter 1. Next, since you're in a NetBeans/Tomcat (or Eclipse/Tomcat) environment, just save the project and click the Run (or Run on Server in Eclipse) button to start Tomcat and deploy and run the application. If the application successfully starts, you'll see in your browser something like what's shown in Figure 4-26.

Figure 4-26. Running the HOGMviaJPA_RESOURCELOCAL_Tomcat7 application

Press the Generate Lucky Number button a few times to persist some lucky numbers into the MongoDB database (tomcat_db) collection (jpa_rl). Open a command prompt and type the commands from Figure 4-27 to see the result of your work. You can monitor Tomcat log messages in case anything unwanted happens.

```
D:\mongodb\bin>mongo tomcat_db
MongoDB shell version: 2.2.2
connecting to: tomcat_db
> show collections
jdbc
jpa
jpa_rl
jta
system.indexes
> db.jpa_rl.find();
{ "_id" : "08c12a62-9c6d-479e-95c7-ad74ab9cd01a", "luckynumber" : 324143 }
{ "_id" : "b40e1cad-bb0c-42f8-9132-627de5d1887c", "luckynumber" : 464324 }
```

Figure 4-27. Checking the jpa_rl collection content

The complete source code for this application is named HOGMviaJPA_RESOURCELOCAL_Tomcat7 and it's available in the Apress repository. It comes as a NetBeans project and was tested under Tomcat 7.

With this example, we finish the set of applications based on bootstrapping Hibernate OGM via both Hibernate Native API and JPA.

If you are not a Maven fan, but still want to test these applications, you can manually add the needed JARs under the Libraries node (in NetBeans/Eclipse) and compile and run the application using the NetBeans/Eclipse interface tools (as discussed in the section in Chapter 1) for getting the Hibernate OGM and MongoDB JARs locally).

If you're not a fan of IDEs either, you can edit the source code in your favorite editor, even Notepad, and compile the applications manually using Ant from the command line. For example, the Ant script (build.xml) in Listing 4-36 can be used to compile an application deployed under Tomcat. Just install Ant (http://ant.apache.org/) and put it in your classpath. Place the Ant script in the application root folder, open a command prompt, navigate to that folder and type build. This will compile the application and build the application WAR:

Listing 4-36. build.xml

```xml
<project name="hibernate" default="war">

<property name="sourcedir" value="${basedir}/WEB-INF/src"/>
<property name="targetdir" value="${basedir}/WEB-INF/classes"/>
<property name="librarydir" value="${basedir}/WEB-INF/lib"/>
<property name="builddir" value="${basedir}/build"/>

<path id="libraries">
    <fileset dir="${librarydir}">
        <include name="*.jar"/>
    </fileset>
</path>

<target name="clean">
    <delete dir="${targetdir}"/>
    <mkdir dir="${targetdir}"/>
    <delete dir="${builddir}"/>
    <mkdir dir="${builddir}"/>
</target>

<target name="compile" depends="clean, copy-resources">
    <javac srcdir="${sourcedir}"
           destdir="${targetdir}"
           classpathref="libraries"/>
</target>

<target name="copy-resources">
    <copy todir="${targetdir}">
        <fileset dir="${sourcedir}">
            <exclude name="**/*.java"/>
        </fileset>
    </copy>
</target>
```

```
<target name="war" depends="compile">
  <jar jarfile="${builddir}/{app_name}.war" basedir="${basedir}"/>
</target>

</project>
```

Obviously, you have to deal with application server and browser start/stop maneuvers.

Synthesis

Developing and testing these applications gave birth to this section. After analyzing these applications, we can come to some general conclusions regarding Hibernate OGM and MongoDB when integrated in different application environments. Clearly, Hibernate OGM is capable of running in many different environments and architectures and can be used with a number of frameworks and tools.

Moreover, depending on the environment (especially EE and JTA standalone) and the bootstrapping (via Hibernate Native API or JPA), we can extract a bunch of mandatory and/or recommended settings that Hibernate OGM needs for correctly serving Java applications.

Hibernate OGM via JPA in an EE Container

When you use Hibernate OGM via JPA in an EE container, you'll want to include the following settings in the persistence.xml file:

- Set the transaction type to JTA using the transaction-type JTA attribute of the persistence-unit tag.

- Set the JTA platform to the correct EE container using the hibernate.transaction.jta. platform property.

- Specify a JTA data source. This should be tested and can be skipped in some cases. For GlassFish you can use the built-in data source jdbc/sample (this is the associated JNDI name) and for JBoss AS you can use java:/DefaultDS (prior to version 7) or java:jboss/ datasources/ExampleDS (version 7 and above). The data source is specified using the jta-data-source tag.

Hibernate OGM via Hibernate Native API in an EE Container

When you use Hibernate OGM via Hibernate Native API in an EE container, you should include the following settings in the hibernate.cfg.xml file (or a programmatic version of it):

- Set the property hibernate.transaction.factory_class to org.hibernate.transaction. JTATransactionFactory, if you manually demarcate transaction boundaries, or to org. hibernate.transaction.CMTTransactionFactory, if you use declarative transaction demarcation.

- Set the property hibernate.current_session_context_class to jpa to indicate the strategy for scoping the "current" Session instances.

- Set the JTA platform to the correct EE container using the hibernate.transaction.jta. platform property

Hibernate OGM via JPA in Standalone JTA

When you use Hibernate OGM via JPA in an non-EE container (standalone JTA, like Tomcat), you should include the following settings in `persistence.xml` file:

- Set the transaction type to JTA using the `transaction-type` JTA attribute of the `persistence-unit` tag.

- Set the JTA platform (this is the standalone JTA—JOTM, JBoss JTA, Bitronix, and so forth—not a container built-in to JTA) using the `hibernate.transaction.jta.platform` property.

- Check the documentation specific to the selected standalone JTA because it may require some specific properties to be set.

Hibernate OGM via Hibernate Native API in Standalone JTA

When you use Hibernate OGM via Hibernate Native API in a non-EE container (a standalone JTA, like Tomcat), you should include the following settings in the `hibernate.cfg.xml` file (or a programmatic version of it):

- Set the property `hibernate.transaction.factory_class` to `org.hibernate.transaction.JTATransactionFactory`, if you manually demarcate transaction boundaries, or to `org.hibernate.transaction.CMTTransactionFactory`, if you use declarative transaction demarcation.

- Set the property `hibernate.current_session_context_class` to `jpa` to indicate the strategy for scoping the current `Session` instances.

- Set the JTA platform (this is the standalone JTA—JOTM, JBoss JTA, Bitronix, and so forth—not a container built-in to JTA) using the `hibernate.transaction.jta.platform` property.

- Check the documentation specific to the selected standalone JTA because it may require some specific properties to be set.

Hibernate OGM via JPA in Non-JTA

When you use Hibernate OGM via JPA in a non-JTA environment (like Tomcat), you should include the following settings in `persistence.xml` file:

- Set the transaction type to `RESOURCE_LOCAL` using the `transaction-type` JTA attribute of `persistence-unit` tag.

- Don't specify any JTA platform, but provide the JBoss JTA JARs to the application.

- Manage both the `EntityManager` and its JTA-transaction by yourself.

Hibernate OGM via Hibernate Native API in Non-JTA

When you use Hibernate OGM via Hibernate Native API in a non-JTA environment (like Tomcat), you should include the following settings in the `hibernate.cfg.xml` file (or a programmatic version of it):

- Set the property `hibernate.transaction.factory_class` to `org.hibernate.transaction.JDBCTransactionFactory`.

- Set the property `hibernate.current_session_context_class` to `thread`.

- Use Hibernate's Transaction and the built-in *session-per-request* functionality instead of calling the JDBC API.

■ **Note**   Values accepted by the `hibernate.transaction.jta.platform` property (indicating the JTA platform) are available in Chapter 2 in the section "*Bootstrap Hibernate OGM Using JPA*".

Summary

In this chapter, you saw how to integrate Hibernate OGM with different kinds of applications by varying the container environment, bootstrapping procedure, and involved frameworks and tools. The list of applications presented in this chapter includes:

- Java SE and Mongo DB—the HelloWorld Example

- Hibernate OGM (via Hibernate Native API) in a non-JTA environment (JDBC Transactions, Tomcat 7)

- Hibernate OGM (via Hibernate Native API) in a standalone JTA environment (JBoss JTA, Tomcat 7)

- Hibernate OGM (via Hibernate Native API) in a built-in JTA environment (no EJB, GlassFish 3)

- Hibernate OGM (via Hibernate Native API) in a built-in JTA environment (EJB/BMT, GlassFish 3)

- Hibernate OGM (via Hibernate Native API) in a built-in JTA environment (EJB/CMT, GlassFish 3)

- Hibernate OGM (via JPA) in a built-in JTA environment (GlassFish AS 3)

- Hibernate OGM (via JPA) in a built-in JTA environment (JBoss AS 7)

- Hibernate OGM (via JPA) in a built-in JTA environment (JBoss AS 7 and Seam application)

- Hibernate OGM (via JPA) in a built-in JTA environment (GlassFish and Spring application)

- Hibernate OGM (via JPA) JPA/JTA in a standalone JTA environment (Tomcat)

- Hibernate OGM in a non- JTA environment (RESOURCE_LOCAL, Apache Tomcat 7)

CHAPTER 5

■ ■ ■

Hibernate OGM and JPA 2.0 Annotations

Mapping Java entities in Hibernate OGM can be divided into supported and non-supported annotations. Practically, Hibernate OGM supports the mandatory annotations like @Entity and @Id, as well as all the commonly used annotations like @Table and @Column. However, in the 4.0.0.Beta2 release, it doesn't support some "pretentious" annotations, like @Inheritance and @DiscriminatorColumn. Unsupported annotations may cause errors or work inappropriately, or may be entirely ignored.

Hibernate OGM translates each entity in accordance with the official specification, but adapted to MongoDB capabilities. This means that some annotations will work exactly as expected, while others will have some limitations, and a few may not work at all. Since Hibernate OGM has the responsibility for creating a symbiosis between JPA annotations and MongoDB storage, it's no surprise that it will take more time and releases to make this symbiosis work smoothly in practice.

I'll start off with a brief discussion of Java supported types in OGM, then move on to the eager/lazy loading mechanism and cascading facility. Then we'll follow a simple scenario to explore the annotations: a brief overview, a look at OGM support, some case studies, and, finally the results of that annotation in MongoDB after passing through Hibernate OGM. In previous chapters, especially in Chapter 4, you saw some Java entities and some of the supported annotations. In this chapter, we'll take a closer look at those and at more annotations, such as @Id, @Column, @Table, @Embedded, @Enumerated, @Temporal. Finally, we'll delve into association annotations.

Java Supported Types

Java entities go hand in hand with Java types since they encapsulate all kinds of data: numbers, strings, URLs, objects, custom types, and so on. Practically, each persistable field of an entity is characterized by a Java type and must be represented in a MongoDB document field. One of the main concerns of Hibernate OGM, therefore, was (and is) to provide as much support as possible for Java types.

According to the official documentation, Hibernate OGM 4.0.0.Beta.2 supports the following Java types (though this list may change in future releases):

- Boolean
- Byte
- Calendar (may change)
- Class (may change)
- Date (may change)
- Double

- Integer

- Long

- Byte Array

- String

These types are supported natively. Other supported types, such as BigDecimal, BigInteger, URL, and UUID, are stored in MongoDB as strings.

Eager and Lazy Loading Considerations

As you probably know, JPA can load data from a database eagerly (fetch immediately) or lazily (fetch when needed). These notions usually come into play when two (or more) entities are involved in an association. For example, if one entity is the parent and the other is the child (meaning that the parent entity defines a collection of child entities), the possibilities are:

- eager loading—a child is fetched when its parent is fetched.

- lazy loading—a child is fetched only when you try to access it.

Eager loading is natively supported in all JPA implementations, while lazy loading is implementented in different ways or not supported. Hibernate (including Hibernate OGM) supports lazy loading using proxy objects instead of instances of the entity classes.

Hibernate uses proxies as a solution for "breaking up" the interconnected data received from a database into smaller pieces that can be easily stored in memory. It may be useful to be aware that Hibernate dynamically generates proxies for objects that are lazily loaded. Chances are, you aren't aware of proxy objects, and won't be until you get some exceptions of type LazyInitializationException, or until you try to test lazy loading in a debugger and notice the presence of some not-null objects with null properties. Not knowing when you're "working" on a proxy object instead of an entity object can cause weird results or exceptions. We'll discuss this more later on in the chapter.

Cascadable Operations Considerations

Since version 1.0, JPA supports cascadable operations. Put simply, if you apply some operations to an entity and those operations can be propagated to an associated entity, those operations are cascadable. JPA has five cascadable operations: persist, merge, remove, refresh, and detach (the last was added in JPA 2.0).

Programmatically, you can indicate which operations should be persisted using the Java enum CascadeType (http://docs.oracle.com/javaee/6/api/javax/persistence/CascadeType.html). For example, you can indicate that the persist and merge operations should be persisted in one-to-many associations:

```
...
@OneToMany(cascade = {CascadeType.PERSIST,CascadeType.MERGE},
           mappedBy = "...")
    public Set<...> get...() {
        return this...;
    }
...
```

When all five operations should be propagated, use CascadeType.ALL:

```
...
@OneToMany(cascade = {CascadeType.ALL},
           mappedBy = "...")
    public Set<...> get...() {
        return this...;
    }
...
```

Hibernate OGM supports all cascadable operations and everything works as expected. In this chapter, you'll see several examples and you may be inspired to explore cascading techniques on those examples yourself.

Entity Mapping

Let's take look now at entity mapping in Hibernate OGM. More specifically, let's see how Hibernate OGM maps JPA 2.0 annotations, including annotations for persistable classes and for fields and relationships. I won't follow a strict JPA 2.0 classification of annotations, but rather an approach that allows me to introduce annotations one by one, so I can test the entity at each step based only on the annotations we've already seen.

■ **Note** For testing purposes I used a MongoDB database named mapping_entities_db. Before performing each test, you should drop all the existing collections from this database (you can use the db.dropDatabase command). Otherwise, you may get various errors, depending on the test.

Let's begin!

@Entity Annotation

Mapped by the javax.persistence.Entity annotation.
    Official documentation: http://docs.oracle.com/javaee/6/api/javax/persistence/Entity.html.

Brief Overview

@Entity marks a class as an entity. By default, the entity name is the same as the annotated unqualified class name, but it can be replaced using the name element (for example, @Entity(name="*MyEntityName*")).

OGM Support

Hibernate OGM, like any other entity consumer, uses this annotation simply as a flag to recognize an entity class, so it has no direct effect on the persistence layer, MongoDB in our case.

Example

```
import javax.persistence.Entity;
...

@Entity
public class PlayerEntity implements Serializable {
...
```

In this case, the entity name is PlayerEntity.

@Id Annotation

Mapped by the javax.persistence.Id annotation.
Official documentation: http://docs.oracle.com/javaee/6/api/javax/persistence/Id.html.

Brief Overview

The @Id annotation is applied to an entity field (or property) to mark it as the primary key of that entity. Primary key values are set explicitly, or automatically using generators (dedicated algorithms) that guarantee uniqueness, consistency, and scalability. Usually, primary key types are represented as numbers or strings, but they can also be dates.

MongoDB is aware of primary keys and has a reserved field for them, _id (as you know from Chapter 2). If _id value is not specified, MongoDB automatically fills it with "MongoDB Id Object". But you can put any unique info into this field (a number, a timestamp, a string, and so forth).

OGM Support

Hibernate OGM supports the @Id annotation and a consistent set of generators, including the four standard JPA generators. Some of the Hibernate generators are available as well, through a generic generator; they will be listed later. For maximum scalability, Hibernate OGM recommends generators based on UUID (either uuid or uuid2). You'll also see some of the supported id generators and their effects in MongoDB, but, obviously, it's impossible to cover all kinds of generators. Remember to test your own generators (custom generators, for example). That I omitted a generator here doesn't mean it is, or is not, supported.

Example of a Simple @Id

By "simple @Id" I mean a primary key that doesn't have an explicit generator. In this case, you have to manually set a unique id value for each entity instance you need to persist, otherwise an error of type "*org.hibernate. HibernateException: trying to insert an already existing entity*" will result from the persisting operation.

As long as you set the primary keys correctly, everything works perfectly and the data can be found in MongoDB. For example, the following Players entity uses a simple @Id of type int:

```
import javax.persistence.Id;
...

@Entity
public class Players implements Serializable {
```

```
@Id
private int id;
private String name;
private String surname;
private int age;

//constructors, getters and setters
...
}
```

Next, I create three `Players` and use the `setId` method to manually specify ids 1, 2 and 3. Persist these `Players` into a MongoDB collection and you'll obtain three documents, as shown in Figure 5-1.

```
{ "_id" : 1, "age" : 31, "name" : "Federer", "surname" : "Roger" }
{ "_id" : 2, "age" : 25, "name" : "Murray", "surname" : "Andy" }
{ "_id" : 3, "age" : 26, "name" : "Nadal", "surname" : "Rafael" }
```

Figure 5-1. *Persisting three Players instances into a MongoDB collection*

Example of @Id and the AUTO Strategy

JPA comes with four strategies that can be applied to primary key generation: AUTO, IDENTITY, SEQUENCE and TABLE. AUTO lets the persistence provider choose the right strategy with respect to the database (table, sequence, or identity). Normally, this is the primary key generation strategy that's the default for the database. Thus, if you used AUTO, Hibernate OGM should pick the appropriate strategy based on the underlying database—MongoDB (which, in this case would be sequence). This strategy has the advantage of making the code very portable, though database migration can become an issue.

You can set the AUTO strategy using the `@GeneratedValue` annotation, like this:

```
import javax.persistence.GeneratedValue;
import javax.persistence.GenerationType;
import javax.persistence.Id;
...

@Entity
public class Players implements Serializable {

    @Id
    @GeneratedValue(strategy=GenerationType.AUTO)
    private int id;
    private String name;
    private String surname;
    private int age;

    //constructors, getters and setters
...
}
```

I'll now persist a few instances of this entity using Hibernate OGM, with the result in MongoDB shown in Figure 5-2.

```
{ "_id" : 1, "age" : 27, "name" : "Tsonga", "surname" : "Jo-Wilfried" }
{ "_id" : 2, "age" : 27, "name" : "Berdych", "surname" : "Tomas" }
{ "_id" : 3, "age" : 25, "name" : "Djokovic", "surname" : "Novak" }
{ "_id" : 4, "age" : 26, "name" : "Nadal", "surname" : "Rafael" }
{ "_id" : 5, "age" : 31, "name" : "Federer", "surname" : "Roger" }
```

Figure 5-2. Persisting several Players instances into a MongoDB collection

Notice that when a document is persisted, Hibernate OGM tells the database to insert a sequentially generated number using a behind-the-scene collection, named hibernate_sequences. After inserting five documents (records), the content of hibernate_sequences is similar to what you see in Figure 5-3. As you can see, it stores the id value for the next insert.

```
> db.hibernate_sequences.find();
{ "_id" : "Players", "sequence_value" : 6 }
```

Figure 5-3. The hibernate_sequences collection content

Example of @Id and IDENTITY strategy

The IDENTITY strategy requires the persistence provider to assign primary keys (of type short (Short), int (Integer) or long (Long)) for the entity using a database identity column. In relational databases (MySQL, Microsoft SQL Server, IBM DB2, HypersonicSQL, and Sybase), tables usually contain an auto-increment column that tells the database to insert a sequentially generated number when a record is inserted. Attaching the IDENTITY strategy to the auto-increment column enables the entity to automatically generate a sequential number as the primary key when inserted into the database. In the MongoDB world, you're essentially leveraging the generated _id from MongoDB as the primary key for the persisted object.

Hibernate OGM supports this strategy, but since it acts exactly like the AUTO strategy, OGM doesn't use the generated _id from MongoDB as the primary key for the persisted object. In any case, it's a well-known fact that this strategy has some problems, especially with regard to portability and performance.

Setting the IDENTITY strategy can be accomplished using the @GeneratedValue annotation, like this:

```
import javax.persistence.GeneratedValue;
import javax.persistence.GenerationType;
import javax.persistence.Id;
...

@Entity
public class Players implements Serializable {

    @Id
    @GeneratedValue(strategy=GenerationType.IDENTITY)
    private Long id;
    private String name;
    private String surname;
    private int age;

    //constructors, getters and setters
...
}
```

If you persist several instances of the Players entity using Hibernate OGM, MongoDB will reveal the Players collection, as shown in Figure 5-4.

```
> db.Players.find().pretty();          > db.hibernate_sequences.find().pretty();
{                                      { "_id" : "Players", "sequence_value" : 6 }
        "_id" : NumberLong(1),
        "age" : 27,
        "name" : "Berdych",
        "surname" : "Tomas"

}
{
        "_id" : NumberLong(2),
        "age" : 27,
        "name" : "Tsonga",
        "surname" : "Jo-Wilfried"

}
...
```

Figure 5-4. *Persisting several Players instances into a MongoDB collection using the IDENTITY strategy*

Actually, I expected to see something more like this (and no hibernate_sequences collection):

```
{ "_id" : ObjectId("4eaafff900694710bfb8fa5b"),
  "id" : NumberLong(1),
  ...
}
```

or, even better:

```
{ "_id" : ObjectId("4eaafff900694710bfb8fa5b"),
  ...
}
```

■ **Note** More details about ObjectId and how it's generated are available in the MongoDB official documentation at: http://docs.mongodb.org/manual/reference/object-id/

Example of @Id and the SEQUENCE strategy

The SEQUENCE strategy (called seqhilo in Hibernate) requires the persistence provider to assign primary keys (of type short, int, or long) for the entity using a database sequence. Instead of generating a primary key value during commit, this strategy generates groups of primary keys before commit, which is useful when the primary key value is needed earlier. (It's possible that some of the IDs in a given allocation will not be used, which can cause gaps in sequence values.)

Hibernate OGM supports this strategy by keeping the sequence information in a collection named hibernate_sequences. To show how this strategy works, I've configured a sequence generator with an initial value of 5 and a size allocation (the number of primary keys in a group) of 2, using the @SequenceGenerator annotation, like this:

```
@SequenceGenerator(name="mongodb_sequence", initialValue=5, allocationSize=2)
```

Next, I defined an int primary key and indicated the SEQUENCE strategy:

```java
import javax.persistence.GeneratedValue;
import javax.persistence.GenerationType;
import javax.persistence.Id;
import javax.persistence.SequenceGenerator;
...

@Entity
@SequenceGenerator(name="mongodb_sequence", initialValue=5, allocationSize=2)
public class Players implements Serializable {

    @Id
    @GeneratedValue(strategy=GenerationType.SEQUENCE, generator="mongodb_sequence")
    private int id;
    private String name;
    private String surname;
    private int age;

    //constructors, getters and setters
...
}
```

After persisting the first object, the hibernate_sequences and Players collections look like what's shown in Figure 5-5.

```
> db.hibernate_sequences.find();
{ "_id" : "Players", "sequence_value" : 9 }
> db.Players.find();
{ "_id" : 5, "age" : 28, "name" : "Tipsarevic", "surname" : "Janko" }
```

Figure 5-5. *Persisting one Players instance into a MongoDB collection using the SEQUENCE strategy*

Notice that the id of the first object (document) is the initial value of the generated sequence, while the generated sequence allocation size is calculated as the (allocation size * 2) + initial value, which is (2*2) + 5 = 9 (sequence_value field).

I then persisted three more objects and the result is shown in Figure 5-6.

```
> db.hibernate_sequences.find();
{ "_id" : "Players", "sequence_value" : 11 }
> db.Players.find();
{ "_id" : 5, "age" : 28, "name" : "Tipsarevic", "surname" : "Janko" }
{ "_id" : 6, "age" : 27, "name" : "Berdych", "surname" : "Tomas" }
{ "_id" : 7, "age" : 25, "name" : "Murray", "surname" : "Andy" }
```

Figure 5-6. *Persisting three more Players instances into a MongoDB collection using the SEQUENCE strategy*

So, when I persisted an object with id equal to 7, the sequence automatically increased with the allocation size value—2. Here the process is redundant.

Note that you can add the optional catalog element to the sequence generator:

```java
@SequenceGenerator(name="mongodb_sequence", catalog="MONGO",
                                  initialValue=5, allocationSize=2)
```

Now, the hibernate_sequences collection name becomes MONGO.hibernate_sequences. Moreover, if you add a schema element, like this:

```
@SequenceGenerator(name="mongodb_sequence", catalog="MONGO",
                                      schema="MONGOSEQ", initialValue=5, allocationSize=2)
```

Then, the hibernate_sequences collection name becomes MONGO.MONGOSEQ.hibernate_sequences. Everything seems to work as expected!

Example of @Id and TABLE Strategy

The TABLE strategy (called MultipleHiLoPerTableGenerator in Hibernate) requires the persistence provider to assign primary keys (of type short, int or long) for the entity using an underlying database table. This strategy is very widely used thanks to excellent performance, portability, and clustering. JPA providers are free to decide which approach to use to accomplish this task. The generator can be configured using the standard @TableGenerator annotation.

Hibernate OGM supports this strategy by creating a collection named hibernate_sequences; for MongoDB, the underlying table is a collection. To show how this strategy works, I've configured a table generator with an initial value of 5 and a size allocation (the number of primary keys in a group) of 2 using the @TableGenerator annotation, like this:

```
@TableGenerator(name="mongodb_table", initialValue=5, allocationSize=2)
```

Next, I define an int primary key and indicate the TABLE strategy, as shown in Listing 5-1.

Listing 5-1. Using the TABLE Strategy

```
import javax.persistence.GeneratedValue;
import javax.persistence.GenerationType;
import javax.persistence.Id;
import javax.persistence.TableGenerator;
...

@Entity
@TableGenerator(name="mongodb_table", initialValue=5, allocationSize=2)
public class Players implements Serializable {

    @Id
    @GeneratedValue(strategy=GenerationType.TABLE, generator="mongodb_table")
    private int id;
    private String name;
    private String surname;
    private int age;

    //constructors, getters and setters
...
}
```

After persisting the first object, the hibernate_sequences and Players collections have the content shown in Figure 5-7.

```
> db.hibernate_sequences.find();
{ "_id" : "Players", "sequence_value" : 10 }
> db.Players.find();
{ "_id" : 6, "age" : 24, "name" : "Del Potro", "surname" : "Juan Martin" }
```

Figure 5-7. *Persisting one Players instance to a MongoDB collection using the TABLE strategy*

Notice that the id of the first object (document) is the initial value + 1, while the sequence allocation size is calculated as the (allocation size * 2) + initial value + 1, which is (2*2) + 5 + 1= 10 (sequence_value field).

Next, I persisted three more objects and got the results shown in Figure 5-8:

```
> db.hibernate_sequences.find();
{ "_id" : "Players", "sequence_value" : 12 }
> db.Players.find();
{ "_id" : 6, "age" : 24, "name" : "Del Potro", "surname" : "Juan Martin" }
{ "_id" : 7, "age" : 27, "name" : "Berdych", "surname" : "Tomas" }
{ "_id" : 8, "age" : 24, "name" : "Del Potro", "surname" : "Juan Martin" }
```

Figure 5-8. *Persisting three more Players instances to a MongoDB collection using the TABLE strategy*

So, when I persisted the object with id equal to 8, the sequence was automatically increased by 1 + the allocation size value, by 3. For this, the process is redundant.

Notice that you can change the name of the hibernate_sequences by adding the table element in a table generator:

```
@TableGenerator(name="mongodb_table", table="pk_table", initialValue=5, allocationSize=2)
```

Example of @Id and GenericGenerator—UUID and UUID2

UUID and UUID2 are two of the many generators Hibernate provides in addition to the four standard JPA generators. UUID generates a 128-bit UUID based on a custom algorithm, while UUID2 generates an IETF RFC 4122-compliant (variant 2) 128-bit UUID. For MongoDB, these kinds of primary keys are represented as strings.

Hibernate OGM supports both generators, but in some environments, UUID generates some warnings. In GlassFish, for example, using the UUID generator throws this warning: "*WARN: HHH000409: Using org.hibernate. id.UUIDHexGenerator which does not generate IETF RFC 4122 compliant UUID values; consider using org.hibernate. id.UUIDGenerator instead*". In simple translation, "use UUID2". So it's better to use UUID2, as shown in Listing 5-2.

Listing 5-2. Using UUID2

```
import javax.persistence.GeneratedValue;
import javax.persistence.Id;
import org.hibernate.annotations.GenericGenerator;
...

@Entity
@GenericGenerator(name="mongodb_uuidgg", strategy="uuid2")
public class Players implements Serializable {

    @Id
    @GeneratedValue(generator="mongodb_uuidgg")
    private String id;
    private String name;
```

```
    private String surname;
    private int age;

    //constructors, getters and setters
...
}
```

If I now persist several instances of the Players entity using Hibernate OGM, MongoDB will reveal the Players collection shown in Figure 5-9.

```
> db.Players.find().pretty();
{
        "_id" : "991f1149-3b90-4627-a4bd-728fab03ee91",
        "age" : 30,
        "name" : "Ferrer",
        "surname" : "David"
}
{
        "_id" : "7ad82afc-12bd-43d0-9d24-6fd5305f213a",
        "age" : 28,
        "name" : "Tipsarevic",
        "surname" : "Janko"
}
{
        "_id" : "098c9f5c-8ca6-4658-b03d-939d7e7a2bd1",
        "age" : 27,
        "name" : "Berdych",
        "surname" : "Tomas"
}
```

Figure 5-9. Persisting several Players instances into a MongoDB collection using the UUID2 strategy

Example of @Id and Custom Generator

Sometimes, all the primary key generators in the world are just not enough to meet the needs of the application. In such cases, a custom generator becomes mandatory, but before writing one, you need to know if your persistence environment will support it. In this case, Hibernate OGM and MongoDB worked perfectly with my custom generator, as you'll see.

Creating a new Hibernate custom generator is a very simple task if you follow these steps:

- create a new class that implements the org.hibernate.id.IdentifierGenerator interface

- override the IdentifierGenerator.generate method; provide the generator business logic and return the new primary key as a Serializable object

Based on these two steps, I wrote a custom generator that creates primary keys of type: *XXXX*_long-number (for example, SFGZ_3495832849584739405). Listing 5-3 shows the custom generator.

Listing 5-3. A Custom Primary Key Generator

```
package hogm.mongodb.generator;

import java.io.Serializable;
import java.util.Random;
import org.hibernate.HibernateException;
import org.hibernate.engine.spi.SessionImplementor;
import org.hibernate.id.IdentifierGenerator;
```

```java
public class CustomGenerator implements IdentifierGenerator {

    @Override
    public Serializable generate(SessionImplementor sessionImplementor,
            Object object) throws HibernateException {

        Random rnd = new Random();
        String str = "";

        for (int i = 0; i <= 3; i++) {
            str = str + (char) (rnd.nextInt(26) + 'a');
        }

        str = str + "_";
        str = str + String.valueOf(rnd.nextLong());
        str=str.toUpperCase();

        return str;
    }
}
```

Testing the custom generator is pretty straightforward. First, I use the @GenericGenerator annotation and indicate the custom generator's fully qualified class name as the generator strategy:

```java
@GenericGenerator(name="mongodb_custom_generator",
                        strategy="hogm.mongodb.generator.CustomGenerator")
```

Next, I define a String primary key field and use the @GeneratedValue annotation shown in Listing 5-4.

Listing 5-4. Using the GeneratedValue Annotation

```java
import javax.persistence.GeneratedValue;
import javax.persistence.Id;
import org.hibernate.annotations.GenericGenerator;
...


@Entity
@GenericGenerator(name="mongodb_custom_generator",
                        strategy="hogm.mongodb.generator.CustomGenerator")

public class Players implements Serializable {

    @Id
    @GeneratedValue(generator="mongodb_custom_generator")
    private String id;
    private String name;
    private String surname;
    private int age;

    //constructors, getters and setters
...
}
```

Again, I persist several instances of the Players entity using Hibernate OGM, and MongoDB reveals the Players collection in Figure 5-10.

```
> db.Players.find().pretty();
{
        "_id" : "BDMU_2220843745796377247",
        "age" : 31,
        "name" : "Federer",
        "surname" : "Roger"
}
{
        "_id" : "PRNN_-43169740083129546112",
        "age" : 28,
        "name" : "Tipsarevic",
        "surname" : "Janko"
}
{
        "_id" : "IZRK_-8205773235493384459",
        "age" : 25,
        "name" : "Murray",
        "surname" : "Andy"
}
```

Figure 5-10. Persisting several Players instances into a MongoDB collection using a custom generator

The complete application that demonstrates @Id annotation is available in the Apress repository and is named HOGM_MONGODB_Id. It comes as a NetBeans project and was tested under GlassFish 3 AS.

@EmbeddedId Annotation

Mapped by the javax.persistence.EmbeddedId annotation.
Official documentation: http://docs.oracle.com/javaee/6/api/javax/persistence/EmbeddedId.html.

Brief Overview

The @EmbeddedId annotation denotes a composite primary key that's an embeddable class. You are forced to write a new serializable class that must: be annotated with the @Embeddable annotation (no need of @Entity or other annotations for this class); define primary key fields; and define getters and setters for the primary key fields. @Embeddable allows you to specify a class whose instances are stored as an intrinsic part of the owning entity. The entity itself must define a primary key field of the type of the class annotated with @Embeddable. This field should be annotated with @EmbeddedId.

If you prefer this kind of composite key, there's no need to specify the @Id annotation anymore. For MongoDB, a composite key should be stored in the _id field as an embedded document.

OGM Support

Hibernate OGM supports composite keys defined with the @EmbeddedId annotation. It transforms the Java composite key into an embedded document in the _id field of MongoDB and the primary key fields become the embedded document fields.

Example

Creating this kind of composite key comprises two main steps: first, you write the serializable primary key class and annotate it with @Embeddable, and, second, you choose the appropriate entity property or persistence field that will become the composite primary key and annotate it with @EmbeddedId. For example, suppose you have a primary key class:

```
import javax.persistence.Embeddable;
...

@Embeddable
public class RankingAndPrizeE implements Serializable {

    private int ranking;
    private String prize;

    //constructors, getters and setters
...
}
```

Then, in the Players entity, you create a composite primary key field:

```
import javax.persistence.EmbeddedId;
...

@Entity
public class Players implements Serializable {

  @EmbeddedId
  private RankingAndPrizeE id;
  private String name;
  private String surname;
  private int age;

  //constructors, getters and setters
...
}
```

Now persist several instances of the Players entity using Hibernate OGM, and MongoDB will reveal the Players collection shown in Figure 5-11.

```
> db.Players.find().pretty();
{
        "_id" : {
                "prize" : "$13,139,293",
                "ranking" : 6
        },
        "age" : 27,
        "name" : "Berdych",
        "surname" : "Tomas"
}
{
        "_id" : {
                "prize" : "$45,686,497",
                "ranking" : 1
        },
        "age" : 25,
        "name" : "Djokovic",
        "surname" : "Novak"
}
{
        "_id" : {
                "prize" : "$50,061,827",
                "ranking" : 4
        },
        "age" : 26,
        "name" : "Nadal",
        "surname" : "Rafael"
}
```

Figure 5-11. *Defining a composite key using @EmbeddedId*

The complete application that demonstrates the @EmbeddedId annotation is available in the Apress repository and is named HOGM_MONGODB_Id. It comes as a NetBeans project and was tested under GlassFish 3 AS.

@IdClass Annotation

Mapped by the javax.persistence.IdClass annotation.
Official documentation: http://docs.oracle.com/javaee/6/api/javax/persistence/IdClass.html.

Brief Overview

The @IdClass annotation denotes a composite primary key that is mapped to multiple fields or properties of the entity. This approach forces you to write a new serializable class that defines the primary key fields and overrides the equals and hashCode methods. The primary key fields defined in the primary key class must also appear in the entity class in exactly the same way, except that they must have getter and setter methods. Moreover, the entity class is annotated with @IdClass.

If you prefer this kind of composite key, you'll have multiple @Id annotations in the entity—one per primary key field. For MongoDB, a composite key should be stored in the _id field as an embedded document.

OGM Support

Hibernate OGM supports composite keys defined with the @IdClass annotation. It transforms the Java composite key into an embedded document in the MongoDB _id field and the primary key fields become the embedded document fields.

Example

Creating this kind of composite key comprises two main steps: first, you write the serializable primary key class and, second, you annotate the entity class with @IdClass and define the primary keys fields as in the primary keys class. The first step is shown in Listing 5-5.

Listing 5-5. The Serializable Primary Key Class

```java
package hogm.mongodb.entity;

import java.io.Serializable;

public class RankingAndPrizeC implements Serializable {

    private int ranking;
    private String prize;

    public RankingAndPrizeC() {
    }

    @Override
    public boolean equals(Object arg0) {

        //implement equals here
        return false;
    }

    @Override
    public int hashCode() {

        //implement hashCode here
        return 0;
    }
}
```

And the second step is shown in Listing 5-6.

Listing 5-6. Define the Primary Keys Fields

```java
import javax.persistence.Id;
import javax.persistence.IdClass;
...

@Entity
@IdClass(hogm.mongodb.entity.RankingAndPrizeC.class)
public class Players implements Serializable {

    @Id
    private int ranking;
    @Id
    private String prize;
    private String name;
```

```
    private String surname;
    private int age;

    //constructors, getters and setters
...
```

Now persist several instances of the `Players` entity using Hibernate OGM. MongoDB will reveal the the `Players` collection shown in Figure 5-12.

```
> db.Players.find().pretty();
{
        "_id" : {
                "prize" : "$50,061,827",
                "ranking" : 4
        },
        "age" : 26,
        "name" : "Nadal",
        "surname" : "Rafael"
}
> db.Players.find().pretty();
{
        "_id" : {
                "prize" : "$50,061,827",
                "ranking" : 4
        },
        "age" : 26,
        "name" : "Nadal",
        "surname" : "Rafael"
}
```

Figure 5-12. *Define a composite key using @IdClass*

The complete application that demonstrates the `@IdClass` annotation is available in the Apress repository and is named `HOGM_MONGODB_Id`. It comes as a NetBeans project and was tested under GlassFish 3 AS.

@Table Annotation

Mapped by the `javax.persistence.Table` annotation.
Official documentation: `http://docs.oracle.com/javaee/6/api/javax/persistence/Table.html`.

Brief Overview

In a relational database, each entity is represented as a table (known as a primary table) whose name is, by default, the same as the entity (an unqualified entity class name). If you want to set another name for a table, you can use the `@Table` annotation and the `name` element. You can also specify a catalog and a schema by adding the `catalog` and `schema` elements.

MongoDB associates the notion of table with collection. The default collection name is the same as the mapped entity.

OGM Support

Hibernate OGM supports `@Table` annotation. It will supply the `name` element value as the name of the corresponding collection. Moreover, if you specify the `catalog` element as well, Hibernate OGM will add the catalog value as a prefix to the schema name (or collection name, if the schema is missing) and will separate it from the schema name (or collection name) with a dot. And if you specify the schema element, Hibernate OGM will add the schema value between the catalog name (if that exists) and the collection name separated by dots. As you can see, when catalog, schema, and collection names are present, Hibernate OGM concatenates a final name based on the relational model hierarchy: catalogs contain schemas, and schemas contain tables.

Example

Testing @Table annotation is a straightforward task, since all you need to do is add this annotation at the class level and see what happens. Here's the Players entity annotated with @Table:

```java
import javax.persistence.Table;
...


@Entity
@Table(catalog="ATP", schema="public", name="atp_players")
public class Players implements Serializable {

    @Id
    @GeneratedValue(strategy=GenerationType.AUTO)
    private int id;
    private String name;
    private String surname;
    private int age;

    //constructors, getters and setters
    ...
}
```

Figure 5-13 shows the effect of the @Table annotation on MongoDB:

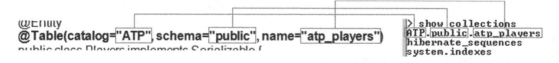

Figure 5-13. *Mapping @Table annotation in MongoDB*

The complete application that demonstrates the @Table annotation is available in the Apress repository and is named HOGM_MONGODB_TableColumn. It comes as a NetBeans project and it was test it under GlassFish 3 AS.

@Column Annotation

Mapped by the javax.persistence.Column annotation.
   Official documentation: http://docs.oracle.com/javaee/6/api/javax/persistence/Column.html.

Brief Overview

In a relational database, each entity's persistent property or field is represented in the database as a column of the corresponding table, and the field name provides the column name. You can explicitly provide a column name (different from the field name) by annotating its field with the @Column annotation and specifying the desired name as the value of the name element. Moreover, the @Column elements let you set some data restrictions, such as length (using the length element), whether the database column is nullable (the nullable element), and so on. All of the supported elements are listed in the official documentation.

MongoDB stores each entity instance as a document. Each document is made of the document's fields that are characterized by name and value. Apart from the reserved _id field, the rest of the document's field names reflect the entity persistence property or field names (or, from the relational model perspective, the column names).

OGM Support

Hibernate OGM supports the @Column annotation. It will supply each name element value as the name of the corresponding document's field. Besides name, the rest of @Column elements seem to be ignored. Moreover, adding an @Column annotation to the primary key persistence field will be ignored and the MongoDB _id field name will be used instead, so you can use any name you like for the primary key field in the entity.

Example

Testing @Column annotation is a straightforward task, since all you need to do is add this annotation at field (or property) level and see what happens. Here's the Players entity annotated with @Column:

```
import javax.persistence.Column;
...

@Entity
@Table(catalog="ATP", schema="public", name="atp_players")
public class Players implements Serializable {

    @Id
    @GeneratedValue(strategy=GenerationType.AUTO)
    private int id;
    @Column(name="player_name")
    private String name;
    @Column(name="player_surname")
    private String surname;
    @Column(name="player_age")
    private int age;

    //constructors, getters and setters
    ...
}
```

Figure 5-14 shows the effect of @Column annotation on MongoDB.

```
private int id;
@Column(name="player_name")
private String name;
@Column(name="player_surname")
private String surname;
@Column(name="player_age")
private int age;
```

```
> db.ATP.public.atp_players.find().pretty();
{
    "_id" : 1,
    "player_age" : 25,
    "player_name" : "Murray",
    "player_surname" : "Andy"
```

Figure 5-14. *Mapping @Column annotation in MongoDB*

The complete application for demonstrating the @Column annotation is available in the Apress repository and is named HOGM_MONGODB_TableColumn. It comes as a NetBeans project and was tested under GlassFish 3 AS.

@Temporal Annotation

Mapped by the javax.persistence.Temporal annotation.
    Official documentation: http://docs.oracle.com/javaee/6/api/javax/persistence/Temporal.html.

Brief Overview

@Temporal annotation indicates a persistence field or property that represents a date, time, or date-time (timestamp) value. The supported values are of type java.util.Date and java.util.Calendar. The type used in mapping java.util.Date or java.util.Calendar can be indicated using TemporalType as DATE (mapped as java.sql.Date), TIME (mapped as java.sql.Time) or TIMESTAMP (mapped as java.sql.Timestamp).

    MongoDB supports date/time fields in its documents. MongoDB dates follow the format defined by the BSON official documentation (see http://bsonspec.org/#/specification) and they can be created in MongoDB shell using Date or ISODate constructors, like this:

```
var mydate = new Date()
var mydate = new Date("Sun Feb 16 2013")
var mydate = new Date("Sun Feb 16 2013 08:22:05")
var mydate_iso = ISODate()
var mydate_iso = ISODate("2013-02-16T08:22:05")
```

OGM Support

Hibernate OGM supports the @Temporal annotation. Each temporal field (independent of its type) will be converted into a MongoDB ISO date consisting of year, month, day, hour, minute, and second (year-month-dayThour:minute:second). For example, a Java date defined using the Gregorian calendar would look like this:

```
private static final Calendar calendar = GregorianCalendar.getInstance();
calendar.clear();
calendar.set(1987, Calendar.MAY, 22); //22.05.1987
```

    That date is represented in MongoDB like this:

```
ISODate("1987-05-22T00:00:00Z")
```

Notice that in this example I didn't indicate the hour, minute and second. Adding a sample time transforms the calendar settings to this:

```
calendar.set(1987, Calendar.MAY, 22, 12, 40, 01); //22.05.1987 12:40:01
```

And the MongoDB representation becomes:

```
ISODate("1987-05-22T12:40:01Z")
```

If you don't clear the calendar settings by calling the clear method, and you don't specify a time (hour, minute and second), the current time will be automatically set.

Example

First I define in the entity a java.util.Date field representing each player's birthday. Then I annotate it with @Temporal (javax.persistence.TemporalType.DATE), as you can see in Listing 5-7.

Listing 5-7. Defining a Field to Represent Each Player's Birthday

```
import java.util.Date;
import javax.persistence.Temporal;
...

@Entity
@Table(catalog="ATP", schema="public", name="atp_players")
public class Players implements Serializable {

    @Id
    @GeneratedValue(strategy=GenerationType.AUTO)
    private int id;
    @Column(name="player_name")
    private String name;
    @Column(name="player_surname")
    private String surname;
    @Column(name="player_age")
    private int age;
    @Temporal(javax.persistence.TemporalType.DATE)
    private Date birth;

    //constructors, getters and setters
...
}
```

Second, I defined the players' birthdays using the Gregorian calendar, like this:

```
private static final Calendar calendar = GregorianCalendar.getInstance();
calendar.clear();
calendar.set(1987, Calendar.MAY, 22);   //22.05.1987
calendar.clear();
calendar.set(1981, Calendar.AUGUST, 8); //08.08.1981
...
```

Now I'll persist several instances of the Players entity using Hibernate OGM. MongoDB will reveal the Players collection shown in Figure 5-15. Notice the birth document field.

```
> db.ATP.public.atp_players.find().pretty();
{
        "_id" : 1,
        "birth" : ISODate("1986-06-03T00:00:00Z"),
        "player_age" : 26,
        "player_name" : "Nadal",
        "player_surname" : "Rafael"
}
{
        "_id" : 2,
        "birth" : ISODate("1982-04-02T00:00:00Z"),
        "player_age" : 30,
        "player_name" : "Ferrer",
        "player_surname" : "David"
}
...
```

Figure 5-15. *Mapping the @Temporal annotation in MongoDB*

The complete application for demonstrating the @Temporal annotation is available in the Apress repository and is named HOGM_MONGODB_Temporal. It comes as a NetBeans project and it was test it under GlassFish 3 AS.

@Transient Annotation

Mapped by the javax.persistence.Transient annotation.
Official documentation: http://docs.oracle.com/javaee/6/api/javax/persistence/Transient.html.

Brief Overview

First, a word of caution: If you're not familiar with @Transient annotation, be carefully not to confuse it with the Java transient keyword. The transient keyword is used to indicate non-serializable fields, while the @Transient annotation is specific to JPA and indicates fields that must not be persisted to the underlying database. Moreover, this annotation doesn't imply any support from the database; only the JPA provider should know how to deal with it.

OGM Support

Hibernate OGM supports the @Transient annotation. When an entity class is passed to OGM, it persists only the fields that are not annotated with @Transient.

Example

Here I've annotated some of the Players entity fields with @Transient, like so:

```
import javax.persistence.Transient;
...

@Entity
@Table(catalog="ATP", schema="public", name="atp_players")
public class Players implements Serializable {
```

```
@Id
@GeneratedValue(strategy=GenerationType.AUTO)
private int id;
@Column(name="player_name")
private String name;
@Column(name="player_surname")
private String surname;
@Column(name="player_age")
@Transient
private int age;
@Temporal(javax.persistence.TemporalType.DATE)
@Transient
private Date birth;

//constructors, getters and setters
...
}
```

If you persist several instances of the Players entity using Hibernate OGM, MongoDB will reveal the Players collection shown in Figure 5-16. Notice that the age and birth document fields are missing, which means that OGM does not persist them based on the @Transient state.

```
> db.ATP.public.atp_players.find().pretty();
{ "_id" : 1, "player_name" : "Berdych", "player_surname" : "Tomas" }
{ "_id" : 2, "player_name" : "Djokovic", "player_surname" : "Novak" }
```

Figure 5-16. Mapping @Transient annotation in MongoDB

The complete application for demonstrating the @Transient annotation is available in the Apress repository and is named HOGM_MONGODB_Transient. It comes as a NetBeans project and was tested under GlassFish 3 AS.

@Embedded and @Embeddable Annotations

Mapped by the javax.persistence.Embedded and javax.persistence.Embeddable annotations.
    Official documentation: http://docs.oracle.com/javaee/6/api/javax/persistence/Embedded.html

http://docs.oracle.com/javaee/6/api/javax/persistence/Embeddable.html

Brief Overview

When a persistence field or property is annotated with @Embedded, this denotes an instance of an embeddable class. This class is not an entity and doesn't have an id or table; it's just a logical part of the entity that contains the embedded field, and it was intentionally separated and marked as embeddable using the @Embeddable annotation at the class level. The reasons for separation vary, from the wish to have straightforward code to not wanting to persist the embeddable part, and thus marking its fields as transient using the @Transient annotation. By default, each non-transient property or field of the embedded object is mapped to the database table for the entity.
    From the MongoDB perspective, embeddable objects are stored as nested documents within the entity's documents.

OGM Support

Hibernate OGM supports @Embedded and @Embeddable annotations. Moreover, as you can see here, Hibernate OGM also supports the @Transient annotation for embeddable fields (mapped by javax.persistence.Transient, with more details at http://docs.oracle.com/javaee/6/api/javax/persistence/Transient.html). OGM knows how to convert each instance of the embeddable class into a nested document inside the document representing each owner entity instance. Any field of the embeddable class that is annotated as transient will not be persisted in the nested document.

Don't try to use the @SecondaryTable annotation (javax.persistence.SecondaryTable) because OGM doesn't support it.

Example

First, I define an embeddable class that contains some details for each player: birthplace, residence, height, weight, and so on. The class is very simple, but the @Embeddable annotations makes it special:

```
import javax.persistence.Embeddable;
...

@Embeddable
public class Details implements Serializable {

    private String birthplace;
    private String residence;
    private String height;
    private String weight;
    private String plays;
    private int turnedpro;
    private String coach;
    private String website;

    //constructors, getters and setters
...
}
```

Next, in the Players entity, I create a field of type Details and annotate it as @Embedded, as Listing 5-8 shows.

Listing 5-8. Creating the Embedded Details Field

```
import javax.persistence.Embedded;
...

@Entity
@Table(catalog="ATP", schema="public", name="atp_players")
public class Players implements Serializable {

    private static final long serialVersionUID = 1L;

    @Id
    @GeneratedValue(strategy=GenerationType.AUTO)
    private int id;
    @Column(name="player_name")
```

```
    private String name;
    @Column(name="player_surname")
    private String surname;
    @Column(name="player_age")
    private int age;
    @Temporal(javax.persistence.TemporalType.DATE)
    private Date birth;
    @Embedded
    private Details details;

  //constructors, getters and setters
...
}
```

If you now persist several instances of the Players entity using Hibernate OGM, MongoDB will reveal the Players collection shown in Figure 5-17. Note the nested document.

```
> db.ATP.public.atp_players.find().pretty();
{
        "_id" : 1,
        "birth" : ISODate("1986-06-03T00:00:00Z").
        "details" : {
                "birthplace" : "Manacor, Mallorca, Spain",
                "coach" : "Toni Nadal",
                "height" : "185 cm",
                "plays" : "Left-handed",
                "residence" : "Manacor, Mallorca, Spain",
                "turnedpro" : 2001,
                "website" : "http://www.rafaelnadal.com",
                "weight" : "188 lbs (85 kg)"
        },
        "player_age" : 26,
        "player_name" : "Nadal",
        "player_surname" : "Rafael"
}
...
```

Figure 5-17. Mapping @Embeddable and @Embedded annotations in MongoDB

I've also annotated the embeddable fields birthplace and residence as transient:

```
import javax.persistence.Transient;
...

@Embeddable
public class Details implements Serializable {

    @Transient
    private String birthplace;
    @Transient
    private String residence;
...
}
```

I persisted more players and Hibernate OGM worked perfectly. The transient fields were not persisted, as you can see in Figure 5-18.

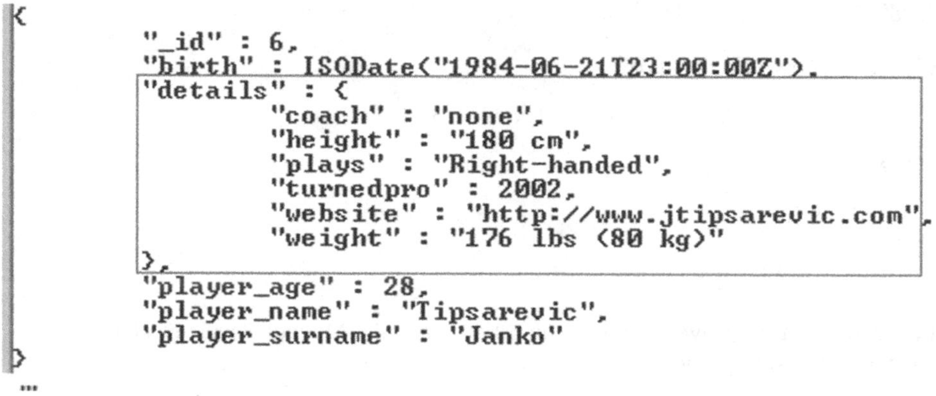

```
"_id" : 6,
"birth" : ISODate("1984-06-21T23:00:00Z"),
"details" : {
        "coach" : "none",
        "height" : "180 cm",
        "plays" : "Right-handed",
        "turnedpro" : 2002,
        "website" : "http://www.jtipsarevic.com",
        "weight" : "176 lbs (80 kg)"
},
"player_age" : 28,
"player_name" : "Tipsarevic",
"player_surname" : "Janko"
```

Figure 5-18. *Using @Transient for a few embeddable fields (or properties)*

For the sake of completeness, it's worth noting that if you annotate all the embeddable fields as transient, OGM will completely skip the nested document, as you can see in Figure 5-19.

```
"_id" : 9,
"birth" : ISODate("1982-04-02T00:00:00Z"),
"player_age" : 30,
"player_name" : "Ferrer",
"player_surname" : "David"
```

Figure 5-19. *Using @Transient for all embeddable fields (or properties)*

The complete application that demonstrates the @Embeddable and @Embedded annotations is available in the Apress repository and is named HOGM_MONGODB_Embedded. It comes as a NetBeans project and was tested under GlassFish 3 AS.

■ **Note** An embeddable object can be shared among multiple classes. In a relational model, this feature is supported by allowing each embedded mapping to override the columns used in the embeddable, which is accomplished using the @AttributeOverride annotation. In MongoDB and Hibernate OGM, you don't need to override columns. Everything will work as expected without any special treatment; just use @Embedded in each class you want to embed the same embeddable class.

@Enumerated Annotation

Mapped by the javax.persistence.Enumerated annotation.
Official documentation: http://docs.oracle.com/javaee/6/api/javax/persistence/Enumerated.html.

Brief Overview

Sometimes a Java enum type can be appropriate for representing a column in the database. JPA provides conversion between database columns and Java enum types via the @Enumerated annotation. An enum type is, by default, ordinal; it persists the enumerated type property or field as an integer, but it can also be made a string by setting the EnumType value as STRING.

MongoDB treats a column that stores Java enum type values as an ordinary document field.

OGM Support

Hibernate OGM supports the @Enumerated annotation. It knows how to convert a Java enum type into a MongoDB document field and how to restore it. Both EnumType.ORDINAL and EnumType.STRING are supported. OGM stores STRING values in MongoDB between quotes, to indicate string values. ORDINAL values, on the other hand, are stored without quotes, indicating numeric values.

Example

First, I define a Java enum type representing the highest ranking of our players in the history of the ATP World Tour. Then I define the corresponding field that will be persisted or restored by Hibernate OGM and I mark it with the @Enumerated annotation. Listing 5-9 shows part of the code for the entity.

Listing 5-9. A Java Enum Type

```java
import javax.persistence.EnumType;
import javax.persistence.Enumerated;
...

@Entity
@Table(catalog="ATP", schema="public", name="atp_players")
public class Players implements Serializable {

    public static enum Ratings {

        FIRST,
        SECOND,
        THIRD,
        FOURTH,
        FIFTH,
        SIXTH,
        SEVENTH,
        EIGHTH,
        NINTH,
        TENTH
    }


    @Id
    @GeneratedValue(strategy=GenerationType.AUTO)
    private int id;
    @Column(name="player_name")
    private String name;
```

```
    @Column(name="player_surname")
    private String surname;
    @Column(name="player_age")
    private int age;
    @Temporal(javax.persistence.TemporalType.DATE)
    private Date birth;
    @Column(name="player_best_rating")
    @Enumerated(EnumType.STRING)
    private Ratings best_rating;

//constructors, getters and setters
...
}
```

As usual, I now persist several instances of the Players entity using Hibernate OGM, and MongoDB reveals the Players collection shown in Figure 5-20.

```
> db.ATP.public.atp_players.find().pretty();
{
        "_id" : 1,
        "birth" : ISODate("1987-05-22T00:00:00Z"),
        "player_age" : 25,
        "player_best_rating" : "FIRST",
        "player_name" : "Djokovic",
        "player_surname" : "Novak"
}
```

Figure 5-20. Mapping @Enumerated in MongoDB

The complete application that demonstrates the @Enumerated annotation is available in the Apress repository and is named HOGM_MONGODB_Enumerated. It comes as a NetBeans project and was tested under GlassFish 3 AS.

@Cacheable Annotation

Mapped by the javax.persistence.Cacheable annotation.
Official documentation: http://docs.oracle.com/javaee/6/api/javax/persistence/Cacheable.html.

Brief Overview

Caching is one of the most important ways of increasing performance, by reducing database traffic when executing queries, joins, and so on. As you may know, JPA 2.0 contains two levels of cache:

- The *first-level cache* is not directly related to performance and is meant for reducing the number of queries in transactions. It's also known as the *persistent context cache* and it lives as long as the persistence context lives, usually until the end of transaction. When the persistent context is closed, the first-level cache is cleared, and further queries must use the database again. See Figure 5-21.

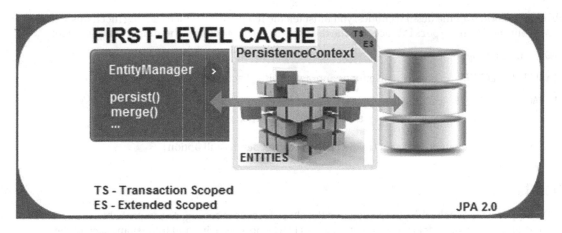

Figure 5-21. *JPA 2.0 first-level cache*

- The *second-level cache* is directly related to performance. In this case, the caching mechanism is placed between the persistence context and the database and it acts a server-side device to keep objects loaded into memory. With this approach, the objects are available for the entire application directly from memory without involving the database. The JPA provider is responsible for implementing the second-level cache, but the implementation itself is pretty subjective, because the specification is not very clear. Therefore, each implementation is free to decide how to implement caching capabilities and how sophisticated they will be. See Figure 5-22.

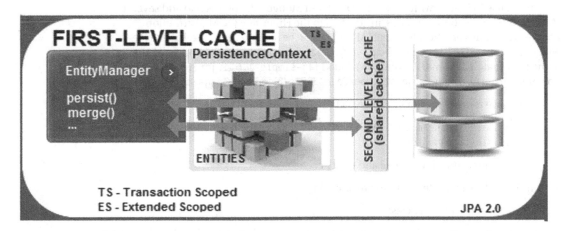

Figure 5-22. *JPA 2.0 second-level cache*

By default, entities are not part of the second-level cache. JPA 2.0 provides the @Cacheable annotation that can be used to explicitly inform the JPA provider about cacheable or non-cacheable entities. The @Cacheable annotation takes a Boolean value (true is the default for cacheable entities; false, for non-cacheable entities). After spreading the @Cacheable annotation over the desired entities, you must tell the JPA provider which caching mechanism to use and, for this, you must add into the persistence.xml file the shared-cache-mode tag. The supported values are:

- NONE - no caching

- ENABLE_SELECTIVE—caching for all entities annotated with @Cacheable(true)

- DISABLE_SELECTIVE—caching for all entities except those annotated with @Cacheable(false)

- ALL—caching for all entities

- UNSPECIFIED—undefined behavior (might be the JPA provider default option)

OGM Support

Hibernate OGM supports the @Cacheable annotation and the shared-cache-mode tag. As you probably know, there are several second-level cache providers for Hibernate, such as EHCache, OSCache, and Infinispan. Each of these cache providers comes with some specific settings and specific features, has strong points and gaps, and provides better or worse performance. But it's not our focus here to look at the different cache providers, so we've arbitrarily chosen EHCache to test the Hibernate OGM support for the @Cacheable annotation and the shared-cache-mode tag. Feel free to use any other supported second-level cache provider.

Example

You might be interested only in the final result and conclusions but, if you want to reproduce the same test, here are the main steps for setting up the EHCache second-level cache. (If you've never used Hibernate OGM and a second-level cache, this is a good opportunity to try them out.)

1. In order to use EHCache with Hibernate OGM and MongoDB, you need to add several JARs to your application's libraries, in addition to the Hibernate OGM distribution and MongoDB driver. The additional JARs are: ehcache-core-2.4.3.jar, hibernate-ehcache-4.1.4.Final.jar, slf4j-api-1.6.1.jar (all available in the optional JARs set of the Hibernate 4.1.4 Final distribution) and slf4j-simple-1.6.1.jar (which you can download from http://www.java2s.com/Code/Jar/s/Downloadslf4jsimple161jar.htm).

2. Next, you have to write the persistence.xml file. You have to:

   - set the shared-cache-mode as ENABLE_SELECTIVE (only the entities annotated as @Cacheable(true) will be cached).

   - turn on the second-level cache and query cache.

   - indicate the second-level cache provider class.

   - set up the region factory class.

   - specify the location of the EHCache configuration file, ehcache.xml, to be used by the cache provider/region-factory (the ehcache.xml content is not really relevant so I won't list it here. You can check it out in the Apress repository under the application named HOGM_MONGODB_Cache).

   - set the JTA platform.

   - add specific properties for configuring the MongoDB connection.

If you complete these steps, you'll end up with a persistence.xml file, like the one in Listing 5-10.

Listing 5-10. Persistence.xml

```xml
<?xml version="1.0" encoding="UTF-8"?>
<persistence version="2.0" xmlns="http://java.sun.com/xml/ns/persistence" xmlns:xsi=
"http://www.w3.org/2001/XMLSchema-instance" xsi:schemaLocation="http://java.sun.com/xml/ns/persistence
http://java.sun.com/xml/ns/persistence/persistence_2_0.xsd">
    <persistence-unit name="HOGM_MONGODB_L2Cache-ejbPU" transaction-type="JTA">
        <provider>org.hibernate.ogm.jpa.HibernateOgmPersistence</provider>
        <class>hogm.mongodb.entity.Players</class>
        <class>hogm.mongodb.entity.Tournaments</class>
        <shared-cache-mode>ENABLE_SELECTIVE</shared-cache-mode>
        <properties>
            <property name="hibernate.cache.use_second_level_cache" value="true"/>
            <property name="hibernate.cache.use_query_cache" value="true"/>
            <property name="hibernate.cache.provider_class"
                      value="org.hibernate.cache.EhCacheProvider"/>
            <property name="hibernate.cache.region.factory_class"
                      value="org.hibernate.cache.ehcache.SingletonEhCacheRegionFactory"/>
            <property name="hibernate.cache.provider_configuration_file_resource_path"
                      value="ehcache.xml"/>
            <property name="hibernate.transaction.jta.platform"
                      value="org.hibernate.service.jta.platform.internal.SunOneJtaPlatform"/>
            <property name="hibernate.ogm.datastore.provider" value="mongodb"/>
            <property name="hibernate.ogm.datastore.grid_dialect"
                      value="org.hibernate.ogm.dialect.mongodb.MongoDBDialect"/>
            <property name="hibernate.ogm.mongodb.database" value="mapping_entities_db"/>
            <property name="hibernate.ogm.mongodb.host" value="127.0.0.1"/>
            <property name="hibernate.ogm.mongodb.port" value="27017"/>
        </properties>
    </persistence-unit>
</persistence>
```

Notice that there are two entities specified in the persistence.xml file—Players and Tournaments. In order to test the ENABLE_SELECTIVE caching mechanism, I've annotated the Players entity with @Cacheable(true) and the Tournaments entity with @Cacheable(false). Our test will check to make sure the Players objects are cacheable, while the Tournaments objects should not be cacheable. Here's the listing for the Players entity:

```java
import javax.persistence.Cacheable;
...

@Entity
@Cacheable(true)
@Table(catalog = "ATP", schema = "public", name = "atp_players")
public class Players implements Serializable {

    //fields declaration
    //constructors, getters and setters
...
}
```

And, the listing for the Tournaments entity is:

```java
import javax.persistence.Cacheable;

@Entity
@Cacheable(false)
public class Tournaments implements Serializable {

    //fields declaration
    //constructors, getters and setters
...
}
```

Before starting to write the test, you need to populate the MongoDB collections associated with these two entities with at least five documents each, with ids 1, 2, 3, 4 and 5 (you'll see why we need five documents in the test section). When that's done, you're ready to write a simple JUnit test to check whether the second-level cache is working. To do this, you need to use the second-level cache API, which is pretty poor but at least it allows us to query and remove entities from the cache using the javax.persistence.Cache interface. It provides the method contains for checking whether the cache contains data for the given entity and two methods for removing data from cache: evict for removing a particular entity and evictAll for clearing the cache.

So, we are ready to write the test. All we need is a simple scenario for the Players and Tournaments entities, like this:

- Use the contains method to check whether the Players objects are in the cache (this should return false).

- Use the EntityManager find method to query the Players objects (this query is executed against the MongoDB database and the extracted objects should be placed in the second-level cache, thanks to ENABLE_SELECTIVE effect).

- Call the contains method again to check whether the Players objects are in the cache (this should return true).

- Use the evict method to remove the Players objects from the cache.

- Check whether the Players objects were removed from the cache when the contains method was called again (this should return false).

The scenario for Tournaments follows:

- Use the contains method to check whether the Tournaments objects are in cache (this should return false).

- Use the EntityManager find method to query the Tournaments objects (this query is executed against the MongoDB database and the extracted objects should NOT be placed in second-level cache thanks to ENABLE_SELECTIVE effect).

- Call the contains method again to check whether the Tournaments objects are in the cache (this should return false).

- Clear the cache by calling the evictAll method.

Finally, translate the scenario into a JUnit test, like the one in Listing 5-11.

Listing 5-11. A JUnit Test

```java
package tests;

import hogm.mongodb.entity.Players;
import hogm.mongodb.entity.Tournaments;
import javax.persistence.Cache;
import javax.persistence.CacheRetrieveMode;
import javax.persistence.CacheStoreMode;
import javax.persistence.EntityManager;
import javax.persistence.EntityManagerFactory;
import javax.persistence.Persistence;
import org.junit.After;
import org.junit.AfterClass;
import static org.junit.Assert.*;
import org.junit.Before;
import org.junit.BeforeClass;
import org.junit.Test;

public class CacheTest {

    private static EntityManagerFactory emf;
    private EntityManager em;

    public CacheTest() {
    }

    @BeforeClass
    public static void setUpClass() {
    }

    @AfterClass
    public static void tearDownClass() {
    }

    @Before
    public void setUp() {
        emf = Persistence.createEntityManagerFactory("HOGM_MONGODB_L2Cache-ejbPU");
        em = emf.createEntityManager();

        em.setProperty("javax.persistence.cache.retrieveMode", CacheRetrieveMode.USE);
        em.setProperty("javax.persistence.cache.storeMode", CacheStoreMode.USE);
    }

    @After
    public void tearDown() {
        if (em != null) {
            em.clear();
            em.close();
        }
    }
```

```java
@Test
public void testCache_ENABLE_SELECTIVE() {

    Cache cache = em.getEntityManagerFactory().getCache();

    //TESTING PLAYERS OBJECT CACHING

    // players objects shouldn't be in second-level cache at this moment
    for (int i = 1; i < 5; i++) {
        assertFalse(cache.contains(Players.class, i));
    }

    // finding the players objects should place them into second-level cache
    for (int i = 1; i < 5; i++) {
        em.find(Players.class, i);
    }

    // players objects should be in second-level cache at this moment,
    // but we delete them from cache one by one
    for (int i = 1; i < 5; i++) {
        assertTrue(cache.contains(Players.class, i));
        cache.evict(Players.class, i);
    }

    // players objects shouldn't be in second-level cache at this moment
    for (int i = 1; i < 5; i++) {
        assertFalse(cache.contains(Players.class, i));
    }

    //TESTING TOURNAMENTS OBJECT CACHING

    // tournaments objects shouldn't be in second-level cache at this moment
    for (int i = 1; i < 5; i++) {
        assertFalse(cache.contains(Tournaments.class, i));
    }

    // finding the tournaments objects shouldn't place them into second-level cache
    for (int i = 1; i < 5; i++) {
        em.find(Tournaments.class, i);
    }

    // players objects shouldn't be in second-level cache at this moment either
    for (int i = 1; i < 5; i++) {
        assertFalse(cache.contains(Tournaments.class, i));
    }

    cache.evictAll();
}
}
```

And the result of the test is 100 percent favorable, as shown in Figure 5-23, which means that Hibernate OGM supports @Cacheable and shared-cache-mode.

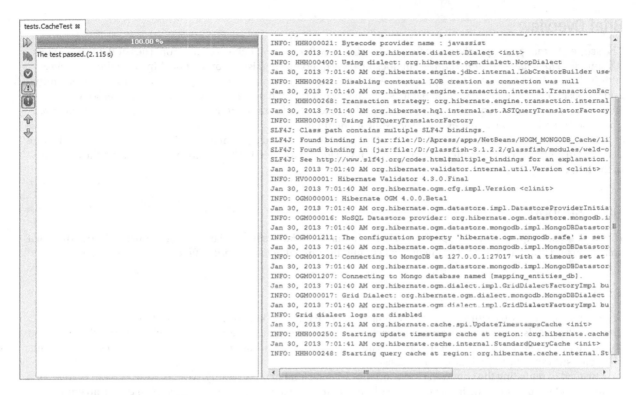

Figure 5-23. *Testing @Cacheable annotation*

In addition, you can easily test DISABLE_SELECTIVE and ALL by writing your own scenarios.

Note that you can programmatically control the cache behavior on retrieving and storing entities by setting the following EntityManager properties (within the setUp method, as in Listing 5-11). For the sake of completeness I set them to default values (USE), but I also tested BYPASS and REFRESH values and everything worked as expected:

- javax.persistence.cache.retrieveMode controls how data is read from the cache for calls to the EntityManager.find method and from queries. It defaults to the value USE, which means that data is retrieved from the second-level cache, if available. If it's not available, the data is retrieved from the database. You can easily bypass the second-level cache and go directly to database by specifying the value BYPASS.

- javax.persistence.cache.storeMode controls how data is stored in the cache. It defaults to the USE value, which means that the cache data is created or updated when data is read from or committed to the database without refreshing the cache upon a database read. Forcing the refresh is available by setting the REFRESH value. Finally, you can leave the cache unmodified by setting the BYPASS value.

Everything you need to know to understand the JPA 2.0 second-level cache API is nicely condensed in the Java EE 6 tutorial available at http://docs.oracle.com/javaee/6/tutorial/doc/gkjia.html.

The complete application for demonstrating the @Cacheable annotation is available in the Apress repository and is named HOGM_MONGODB_Cache. It comes as a NetBeans project and it was tested under GlassFish 3 AS.

@MappedSuperclass Annotation

Mapped by the javax.persistence.MappedSuperclass annotation.

Official documentation: http://docs.oracle.com/javaee/6/api/javax/persistence/MappedSuperclass.html.

Brief Overview

The scope of a mapped superclass is to feed its subclasses with common behavior and properties or fields mappings. It's similar to *table per class inheritance*, but doesn't allow querying, persisting, or relationships with the superclass (this is the big disadvantage of this approach). Also known as the *concrete class*, a mapped superclass is not an entity and it doesn't have a separate table in database. Mapping information may be overridden in the corresponding subclasses using the AttributeOverride and AssociationOverride annotations (or corresponding XML elements). The subclasses are entities, so they are responsible for defining tables.

MongoDB will contain one collection per entity (per subclass) and documents will look exactly as the fields were declared in entities (including the inherited ones). If you look at a collection's content, nothing betrays the existence of the mapped superclass.

OGM Support

Hibernate OGM supports the @MappedSuperclass annotation. It knows how to convert each subclass into a MongoDB collection and populate it with documents that contain the unified fields (inherited fields + entity fields).

Example

My example is based on a simple, common scenario. I start with some kind of generic or abstract object, like the players. "Players" is a very generic notion, since there are many kinds of players—tennis players, baseball players and so on. All players have some common characteristics, such as name, surname, age, and birthday, and some particular characteristics specific to their discipline (category).

Instead of repeating the common characteristics for each kind of player entity, we can place them in a superclass, an abstract class annotated with @MappedSuperclass. Then, for each category of players, we can define an entity that inherits the common characteristics from the superclass and provide more specific characteristics.

So, the mapped superclass is called Players and looks like this:

```
import javax.persistence.MappedSuperclass;
...


@MappedSuperclass
public abstract class Players implements Serializable {

    @Id
    @GeneratedValue(strategy=GenerationType.AUTO)
    protected int id;
    @Column(name="player_name")
    protected String name;
    @Column(name="player_surname")
    protected String surname;
    @Column(name="player_age")
    protected int age;
    @Temporal(javax.persistence.TemporalType.DATE)
    protected Date birth;

    //getters and setters
...
}
```

Next, we set up two categories of players: tennis players and baseball players. One distinguishing characteristic of a tennis player might be which hand he or she uses to play. For a baseball player, it might be the position on the team. So, we can write the TennisPlayers entity to inherit the superclass field and create a new one, like below:

```
import javax.persistence.AttributeOverride;
...

@Entity
@AttributeOverride(name="age", column=@Column(name="tenis_player_age"))
public class TennisPlayers extends Players implements Serializable {

    protected String handplay;

    //constructors, getters and setters
...
}
```

Following the rule, the BaseballPlayers entity is listed below:

```
import javax.persistence.AttributeOverride;
...

@Entity
@AttributeOverride(name="age", column=@Column(name="baseball_player_age"))
public class BaseballPlayers extends Players implements Serializable {

    protected String position;

    //constructors, getters and setters
...
}
```

Now persist several instances of the TennisPlayers and BaseballPlayers entities using Hibernate OGM. MongoDB will reveal the TennisPlayers and BaseballPlayers collections, as shown in Figure 5-24. Notice the inherited fields and the new fields together in the documents, and the effect of @AttributeOverride annotation:

```
TennisPlayers collection
> db.TennisPlayers.find().pretty();
{
        "_id" : 1,
        "birth" : ISODate("1985-09-16T23:00:00Z"),
        "handplay" : "Right-handed",
        "player_name" : "Berdych",
        "player_surname" : "Tomas",
        "tenis_player_age" : 27
}
{
        "_id" : 2,
        "birth" : ISODate("1987-05-15T00:00:00Z"),
        "handplay" : "Right-handed",
        "player_name" : "Murray",
        "player_surname" : "Andy",
        "tenis_player_age" : 25
}
```

```
BaseballPlayers collection
> db.BaseballPlayers.find().pretty();
{
        "_id" : 1,
        "baseball_player_age" : 37,
        "birth" : ISODate("1975-07-27T00:00:00Z"),
        "player_name" : "Rodriguez",
        "player_surname" : "Alex",
        "position" : "Third baseman / Shortstop"
}
{
        "_id" : 2,
        "baseball_player_age" : 33,
        "birth" : ISODate("1979-03-13T00:00:00Z"),
        "player_name" : "Santana",
        "player_surname" : "Johan",
        "position" : "Starting pitcher"
}
{
        "_id" : 3,
        "baseball_player_age" : 32,
        "birth" : ISODate("1980-07-21T00:00:00Z"),
        "player_name" : "Sabathia",
        "player_surname" : "CC",
        "position" : "Starting pitcher"
}
```

Figure 5-24. *Testing @MappedSuperclass annotation in MongoDB*

The complete application that demonstrates the @MappedSuperclass annotation is available in the Apress repository and is named HOGM_MONGODB_MappedSuperclass. It comes as a NetBeans project and it was tested under GlassFish 3 AS.

@ElementCollection Annotation

Mapped by the javax.persistence.ElementCollection annotation.

Official documentation: http://docs.oracle.com/javaee/6/api/javax/persistence/ElementCollection.html

Brief Overview

The @ElementCollection annotation is used to indicate a collection of instances (a basic Java type or embeddable class). Don't confuse Java collections with MongoDB collections. The Java collection data is stored in a separate table (the *collection table)* that can be specified using the @CollectionTable annotation, which indicates the collection table name and any joins. Since the data is stored in a separate table, this is not similar to @Embeddable objects that are embedded in the source object's table. It's more like a one-to-many embeddable relationship. A key feature of @ElementCollection is its ability to easily define collections of simple values (objects) without defining new classes but having separate tables for them. A drawback is that you can't control the propagation level of persisting, merging, or removing data, since the target objects are strictly related to the source objects and they act as one. Nevertheless, the fetch type (EAGER and LAZY) is available, so you can load source objects without the target objects.

OGM Support

Hibernate OGM provides partial support for the @ElementCollection annotation. Though I encountered no errors or bugs during testing, it doesn't really do what the specification says. The @CollectionTable annotation is not supported and the Java collection data is stored in MongoDB as nested collections in the entity collection, not in separate collections.

Example

To demonstrate @ElementCollection for a collection of embeddable class instances, I defined a simple class representing, for each player, the list of tournaments won or finals played in 2012:

```
import javax.persistence.Embeddable;
...

@Embeddable
public class Wins2012 implements Serializable {

    private String titlesfinals;

    //constructors, getters and setters
...
}
```

Typically, such a class would contain more than one field, but for testing purposes there's no need to add more fields.

In addition, for a collection of simple objects, I used a List<String> to hold the ranking history for each player between 2008 and 2012.

Both collections were defined in the Players entity, as shown in Listing 5-12 (elements like targetClass ("*the basic or embeddable class that is the element type of the collection*") and fetch ("*whether the collection should be lazily loaded or must be eagerly fetched*") are optional).

Listing 5-12. Defining Two Collections

```
import javax.persistence.AttributeOverride;
import javax.persistence.AttributeOverrides;
import javax.persistence.FetchType;
...

@Entity
@Table(catalog = "ATP", schema = "public", name = "atp_players")
public class Players implements Serializable {

    private static final long serialVersionUID = 1L;
    @Id
    @GeneratedValue(strategy = GenerationType.AUTO)
    private int id;
    @Column(name = "player_name")
    private String name;
    @Column(name = "player_surname")
    private String surname;
    @Column(name = "player_age")
    private int age;
    @Temporal(javax.persistence.TemporalType.DATE)
    private Date birth;
    @ElementCollection(targetClass=hogm.mongodb.entity.Wins2012.class,
                                    fetch = FetchType.EAGER)
    @CollectionTable(name = "EC_TABLE")  //not supported by OGM
    @AttributeOverrides({
        @AttributeOverride(name = "titlesfinals",
        column = @Column(name = "EC_titlesfinals"))
    })
    private List<Wins2012> wins = new ArrayList<Wins2012>();
    @ElementCollection(targetClass=java.lang.String.class,
                                    fetch = FetchType.LAZY)
    @CollectionTable(name = "RANKING_TABLE")  //not supported by OGM
    private List<String> rankinghistory08_12 = new ArrayList<String>();

//constructors, getters and setters
...
}
```

Next, I persist a few Players instances and the result is shown in Figure 5-25. Notice that there are no separate MongoDB collections for the two Java collections—the @AttributeOverrides worked perfectly.

@ElementCollection

[Insert Tenis Player] [Go to see lazy loading (you need a document with _id:1)]

```
...
K
        "_id" : 2,
        "birth" : ISODate("1985-09-16T23:00:00Z"),
        "player_age" : 27,
        "player_name" : "Berdych",
        "player_surname" : "Tomas",                          @ElementCollection
        "rankinghistory08_12" : [                            generates nested
                {                                            collections, "wins" and
                        "rankinghistory08_12" : "2011: 7"    "rankinghistory08-12"
                },
                {
                        "rankinghistory08_12" : "2010: 6"
                },
                {
                        "rankinghistory08_12" : "2009: 20"
                },
                {
                        "rankinghistory08_12" : "2008: 20"
                },
                {
                        "rankinghistory08_12" : "2012: 6"
                }
        ],
        "wins" : [
                {
                        "EC_titlesfinals" : "Stockholm"
                },
                {
                        "EC_titlesfinals" : "Montpellier"
                }
        ]
D
...
```

Figure 5-25. *Testing @ElementCollection annotation in MongoDB*

The complete application for demonstrating the @ElementCollection annotation is available in the Apress repository and is named HOGM_MONGODB_ElementCollection. It comes as a NetBeans project and was tested under GlassFish 3 AS. Before you continue with this section, please download the corresponding NetBeans project and ensure that you can successfully run the application under GlassFish AS 3.

While testing, you may have noticed in the web GUI a button labeled, "Go to see lazy loading (you need a document with _id:1)." If you press this button, the wins collection is loaded using the EAGER mechanism and the rankinghistory08_12 collection is loaded using the LAZY mechanism (for a single player, with id:1). The result will be similar to what's shown in Figure 5-26.

Id	Name	Surname	Age	Birth	Wins (EAGER)	Rankings History 2008-2012 (LAZY)
1	Berdych	Tomas	27	Tue Sep 17 00:00:00 WET 1985	Stockholm Montpellier	[2011: 7, 2008: 20, 2009: 20, 2010: 6, 2012: 6]

Figure 5-26. *Testing LAZY loading for @ElementCollection annotation in MongoDB*

The results in Figure 5-26 give rise to an obvious question: how do I know that the wins collection was loaded eagerly and the rankinghistory08_12 was loaded lazily? In other words, how do I know that lazy loading worked?

Well, such questions are common when Hibernate (including Hibernate OGM) JPA is involved, because the proxy objects used by Hibernate behind the scene can be confusing. Nevertheless, the question as to whether lazy loading is working can be solved in several ways. You can choose to write JUnit tests to monitor database transfers or any other complex solutions, or you can create a simple test, like the one I'll describe. Note that this test was performed in the NetBeans IDE and is specific to the example presented in this section, but it can be easily adjusted to other cases. Here are the steps in the test:

- Set `FetchType.EAGER` for both collections, `wins` and `rankinghistory08_12`.

- In the `hogm.mongodb.ejb.SampleBean` stateless bean, locate the following line of code in method `loadAction`:

  `Players p = em.find(Players.class, 1);`

- After this line, place a NetBeans line breakpoint as shown in Figure 5-27.

```
64          Players p = em.find(Players.class, 1);
□          first.add(p);
```

Figure 5-27. *Adding a line breakpoint in NetBeans*

- Deploy and start the application in debug mode (press the Debug Project button on NetBeans toolbar).

- After the application starts, press the button labeled "Go to see lazy loading (you need a document with _id:1)". This will cause debugger to execute the code until the line breakpoint and leave the application suspended at that point.

- The `Players` instance is loaded and the `p` variable is listed in NetBeans debugger (see the `Variables` window in Figure 5-28). Don't expand the `p` tree node, since this will be interpreted as an explicit request to see the `p` content.

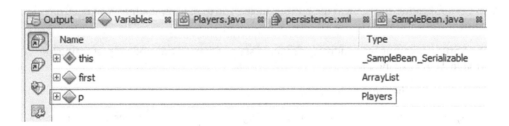

Figure 5-28. *The Variables window in NetBeans*

- Next, shut down the MongoDB server (you can press Ctrl+C in server shell).

- Now you can expand the `p` node and the `wins` and `rankinghistory08_12` sub-nodes as shown in Figure 5-29. Since the MongoDB server is closed, and the collections data is available, we can conclude that the data was eagerly loaded.

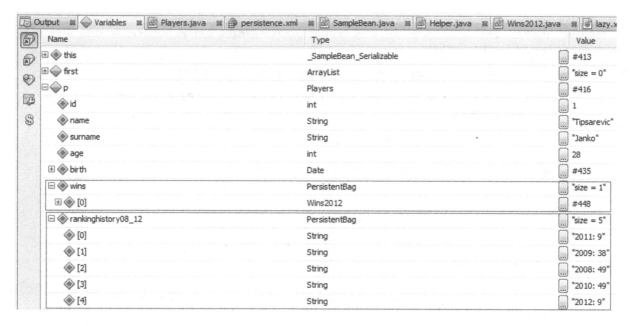

Figure 5-29. *Expanding the "p" node*

- Next, close the application, stop the debugger and restart the MongoDB server.

- Set FetchType.LAZY for the rankinghistory08_12 collection and FetchType.EAGER for wins collection.

- Again, start the application in debugging mode.

- After the application starts, press the button labeled "Go to see lazy loading (you need a document with _id:1)".

- In the NetBeans Variables window, you should see a collapsed tree node representing the p variable. Don't expand the node.

- Again, shut down the MongoDB server.

- Now, expand the p node and the wins and rankinghistory08_12 sub-nodes as shown in Figure 5-30. Notice that the wins collection contains data, since it was eagerly loaded, but the rankinghistory08_12 node reveals an error indicating it can't connect to the MongoDB server. This means that the data for the rankinghistory08_12 collection wasn't loaded eagerly and it should be loaded now, when you explicitly expanded the rankinghistory08_12 node. Therefore, lazy loading is working in Hibernate OGM.

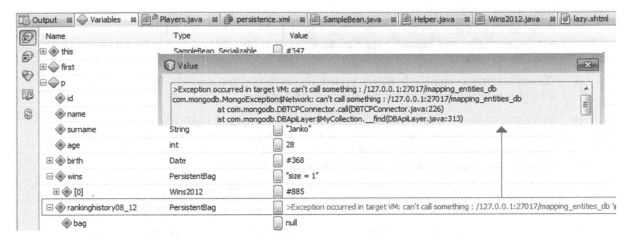

Figure 5-30. *Expanding the "p" node*

You can easily perform similar tests for other cases, such as for associations.

JPA Lifecycle Events @EntityListeners, @ExcludeDefaultListeners, @ExcludeSuperclassListeners Annotations

Mapped by the `javax.persistence.EntityListeners`, `javax.persistence.ExcludeDefaultListeners` and `javax.persistence.ExcludeSuperclassListeners` annotations.

Official documentation:

```
http://docs.oracle.com/javaee/6/api/javax/persistence/EntityListeners.html
http://docs.oracle.com/javaee/6/api/javax/persistence/ExcludeDefaultListeners.html
http://docs.oracle.com/javaee/6/api/javax/persistence/ExcludeSuperclassListeners.html
```

Brief Overview

JPA comes with a set of *callback methods* that reflect the lifecycle of entities. In a practical sense, an entity lifecycle consists of a suite of events, like persist, update, remove, and so on. For each event, JPA lets you define a supported callback method and when an event is fired, JPA automatically calls the corresponding callback method. You are responsible for writing the callback method implementation.

When callback methods are defined within the entity body, they are internal callback methods and when they are defined outside the entity body, in a separate class, they are external callback methods. In addition, default callback methods are listeners that can be applied by default to all the entity classes. To relate these concepts to annotations, here are the typical cases:

- Internal callback methods don't need annotations. The callback methods are simply defined in the entity body or mapped superclasses.

- External callback methods don't need annotations. But, the entities and mapped superclasses that use these methods need to be annotated with @EntityListeners({*ExternalListener_1.class*, *ExternalListeners_2.class*, ...}).

- Default callback methods don't need annotations. Actually there are no annotations for these callbacks; that's why the default listeners are defined in an XML file named orm.xml, which goes in the same location as persistence.xml or in any other location indicated in persistence.xml.

- Default listeners are applied by default to all the entity classes. You can turn off this behavior for an entity by annotating it with @ExcludeDefaultListeners.

- By default, entities inherit the callback methods from their mapped superclasses (the invocation of superclass listeners is inherited in the entity class). You can obtain the opposite effect by annotating the entity class with @ExcludeSuperclassListeners. Moreover, you can override the mapped superclasses callback methods in subclasses.

The internal callback methods can be marked with the following annotations:

- @PrePersist is executed before a new entity is persisted (added to the EntityManager).

- @PostPersist is executed after storing a new entity in the database (during commit or flush).

- @PostLoad is executed after an entity has been retrieved from the database.

- @PreUpdate is executed when an entity is identified as modified by the EntityManager.

- @PostUpdate is executed after updating an entity in the database (during commit or flush).

- @PreRemove is executed when an entity is marked for removal in the EntityManager.

- @PostRemove is executed after deleting an entity from the database (during commit or flush).

The external callback methods and default callback methods are the same except that they take one argument that specifies the entity that's the source of the lifecycle event.

Note that when all listeners appear in an application, there's a strict order of invocation. Default callback methods happen first, external callback methods are second, and internal callback methods execute last.

OGM Support

Hibernate OGM supports @EntityListeners, @ExcludeDefaultListeners, and @ExcludeSuperclassListeners annotations. It also supports listeners for entities and for mapped superclasses.

Example

For this example I used the classes defined in the section about mapped superclasses—the abstract mapped superclass, Players, and the two entities, TennisPlayers and BaseballPlayers. With these three classes, I can test the listeners quite well. Notice that the callback methods mark their presence only through some log messages.

In order of invocation, I defined first a default listener in the orm.xml file (don't forget to save this file in the same location as persistence.xml):

```
<entity-mappings xmlns="http://java.sun.com/xml/ns/persistence/orm"
 xmlns:xsi="http://www.w3.org/2001/XMLSchema-instance"
 xsi:schemaLocation="http://java.sun.com/xml/ns/persistence/orm
 http://java.sun.com/xml/ns/persistence/orm_1_0.xsd" version="1.0">
  <persistence-unit-metadata>
    <persistence-unit-defaults>
```

```
     <entity-listeners>
       <entity-listener class="hogm.mongodb.listeners.DefaultListener" />
     </entity-listeners>
   </persistence-unit-defaults>
 </persistence-unit-metadata>
</entity-mappings>
```

The `hogm.mongodb.listeners.DefaultListener` implements only the `onPrePersist` and `onPostPersist` methods, as shown in Listing 5-13.

Listing 5-13. The onPrePersist and onPostPersist Methods

```
package hogm.mongodb.listeners;

import java.util.logging.Level;
import java.util.logging.Logger;
import javax.persistence.PostPersist;
import javax.persistence.PrePersist;

public class DefaultListener {

    @PrePersist
    void onPrePersist(Object o) {
        Logger.getLogger(DefaultListener.class.getName()).
                                   log(Level.INFO, "PREPARING THE PERSIST SOME OBJECT ...");
    }

    @PostPersist
    void onPostPersist(Object o) {
        Logger.getLogger(DefaultListener.class.getName()).
                                   log(Level.INFO, "AN OBJECT WAS PERSISTED ...");
    }
}
```

By default, these methods will be called for all three entities when an object is persisted.

I also define two external listeners, one to implement the callback methods specific to update operations and the other for delete operations. These listeners will be available only for the `BaseballPlayers` entity, using the `@EntityListeners` annotation. The first listener is shown in Listing 5-14.

Listing 5-14. The Update Listener

```
package hogm.mongodb.listeners;
import java.util.logging.Level;
import java.util.logging.Logger;
import javax.persistence.PostUpdate;
import javax.persistence.PreUpdate;

public class BaseballExternalUpdateListeners {
```

```
    @PreUpdate
    void onPreUpdate(Object o) {
        Logger.getLogger(BaseballExternalUpdateListeners.class.getName()).log(Level.INFO,
            "PREPARING THE UPDATE THE FIRST BASEBALL PLAYER OBJECT ...{0}", o.toString());
    }

    @PostUpdate
    void onPostUpdate(Object o) {
        Logger.getLogger(BaseballExternalUpdateListeners.class.getName()).log(Level.INFO,
            "THE FIRST BASEBALL PLAYER OBJECT WAS UPDATED...{0}", o.toString());
    }
}
```

And the second one is in Listing 5-15.

Listing 5-15. The Delete Listener

```
package hogm.mongodb.listeners;

import java.util.logging.Level;
import java.util.logging.Logger;
import javax.persistence.PostRemove;
import javax.persistence.PreRemove;

public class BaseballExternalRemoveListeners {

    @PreRemove
    void onPreRemove(Object o) {
        Logger.getLogger(BaseballExternalRemoveListeners.class.getName()).log(Level.INFO,
          "PREPARING THE DELETE FOR THE FIRST BASEBALL PLAYER OBJECT ...{0}", o.toString());
    }

    @PostRemove
    void onPostRemove(Object o) {
        Logger.getLogger(BaseballExternalRemoveListeners.class.getName()).log(Level.INFO,
          "THE FIRST TENNIS PLAYER OBJECT WAS REMOVED ...{0}", o.toString());
    }
}
```

The mapped superclass, Players, will reject default listeners and implement three internal callback methods: onPrePersist, onPostPersist and onPostLoad. These listeners are inherited only by the BaseballPlayers entity, because the TennisPlayers entity will be annotated with @ExcludeSuperclassListeners. The Players mapped superclass is shown in Listing 5-16.

Listing 5-16. The Players Mapped Superclass

```
package hogm.mongodb.entity;

import java.io.Serializable;
import java.util.Date;
import java.util.logging.Level;
import java.util.logging.Logger;
import javax.persistence.Column;
```

```java
import javax.persistence.ExcludeDefaultListeners;
import javax.persistence.GeneratedValue;
import javax.persistence.GenerationType;
import javax.persistence.Id;
import javax.persistence.MappedSuperclass;
import javax.persistence.PostLoad;
import javax.persistence.PostPersist;
import javax.persistence.PrePersist;
import javax.persistence.Temporal;

@MappedSuperclass
@ExcludeDefaultListeners
public abstract class Players implements Serializable {

    @Id
    @GeneratedValue(strategy = GenerationType.AUTO)
    protected int id;
    @Column(name = "player_name")
    protected String name;
    @Column(name = "player_surname")
    protected String surname;
    @Column(name = "player_age")
    protected int age;
    @Temporal(javax.persistence.TemporalType.DATE)
    protected Date birth;

    @PrePersist
    void onPrePersist() {
        Logger.getLogger(Players.class.getName()).log(Level.INFO,
            "PREPARING THE PERSIST A (BASEBALL) PLAYER OBJECT ...");
    }

    @PostPersist
    void onPostPersist() {
        Logger.getLogger(Players.class.getName()).log(Level.INFO,
            "THE (BASEBALL) PLAYER OBJECT WAS PERSISTED ...");
    }

    @PostLoad
    void onPostLoad() {
        Logger.getLogger(Players.class.getName()).log(Level.INFO,
            "THE FIRST (BASEBALL) PLAYER OBJECT WAS LOADED ...");
    }

    //constructors, getters and setters
...
}
```

Next up is the TennisPlayers entity, shown in Listing 5-17. It will implement all the internal listeners and accept the default listeners but not the superclass listeners (notice the presence of @ExcludeSuperclassListeners annotations:

Listing 5-17. The TennisPlayers Entity

```java
import java.io.Serializable;
import java.util.logging.Level;
import java.util.logging.Logger;
import javax.persistence.AttributeOverride;
import javax.persistence.Column;
import javax.persistence.Entity;
import javax.persistence.ExcludeSuperclassListeners;
import javax.persistence.PostLoad;
import javax.persistence.PostPersist;
import javax.persistence.PostRemove;
import javax.persistence.PostUpdate;
import javax.persistence.PrePersist;
import javax.persistence.PreRemove;
import javax.persistence.PreUpdate;

@Entity
@ExcludeSuperclassListeners
@AttributeOverride(name = "age", column =
@Column(name = "tenis_player_age"))
public class TennisPlayers extends Players implements Serializable {

    protected String handplay;

    @PrePersist
    @Override
    void onPrePersist() {
        Logger.getLogger(TennisPlayers.class.getName()).log(Level.INFO,
            "PREPARING THE PERSIST A TENNIS PLAYER OBJECT ...");
    }

    @PostPersist
    @Override
    void onPostPersist() {
        Logger.getLogger(TennisPlayers.class.getName()).log(Level.INFO,
            "THE TENNIS PLAYER OBJECT WAS PERSISTED ...");
    }

    @PostLoad
    @Override
    void onPostLoad() {
        Logger.getLogger(TennisPlayers.class.getName()).log(Level.INFO,
            "THE FIRST TENNIS PLAYER OBJECT WAS LOADED ...");
    }
```

```java
@PreUpdate
void onPreUpdate() {
    Logger.getLogger(TennisPlayers.class.getName()).log(Level.INFO,
        "PREPARING THE UPDATE THE FIRST TENNIS PLAYER OBJECT ...");
}

@PostUpdate
void onPostUpdate() {
    Logger.getLogger(TennisPlayers.class.getName()).log(Level.INFO,
        "THE FIRST TENNIS PLAYER OBJECT WAS UPDATED...");
}

@PreRemove
void onPreRemove() {
    Logger.getLogger(TennisPlayers.class.getName()).log(Level.INFO,
        "PREPARING THE DELETE FOR THE FIRST TENNIS PLAYER OBJECT ...");
}

@PostRemove
void onPostRemove() {
    Logger.getLogger(TennisPlayers.class.getName()).log(Level.INFO,
        "THE FIRST TENNIS PLAYER OBJECT WAS REMOVED ...");
}

public String getHandplay() {
    return handplay;
}

//constructors, getters and setters
...
}
```

And, finally, the BaseballPlayers entity is shown in Listing 5-18. It doesn't define any internal listeners. It uses the defined external listeners, specified using the @EntityListeners annotation, and inherits the listeners from the mapped superclass. It will not accept default listeners, since the mapped superclass excludes default listeners.

Listing 5-18. The BaseballPlayers Entity

```java
package hogm.mongodb.entity;

import hogm.mongodb.listeners.BaseballExternalRemoveListeners;
import hogm.mongodb.listeners.BaseballExternalUpdateListeners;
import java.io.Serializable;
import javax.persistence.AttributeOverride;
import javax.persistence.Column;
import javax.persistence.Entity;
import javax.persistence.EntityListeners;

@Entity
@EntityListeners({BaseballExternalUpdateListeners.class,
                               BaseballExternalRemoveListeners.class})
```

```
@AttributeOverride(name = "age", column =
@Column(name = "baseball_player_age"))
public class BaseballPlayers extends Players implements Serializable {

    protected String position;

    //constructors, getters and setters
...
```

Done! I know it's confusing, but testing all three annotations for entities and mapped superclasses in a single application is pretty sophisticated. In a real application you wouldn't mix all of this stuff together. Figure 5-31 should help to clarify things.

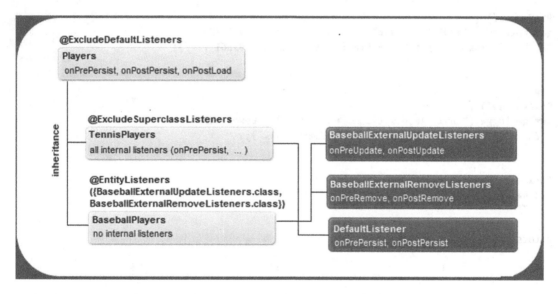

Figure 5-31. *Testing JPA listeners*

Here's the simple scenario I tested:

- Insert two tennis players and one baseball player.
- Load first tennis player.
- Update first tennis player.
- Delete first tennis player.
- Update first baseball player.
- Load first baseball player.
- Delete second tennis player.
- Delete first baseball player.

In Figure 5-32, you can see each step from the listener's call perspective. It looks like Hibernate OGM has done a great job and everything works exactly as expected and each callback method was called at the appropriate moment.

Log	Description
INFO: PREPARING TO PERSIST SOME OBJECT ... INFO: PREPARING TO PERSIST A TENNIS PLAYER OBJECT ... INFO: AN OBJECT WAS PERSISTED ... INFO: THE TENNIS PLAYER OBJECT WAS PERSISTED ...	**Insert first tennis player** default listeners (onPrePersist and onPostPersist) and internal listeners (onPrePersist and onPostPersist) are called by JPA
INFO: PREPARING TO PERSIST SOME OBJECT ... INFO: PREPARING TO PERSIST A TENNIS PLAYER OBJECT ... INFO: AN OBJECT WAS PERSISTED ... INFO: THE TENNIS PLAYER OBJECT WAS PERSISTED ...	**Insert second tennis player** default listeners (onPrePersist and onPostPersist) and internal listeners (onPrePersist and onPostPersist) are called by JPA
INFO: PREPARING TO PERSIST A (BASEBALL) PLAYER OBJECT ... INFO: THE (BASEBALL) PLAYER OBJECT WAS PERSISTED ...	**Insert first baseball player** inherited onPrePersist and onPostPersist listeners are called by JPA
INFO: THE FIRST TENNIS PLAYER OBJECT WAS LOADED ...	**Load first tennis player** the internal listener, onPostLoad is called by JPA
INFO: THE FIRST TENNIS PLAYER OBJECT WAS LOADED ... INFO: PREPARING TO UPDATE THE FIRST TENNIS PLAYER OBJECT ... INFO: THE FIRST TENNIS PLAYER OBJECT WAS UPDATED...	**Update first tennis player** the internal listeners, onPostLoad, onPreUpdate and onPostUpdate are called by JPA
INFO: THE FIRST TENNIS PLAYER OBJECT WAS LOADED ... INFO: PREPARING TO DELETE FOR THE FIRST TENNIS PLAYER OBJECT ... INFO: THE FIRST TENNIS PLAYER OBJECT WAS REMOVED ...	**Delete first tennis player** the internal listeners, onPostLoad, onPreRemove and onPostRemove are called by JPA
INFO: THE FIRST (BASEBALL) PLAYER OBJECT WAS LOADED ... INFO: PREPARING TO UPDATE THE FIRST BASEBALL PLAYER OBJECT ...ho· INFO: THE FIRST BASEBALL PLAYER OBJECT WAS UPDATED...hogm.mongodb	**Update first baseball player** the inherited listener onPostLoad and the external listeners. onPreUpdate and onPostUpdate are called by JPA
INFO: THE FIRST (BASEBALL) PLAYER OBJECT WAS LOADED ...	**Load first baseball player** the inherited listener, onPostLoad is called by JPA
INFO: THE FIRST TENNIS PLAYER OBJECT WAS LOADED ... INFO: PREPARING TO DELETE FOR THE FIRST TENNIS PLAYER OBJECT ... INFO: THE FIRST TENNIS PLAYER OBJECT WAS REMOVED ...	**Delete the second tenis player** the internal listeners, onPostLoad, onPreRemove and onPostRemove are called by JPA
INFO: THE FIRST (BASEBALL) PLAYER OBJECT WAS LOADED ... INFO: PREPARING TO DELETE FOR THE FIRST BASEBALL PLAYER OBJECT .c INFO: THE FIRST TENNIS PLAYER OBJECT WAS REMOVED ...hogm.mongodb.·	**Delete first baseball player** the inherited onPostLoad listener and the external, onPreRemove and onPostRemove listeners are called by JPA

Figure 5-32. *Results of testing JPA listeners*

The complete application that demonstrates the JPA listeners is available in the Apress repository and is named HOGM_MONGODB_Listeners. It comes as a NetBeans project and was tested under GlassFish 3 AS.

@Version Annotation

Mapped by the javax.persistence.Version annotation.
Official documentation: http://docs.oracle.com/javaee/6/api/javax/persistence/Version.html

Brief Overview

An @Version field or property has a double role: to guarantee data integrity when performing merge operations (updates) and to provide optimistic concurrency control. Version fields (only one version field per entity class is allowed) team well with JPA *optimistic locking,* which is applied on transaction commit and is responsible for checking every object to be updated or deleted. The goal is to avoid possible conflicts that can occur when JPA deals with simultaneous updates to the same data by two concurrent threads (users). When a conflict arises, the persistent provider throws an exception. In other words, optimistic locking assumes that the data will not be modified between read-write data operations.

The field annotated with @Version is persisted to the database with an initial value of, usually, 0 and it's automatically incremented (usually by 1) for each update operation (the calling of the merge method). Practically, when JPA "bakes" an entity update statement, it adds to the WHERE clause, beside the update scope, the right "words" for incrementing the version field and for matching the old version value (the read value):

```
UPDATE table_name SET field_1 = value_1, ... field_n = value_n, version = (version  + 1)
WHERE id = some_id  and version = read_version
```

If, in the meantime, the same entity is updated by another user (thread), the persistence provider will throw an OptimisticLockException since it can't locate the correct old version value. Optimistic locking can provide better scalability, but the drawback is that the user/application must refresh and retry failed updates.

Optimistic locking is specific to JPA 1.0 and is the most common style (used and recommended) of locking. JPA 2.0 also comes with *pessimistic locking*, which locks the database row when data is being read or written to. This is rarely used, though, since it can hinder scalability and cause deadlocks and risk states. Both optimistic and pessimistic locking are layered on top of @Version annotation and are controllable through the JPA API.

More details about JPA 2.0 locking can be found in this excellent article, "*JPA 2.0 Concurrency and locking*" (https://blogs.oracle.com/carolmcdonald/entry/jpa_2_0_concurrency_and).

OGM Support

Hibernate OGM supports @Version annotation and the field annotated with @Version is stored in MongoDB like any other field. You can also control locking mechanisms using the EntityManager find, refresh, and lock methods. Since OGM doesn't support native query or named queries, you can't use the Query and NamedQuery locking methods.

Example

First, I define an @Version field in the Players entity, as shown in Listing 5-19. I named it version and set it as type Long (you can choose from int, Integer, short, Short, long, java.sql.Timestamp).

Listing 5-19. Defining the @Version Field

```
import javax.persistence.Version;
...

@Entity
@Table(name = "atp_players")
public class Players implements Serializable {

    private static final long serialVersionUID = 1L;
    @Id
    @GeneratedValue(strategy = GenerationType.AUTO)
    private int id;
    @Version
    private Long version;
    @Column(name = "player_name")
    private String name;
    @Column(name = "player_surname")
    private String surname;
    @Column(name = "player_age")
    private int age;
    private int facade; //used for simulating updated

    public Long getVersion() {
        return version;
    }
```

```
    protected void setVersion(Long version) {
        this.version = version;
    }

    //constructors, getters and setters
...
}
```

Notice that since the @Version field should not normally be modified by the application, the corresponding setter method was declared protected.

Now, let's check if the @Version field is automatically incremented on each update operation. For this, persist some players and find a reason to call the merge method several times, for example, to update the facade field with some random numbers. While merging, monitor the atp_players collection documents in the MongoDB shell. In Figure 5-33, the left side presents the document (_id:1) before calling merge for first time. On the right-side, notice that after I called merge three times, the value of the version field grew from 0 to 3.

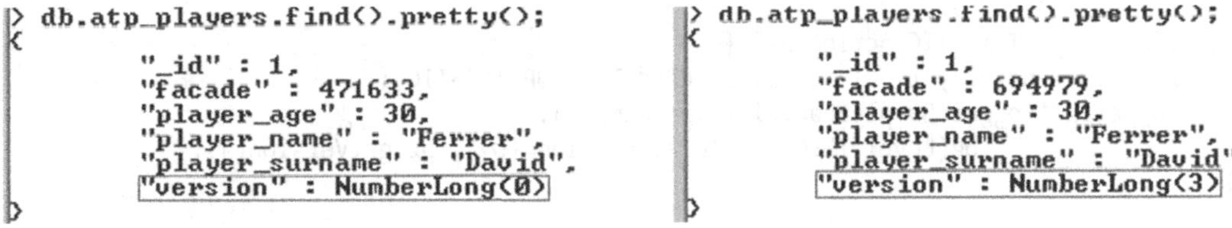

Figure 5-33. *Monitoring version field incrementation while calling the merge method*

So, OGM successfully increased the version field each time merge was called.

■ **Note** If you can't obtain a document with _id:1, you should drop the hibernate_sequences collection and repeat the persist operation. You need this _id:1 because in the next test we use the EntityManager find method with this id. I realize that using auto-generated keys and the find method like this is unusual and not realistic, but it's just for teaching purposes.

Testing whether the optimistic locking is actually working (LockModeType.OPTIMISTIC) is not simple; it usually requires writing a JUnit test to simulate concurrent transactions. However, I prefer to a different approach and I want to shape a stateful bean according to the following scenario:

- Declare a stateful bean and inject the OGM EntityManager; as a session bean, it will maintain the conversational state over multiple requests:

```
@Named("bean")
@Stateful
@SessionScoped
public class SampleBean {

    @PersistenceContext(unitName = "PU_name")
    private EntityManager em;
...
```

- Declare two Players objects, p1 and p2:

```
Players p1 = null;
Players p2 = null;
```

- Create a business method that populates p1 with the first player in the database and displays the read version field. Note that I specified the locking mode as OPTIMISTIC (which is the default):

```
public void read_OPTIMISTIC_Action_1() {
        p1 = em.find(Players.class, 1, LockModeType.OPTIMISTIC);
        Logger.getLogger(SampleBean.class.getName()).
                    log(Level.INFO, "READ 1, version={0}", p1.getVersion());
    }
```

- Repeat the previous step for p2:

```
public void read_OPTIMISTIC_Action_2() {
        p2 = em.find(Players.class, 1, LockModeType.OPTIMISTIC);
        Logger.getLogger(SampleBean.class.getName()).
                    log(Level.INFO, "READ 2, version={0}", p2.getVersion());
    }
```

- Create a business method for updating p1. After the update, read p1 again and display the version. This was incremented by 1 and the update is successfully accomplished since the document wasn't modified between read and write operations:

```
public void update_OPTIMISTIC_Action_1() {
        p1.setFacade(new Random().nextInt(1000000));
        em.merge(p1);
        em.flush();
        p1 = em.find(Players.class, 1, LockModeType.OPTIMISTIC);
        Logger.getLogger(SampleBean.class.getName()).
                    log(Level.INFO, "UPDATE 1, version={0}",   p1.getVersion());
    }
```

- Write a business method for updating p2. Before calling merge, display the read version. This value should be smaller than the current version in the database, indicating that between p2 read and write operations, another thread has modified the document. Therefore, when the merge method is called, I'll get an OptimisticLockException:

```
public void update_OPTIMISTIC_Action_2() {
        Logger.getLogger(SampleBean.class.getName()).
                    log(Level.INFO, "UPDATE 2, version={0}", p2.getVersion());
        p2.setFacade(new Random().nextInt(1000000));
        em.merge(p2);
        em.flush();
        //there is no need to check version,
        // now the OptimisticLockException exception should be on screen
    }
```

For a successful test, I need to call these four methods precisely in order: read_OPTIMISTIC_Action_1(), read_OPTIMISTIC_Action_2(), update_OPTIMISTIC_Action_1() and update_OPTIMISTIC_Action_2(). The output of GlassFish log is shown in Figure 5-34.

```
INFO: READ 1, version=3
INFO: READ 2, version=3
INFO: UPDATE 1, version=4
INFO: UPDATE 2, version=3
Caused by: javax.persistence.OptimisticLockException
        at org.hibernate.ejb.AbstractEntityManagerImpl
        at org.hibernate.ejb.AbstractEntityManagerImpl
        at org.hibernate.ejb.AbstractEntityManagerImpl
        at org.hibernate.ejb.AbstractEntityManagerImpl
        at org.hibernate.ejb.AbstractEntityManagerImpl
        at org.hibernate.ogm.jpa.impl.OgmEntityManager
        at com.sun.enterprise.container.common.impl.En
   ...
Caused by: org.hibernate.StaleObjectStateException: Row was updated or deleted by another transaction
        at org.hibernate.event.internal.DefaultMergeEventListener.entityIsDetached(DefaultMergeEventLi
   ...
```

Figure 5-34. *Obtaining the OptimisticLockException for LockModeType.OPTIMISTIC*

If I change LockModeType.OPTIMISTIC into LockModeType.OPTIMISTIC_FORCE_INCREMENT, I can easily test the optimistic force-increment mechanism. If you ran the preceding test, drop all the atp_players collections and again, persist one Players instance. Then use one of the next two method call sequences: read_OPTIMISTIC_Action_1, read_OPTIMISTIC_Action_2, update_OPTIMISTIC_Action_1 or read_OPTIMISTIC_Action_1, read_OPTIMISTIC_Action_2, update_OPTIMISTIC_Action_2, update_OPTIMISTIC_Action_1. Because the version field is incremented before each commit, not just for the updates commit, you'll see something like what's shown in Figure 5-35 (the first call sequence).

After persisting ...
```
> db.atp_players.find().pretty();
{
        "_id" : 1,
        "facade" : 990167,
        "player_age" : 27,
        "player_name" : "Berdych",
        "player_surname" : "Tomas",
        "version" : NumberLong(0)
}
...
```

After read p1 ...
```
> db.atp_players.find().pretty();
{
        "_id" : 1,
        "facade" : 990167,
        "player_age" : 27,
        "player_name" : "Berdych",
        "player_surname" : "Tomas",
        "version" : NumberLong(1)
}
```

After read p2 ...
```
> db.atp_players.find().pretty();
{
        "_id" : 1,
        "facade" : 990167,
        "player_age" : 27,
        "player_name" : "Berdych",
        "player_surname" : "Tomas",
        "version" : NumberLong(2)
}
```

After update p1 ...
```
javax.persistence.OptimisticLockException
org.hibernate.ejb.AbstractEntityManagerImpl.
org.hibernate.ejb.AbstractEntityManagerImpl.
org.hibernate.ejb.AbstractEntityManagerImpl.
org.hibernate.ejb.AbstractEntityManagerImpl.
org.hibernate.ejb.AbstractEntityManagerImpl.
org.hibernate.ogm.jpa.impl.OgmEntityManager.
```

Figure 5-35. *Obtaining the OptimisticLockException for LockModeType. OPTIMISTIC_FORCE_INCREMENT*

The complete application that demonstrates the @Version annotation is available in the Apress repository and is named HOGM_MONGODB_Version. It comes as a NetBeans project and was tested under GlassFish 3 AS.

@Access Annotation

Mapped by the javax.persistence.Access annotation
Official documentation: http://docs.oracle.com/javaee/6/api/javax/persistence/Access.html

Brief Overview

By default, an entity provides data to be persisted through its persistent fields. Moreover, when data is extracted from a database, it populates the same persistent fields. In annotations terms, this is @Access(AccessType.FIELD). Another approach involves obtaining the data to persist by accessing fields indirectly as properties, using get methods. Similarly, the extracted data populates entity through the set methods. In annotations terms, this is @Access(AccessType.PROPERTY).

In JPA 1.x, the access type was restricted to be a field or property based on the entity hierarchy. Starting with JPA 2.0, an embeddable class can have an access type different from the access type of the entity in which it's embedded.

OGM Support

Hibernate OGM supports the @Access annotation according to the JPA 2.0 specification. It can extract data to persist from an embeddable class via one access type and from the entity via the other access type. Of course, I'm talking about the entity that embeds the embeddable class.

Example

For this example, I define an embeddable class, named Details:

```
import javax.persistence.Access;
import javax.persistence.AccessType;
...

@Embeddable
@Access(AccessType.FIELD)
public class Details implements Serializable {

    private String birthplace;
    private String residence;
    private String height;
    private String weight;
    private String plays;
    private int turnedpro;
    private String coach;
    private String website;

    //constructors, getters and setters
...
}
```

Note the @Access annotation. (I chose arbitrarily to use the access type FIELD). Now the entity, named Players is annotated with @Access(AccessType.PROPERTY). In order to use property access, I need to provide get and set methods based on the Java bean property convention for non-transient fields. I must also move all the JPA annotations from the field level to their getters. Listing 5-20 shows the complete listing for the Players entity.

Listing 5-20. The Complete Players Entity

```java
import javax.persistence.Access;
import javax.persistence.AccessType;
...

@Entity
@Access(AccessType.PROPERTY)
@Table(catalog = "ATP", schema = "public", name = "atp_players")
public class Players implements Serializable {

    private int id;
    private String name;
    private String surname;
    private int age;
    private Date birth;
    private Details details;

    @Column(name = "player_name")
    public String getName() {
        return name;
    }

    public void setName(String name) {
        this.name = name;
    }

    @Column(name = "player_surname")
    public String getSurname() {
        return surname;
    }

    public void setSurname(String surname) {
        this.surname = surname;
    }

    @Column(name = "player_age")
    public int getAge() {
        return age;
    }

    public void setAge(int age) {
        this.age = age;
    }

    @Temporal(javax.persistence.TemporalType.DATE)
    public Date getBirth() {
        return birth;
    }
```

```java
    public void setBirth(Date birth) {
        this.birth = birth;
    }

    @Embedded
    public Details getDetails() {
        return details;
    }

    public void setDetails(Details details) {
        this.details = details;
    }

    @Id
    @GeneratedValue(strategy = GenerationType.AUTO)
    public int getId() {
        return id;
    }

    public void setId(int id) {
        this.id = id;
    }
}
```

Now, the entity class has the PROPERTY access type and the embeddable class has the FIELD access type. This was not possible until JPA 2.0, because the embeddable object's access type was determined by the access type of the entity class in which it was declared.

Done! Make sure everything works as expected by persisting several entity instances.

The complete application that demonstrates the @Access annotation is available in the Apress repository and is named HOGM_MONGODB_Access. It comes as a NetBeans project and was tested under GlassFish 3 AS.

■ **Note** Obviously, you don't always need to explicitly specify the access type, but sometimes you do to avoid mapping problems. For example, you may have two entities that define different access types, but both embed the same embeddable class. In this case, you must explicitly set the access type of the embeddable class. The same kind of situation can occur with inheritance—each entity inherits the access type from its parent entity, which may not always be desirable. Starting with JPA 2.0, you can explicitly override the access type locally, in any entity involved in this inheritance.

There are some misconceptions regarding the access type FIELD in Hibernate. To avoid certain "traps," you should know that Hibernate is fully capable of populating entities when this access type is set. A problem can occur when you need to access those values from your code, because in this case Hibernate requires dedicated methods. This is one of the well-known Hibernate proxy pitfalls. To learn the details, a good place to start is at http://blog.xebia.com/2008/03/08/advanced-hibernate-proxy-pitfalls/.

Associations

In Chapter 2, you saw how OGM stores associations using the IN_ENTITY, GLOBAL_COLLECTION, or COLLECTION strategies. Now I'll discuss how OGM stores a different kind of database association. I'll use IN_ENTITY for most of the examples. There are several types of database associations:

- One-To-One

- One-To-Many and Many-To-One

- Many-To-Many

Direction in Entity Associations

I want to add here a short overview of direction in entity associations, because I think it will be useful for the last part of this chapter. Entity associations have the following characteristics:

- The directionality of association can be from one side (unidirectional) or from both sides (bidirectional) of the relationship.

- In unidirectional associations, one of the sides is defined as the owning side; the opposite side is not aware of the association.

- In bidirectional associations, both sides have references to the other side.

- In a bidirectional association, one side is defined as the owning side (the *owner*), while the opposite side is the owned side (*non-owner*).

- Programmatically speaking, in a bidirectional association, declaration is asymmetric, meaning that only one side provides information about directionality by setting the mappedBy element in the association-specific annotation. In bidirectional one-to-one and many-to-many associations, either side can use the mappedBy element, while in a bidirectional one-to-many association, mappedBy can't be declared on the many-to-one side.

- The value of the annotation's element is the name of the field (or property) on the owning side of the association that references the entity on the owned side.

@OneToOne Annotation

Mapped by the javax.persistence.OneToOne annotation.
   Official documentation: http://docs.oracle.com/javaee/6/api/javax/persistence/OneToOne.html

Brief Overview

In relational database terms, a one-to-one association occurs when there is exactly one record in a table that corresponds to exactly one record in a related table; both tables contain the same number of records and each row of the first table is linked to another row in the second table. JPA maps both unidirectional and bidirectional one-to-one associations using @OneToOne annotation. In bidirectional associations, the non-owning side must use the mappedBy element of the @OneToOne annotation to specify the association field or property of the owning side (either side can be the owner). Such an association supports fetching (eager or lazy), cascading, and orphan removal.

OGM Support

Hibernate OGM supports @OneToOne annotations that conform to the JPA 2.0 specification. As you know, by default, OGM stores data in MongoDB using the IN_ENTITY strategy, which doesn't imply any additional collections–each entity class is represented by a single collection. It's easy to distinguish the following cases:

- For a unidirectional one-to-one association, OGM stores the navigation information for associations in the collection representing the owner side of the association. Each document from this collection contains a field for storing the corresponding foreign key. See Figure 5-36.

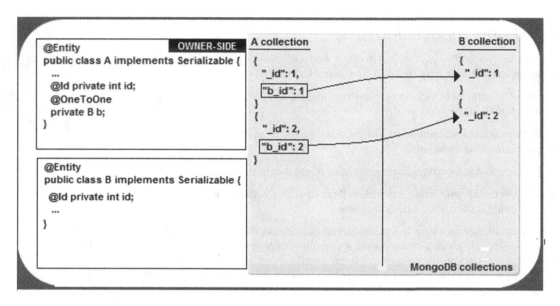

Figure 5-36. *IN_ENTITY: one-to-one unidirectional association*

- For a bidirectional one-to-one association, the navigation information is stored like this: the collection representing the entity that uses mappedBy (the non-owner side of the association) contains fields that store one foreign key per embedded collection, while the collection representing the owner side of the association contains, in each document, a field that stores the corresponding foreign key. See Figure 5-37.

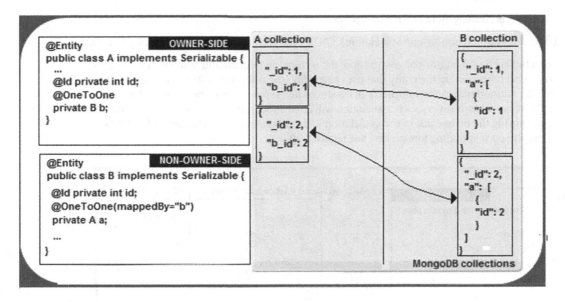

Figure 5-37. *IN_ENTITY: one-to-one bidirectional association*

For the GLOBAL_COLLECTION strategy, there are also some straightforward cases:

- For a unidirectional one-to-one association, GLOBAL_COLLECTION has no effect (similar to IN_ENTITY).

- For a bidirectional one-to-one association, the navigation information is stored like this: the collection representing the entity that uses mappedBy (the non-owner side) doesn't contain navigation information; it's stored in the global Associations collection. The collection representing the owner side of the association contains, in each document, a field that stores the corresponding foreign key. See Figure 5-38.

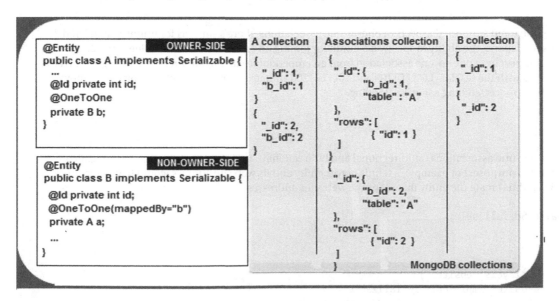

Figure 5-38. *GLOBAL_COLLECTION: one-to-one bidirectional association*

For the COLLECTION strategy, here are the possibilities:

- For unidirectional one-to-one associations, COLLECTION has no effect (similar to IN_ENTITY).

- For a bidirectional one-to-one association, the navigation information is stored like this: the collection representing the entity that uses mappedBy (the non-owner side of the association) doesn't contain navigation information; it's stored in a separate collection prefixed with the word associations (every such association will have a separate collection). The collection representing the owner side of the association will contain, in each document, a field that stores the corresponding foreign key. See Figure 5-39.

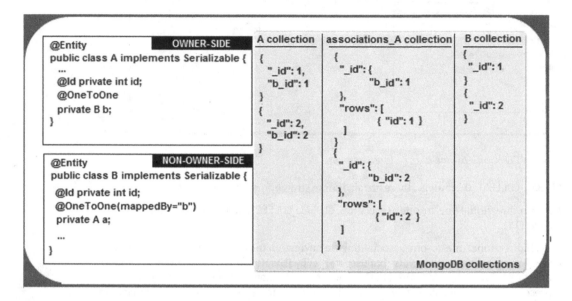

Figure 5-39. *COLLECTION: one-to-one bidirectional association*

To sum up the main supported aspects of one-to-one associations, there's support for unidirectional and bidirectional associations; the ability to specify a column for joining an entity association or element collection (using @JoinColumn), support for a one-to-one association from an embeddable class to another entity using @JoinTable and @JoinColumns with the GLOBAL_COLLECTION and COLLECTION strategies, cascading(all) and orphan removal. Moreover, OGM supports fetching using lazy loading.

Example

To illustrate one-to-one associations (unidirectional and bidirectional), I need two entities that are logically appropriate for this purpose. For example, a tennis player entity and its web site address would have such an association. I can thus create the entity that maps the web sites addresses:

```
import java.io.Serializable;
...

@Entity
@Table(name = "players_websites")
public class Websites implements Serializable {
```

```
    @Id
    @GeneratedValue(strategy = GenerationType.AUTO)
    private int id;
    private String http_address;
    //constructors, getters and setters
...
}
```

Next, I create the Players entity and define a unidirectional one-to-one association:

```
import javax.persistence.JoinColumn;
import javax.persistence.OneToOne;
...

@Entity
@Table(name = "atp_players")
public class Players implements Serializable {

    private static final long serialVersionUID = 1L;
    @Id
    @GeneratedValue(strategy = GenerationType.AUTO)
    private int id;
    @Column(name = "player_name")
    private String name;
    @Column(name = "player_surname")
    private String surname;
    @Column(name = "player_age")
    private int age;
    @Temporal(javax.persistence.TemporalType.DATE)
    @Column(name = "player_birth")
    private Date birth;
    @OneToOne(cascade = {CascadeType.PERSIST, CascadeType.REMOVE})
    @JoinColumn(name = "website_fk", unique = true, nullable = false, updatable = false)
    private Websites website;

    //constructors, getters and setters
...
}
```

Now I'll persist several players and their web site addresses to get something like what's shown in Figure 5-40. Notice that each document within the atp_players collection contains a field named website_pk that stores the foreign key from the players_websites collection. This is how OGM maps the one-to-one unidirectional association using the IN_ENTITY strategy.

```
> db.atp_players.find().pretty();
{
        "_id" : 1,
        "player_age" : 25,
        "player_birth" : ISODate("1987-05-22T00:00:00Z"),
        "player_name" : "Djokovic",
        "player_surname" : "Novak",
        "website_fk" : 1
}
{
        "_id" : 2,
        "player_age" : 31,
        "player_birth" : ISODate("1981-08-08T00:00:00Z"),
        "player_name" : "Federer",
        "player_surname" : "Roger",
        "website_fk" : 2
}
> db.players_websites.find().pretty();
{ "_id" : 1, "http_address" : "http://www.novakdjokovic.com" }
{ "_id" : 2, "http_address" : "http://www.rogerfederer.com" }
```

Figure 5-40. One-to-one unidirectional association

Moreover, I can easily transform this association into a bidirectional one by modifying the Websites entity, adding the @OneToOne annotation and the mappedBy element:

```
import javax.persistence.OneToOne;
...

@Entity
@Table(name = "players_websites")
public class Websites implements Serializable {

    @Id
    @GeneratedValue(strategy = GenerationType.AUTO)
    private int id;
    private String http_address;
    @OneToOne(mappedBy = "website")
    private Players player_website;

    //constructors, getters and setters
...
}
```

This time, the atp_players and players_websites collections look like what's shown in Figure 5-41. As you can see, the owner of the association, atp_players, still contains the field for storing foreign keys, while the non-owning side, players_websites, stores the foreign keys in embedded collections.

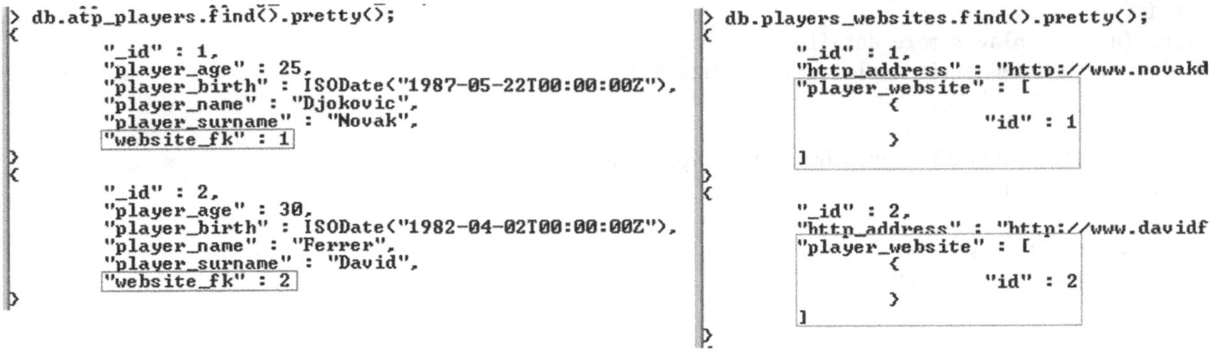

Figure 5-41. *One-to-one bidirecional association*

My next goal is to create a one-to-one association from an embeddable class to another entity. For this, I need an embeddable class that stores some player details and an entity that stores even more details. The embeddable class will define a one-to-one association to this entity. Here's the embeddable class, which is named `Details`:

```
import javax.persistence.Embeddable;
import javax.persistence.OneToOne;
...

@Embeddable
@Table(name = "player_details")
public class Details implements Serializable {

    private String birthplace;
    private String residence;
    private String height;
    private String weight;
    private String plays;
    private int turnedpro;
    private String coach;
    @OneToOne(cascade={CascadeType.PERSIST, CascadeType.REMOVE})
    private MoreDetails more;

    //constructors, getters and setters
...
}
```

The `MoreDetails` field references the following entity:

```
import java.io.Serializable;
...
```

```
@Entity
@Table(name = "player_more_details")
public class MoreDetails implements Serializable {

    @Id
    @GeneratedValue(strategy = GenerationType.AUTO)
    private int id;
    private int ranking;
    private String prizes;
  //constructors, getters and setters
...
}
```

The final step consists of adding the embeddable class in the Players entity:

import javax.persistence.Embedded;

```
@Entity
@Table(name = "atp_players")
public class Players implements Serializable {

    @Id
    @GeneratedValue(strategy = GenerationType.AUTO)
    private int id;
    ...
    @Embedded
    private Details details;

    //constructors, getters and setters
...
}
```

Now, MongoDB will reveal two collections, atp_players and player_more_details, as shown in Figure 5-42. Notice that the atp_players nested documents (the details field), used for storing the embeddable class, contains a field, named more_id, that stores the foreign keys referencing the player_more_details documents.

```
> db.atp_players.find().pretty();
{
        "_id" : 1,
        "details" : {
                "birthplace" : "Javea, Spain",
                "coach" : "Javier Piles",
                "height" : "175 cm",
                "more_id" : 1,
                "plays" : "Right-handed",
                "residence" : "Valencia, Spain",
                "turnedpro" : 2000,
                "weight" : "160 lbs (73 kg)"
        },
        "player_age" : 30,
        "player_birth" : ISODate("1982-04-02T00:00:00Z"),
        "player_name" : "Ferrer",
        "player_surname" : "David",
        "website_fk" : 1
}
{
        "_id" : 2,
        "details" : {
                "birthplace" : "Dunblane, Scotland",
                "coach" : "Ivan Lendl",
                "height" : "190 cm",
                "more_id" : 2,
                "plays" : "Right-handed",
                "residence" : "London, England",
                "turnedpro" : 2005,
                "weight" : "185 lbs (84 kg)"
        },
        "player_age" : 25,
        "player_birth" : ISODate("1987-05-15T00:00:00Z"),
        "player_name" : "Murray",
        "player_surname" : "Andy",
        "website_fk" : 2
}
> db.player_more_details.find().pretty();
{ "_id" : 1, "prizes" : "$17,178,869", "ranking" : 5 }
{ "_id" : 2, "prizes" : "$24,934,421", "ranking" : 3 }
{ "_id" : 3, "prizes" : "$50,061,827", "ranking" : 4 }
```

Figure 5-42. *One-to-one association and an embeddable class*

I've played a little with the one-to-one associations for storing, retrieving, and removing some Players instances. In Figure 5-43, you can see a sample of GlassFish log messages resulting from a simple scenario: insert one player, list it, delete it, and list it again. (Notice the cascading effect on persist and remove).

```
INFO: PLAYERS INFORMATION ...
INFO: ************** PLAYER WITH ID: 1 *****************
INFO: PLAYER: Name:Del Potro, Surname:Juan Martin, Age:24, Birth:9/23/88 12:00 AM
INFO: DETAILS: Birthplace:Tandil, Argentina, Coach:Franco Davin, Height:198 cm, Weight:214 lbs (97 kg), Reside
INFO: MORE DETAILS: Prizes:$10,853,349, Ranking:7
INFO: WEBSITE: hogm.mongodb.entity.Players@758760bd
INFO: ****************************************************
INFO: NO MORE PLAYERS AVAILABLE ...
INFO: WEBSITES INFORMATION ...
INFO: ************** WEBSITE WITH ID: 1 ****************
INFO: WEBSITE: Url:none, This website belongs to :Del Potro Juan Martin
INFO: ****************************************************
INFO: NO MORE WEBSITES AVAILABLE ...
INFO: REMOVING FIRST PLAYER (_id:1 - _id:10) ...
INFO: PLAYER SUCCESSFULLY REMOVED ...
INFO: PLAYERS INFORMATION ...
INFO: NO MORE PLAYERS AVAILABLE ...
INFO: WEBSITES INFORMATION ...
INFO: NO MORE WEBSITES AVAILABLE ...
```

Figure 5-43. *Testing one-to-one associations (persist, retrieve, list, and remove)*

The complete application for demonstrating the @OneToOne annotation is available in the Apress repository and is named HOGM_MONGODB_OneToOne. It comes as a NetBeans project and was tested under GlassFish 3 AS.

@OneToMany and @ManyToOne Annotation

Mapped by the javax.persistence.OneToMany and javax.persistence.ManyToOne annotations
Official documentation: http://docs.oracle.com/javaee/6/api/javax/persistence/OneToMany.html

http://docs.oracle.com/javaee/6/api/javax/persistence/ManyToOne.html

Brief Overview

In relational database terms, a one-to-many association occurs when each record in one table corresponds to many records in a related table. The tables don't contain the same number of records and each row from the first table is linked to more rows in the second table. This kind of association is mapped by JPA using the @OneToMany annotation.

When rows from the second table have an inverse association back to the first table, this is a bidirectional association and is indicated by the @ManyToOne annotation. In bidirectional associations, the mappedBy element must be used to specify the association field or property of the entity that is the owner of the association.

Both, @OneToMany and @ManyToOne can be used in an embeddable class to specify an association to a collection of entities, or to specify an association from the embeddable class to an entity class.

Such associations support fetching (eager or lazy), cascading, and orphan removal (only on @OneToMany, not on @ManyToOne).

OGM Support

Hibernate OGM supports @OneToMany and @ManyToOne annotations. As you know, by default, OGM stores data in MongoDB using the IN_ENTITY strategy, which does not imply any additional collection—each entity class is represented by a single collection. We can easily distinguish the following cases:

- For unidirectional one-to-many associations, OGM stores the navigation information for associations in the collection representing the owner side of the association, in fields that store the foreign keys in embedded collections. See Figure 5-44.

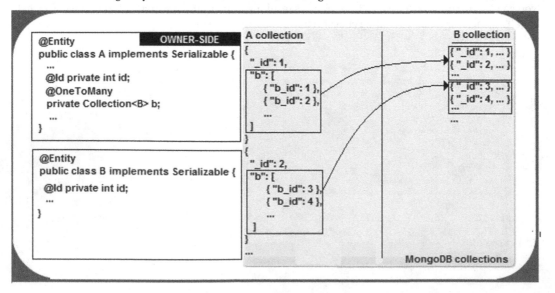

Figure 5-44. *IN_ENTITY: one-to-many unidirectional association*

- For unidirectional many-to-one associations, OGM stores the navigation information in the collection representing the owner side of the association; each document will contain a field for storing the corresponding foreign key. See Figure 5-45.

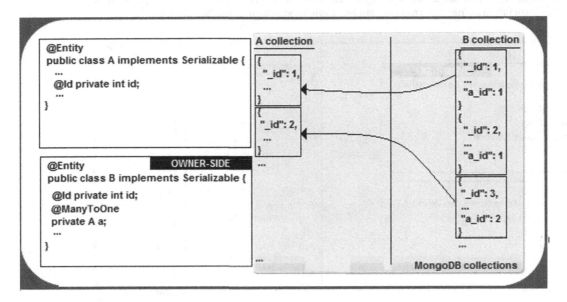

Figure 5-45. *IN_ENTITY: many-to-one unidirectional association*

- For a bidirectional one-to-many association, the navigation information is stored like this: the collection representing the entity that uses mappedBy (the non-owner side of the association) will contain fields that store the foreign keys in embedded collections. The collection representing the owner side of the association will contain, in each document, a field that stores the corresponding foreign key. See Figure 5-46.

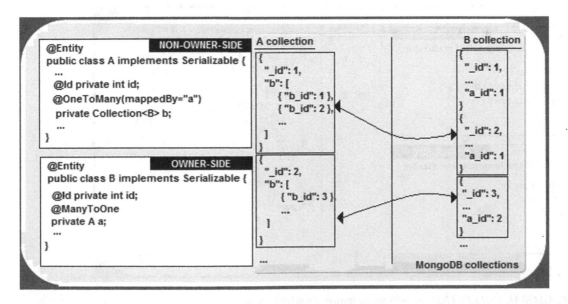

Figure 5-46. *IN_ENTITY: one-to-many bidirectional association*

For the GLOBAL_COLLECTION strategy, there are also some straightforward cases:

- For unidirectional one-to-many associations, OGM stores the navigation information for associations inside the global collection, named Associations. The collection representing the association owner does not contain any navigation information. See Figure 5-47.

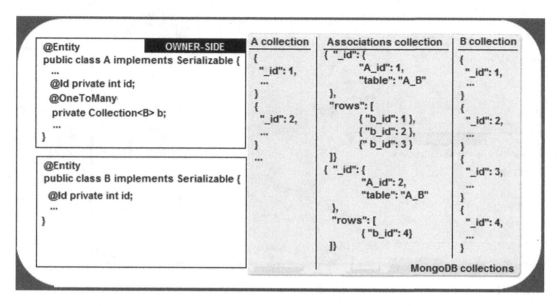

Figure 5-47. GLOBAL_COLLECION: one-to-many unidirectional association

- For unidirectional many-to-one association, GLOBAL_COLLECTION doesn't have any effect. See Figure 5-48.

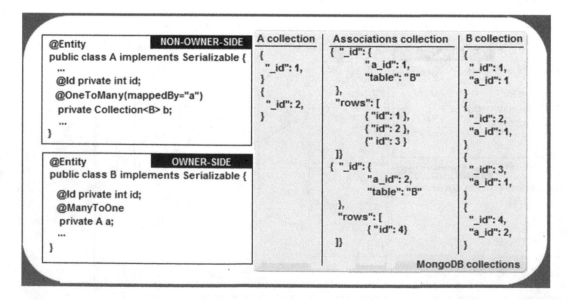

Figure 5-48. GLOBAL_COLLECTION: one-to-many bidirectional association

- For a bidirectional one-to-many association, the navigation information is stored like this: the collection representing the entity that uses mappedBy (the non-owning @OneToMany entity) will not contain navigation information. This information is now stored in the Associations collection. The other side (the owner) will contain, in each document, a field that stores the corresponding foreign key.

For the COLLECTION strategy, we have:

- For unidirectional one-to-many associations, OGM stores the navigation information for associations in a new collection prefixed with the word associations. The collection representing the association owner does not contain navigation information. See Figure 5-49.

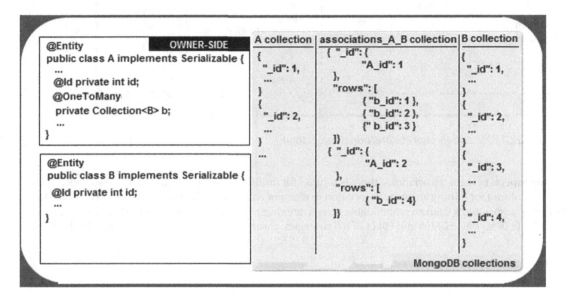

Figure 5-49. *COLLECTION: one-to-many unidirectional association*

- For unidirectional many-to-one associations, COLLECTION doesn't have any effect

- For a bidirectional one-to-many association, the navigation information is stored like this: the collection representing the entity that uses mappedBy (the non-owning @OneToMany entity) does not contain navigation information. This information is stored in a new collection prefixed with the word associations. The other side (the owner) will contain, in each document, a field that stores the corresponding foreign key. See Figure 5-50.

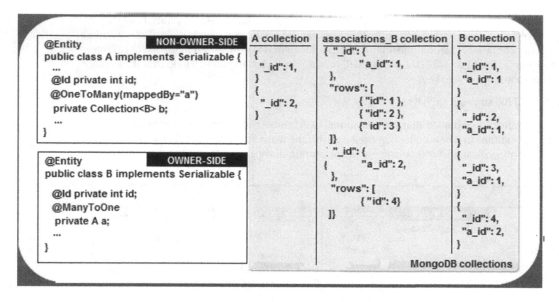

Figure 5-50. *COLLECTION: one-to-many bidirectional association*

For the main aspects of these associations, there is support for unidirectional and bidirectional associations, the ability to specify a column for joining an entity association or element collection (@JoinColumn), support for one-to-many/many-to-one associations from an embeddable class to another entity or collection of entities, @JoinTable and @JoinColumns with GLOBAL_COLLECTION and COLLECTION strategies, cascading(all), orphan removal, and fetching with lazy loading.

Example

As an example of a one-to-many association (unidirectional and bidirectional), I need two entities that should be logically appropriate for this purpose. A tennis player who has many photos for his fans can be a good test case for a one-to-many association, when we store the player and his photos. The photos can be mapped in the Photos entity, like so:

```
import java.io.Serializable;
...

@Entity
@Table(name = "players_photos")
public class Photos implements Serializable {

    @Id
    @GeneratedValue(strategy = GenerationType.AUTO)
    private int id;
    private String photo;

    //constructors, getters and setters
...
}
```

Now, each player has a collection of Photos, so the Players entity should define a @OneToMany association, like this:

```java
import javax.persistence.CascadeType;
import javax.persistence.OneToMany;
...

@Entity
@Table(name = "atp_players")
public class Players implements Serializable {

    @Id
    @GeneratedValue(strategy = GenerationType.AUTO)
    private int id;
      ...

    @OneToMany(cascade=CascadeType.ALL)
    private Collection<Photos> photos;

    //constructors,getters and setters
...
}
```

Persist several players and their photos to get something similar to what's shown in Figure 5-51. Notice that each document in the atp_players collection contains a field named photos, which stores (in a nested collection) the corresponding foreign keys from the players_photos collection. This is how OGM maps the one-to-many unidirectional association using IN_ENTITY strategy.

```
> db.atp_players.find().pretty();
{
        "_id" : 1,
        "photos" : [
                {
                        "photos_id" : 1
                },
                {
                        "photos_id" : 2
                }
        ],
        "player_age" : 30,
        "player_birth" : ISODate("1982-04-02T00:00:00Z"),
        "player_name" : "Ferrer",
        "player_surname" : "David"

        "_id" : 2,
        "photos" : [
                {
                        "photos_id" : 3
                },
                {
                        "photos_id" : 4
                },
                {
                        "photos_id" : 5
                },
                {
                        "photos_id" : 6
                }
        ],
        "player_age" : 24,
        "player_birth" : ISODate("1988-09-23T00:00:00Z"),
        "player_name" : "Del Potro",
        "player_surname" : "Juan Martin"
```

```
> db.players_photos.find().pretty();
{ "_id" : 1, "photo" : "ferrer_1.png" }
{ "_id" : 2, "photo" : "ferrer_2.png" }
{ "_id" : 3, "photo" : "delpotro_1.png" }
{ "_id" : 4, "photo" : "delpotro_2.png" }
{ "_id" : 5, "photo" : "delpotro_3.png" }
{ "_id" : 6, "photo" : "delpotro_4.png" }
```

Figure 5-51. *Unidirectional one-to-many association*

Because I've used generics to specify the element type, the associated target entity type isn't specified. When generics aren't used, I need to specify the target entity class using the targetEntity element. For example, I can redefine the @OneToMany association, like this:

```
...
@OneToMany(targetEntity=hogm.mongodb.entity.Photos.class, cascade=CascadeType.ALL)
    private Collection photos;
...
```

If you think about the association from the opposite direction, many photos belong to the same player, which describes a unidirectional many-to-one association. Implementing such an association means we write the Players entity like this:

```
import java.io.Serializable;
...

@Entity
@Table(name = "atp_players")
public class Players implements Serializable {

    @Id
    @GeneratedValue(strategy = GenerationType.AUTO)
    private int id;
    @Column(name = "player_name")
    private String name;
    @Column(name = "player_surname")
    private String surname;
    @Column(name = "player_age")
    private int age;
    @Temporal(javax.persistence.TemporalType.DATE)
    @Column(name = "player_birth")
    private Date birth;

  //constructors, getters and setters
...
}
```

In addition, the Photos entity must define an @ManyToOne field (or property), like this:

```
import javax.persistence.JoinColumn;
import javax.persistence.ManyToOne;
...

@Entity
@Table(name = "players_photos")
public class Photos implements Serializable {

    @Id
    @GeneratedValue(strategy = GenerationType.AUTO)
    private int id;
    private String photo;
```

```
@ManyToOne
@JoinColumn(name = "player_fk", unique = true, nullable = false, updatable = false)
private Players player_photos;

    //constructors, getters and setters
...
}
```

Persist several players and their photos to get something like what's shown in Figure 5-52. Notice that each document in the players_photos collection contains a field named player_pk that stores the corresponding foreign keys from the atp_players collection. This is how OGM maps the many-to-one unidirectional association using IN_ENTITY strategy.

```
> db.atp_players.find().pretty();
{
        "_id" : 1,
        "player_age" : 25,
        "player_birth" : ISODate("1987-05-15T00:00:00Z"),
        "player_name" : "Murray",
        "player_surname" : "Andy"
}
{
        "_id" : 2,
        "player_age" : 28,
        "player_birth" : ISODate("1984-06-21T23:00:00Z"),
        "player_name" : "Tipsarevic",
        "player_surname" : "Janko"
}

> db.players_photos.find().pretty();
{ "_id" : 1, "photo" : "murray_1.png", "player_fk" : 1 }
{ "_id" : 2, "photo" : "murray_2.png", "player_fk" : 1 }
{ "_id" : 3, "photo" : "murray_3.png", "player_fk" : 1 }
{ "_id" : 4, "photo" : "murray_4.png", "player_fk" : 1 }
{ "_id" : 5, "photo" : "tipsarevic_1.png", "player_fk" : 2 }
{ "_id" : 6, "photo" : "tipsarevic_2.png", "player_fk" : 2 }
{ "_id" : 7, "photo" : "tipsarevic_3.png", "player_fk" : 2 }
```

Figure 5-52. *Unidirectional many-to-one association*

I can easily change the unidirectional one-to-many and many-to-one association into a bidirectional one by adjusting the Players entity (Photos remains unchanged). I need to specify the association field of the entity that is the owner of the relationship. Therefore, in the Players entity, I make this adjustemnt:

```
...
@OneToMany(cascade=CascadeType.ALL, mappedBy = "player_photos")
    private Collection<Photos> photos;
...
```

This time, the atp_players and players_photos collections look like what's shown in Figure 5-53.

```
> db.atp_players.find().pretty();
<
        "_id" : 1,
        "photos" : [
                {
                        "id" : 1
                },
                {
                        "id" : 2
                }
        ],
        "player_age" : 27,
        "player_birth" : ISODate("1985-04-16T23:00:00Z"),
        "player_name" : "Tsonga",
        "player_surname" : "Jo-Wilfried"
>
<
        "_id" : 2,
        "photos" : [
                {
                        "id" : 3
                },
                {
                        "id" : 4
                },
                {
                        "id" : 5
                }
        ],
        "player_age" : 25,
        "player_birth" : ISODate("1987-05-22T00:00:00Z"),
        "player_name" : "Djokovic",
        "player_surname" : "Novak"
>
```

```
> db.players_photos.find().pretty();
{ "_id" : 1, "photo" : "tsonga_1.png", "player_fk" : 1 }
{ "_id" : 2, "photo" : "tsonga_2.png", "player_fk" : 1 }
{ "_id" : 3, "photo" : "novak_1.png", "player_fk" : 2 }
{ "_id" : 4, "photo" : "novak_2.png", "player_fk" : 2 }
{ "_id" : 5, "photo" : "novak_3.png", "player_fk" : 2 }
```

Figure 5-53. *Bidirectional one-to-many association*

Finally, I've played a little with these associations for storing, retrieving, and removing some Players instances. In Figure 5-54, you can see a sample of GlassFish log messages following a simple scenario: insert one player, list it, delete it, and list it again. (Notice the cascading effect on persist and remove.)

```
INFO: PLAYERS INFORMATION ...
INFO: ************** PLAYER WITH ID: 1 *****************
INFO: PLAYER: Name:Ferrer, Surname:David, Age:30, Birth:4/2/82 12:00 AM
INFO: PHOTO: Name:ferrer_1.png
INFO: PHOTO: Name:ferrer_2.png
INFO: ***************************************************
INFO: NO MORE PLAYERS AVAILABLE ...
INFO: PHOTOS INFORMATION ...
INFO: ************** PHOTO WITH ID: 1 *****************
INFO: PHOTO: Photo :ferrer_1.png, This photo belongs to :Ferrer David
INFO: ***************************************************
INFO: ************** PHOTO WITH ID: 2 *****************
INFO: PHOTO: Photo :ferrer_2.png, This photo belongs to :Ferrer David
INFO: ***************************************************
INFO: NO MORE PHOTOS AVAILABLE ...
INFO: REMOVING FIRST PLAYER (_id:1 - _id:10) ...
INFO: PLAYER SUCCESSFULLY REMOVED ...
INFO: PLAYERS INFORMATION ...
INFO: NO MORE PLAYERS AVAILABLE ...
INFO: PHOTOS INFORMATION ...
INFO: NO MORE PHOTOS AVAILABLE ...
```

Figure 5-54. *Testing one-to-many associations*

The complete application for demonstrating the @OneToMany/@ManyToOne annotations is available in the Apress repository and is named HOGM_MONGODB_OneToMany. It comes as a NetBeans project and was tested under GlassFish 3 AS.

@ManyToManyAnnotation

Mapped by the javax.persistence.ManyToMany annotation.

Official documentation: http://docs.oracle.com/javaee/6/api/javax/persistence/ManyToMany.html

Brief Overview

In relational database terms, a many-to-many association occurs when many records in one table each correspond to many records in a related table. This kind of association is mapped by JPA using the @ManyToMany annotation.

When rows from the second table have an inverse association back to the first table, it's a bidirectional association. In a bidirectional many-to-many association, the relational model usually uses three tables, two tables for data and an additional table known as a *junction table,* which holds a composite key made of two fields: the two foreign key fields that refer to the primary keys of first and second tables. The same pair of foreign keys can occur only once. In JPA, the junction table can be specified using the @JoinTable annotation on the owning side, which can be either side.

Practically, in JPA, the main difference between @ManyToMany and @OneToMany is that @ManyToMany always makes use of this intermediate relational join table to store the association, while @OneToMany can use either a join table or a foreign key in a target object's table referencing the source object table's primary key. The non-owning side (which can be either of the two sides) should use the mappedBy element to specify the association field or property of the owning side. Technically, mappedBy will keep the database correctly updated if you only add or remove from the owning side, but this can cause issues, such as orphans (records without links) that must be removed from the application code. Without mappedBy, duplicate records in the join table may appear since you'll have two different associations. In a bidirectional many-to-many association, it is recommended you add data from both sides.

@ManyToMany can be used in an embeddable class to specify an association to a collection of entities. Such an association supports fetching (eager or lazy) and cascading, but doesn't support orphan removal, which is allowed only for associations with single cardinality on the source side.

OGM Support

Hibernate OGM supports the @ManyToMany annotation. As you know, by default, OGM stores data in MongoDB using the IN_ENTITY strategy, which does not imply any additional collection, only entity collections. For unidirectional many-to-many associations, OGM stores the navigation information for associations in the owner collection, in fields that store the foreign keys in embedded collections. If the association is bidirectional, both sides will contain embedded collections for storing the corresponding navigation information (foreign keys). For the GLOBAL_COLLECTION and COLLECTION strategies, a third collection will be used as described in Chapter 2, in the section called "*Association Storing.*" In the case of the COLLECTION strategy, if mappedBy is not specified, it's assumed to be two difference associations and you'll get two join collections (one per association).

The main aspects of these associations include supports for unidirectional and bidirectional associations, the ability to specify a column for joining an entity association or element collection (@JoinColumn), support for one-to-many/many-to-one associations from an embeddable class to another collection of entities, @JoinTable and @JoinColumns with the GLOBAL_COLLECTION and COLLECTION strategies, and cascading(all). In addition, OGM supports fetching with lazy loading.

Example

To demonstrate a many-to-many association, I need two entities that should be logically appropriate for this purpose. For example, a tennis player might participate in several tournaments, and each tournament would contain several players. This can be a good test case for a many-to-many association when we store the players, the tournaments, and the association. To start, let's suppose that only the players are aware of the tournaments. In other words, let's implement a unidirectional many-to-many association.

For this, the Players entity must define an @ManyToMany association, like this:

```java
import javax.persistence.ManyToMany;
...

@Entity
@Table(name = "atp_players")
public class Players implements Serializable {

    @Id
    @GeneratedValue(strategy = GenerationType.AUTO)
    private int id;
    @Column(name = "player_name")
    private String name;
    @Column(name = "player_surname")
    private String surname;
    @Column(name = "player_age")
    private int age;
    @Temporal(javax.persistence.TemporalType.DATE)
    @Column(name = "player_birth")
    private Date birth;
    @ManyToMany(cascade = CascadeType.PERSIST)
    Collection<Tournaments> tournaments;

    //constructors, getters and setters
...
}
```

The Tournaments entity is pretty straightforward:

```java
import java.io.Serializable;
...

@Entity
@Table(name = "atp_tournaments")
public class Tournaments implements Serializable {

    @Id
    @GeneratedValue(strategy = GenerationType.AUTO)
    private int id;
    private String tournament;

    //constructors, getters and setters
...
}
```

Persist several players and tournaments and define some links from players to tournaments to get something like what's shown in Figure 5-55. Notice that each document in the atp_players collection contains a field named tournaments that stores (in a nested collection) the corresponding foreign keys from the atp_tournaments collection. This is how OGM maps the many-to-many unidirectional association using IN_ENTITY strategy.

```
> db.atp_players.find().pretty();
{
        "_id" : 1,
        "player_age" : 25,
        "player_birth" : ISODate("1987-05-22T00:00:00Z"),
        "player_name" : "Djokovic",
        "player_surname" : "Novak",
        "tournaments" : [
                {
                        "tournaments_id" : 1
                }
        ]
}
{
        "_id" : 2,
        "player_age" : 31,
        "player_birth" : ISODate("1981-08-08T00:00:00Z"),
        "player_name" : "Federer",
        "player_surname" : "Roger",
        "tournaments" : [
                {
                        "tournaments_id" : 4
                },
                {
                        "tournaments_id" : 3
                },
                {
                        "tournaments_id" : 2
                },
                {
                        "tournaments_id" : 1
                }
        ]
}
> db.atp_tournaments.find().pretty();
{ "_id" : 1, "tournament" : "Open Sud de France" }
{ "_id" : 2, "tournament" : "Barclays ATP World Tour Finals" }
{ "_id" : 3, "tournament" : "Sony Open Tennis" }
{ "_id" : 4, "tournament" : "Dubai Duty Free Tennis Championships" }
```

Figure 5-55. *Unidirectional many-to-many association*

The same kind of association can be defined from the Tournaments perspective by translating the @ManyToMany annotation from the Players entity to the Tournaments entity and providing Players for Tournaments, instead of Tournaments for Players.

You can easily transform this unidirectional many-to-many association into a bidirectional association. While the Players entity remains unchanged, the Tournaments entity should be modified like this:

```
import javax.persistence.ManyToMany;
...

@Entity
@Table(name = "atp_tournaments")
public class Tournaments implements Serializable {
```

```
@Id
@GeneratedValue(strategy = GenerationType.AUTO)
private int id;
private String tournament;
@ManyToMany(mappedBy = "tournaments")
Collection<Players> players;

    //constructors, getters and setters
...
}
```

Now, MongoDB will contain nested collections in both entity collections, atp_players and atp_tournaments. Each nested collection will store the foreign keys of the other side. See Figure 5-56.

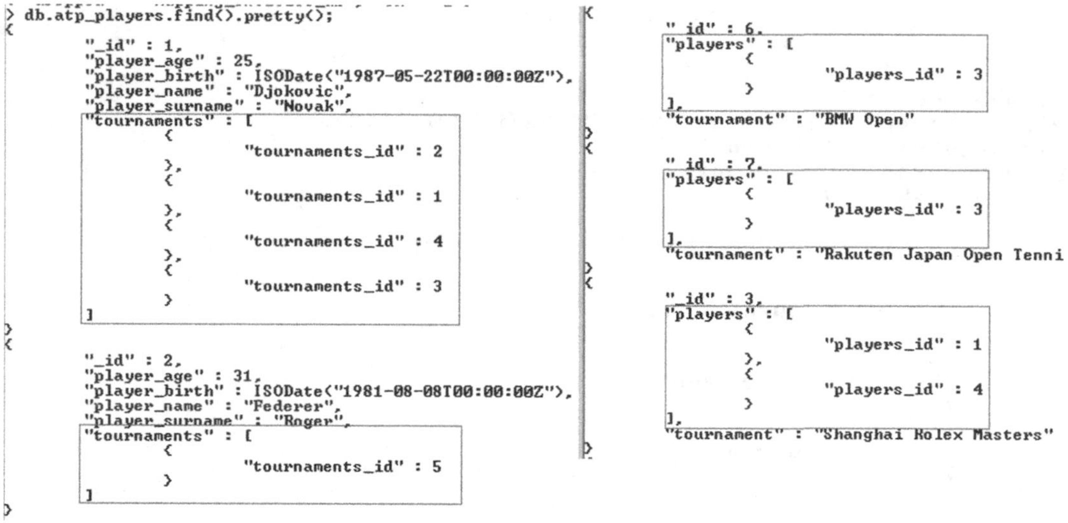

Figure 5-56. *Bidirectional many-to-many association*

Notice that in the preceding cases, I used generics, so I didn't specify the associated target entity type. When generics aren't used, you need to specify the target entity class using the targetEntity element. For example, I can redefine the @ManyToMany associations like this:

```
...
//in Players entity
@ManyToMany(targetEntity = hogm.mongodb.entity.Tournaments.class,cascade = CascadeType.PERSIST)
    Collection tournaments;
...
...
//in Tournaments entity
@ManyToMany(targetEntity = hogm.mongodb.entity.Players.class, mappedBy = "tournaments")
    Collection players;
...
```

When the GLOBAL_COLLECTION or COLLECTION strategy is preferred, I can use @JoinTable (including @JoinColumn) on the owning side of the association to indicate the name of the association table and columns. For GLOBAL_COLLECTION, I can use:

```
...
@ManyToMany(targetEntity = hogm.mongodb.entity.Tournaments.class,
                          cascade = CascadeType.PERSIST)
    @JoinTable(name = "PLAYERS_AND_TOURNAMENTS", joinColumns =
    @JoinColumn(name = "PLAYER_ID", referencedColumnName = "id"),
    inverseJoinColumns =
    @JoinColumn(name = "TOURNAMENT_ID", referencedColumnName = "id"))
    Collection tournaments;
...
```

The result is shown in Figure 5-57.

```
> show collections
Associations
atp_players
atp_tournaments
hibernate_sequences
system.indexes
> db.Associations.find().pretty();
{
        "_id" : {
                "TOURNAMENT_ID" : 1,
                "table" : "PLAYERS_AND_TOURNAMENTS"
        },
        "rows" : [
                {
                        "PLAYER_ID" : 1
                }
        ]
}
{
        "_id" : {
                "PLAYER_ID" : 1,
                "table" : "PLAYERS_AND_TOURNAMENTS"
        },
        "rows" : [
                {
                        "TOURNAMENT_ID" : 1
                },
                {
                        "TOURNAMENT_ID" : 2
                }
        ]
}
```

Figure 5-57. *GLOBAL_COLLECTION and @JoinTable*

And for COLLECTION, the result is shown in in Figure 5-58.

```
> show collections
associations_PLAYERS_AND_TOURNAMENTS
atp_players
atp_tournaments
hibernate_sequences
system.indexes
> db.associations_PLAYERS_AND_TOURNAMENTS.find().pretty();
{
        "_id" : {
                "TOURNAMENT_ID" : 1
        },
        "rows" : [
                {
                        "PLAYER_ID" : 1
                }
        ]
}
{
        "_id" : {
                "PLAYER_ID" : 1
        },
        "rows" : [
                {
                        "TOURNAMENT_ID" : 1
                },
                {
                        "TOURNAMENT_ID" : 2
                }
        ]
}
```

Figure 5-58. *COLLECTION and @JoinTable*

Finally, I played a little with these associations for storing, retrieving, and removing some Players and Tournaments instances. You can test the entire application by downloading it from the Apress repository; it's the HOGM_MONGODB_ManyToMany application (notice that the application doesn't provide orphan removal). It comes as a NetBeans project and was tested under GlassFish 3 AS.

Unsupported JPA 2.0 Annotations

According to the Hibernate OGM Beta 4.0.0Beta 2 documentation, the following are not supported:

- inheritance strategies: @Inheritance nor @DiscriminatorColumn.
- secondary tables: @SecondaryTables, @SecondaryTable
- named queries
- native queries

Summary

In this chapter, you saw how Hibernate OGM implements the JPA 2.0 annotations for working with MongoDB stores. I discussed the main JPA 2.0 annotations and focused on the supported ones:

- `@Entity`
- `@Id`
- `@EmbeddedId`
- `@IdClass`
- `@Table`
- `@Column`
- `@Temporal`
- `@Transient`
- `@Embedded and @Embeddable`
- `@Enumerated`
- `@Cacheable`
- `@MappedSuperclass`
- `@ElementCollection`
- `@EntityListeners, @ExcludeDefaultListeners, @ExcludeSuperclassListeners`
- `@Version`
- `@Access`
- `@OneToOne, @OneToMany, @ManyToOne, @ManyToMany`

The list of unsupported annotations is quite short and will probably be reduced to zero on the next release.

CHAPTER 6

■ ■ ■

Hibernate OGM Querying MongoDB

In previous chapters, we accomplished several tasks in order to organize and store our data in NoSQL MongoDB stores. Now we'll make use of this data by applying different querying techniques to extract only the information we need from a NoSQL MongoDB store.

As I noted in Chapter 1, querying a NoSQL database is a delicate and complex task—there are different situations, and different approaches depending on the native support for NoSQL querying. For MongoDB, there are a number of querying options; it's up to you to choose the one that meets your needs, depending on your queries' complexity, performance parameters, and so on:

- Native query technology, which means using the MongoDB driver querying capabilities without involving Hibernate OGM or any other technology.

- Hibernate ORM/OGM for CRUD, in which Create/Read/Update/Delete operations are implemented by the Hibernate ORM engine.

- Hibernate Search/Apache Lucene, which uses a full-text indexing and query engine (Apache Lucene). Hibernate Search is a powerful querying mechanism with great performance and capabilities and provides a very easy-to-use bridge to Lucene. For complex queries and indexing support, this is the right choice.

- Hibernate OGM JP-QL parser, which uses uses Hibernate Search to retrieve the desired information from a MongoDB store, is good for simple queries. This JP-QL parser is in its infancy, so it will need time to become powerful and support complex queries.

- Other tools, such as DataNucleus, Morphia, and so on that won't be covered in this book.

■ **Note**   Currently, Hibernate OGM via Hibernate Native API doesn't provide support for Hibernate Criteria. Moreover, it doesn't, via JPA, provide support for native and named queries.

We are going to delve into each of these querying possibilities and try to see how it works. We will focus on Hibernate OGM and discuss MongoDB from this perspective. For the sake of completeness, however, we'll start this journey about querying MongoDB by first looking at basic MongoDB querying capabilities, and reserve the subject of Hibernate OGM till the second part of the chapter. In this way, you'll get a complete picture of querying MongoDB and you'll be better able to choose the appropriate querying solution for your needs.

MongoDB Native Query

As you probably know, MongoDB natively provides interactive support through the mongo shell (a full interactive JavaScript environment with a database interface for MongoDB), and programmatic support through the MongoDB driver (which is available for multiple programming languages, such as Java, Ruby, and PHP). In this section, we will skip the shell and concentrate on querying a MongoDB store using the MongoDB driver for Java. You'll need the 2.8.0 version of this driver, which is available for download as a JAR named mongo-java-driver-2.8.0.jar at www.docs.mongodb.org/manual/applications/drivers/.

Before executing any query, you need to configure a MongoDB connection and create a database, then create a collection and populate it with data. For this, please go back to the section in Chapter 4 called "Java SE and Mongo DB—the HelloWorld Example." Once you know how to connect and persist documents to a MongoDB store, you're ready to perform queries.

We'll create a collection called players and try some queries against it. Each document stores some tennis player data: name, surname, age, and birth date (and duplicate documents are allowed). After populating the collection with several documents, you can start with the well-known "select all" query. You can use the find method, which returns a cursor that contains a number of documents. As you can see, it's very easy to iterate the results. This chunk of code uses find to extract all documents:

```
...
Mongo mongo = new Mongo("127.0.0.1", 27017);
DB db = mongo.getDB("players_db");
DBCollection dbCollection = db.getCollection("players");
...
System.out.println("Find all documents in collection:");
        try (DBCursor cursor = dbCollection.find()) {
            while (cursor.hasNext()) {
                System.out.println(cursor.next());
            }
        }
...
```

The result of this query is shown in Figure 6-1.

```
Find all documents in collection:
{ "_id" : ...  , "name" : "Ferrer" , "surname" : "David" , "age" : 30 , "birth" : { "$date" : "1982-04-02T00:00:00.00
{ "_id" : ...  , "name" : "Ferrer" , "surname" : "David" , "age" : 30 , "birth" : { "$date" : "1982-04-02T00:00:00.00
{ "_id" : ...  , "name" : "Tsonga" , "surname" : "Jo-Wilfried" , "age" : 27 , "birth" : { "$date" : "1985-04-16T23:00
{ "_id" : ...  , "name" : "Federer" , "surname" : "Roger" , "age" : 31 , "birth" : { "$date" : "1981-08-08T00:00:00.0
{ "_id" : ...  , "name" : "Del Potro" , "surname" : "Juan Martin" , "age" : 24 , "birth" : { "$date" : "1988-09-23T00
{ "_id" : ...  , "name" : "Murray" , "surname" : "Andy" , "age" : 25 , "birth" : { "$date" : "1987-05-15T00:00:00.000
{ "_id" : ...  , "name" : "Tsonga" , "surname" : "Jo-Wilfried" , "age" : 27 , "birth" : { "$date" : "1985-04-16T23:00
{ "_id" : ...  , "name" : "Federer" , "surname" : "Roger" , "age" : 31 , "birth" : { "$date" : "1981-08-08T00:00:00.0
{ "_id" : ...  , "name" : "Nadal" , "surname" : "Rafael" , "age" : 26 , "birth" : { "$date" : "1986-06-03T00:00:00.00
{ "_id" : ...  , "name" : "Djokovic" , "surname" : "Novak" , "age" : 25 , "birth" : { "$date" : "1987-05-22T00:00.
```

Figure 6-1. *All documents of the players collection*

■ **Note** You can count how many documents are in a collection by calling the getCount method, like this: dbCollection.getCount();.

You can find a single document using the findOne method; this method doesn't return a cursor. The snipped code is:

```
...
System.out.println("Find the first document in collection:");
          DBObject first = dbCollection.findOne();
          System.out.println(first);
...
```

The result will be the first document from the players collection, as shown in Figure 6-2.

```
Find the first document in collection:
{ "_id" : ... , "name" : "Ferrer" , "surname" : "David" , "age" : 30 , "birth" : { "$date" : "1982-04-02T00:00:00.000
```

Figure 6-2. *Extracting the first document of the players collection*

You can also execute conditional queries. For example, we can extract the documents corresponding to the player Rafael Nadal using the find method, like this:

```
...
System.out.println("Find Rafael Nadal documents:");
          BasicDBObject query = new BasicDBObject("name", "Nadal").append("surname", "Rafael");
          try (DBCursor cursor = dbCollection.find(query)) {
              while (cursor.hasNext()) {
                  System.out.println(cursor.next());
              }
          }
...
```

The results are shown in Figure 6-3.

```
Find Rafael Nadal documents:
{ "_id" : ... , "name" : "Nadal" , "surname" : "Rafael" , "age" : 26 , "birth" : { "$date" : "1986-06-03T00:00:00.000
```

Figure 6-3. *Extracting only documents containing Rafael Nadal*

The find method combined with the $gt (greater than) operator lets you extract all players whose age is greater than 25:

```
...
System.out.println("Find players with age > 25:");
          BasicDBObject  query = new BasicDBObject("age", new BasicDBObject("$gt", 25));
          try (DBCursor cursor = dbCollection.find(query)) {
              while (cursor.hasNext()) {
                  System.out.println(cursor.next());
              }
          }
...
```

You can see the results in Figure 6-4.

```
Find players with age > 25:
{ "_id" : ... , "name" : "Ferrer" , "surname" : "David" , "age" : 30 , "birth" : { "$date" : "1982-04-02T00:00:00.000Z
{ "_id" : ... , "name" : "Ferrer" , "surname" : "David" , "age" : 30 , "birth" : { "$date" : "1982-04-02T00:00:00.000Z
{ "_id" : ... , "name" : "Tsonga" , "surname" : "Jo-Wilfried" , "age" : 27 , "birth" : { "$date" : "1985-04-16T23:00:0
{ "_id" : ... , "name" : "Federer" , "surname" : "Roger" , "age" : 31 , "birth" : { "$date" : "1981-08-08T00:00:00.000
{ "_id" : ... , "name" : "Tsonga" , "surname" : "Jo-Wilfried" , "age" : 27 , "birth" : { "$date" : "1985-04-16T23:00:0
{ "_id" : ... , "name" : "Federer" , "surname" : "Roger" , "age" : 31 , "birth" : { "$date" : "1981-08-08T00:00:00.000
{ "_id" :     , "name" : "Nadal" , "surname" : "Rafael" , "age" : 26 , "birth" : { "$date" : "1986-06-03T00:00:00.000Z
```

Figure 6-4. *Extracting only documents with age greater than 25*

The find method combined with the $lt (less than) operator lets you extract all players whose age is less than 28:

```
...
System.out.println("Find players with age < 28:");
        BasicDBObject  query = new BasicDBObject("age", new BasicDBObject("$lt", 28));
        try (DBCursor cursor = dbCollection.find(query)) {
            while (cursor.hasNext()) {
                System.out.println(cursor.next());
            }
        }
...
```

The results are shown in Figure 6-5.

```
Find players with age < 28:
{ "_id" : ... , "name" : "Tsonga" , "surname" : "Jo-Wilfried" , "age" : 27 , "birth" : { "$date" : "1985-04-16T23:00:0
{ "_id" : ... , "name" : "Del Potro" , "surname" : "Juan Martin" , "age" : 24 , "birth" : { "$date" : "1988-09-23T00:0
{ "_id" : ... , "name" : "Murray" , "surname" : "Andy" , "age" : 25 , "birth" : { "$date" : "1987-05-15T00:00:00.000Z"
{ "_id" : ... , "name" : "Tsonga" , "surname" : "Jo-Wilfried" , "age" : 27 , "birth" : { "$date" : "1985-04-16T23:00:0
{ "_id" : ... , "name" : "Nadal" , "surname" : "Rafael" , "age" : 26 , "birth" : { "$date" : "1986-06-03T00:00:00.000Z
{ "_id" : ... , "name" : "Djokovic" , "surname" : "Novak" , "age" : 25 , "birth" : { "$date" : "1987-05-22T00:00:00.00
```

Figure 6-5. *Extracting only documents with age less than 28*

Extracting data that falls within (or outside of) an interval of values can be accomplished using the $gt and $lt, or $gte (greater than or equal) and $lte (less than or equal) operators and the find method. For example, you can obtain all players born between 1 January, 1982 and 31 December, 1985 like this:

```
...
System.out.println("JAVA - Find players with birthday between 1 January, 1982 - 31 December, 1985:");
        Calendar calendar_begin = GregorianCalendar.getInstance();
        calendar_begin.clear();
        calendar_begin.set(1982, Calendar.JANUARY, 1);
        Calendar calendar_end = GregorianCalendar.getInstance();
        calendar_end.clear();
        calendar_end.set(1985, Calendar.DECEMBER, 31);
        BasicDBObject query = new BasicDBObject("birth", new BasicDBObject("$gte",
                            calendar_begin.getTime()).append("$lte", calendar_end.getTime()));
        try (DBCursor cursor = dbCollection.find(query)) {
            while (cursor.hasNext()) {
                System.out.println(cursor.next());
            }
        }
...
```

The results are shown in Figure 6-6:

```
Find players with birthday between 1 January, 1982 - 31 December, 1985:
{ "_id" : ... , "name" : "Ferrer" , "surname" : "David" , "age" : 30 , "birth" : { "$date" : "1982-04-02T00:00:00.000
{ "_id" : ... , "name" : "Ferrer" , "surname" : "David" , "age" : 30 , "birth" : { "$date" : "1982-04-02T00:00:00.000
{ "_id" : ... , "name" : "Tsonga" , "surname" : "Jo-Wilfried" , "age" : 27 , "birth" : { "$date" : "1985-04-16T23:00:0
{ "_id" : ... , "name" : "Tsonga" , "surname" : "Jo-Wilfried" , "age" : 27 , "birth" : { "$date" : "1985-04-16T23:00:0
```

Figure 6-6. *Extracting only documents with births between 1 January, 1982 and 31 December, 1985*

If you prefer to use Joda Time (a replacement for the Java date and time classes, available at http://joda-time.sourceforge.net), you can write the query like this:

```
System.out.println("JODA - Find players with birthday between 1 January, 1982 - 31 December, 1985:");
        DateTime joda_calendar_begin = new DateTime(1982, 1, 1, 0, 0);
        DateTime joda_calendar_end = new DateTime(1985, 12, 31, 0, 0);
        query = new BasicDBObject("birth", new BasicDBObject("$gte",
        joda_calendar_begin.toDate()).append("$lte", joda_calendar_end.toDate()));
        try (DBCursor cursor = dbCollection.find(query)) {
            while (cursor.hasNext()) {
                System.out.println(cursor.next());
            }
        }
```

You can also extract data with specific values using the $in operator and the find method. For example, you can obtain all players with the ages 25, 27, and 30, like this:

```
...
System.out.println("Find players with ages: 25, 27, 30");
        List<Integer> list = new ArrayList<>();
        list.add(25);
        list.add(27);
        list.add(30);
        BasicDBObject  query = new BasicDBObject("age", new BasicDBObject("$in", list));
        try (DBCursor cursor = dbCollection.find(query)) {
            while (cursor.hasNext()) {
                System.out.println(cursor.next());
            }
        }
...
```

The result are shown in Figure 6-7.

```
Find players with ages: 25, 27, 30
{ "_id" : ... , "name" : "Ferrer" , "surname" : "David" , "age" : 30 , "birth" : { "$date" : "1982-04-02T00:00:00.000
{ "_id" : ... , "name" : "Ferrer" , "surname" : "David" , "age" : 30 , "birth" : { "$date" : "1982-04-02T00:00:00.000
{ "_id" : ... , "name" : "Tsonga" , "surname" : "Jo-Wilfried" , "age" : 27 , "birth" : { "$date" : "1985-04-16T23:00:
{ "_id" : ... , "name" : "Murray" , "surname" : "Andy" , "age" : 25 , "birth" : { "$date" : "1987-05-15T00:00:00.000Z
{ "_id" : ... , "name" : "Tsonga" , "surname" : "Jo-Wilfried" , "age" : 27 , "birth" : { "$date" : "1985-04-16T23:00:
{ "_id" : ... , "name" : "Djokovic" , "surname" : "Novak" , "age" : 26 , "birth" : { "$date" : "1987-05-22T00:00:00.0
```

Figure 6-7. *Extracting only documents with age equal to 25, 27, or 30*

When you need to extract data by negation, you can use the $ne (not equal) operator and the find method. For example, you can easily obtain all players with ages not equal to 27, like this:

```
...
System.out.println("Find players with ages different from: 27");
        BasicDBObject  query = new BasicDBObject("age", new BasicDBObject("$ne", 27));
        try (DBCursor cursor = dbCollection.find(query)) {
            while (cursor.hasNext()) {
                System.out.println(cursor.next());
            }
        }
...
```

The results are shown in Figure 6-8:

```
Find players with ages different from: 27
{ "_id" : ... , "name" : "Ferrer" , "surname" : "David" , "age" : 30 , "birth" : { "$date" : "1982-04-02T00:00:00.000Z
{ "_id" : ... , "name" : "Ferrer" , "surname" : "David" , "age" : 30 , "birth" : { "$date" : "1982-04-02T00:00:00.000Z
{ "_id" : ... , "name" : "Federer" , "surname" : "Roger" , "age" : 31 , "birth" : { "$date" : "1981-08-08T00:00:00.000
{ "_id" : ... , "name" : "Del Potro" , "surname" : "Juan Martin" , "age" : 24 , "birth" : { "$date" : "1988-09-23T00:0
{ "_id" : ... , "name" : "Murray" , "surname" : "Andy" , "age" : 25 , "birth" : { "$date" : "1987-05-15T00:00:00.000Z"
{ "_id" : ... , "name" : "Federer" , "surname" : "Roger" , "age" : 31 , "birth" : { "$date" : "1981-08-08T00:00:00.000
{ "_id" : ... , "name" : "Nadal" , "surname" : "Rafael" , "age" : 26 , "birth" : { "$date" : "1986-06-03T00:00:00.000Z
{ "_id" : ... , "name" : "Djokovic" , "surname" : "Novak" , "age" : 25 , "birth" : { "$date" : "1987-05-22T00:00:00.00
```

Figure 6-8. *Extracting only documents with age different from 27*

In the previous examples, we created (inserted) and retrieved (read) data from MongoDB using MongoDB Java driver. You can accomplish an update accomplish by calling the save method. For example, you can replace Rafael Nadal with Rafael Nadal Parera, like this:

```
...
        System.out.println("UPDATING ...");
        BasicDBObject  query = new BasicDBObject("name", "Nadal").append("surname", "Rafael");
        try (DBCursor cursor = dbCollection.find(query)) {
            while (cursor.hasNext()) {
                DBObject item = cursor.next();
                item.put("name", "Nadal Parera");
                dbCollection.save(item);
            }
        }
...
```

And you can delete data by calling the remove method. For example, you can delete all occurrences of Roger Federer, like this:

```
...
        System.out.println("DELETING ...");
        BasicDBObject  query = new BasicDBObject("name", "Federer").append("surname", "Roger");
        try (DBCursor cursor = dbCollection.find(query)) {
            while (cursor.hasNext()) {
```

```
            DBObject item = cursor.next();
            dbCollection.remove(item);
        }
    }
...
```

■ **Note**   For advanced queries using MongoDB drivers, see *The Definitive Guide to MongoDB* by Eelco Plugge, Tim Hawkins, and Peter Membrey (Apress, 2010). Visit www.apress.com/9781430230519.

The complete application containing the preceding snippets of code is available in the Apress repository and is named MONGODB_QUERY. It comes as a NetBeans project and was tested under Java 7.

Hibernate OGM and CRUD Operations

The four essential operations performed against a NoSQL database—Create, Read, Update and Delete—are available in Hibernate OGM out of the box. Actually, independently of JPA or the Hibernate Native API, Hibernate ORM delegates persistence and load queries to the OGM engine, which delegates CRUD operations to DatastoreProvider and GridDialect, and these interact with the NoSQL store.

In Chapters 3 and 4 you saw how to develop applications based on Hibernate OGM via the Hibernate Native API and Java Persistence API. It should be a piece of cake, therefore, to wrap the Players entity in Listing 6-1 into such an application.

Listing 6-1. The Players Entity

```
package hogm.hnapi.entity;

import java.io.Serializable;
...

@Entity
@Table(name = "atp_players")
@GenericGenerator(name = "mongodb_uuidgg", strategy = "uuid2")
public class Players implements Serializable {

    @Id
    @GeneratedValue(generator = "mongodb_uuidgg")
    private String id;
    @Column(name = "player_name")
    private String name;
    @Column(name = "player_surname")
    private String surname;
    @Column(name = "player_age")
    private int age;
    @Column(name = "player_birth")
    @Temporal(javax.persistence.TemporalType.DATE)
    private Date birth;
```

```java
    public String getName() {
        return name;
    }

    public void setName(String name) {
        this.name = name;
    }

    public String getSurname() {
        return surname;
    }

    public void setSurname(String surname) {
        this.surname = surname;
    }

    public int getAge() {
        return age;
    }

    public void setAge(int age) {
        this.age = age;
    }

    public Date getBirth() {
        return birth;
    }

    public void setBirth(Date birth) {
        this.birth = birth;
    }

    public String getId() {
        return id;
    }

    public void setId(String id) {
        this.id = id;
    }
}
```

Once that's done, you have access to CRUD operations. Suppose we have an instance of Players, named player. Using Hibernate OGM via Hibernate Native API, you can obtain the Hibernate session with the getCurrentSession or openSession methods.

- To persist the player instance, use the persist method:

```java
HibernateUtil.getSessionFactory().getCurrentSession().persist(player);
```

- To update the player instance, use the merge method:

  HibernateUtil.getSessionFactory().getCurrentSession().merge(player);

- To find the player instance by id, use the find method:

  HibernateUtil.getSessionFactory().getCurrentSession().get(Players.class, *id*);

- To delete the player instance, use the delete method:

  HibernateUtil.getSessionFactory().getCurrentSession().delete(player);

You can try all of these methods in a sample application named HOGM_MONGODB_HNAPI_CRUD, available in the Apress repository. It comes as a NetBeans project and was tested under GlassFish 3 AS. The interface application looks like Figure 6-9.

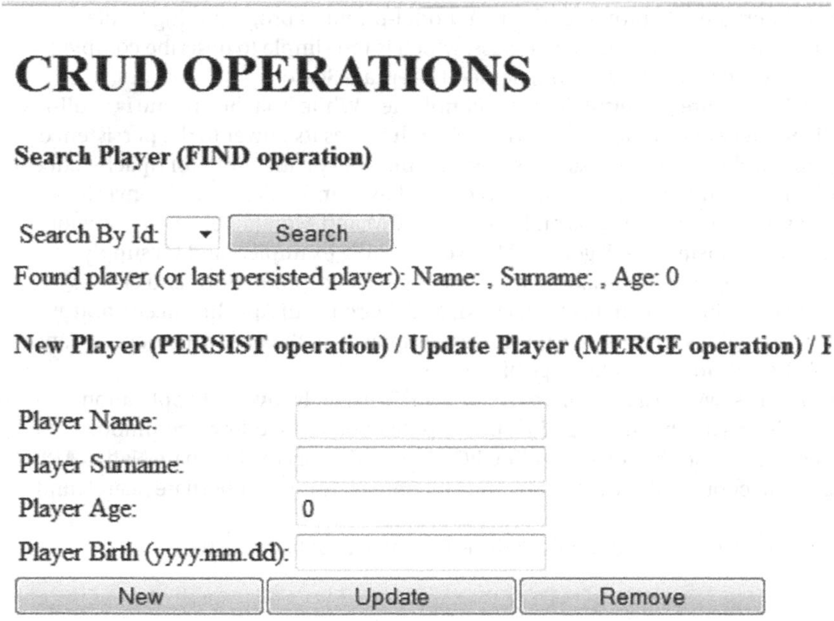

CRUD OPERATIONS

Search Player (FIND operation)

Search By Id: ▾ | Search |
Found player (or last persisted player): Name: , Surname: , Age: 0

New Player (PERSIST operation) / Update Player (MERGE operation) / F

Player Name: [   ]
Player Surname: [   ]
Player Age: [0   ]
Player Birth (yyyy.mm.dd): [   ]
| New | Update | Remove |

Figure 6-9. *Testing Hibernate OGM and CRUD operations*

Using Hibernate OGM via the Java Persistence API (em stands for EntityManager):

- To persist the player instance, use the persist method:

  em.persist(player);

- To update the player instance, use the merge method:

  em.merge(player);

- To find the player instance by id, use the find method:

  ```
  em.find(Players.class, id);
  ```

- To delete the player instance, use the delete method:

  ```
  em.delete (player);
  ```

You can try all of these methods in a sample application named HOGM_MONGODB_JPA_CRUD, available in the Apress repository. It comes as a NetBeans project and was tested under GlassFish 3 AS. The interface application looks like the one in Figure 6-9.

Hibernate Search and Apache Lucene

Basically, Hibernate/JPA and Apache Lucene deal with the same area—querying data. They both provide CRUD operations, a basic data unit (an entity in Hibernate, a document in Lucene) and the same programming concepts. The main difference lies in the fact that Hibernate/JPA promotes domain model-oriented programming, while Lucene deals with only a single, built-in data model—the Document class, which is too simple to describe complex associations. Combined, however, the two yield a higher-level API, named Hibernate Search.

Both Hibernate Search and Apache Lucene are powerful, robust technologies. While Apache Lucene is a full-text indexing and query engine with excellent query performance, Hibernate Search brings its power to the persistence domain model. The symbiosis works fairly well: Hibernate Search "squeezes" the query capabilities of Apache Lucene while providing support for the domain model and the synchronization of databases and indexes, and converting free text queries back to managed objects. Because our focus is on Hibernate OGM and MongoDB, I won't provide a Hibernate Search or Apache Lucene tutorial. Instead we'll get quickly to developing examples, and I'll supply sufficient information for you to understand the new Hibernate Search/Apache Lucene annotations and classes, without going into detail. We are going to combine Hibernate ORM, OGM, and Search with Apache Lucene and MongoDB into applications with query capabilities so you can explore the complexity of the querying process. Once you have a functional application, you'll be able to try a wide range of queries.

We will develop two applications. The first will be a Hibernate OGM/ via Hibernate Native API application and the second Hibernate OGM via JPA (details in Chapters 3 and 4). Both applications will follow a common, straightforward scenario: we'll create an entity (and the corresponding POJO, specific only to Hibernate Native API), persist several instances to a MongoDB collection, and execute some query samples through Hibernate Search and Apache Lucene.

The POJO is named Players and is shown in Listing 6-2 (this POJO is mapped in an hbm.xml file).

Listing 6-2. The Players Class

```
public class Players {

    private String id;
    private String name;
    private String surname;
    private int age;
    private Date birth;

    public String getName() {
        return name;
    }
```

```java
    public void setName(String name) {
        this.name = name;
    }

    public String getSurname() {
        return surname;
    }

    public void setSurname(String surname) {
        this.surname = surname;
    }

    public int getAge() {
        return age;
    }

    public void setAge(int age) {
        this.age = age;
    }

    public Date getBirth() {
        return birth;
    }

    public void setBirth(Date birth) {
        this.birth = birth;
    }

    public String getId() {
        return id;
    }

    public void setId(String id) {
        this.id = id;
    }
}
```

And the Players.hbm.xml file is shown in Listing 6-3.

Listing 6-3. Players.hbm.xml

```xml
<?xml version="1.0" encoding="UTF-8"?>
<!DOCTYPE hibernate-mapping PUBLIC "-//Hibernate/Hibernate Mapping DTD 3.0//EN"
"http://www.hibernate.org/dtd/hibernate-mapping-3.0.dtd">
<hibernate-mapping>
    <class name="hogm.hnapi.pojo.Players" table="atp_players">
        <id name="id" type="string">
            <column name="id" />
            <generator class="uuid2" />
        </id>
        <property name="name" type="string">
            <column name="player_name"/>
        </property>
```

```
        <property name="surname" type="string">
            <column name="player_surname"/>
        </property>
        <property name="age" type="int">
            <column name="player_age"/>
        </property>
        <property name="birth" type="date">
            <column name="player_birth"/>
        </property>
    </class>
</hibernate-mapping>
```

Or, if you prefer the entity version, the POJO becomes what's shown in Listing 6-4. (This entity is used in both applications.)

Listing 6-4. The Entity Version of Players

```java
import java.io.Serializable;
...

@Entity
@Table(name = "atp_players")
@GenericGenerator(name = "mongodb_uuidgg", strategy = "uuid2")
public class Players implements Serializable {

    @Id
    @GeneratedValue(generator = "mongodb_uuidgg")
    private String id;
    @Column(name = "player_name")
    private String name;
    @Column(name = "player_surname")
    private String surname;
    @Column(name = "player_age")
    private int age;
    @Column(name = "player_birth")
    @Temporal(javax.persistence.TemporalType.DATE)
    private Date birth;

    public String getName() {
        return name;
    }

    public void setName(String name) {
        this.name = name;
    }

    public String getSurname() {
        return surname;
    }
```

```java
    public void setSurname(String surname) {
        this.surname = surname;
    }

    public int getAge() {
        return age;
    }

    public void setAge(int age) {
        this.age = age;
    }

    public Date getBirth() {
        return birth;
    }

    public void setBirth(Date birth) {
        this.birth = birth;
    }

    public String getId() {
        return id;
    }

    public void setId(String id) {
        this.id = id;
    }
}
```

Common Steps

No matter which application type (OGM via the Hibernate Native API or via JPA), there are a few common steps to add Hibernate Search or Apache Lucene support:

1. In addition to the Hibernate OGM and MongoDB library (remember it from Chapter 1), we need to add at least two more JARs: `hibernate-search-orm-4.2.0.Final.jar` and `avro-1.6.3.jar`. Both are available in the Hibernate Search distribution, release 4.2.0 Final. Notice that many other JARs, including Apache Lucene and Object/Lucene core mapper, are available in Hibernate OGM and MongoDB library.

2. Next, we need to focus on our POJO (or entity) class. This is the first step to bring Hibernate Search into the equation—Hibernate Search-specific configurations are expressed via annotations. More precisely, we need to use a couple of annotations for mapping the POJO (entity).

   - We'll use the `@Indexed` annotation to mark the `Players` class as indexable (searchable). Entities that are not annotated with `@Indexed` will be ignored by the indexing process.

   - We then specify how the indexing will be done using the `@Field` annotation at the field or property level. There are a few supported attributes but, for now, it's enough to indicate whether the field or property is indexed (using the `index` attribute); whether the field or property is analyzed (using the `analyze` attribute); and whether the field or property is stored in the Lucene index (using the `store` attribute). More attributes and detailed descriptions are available in the official documentation.

- Since we have a Date field, we need to know a few things about how Hibernate Search works with dates. Dates are stored as "*yyyyMMddHHmmssSSS in GMT time (200611072203012 for Nov 7th of 2006 4:03PM and 12ms EST),*" but we can specify the appropriate resolution for storing a date in the index using the @DateBridge annotation (the resolution can be DAY, HOUR, YEAR, MINUTE, SECOND, MONTH and MILISECOND). We use the YEAR resolution.

- For numerical fields, like player age, we can use the @NumericField annotation. This is optional, but it can be useful for enabling efficient range query, and in sorting, and to speed up queries.

- Finally, to indicate a field or property as the document id (primary key), we need to annotate it with @DocumentId. This annotation is optional for entities that already contain an @Id annotation.

- For our needs, the @Indexed, @Field, @NumericField, @DateBridge and @DocumentId annotations are enough to configure the indexing process. Listing 6-5 shows the Players POJO after it has been marked with the Hibernate Search annotations.

Listing 6-5. The Players POJO with Annotations

```
package hogm.hnapi.pojo;

import org.hibernate.search.annotations.Analyze;
import org.hibernate.search.annotations.DateBridge;
import org.hibernate.search.annotations.DocumentId;
import org.hibernate.search.annotations.Field;
import org.hibernate.search.annotations.Index;
import org.hibernate.search.annotations.Indexed;
import org.hibernate.search.annotations.NumericField;
import org.hibernate.search.annotations.Resolution;
import org.hibernate.search.annotations.Store;
...

@Indexed
public class Players {

    @DocumentId
    private String id;
    @Field(index=Index.YES, analyze=Analyze.YES, store=Store.NO)
    private String name;
    @Field(index=Index.YES, analyze=Analyze.NO, store=Store.NO)
    private String surname;
    @NumericField
    @Field(index=Index.YES, analyze=Analyze.NO, store=Store.NO)
    private int age;
    @Field(index=Index.YES, analyze=Analyze.NO, store=Store.NO)
    @DateBridge(resolution = Resolution.YEAR)
    private Date birth;

    public String getName() {
        return name;
    }
```

```java
    public void setName(String name) {
        this.name = name;
    }

    public String getSurname() {
        return surname;
    }

    public void setSurname(String surname) {
        this.surname = surname;
    }

    public int getAge() {
        return age;
    }

    public void setAge(int age) {
        this.age = age;
    }

    public Date getBirth() {
        return birth;
    }

    public void setBirth(Date birth) {
        this.birth = birth;
    }

    public String getId() {
        return id;
    }

    public void setId(String id) {
        this.id = id;
    }
}
```

Or, if we apply these annotations to the Players entity, we get what's shown in Listing 6-6.

Listing 6-6. The Entity Version of Players with Annotations

```java
package hogm.hnapi.entity;

import org.hibernate.search.annotations.Analyze;
import org.hibernate.search.annotations.DateBridge;
import org.hibernate.search.annotations.DocumentId;
import org.hibernate.search.annotations.Field;
import org.hibernate.search.annotations.Index;
import org.hibernate.search.annotations.Indexed;
import org.hibernate.search.annotations.NumericField;
import org.hibernate.search.annotations.Resolution;
import org.hibernate.search.annotations.Store;
...
```

```java
@Entity
@Indexed
@Table(name = "atp_players")
@GenericGenerator(name = "mongodb_uuidgg", strategy = "uuid2")
public class Players implements Serializable {

    private static final long serialVersionUID = 1L;
    @DocumentId
    @Id
    @GeneratedValue(generator = "mongodb_uuidgg")
    private String id;
    @Column(name = "player_name")
    @Field(index=Index.YES, analyze=Analyze.YES, store=Store.NO)
    private String name;
    @Column(name = "player_surname")
    @Field(index=Index.YES, analyze=Analyze.NO, store=Store.NO)
    private String surname;
    @Column(name = "player_age")
    @NumericField
    @Field(index=Index.YES, analyze=Analyze.NO, store=Store.NO)
    private int age;
    @Column(name = "player_birth")
    @Field(index=Index.YES, analyze=Analyze.NO, store=Store.NO)
    @DateBridge(resolution = Resolution.YEAR)
    @Temporal(javax.persistence.TemporalType.DATE)
    private Date birth;

    public String getName() {
        return name;
    }

    public void setName(String name) {
        this.name = name;
    }

    public String getSurname() {
        return surname;
    }

    public void setSurname(String surname) {
        this.surname = surname;
    }

    public int getAge() {
        return age;
    }

    public void setAge(int age) {
        this.age = age;
    }
```

```java
    public Date getBirth() {
        return birth;
    }

    public void setBirth(Date birth) {
        this.birth = birth;
    }

    public String getId() {
        return id;
    }

    public void setId(String id) {
        this.id = id;
    }
}
```

3. Next, we have to provide some basic configuration information in hibernate.cfg.xml (or, in HibernateUtil) for OGM via the Hibernate Native API application, or in persistence.xml, for OGM via JPA.

We have to specify the directory provider; for Apache Lucene, a directory represents the type and place to store index files, and it comes bundled with a file system (FSDirectoryProvider) and an in-memory implementation (RAMDirectoryProvider), though it also supports custom implementations. Hibernate Search is responsible for the configuration and initialization of Lucene resources, including the directory via DirectoryProviders. We want easy access to index files (with the ability to physically inspect indexes with external tools, like Luke), so we'll use the file system to store them by setting the hibernate.search.default.directory_provider property as filesystem. Besides the directory provider, we also have to specify the default base directory for all indexes via the hibernate.search.default.indexBase property. Finally, we can specify the locking strategy (in this case, the filesystem-level lock) by setting the hibernate.search.default.locking_strategy property to single; this is a Java object lock held in memory. Add these configurations in hibernate.cfg.xml (or in HibernateUtil) for OGM via the Hibernate Native API, or in persistence.xml for OGM via JPA, like this:

```xml
//in hibernate.cfg.xml
<property name="hibernate.search.default.directory_provider">filesystem</property>
<property name="hibernate.search.default.indexBase">./Indexes</property>
<property name="hibernate.search.default.locking_strategy">single</property>...
```

Or:

```java
//in HibernateUtil
OgmConfiguration cfgogm = new OgmConfiguration();
...
cfgogm.setProperty("hibernate.search.default.directory_provider","filesystem");
cfgogm.setProperty("hibernate.search.default.indexBase","./Indexes");
cfgogm.setProperty("hibernate.search.default.locking_strategy", "single");
...
```

Or:

```
...
//in persistence.xml
<property name="hibernate.search.default.directory_provider" value="filesystem"/>
<property name="hibernate.search.default.indexBase" value="./Indexes"/>
<property name="hibernate.search.default.locking_strategy" value="single"/>
...
```

Finally, everything is configured and we are ready to start writing Lucene queries. But, from this point on, the code will be specific to each of the two applications. So let's start with the OGM via Hibernate Native API application.

Hibernate Search/Apache Lucene Querying—OGM via Native API

The first goal is to write a "select all" query that will help you become familiar with Lucene style in an OGM via Native API application. Following a step-by-step approach, we can write such a query, like this:

1. Create an `org.hibernate.search.FullTextSession`. This interface will spice up the Hibernate session with full-text search and indexing capabilities. This session provides two ways of writing queries: using the Hibernate Search query DSL (domain search language) or the native Lucene query. The code to accomplish this is:

   ```
   FullTextSession fullTextSession =
   Search.getFullTextSession(HibernateUtil.getSessionFactory().getCurrentSession());
   ```

2. Create an `org.hibernate.search.query.dsl.QueryBuilder` and use the new session to obtain a query builder that helps to simplify the query definition. Notice that we indicate that our query affects only the `Players` class:

   ```
   QueryBuilder queryBuilder = fullTextSession.getSearchFactory().
       buildQueryBuilder().forEntity(Players.class).get();
   ```

3. Create a Lucene query. As you'll see in the official documentation, there are several ways to build a Lucene query using `QueryBuilder`. For this example, we can use the `queryBuilder.all` method, which is a simple approach for obtaining whole documents:

   ```
   org.apache.lucene.search.Query query = queryBuilder.all().createQuery();
   ```

4. Define a sort rule (optional). We can easily define a sort rule using the Lucene sort capabilities. For example, we might need to sort the extracted players by name:

   ```
   org.apache.lucene.search.Sort sort = new Sort(new SortField("name", SortField.STRING));
   ```

5. Wrap the Lucene query in an `org.hibernate.FullTextQuery`. In order to configure the sort rule and execute the query, we need to wrap the Lucene query into a `FullTextQuery`, like this:

   ```
   FullTextQuery fullTextQuery = fullTextSession.createFullTextQuery(query, Players.class);
   ```

6. Specify the object lookup method and database retrieval method. For OGM you must specify object lookup and database retrieval methods (SKIP specifies to not check if

objects are already present in the second level cache or in the persistence context; FIND_BY_ID loads each object by its identifier one by one):

```
fullTextQuery.initializeObjectsWith(ObjectLookupMethod.SKIP,
DatabaseRetrievalMethod.FIND_BY_ID);
```

7. Set the sort rule. You can set the sort rule by calling the setSort method:

```
fullTextQuery.setSort(sort);
```

8. Execute the query. Finally, we execute the query and obtain the results in a java.util.List:

```
List<Players> results = fullTextQuery.list();
```

9. Optionally, clear up the session:

```
fullTextSession.clear();
```

We can put these nine steps in a method named selectAllAction to create our first Hibernate Search/Lucene query. You can find this method in a session bean, named SampleBean, in the package hogm.hnapi.ejb shown in Listing 6-7.

Listing 6-7. The selectAllAction Method

```
package hogm.hnapi.ejb;
...
public class SampleBean {
  ...
  public List<Players> selectAllAction() {

        log.info("Select all Players instance ...");

        FullTextSession fullTextSession =
                Search.getFullTextSession(HibernateUtil.getSessionFactory().getCurrentSession());
        QueryBuilder queryBuilder = fullTextSession.getSearchFactory().
                                        buildQueryBuilder().forEntity(Players.class).get();
        org.apache.lucene.search.Query query = queryBuilder.all().createQuery();
        org.apache.lucene.search.Sort sort = new Sort(new SortField("name", SortField.STRING));

        FullTextQuery fullTextQuery = fullTextSession.createFullTextQuery(query, Players.class);
        fullTextQuery.initializeObjectsWith(ObjectLookupMethod.SKIP,
                                        DatabaseRetrievalMethod.FIND_BY_ID);

        fullTextQuery.setSort(sort);
        List<Players> results = fullTextQuery.list();

        fullTextSession.clear();

        log.info("Search complete ...");

        return results;
    }
...
}
```

The nine steps can be used as a quick guide for writing many other kinds of queries. Now let's see how to write some common queries:

- *Select all players born in 1987*. This query (and similar queries) can be easily written using three methods: queryBuilder.keyword, which indicates we're searching for a specific word; TermContext.onField, which specifies in which Lucene field to look; and TermMatchingContext.matching, which tells what to look for. So, wrapping this query into a method named selectByYearAction looks like what's shown in Listing 6-8.

Listing 6-8. The selectByYearAction Method

```
package hogm.hnapi.ejb;
...
public class SampleBean {
  ...
public List<Players> selectByYearAction() {

        log.info("Search only Players instances 'born in 1987' ...");

        Calendar calendar = GregorianCalendar.getInstance(TimeZone.getTimeZone("UTC"));
        calendar.clear();

        calendar.set(Calendar.YEAR, 1987);

        FullTextSession fullTextSession =
                Search.getFullTextSession(HibernateUtil.getSessionFactory().getCurrentSession());
        QueryBuilder queryBuilder = fullTextSession.getSearchFactory().
                                        buildQueryBuilder().forEntity(Players.class).get();

    org.apache.lucene.search.Query query =
            queryBuilder.keyword().onField("birth").matching(calendar.getTime()).createQuery();

        FullTextQuery fullTextQuery = fullTextSession.createFullTextQuery(query, Players.class);
        fullTextQuery.initializeObjectsWith(ObjectLookupMethod.SKIP,
                                        DatabaseRetrievalMethod.FIND_BY_ID);

        List<Players> results = fullTextQuery.list();

        fullTextSession.clear();

        log.info("Search complete ...");

        return results;
    }
}
```

- *Select only a player named Rafael Nadal*. This query (and similar queries) searches for two words in two different fields, "Rafael" and "Nadal." The query looks for the first word in the player_surname column (surname field), and for the second word in the player_name column (name field). For this, you can use one of the aggregation operators, named must. (Aggregations operators allow you to combine simple queries into more complex queries.)

Wrapping the necessary code into a method named selectRafaelNadalAction shows this. The bool method indicates that we've created a Boolean query—a query that finds documents matching Boolean combinations of other queries. (See Listing 6-9.)

Listing 6-9. The selectRafaelNadalAction Method

```
package hogm.hnapi.ejb;
...
public class SampleBean {

  ...
public List<Players> selectRafaelNadalAction() {

        log.info("Search only Players instances that have the name 'Nadal' and surname 'Rafael' ...");

        FullTextSession fullTextSession =
                Search.getFullTextSession(HibernateUtil.getSessionFactory().getCurrentSession());
        QueryBuilder queryBuilder = fullTextSession.getSearchFactory().
                                        buildQueryBuilder().forEntity(Players.class).get();
        org.apache.lucene.search.Query query = queryBuilder.bool().must(queryBuilder.keyword()
        .onField("name").matching("Nadal").createQuery()).must(queryBuilder.keyword()
.onField("surname").matching("Rafael").createQuery()).createQuery();

        FullTextQuery fullTextQuery = fullTextSession.createFullTextQuery(query, Players.class);
        fullTextQuery.initializeObjectsWith(ObjectLookupMethod.SKIP,
                                            DatabaseRetrievalMethod.FIND_BY_ID);

        List<Players> results = fullTextQuery.list();
        fullTextSession.clear();

        log.info("Search complete ...");

        return results;
    }
}
```

- *Select players with surnames starting with the letter 'J.'* This query (and similar queries) can be written using wildcards. The ? represents a single character and the * represents any character sequence. The TermContext.wildcard method indicates that a wildcard query follows. Wrapping the necessary code into a method named selectJAction shows this. (See Listing 6-10.)

Listing 6-10. The selectJAction Method

```
package hogm.hnapi.ejb;
...
public class SampleBean {

  ...
public List<Players> selectJAction() {

        log.info("Search only Players that surnames begins with 'J' ...");
```

```
FullTextSession fullTextSession =
Search.getFullTextSession(HibernateUtil.getSessionFactory().getCurrentSession());
QueryBuilder queryBuilder = fullTextSession.getSearchFactory().
                                        buildQueryBuilder().forEntity(Players.class).get();

org.apache.lucene.search.Query query = queryBuilder.keyword().wildcard()
                            .onField("surname").matching("J*").createQuery();

FullTextQuery fullTextQuery = fullTextSession.createFullTextQuery(query, Players.class);
fullTextQuery.initializeObjectsWith(ObjectLookupMethod.SKIP,
                                        DatabaseRetrievalMethod.FIND_BY_ID);

List<Players> results = fullTextQuery.list();
fullTextSession.clear();

log.info("Search complete ...");

return results;
    }
}
```

- *Select players with ages in the interval (25,28).* This query (and similar queries) can be treated as range queries. Such a query searches for a value in an interval (boundaries included or not) or for a value below or above the interval boundary (boundaries included or not). You indicate that a range query follows by calling the QueryBuilder.range method. The interval is set by calling the from and to methods, and the interval's boundaries can be excluded by calling the excludeLimit method. Wrapping the necessary code into a method named select25To28AgeAction will show this. (See Listing 6-11.)

Listing 6-11. The select25To28AgeAction Method

```
package hogm.hnapi.ejb;
...
public class SampleBean {
  ...
public List<Players> select25To28AgeAction() {

        log.info("Search only Players that have ages between 25 and 28, excluding limits ...");

        FullTextSession fullTextSession =
                Search.getFullTextSession(HibernateUtil.getSessionFactory().getCurrentSession());
        QueryBuilder queryBuilder = fullTextSession.getSearchFactory().
                                buildQueryBuilder().forEntity(Players.class).get();

        org.apache.lucene.search.Query query = queryBuilder.range()
                                .onField("age").from(25).to(28).excludeLimit().createQuery();

        FullTextQuery fullTextQuery = fullTextSession.createFullTextQuery(query, Players.class);
        fullTextQuery.initializeObjectsWith(ObjectLookupMethod.SKIP,
                                        DatabaseRetrievalMethod.FIND_BY_ID);
```

```
        List<Players>results = fullTextQuery.list();
        fullTextSession.clear();

        log.info("Search complete ...");

        return results;
    }
}
```

■ **Note**   As you can see, you can easy model a range using the from, to, and excludeLimit methods. Beside these, Lucene provides the below and above methods. Using them in a logical approach, you can obtain the well-known operators "<" (less than), ">" (greater than), "<=" (less than or equal to)", and ">=" greater than or equal to).

There are many other kinds of queries you can write, you just have to explore more documentation about Hibernate Search and Apache Lucene. For the queries mentioned, I developed a complete application that's available in the Apress repository and is named HOGM_MONGODB_HNAPI_HS. It comes as a NetBeans project and was tested under GlassFish 3 AS. Figure 6-10 shows this application.

Insert Player																							
All Players				**Select only matching Rafael Nadal documents**				**Surnames J* Players**				**Age between 25 and 28 excluding limits, Players**				**Only Players born in 1987**			
Player Name	Player Surname	Player Age	Player Birth	Player Name	Player Surname	Player Age	Player Birth	Player Name	Player Surname	Player Age	Player Birth	Player Name	Player Surname	Player Age	Player Birth	Player Name	Player Surname	Player Age	Player Birth
Berdych	Tomas	27	16.09.1985	Nadal	Rafael	26	03.06.1986	Tipsarevic	Janko	28	21.06.1984	Berdych	Tomas	27	16.09.1985	Murray	Andy	25	1987
Murray	Andy	25	15.05.1987					Tsonga	Jo-Wilfried	27	16.04.1985	Nadal	Rafael	26	03.06.1986				
Nadal	Rafael	26	03.06.1986									Tipsarevic	Janko	28	21.06.1984				
Tipsarevic	Janko	28	21.06.1984									Tsonga	Jo-Wilfried	27	16.04.1985				
Tsonga	Jo-Wilfried	27	16.04.1985																

Figure 6-10. *The HOGM_MONGODB_HNAPI_HS application*

■ **Note**   You can rebuild the index (deleting it and then reloading all entities from the database) by calling the startAndWait method: fullTextSession.createIndexer().startAndWait();

When you have associations (or embedded objects), you need to provide a few more annotations. Associated objects (and embedded objects) can be indexed as part of the root entity index. For this, the association is marked with @IndexedEmbedded. When the association is bidirectional, the other side must be annotated with @ContainedIn. This helps Hibernate Search keep up to date the associations indexing process.

For example, let's suppose that the Players entity is in a many-to-many association with the Tournaments entity (each player participates in multiple tournaments and each tournament contains multiple players). (And keep in mind that POJOs annotations are specified in .hbm.xml files.) The annotated POJOs are shown in Listing 6-12 and Listing 6-13.

Listing 6-12. The Players POJO

```
package hogm.hnapi.pojo

import org.hibernate.search.annotations.Analyze;
import org.hibernate.search.annotations.DateBridge;
import org.hibernate.search.annotations.DocumentId;
import org.hibernate.search.annotations.Field;
import org.hibernate.search.annotations.Index;
import org.hibernate.search.annotations.Indexed;
import org.hibernate.search.annotations.IndexedEmbedded;
import org.hibernate.search.annotations.Resolution;
import org.hibernate.search.annotations.Store;
...

@Indexed
public class Players {

    @DocumentId
    private String id;
    @Field(index = Index.YES, analyze = Analyze.YES, store = Store.NO)
    private String name;
    @Field(index = Index.YES, analyze = Analyze.NO, store = Store.NO)
    private String surname;
    @Field(index = Index.YES, analyze = Analyze.NO, store = Store.NO)
    private int age;
    @Field(index = Index.YES, analyze = Analyze.NO, store = Store.NO)
    @DateBridge(resolution = Resolution.YEAR)
    private Date birth;
    @IndexedEmbedded
    Collection<Tournaments> tournaments = new ArrayList<Tournaments>(0);

    //getters and setters
...
}
```

Listing 6-13. The Tournaments POJO

```
package hogm.hnapi.pojo

import org.hibernate.search.annotations.Analyze;
import org.hibernate.search.annotations.ContainedIn;
import org.hibernate.search.annotations.DocumentId;
import org.hibernate.search.annotations.Field;
import org.hibernate.search.annotations.Index;
import org.hibernate.search.annotations.Indexed;
import org.hibernate.search.annotations.Store;

@Indexed
public class Tournaments {
```

```
@DocumentId
private String id;
@Field(index = Index.YES, analyze = Analyze.YES, store = Store.NO)
private String tournament;
@ContainedIn
Collection<Players> players = new ArrayList<Players>(0);

//getters and setters
...
}
```

Now wrap these POJOs into entities, as shown in Listing 6-14 and Listing 6-15.

Listing 6-14. The Players Entity

```
package hogm.hnapi.entity;

import org.hibernate.search.annotations.Analyze;
import org.hibernate.search.annotations.DateBridge;
import org.hibernate.search.annotations.DocumentId;
import org.hibernate.search.annotations.Field;
import org.hibernate.search.annotations.Index;
import org.hibernate.search.annotations.Indexed;
import org.hibernate.search.annotations.IndexedEmbedded;
import org.hibernate.search.annotations.Resolution;
import org.hibernate.search.annotations.Store;

@Entity
@Indexed
@Table(name = "atp_players")
@GenericGenerator(name = "mongodb_uuidgg", strategy = "uuid2")
public class Players implements Serializable {

    @DocumentId
    @Id
    @GeneratedValue(generator = "mongodb_uuidgg")
    private String id;
    @Column(name = "player_name")
    @Field(index = Index.YES, analyze = Analyze.YES, store = Store.NO)
    private String name;
    @Column(name = "player_surname")
    @Field(index = Index.YES, analyze = Analyze.NO, store = Store.NO)
    private String surname;
    @Column(name = "player_age")
    @Field(index = Index.YES, analyze = Analyze.NO, store = Store.NO)
    private int age;
    @Column(name = "player_birth")
    @Field
    @DateBridge(resolution = Resolution.YEAR)
    @Temporal(javax.persistence.TemporalType.DATE)
    private Date birth;
    @ManyToMany(cascade = CascadeType.PERSIST,fetch=FetchType.EAGER)
```

229

```
@IndexedEmbedded
private Collection<Tournaments> tournaments= new ArrayList<Tournaments>(0);

    //getters and setters
...
}
```

Listing 6-15. *The Tournaments Entity*

```
package hogm.hnapi.entity;

import org.hibernate.search.annotations.Analyze;
import org.hibernate.search.annotations.ContainedIn;
import org.hibernate.search.annotations.DocumentId;
import org.hibernate.search.annotations.Field;
import org.hibernate.search.annotations.Index;
import org.hibernate.search.annotations.Indexed;
import org.hibernate.search.annotations.Store;

@Entity
@Indexed
@Table(name = "atp_tournaments")
@GenericGenerator(name = "mongodb_uuidgg", strategy = "uuid2")
public class Tournaments implements Serializable {

    @DocumentId
    @Id
    @GeneratedValue(generator = "mongodb_uuidgg")
    private String id;
    @Field(index = Index.YES, analyze = Analyze.YES, store = Store.NO)
    private String tournament;
    @ManyToMany(mappedBy = "tournaments", fetch = FetchType.EAGER)
    @ContainedIn
    private Collection<Players> players = new ArrayList<Players>(0);

    //getters and setters
...
}
```

Now you can write Hibernate Search/Apache Lucene queries. (The official documentation can be a good place to start testing queries for associations.) For testing purposes, I've integrated the preceding POJOs and entities into an application named HOGM_MONGODB_HNAPI_ASSOCIATIONS_HS that can be downloaded from the Apress repository (there are two queries involved). It comes as a NetBeans project and was tested under GlassFish 3 AS. Figure 6-11 shows this application.

| Insert A Set Of Players (before each press drop MongoDB database from shell) |

Players -> Tournaments					Tournaments -> Players	
Player Name	**Player Surname**	**Player Age**	**Player Birth**	**Tournament Name**	**Tournament Name**	**Player**
Tsonga	Jo-Wilfried	27	16.04.1985	BNP Paribas Open Dubai Duty Free Tennis Championships ABN AMRO World Tennis Tournament	Sony Open Tennis	Berdych Tomas 27 16.09.1985 Murray Andy 25 15.05.1987 Del Potro Juan Martin 24 23.09.1988 Federer Roger 31 08.08.1981 Nadal Rafael 26 03.06.1986 Ferrer David 30 02.04.1982
Berdych	Tomas	27	16.09.1985	BNP Paribas Open Open Sud de France Sony Open Tennis Erste Bank Open Rakuten Japan Open Tennis Championships	Gerry Weber Open	Federer Roger 31 08.08.1981 Murray Andy 25 15.05.1987 Nadal Rafael 26 03.06.1986 Ferrer David 30 02.04.1982
Djokovic	Novak	25	22.05.1987	Open Sud de France Barclays ATP World Tour Finals ABN AMRO World Tennis Tournament BNP Paribas Open Aegon Championships Dubai Duty Free Tennis Championships Rakuten Japan Open Tennis Championships China Open	Shanghai Rolex Masters	Murray Andy 25 15.05.1987 Federer Roger 31 08.08.1981 Nadal Rafael 26 03.06.1986 Ferrer David 30 02.04.1982 Del Potro Juan Martin 24 23.09.1988
				Brisbane International BNP Paribas Open Sony Open Tennis Open Sud de France Aegon Championships	If Stockholm Open	Murray Andy 25 15.05.1987 Ferrer David 30 02.04.1982 Del Potro Juan Martin 24 23.09.1988 Nadal Rafael 26 03.06.1986

Figure 6-11. *The HOGM_MONGODB_HNAPI_ASSOCIATIONS_HS application*

■ **Note** You can easily drop a MongoDB database from the shell by typing the command db.dropDatabase();.

Hibernate Search/Apache Lucene Querying—OGM via JPA

Remember the "select all" query we wrote earlier? This time, we'll write the same query for an application based on OGM via JPA. The steps for accomplishing this task are:

1. Create an org.hibernate.search.jpa.FullTextEntityManager. This interface spices up the OGM EntityManager with full-text search and indexing capabilities. Here's the code to accomplish this (em is the EntityManager instance):

```
FullTextEntityManager fullTextEntityManager =
                org.hibernate.search.jpa.Search.getFullTextEntityManager(em);
```

2. Create an org.hibernate.search.query.dsl.QueryBuilder. Use the new entity manager to obtain a query builder that will help simplify the query definition. Note that you indicate that the query affects only the Players class:

```
QueryBuilder queryBuilder = fullTextEntityManager.getSearchFactory().
buildQueryBuilder().forEntity(Players.class).get();
```

3. Create a Lucene query. As the official documentation shows, there are several ways to build a Lucene query using queryBuilder. For this example, we can use the queryBuilder.all method, which is a simple approach for obtaining whole documents:

```
org.apache.lucene.search.Query query = queryBuilder.all().createQuery();
```

4. Define a sort rule (optional). You can easily define a sort rule using the Lucene sort capabilities. For example, you may need to sort the extracted players by name:

```
org.apache.lucene.search.Sort sort = new Sort(new SortField("name", SortField.STRING));
```

5. Wrap the Lucene query in an org.hibernate.FullTextQuery. In order to set the sort rule and execute the query, you need to wrap the Lucene query in a FullTextQuery, like this:

```
FullTextQuery fullTextQuery = fullTextEntityManager.createFullTextQuery(query, Players.class);
```

6. Specify the object lookup method and the database retrieval method. For OGM, you must specify object lookup and database retrieval methods, like this:

```
fullTextQuery.initializeObjectsWith(ObjectLookupMethod.SKIP,
DatabaseRetrievalMethod.FIND_BY_ID);
```

7. Set the sort rule. You can set the sort rule by calling the setSort method, like so:

```
fullTextQuery.setSort(sort);
```

8. Execute the query. Finally, you can execute the query and obtain the results in a java.util.List:

```
...
List<Players> results = fullTextQuery.getResultList();
...
```

9. Clear up the session (optional):

```
fullTextEntityManager.clear();
```

Now, you can put these nine steps in a method named selectAllAction to obtain the Hibernate Search/Lucene query shown in Listing 6-16.

Listing 6-16. The selectAllAction Method

```
package hogm.jpa.ejb;
...
public class SampleBean {
...
public List<Players> selectAllAction() {

        log.info("Select all Players instance ...");
```

```
FullTextEntityManager fullTextEntityManager =
                          org.hibernate.search.jpa.Search.getFullTextEntityManager(em);

QueryBuilder queryBuilder = fullTextEntityManager.getSearchFactory().
                              buildQueryBuilder().forEntity(Players.class).get();
org.apache.lucene.search.Sort sort = new Sort(new SortField("name", SortField.STRING));
org.apache.lucene.search.Query query = queryBuilder.all().createQuery();

FullTextQuery fullTextQuery = fullTextEntityManager.createFullTextQuery(query, Players.class);
fullTextQuery.initializeObjectsWith(ObjectLookupMethod.SKIP,
                              DatabaseRetrievalMethod.FIND_BY_ID);

fullTextQuery.setSort(sort);
List<Players> results = fullTextQuery.getResultList();

fullTextEntityManager.clear();

log.info("Search complete ...");

return results;
    }
}
```

The nine steps can be used as a quick guide for writing many other kinds of queries. In addition, you can see how to write some common queries (these are the same queries from the section *"Hibernate Search/Apache Lucene Querying OGM via Native API,"* rewritten for the OGM via JPA case).

- *Select all players born in 1987.* This query (and similar queries) can be easily written using three methods: QueryBuilder.keyword, which indicates we're searching for a specific word; TermContext.onField, whichspecifies in which Lucene field to look; and TermMatchingContext.matching, which tells what to look for. So, wrapping this query into a method named selectByYearAction looks like what's shown in Listing 6-17.

Listing 6-17. The selectByYearAction Method

```
package hogm.jpa.ejb;
...
public class SampleBean {
...

public List<Players> selectByYearAction() {

    log.info("Search only Players instances born in 1987 ...");

    Calendar calendar = GregorianCalendar.getInstance(TimeZone.getTimeZone("UTC"));
    calendar.clear();

    calendar.set(Calendar.YEAR, 1987);

    FullTextEntityManager fullTextEntityManager =
                          org.hibernate.search.jpa.Search.getFullTextEntityManager(em);
```

```
        QueryBuilder queryBuilder = fullTextEntityManager.getSearchFactory().
                                    buildQueryBuilder().forEntity(Players.class).get();

        org.apache.lucene.search.Query query = queryBuilder.keyword()
                            .onField("birth").matching(calendar.getTime()).createQuery();

        FullTextQuery fullTextQuery = fullTextEntityManager.createFullTextQuery(query, Players.class);
        fullTextQuery.initializeObjectsWith(ObjectLookupMethod.SKIP,
                                            DatabaseRetrievalMethod.FIND_BY_ID);

        List<Players> results = fullTextQuery.getResultList();

        fullTextEntityManager.clear();

        log.info("Search complete ...");

        return results;
    }
}
```

- *Select only the player named Rafael Nadal.* This query (and similar queries) searches for two words in two different fields, "Rafael" and "Nadal." The query looks for the first word in the player_surname column (surname field), and for the second word in the player_name column (name field). For this, you can use one of the aggregation operators, named must. Wrapping the necessary code into a method named selectRafaelNadalAction shows this. The bool method indicates that we have created a Boolean query. (See Listing 6-18.)

Listing 6-18. The selectRafaelNadalAction Method

```
package hogm.jpa.ejb;
...
public class SampleBean {
...
public List<Players> selectRafaelNadalAction() {

        log.info("Search only Players instances that have the name 'Nadal' and surname 'Rafael' ...");

        FullTextEntityManager fullTextEntityManager =
                            org.hibernate.search.jpa.Search.getFullTextEntityManager(em);
        QueryBuilder queryBuilder = fullTextEntityManager.getSearchFactory().
                                    buildQueryBuilder().forEntity(Players.class).get();

        org.apache.lucene.search.Query query = queryBuilder.bool().must(queryBuilder.keyword()
                    .onField("name").matching("Nadal").createQuery()).must(queryBuilder.keyword()
                    .onField("surname").matching("Rafael").createQuery()).createQuery();

        FullTextQuery fullTextQuery = fullTextEntityManager.createFullTextQuery(query, Players.class);
        fullTextQuery.initializeObjectsWith(ObjectLookupMethod.SKIP,
                                            DatabaseRetrievalMethod.FIND_BY_ID);
```

```
        List<Players> results = fullTextQuery.getResultList();
        fullTextEntityManager.clear();

        log.info("Search complete ...");

        return results;
    }
}
```

- *Select players with surnames starting with the letter 'J.'* This query (and similar queries) can be written using wildcards. The ? represents a single character and the * represents any character sequence. The TermContext.wildcard method indicates that a wildcard query follows. Wrapping the necessary code into a method named selectJAction will show this. (See Listing 6-19.)

Listing 6-19. The selectJAction Method

```
package hogm.jpa.ejb;
...
public class SampleBean {
...
public List<Players> selectJAction() {

        log.info("Search only Players that surnames begins with 'J' ...");

        FullTextEntityManager fullTextEntityManager =
                        org.hibernate.search.jpa.Search.getFullTextEntityManager(em);

        QueryBuilder queryBuilder = fullTextEntityManager.getSearchFactory()
                                .buildQueryBuilder().forEntity(Players.class).get();

        org.apache.lucene.search.Query query = queryBuilder.keyword().wildcard()
                                .onField("surname").matching("J*").createQuery();

        FullTextQuery fullTextQuery = fullTextEntityManager.createFullTextQuery(query, Players.class);
        fullTextQuery.initializeObjectsWith(ObjectLookupMethod.SKIP,
                                                DatabaseRetrievalMethod.FIND_BY_ID);

        List<Players> results = fullTextQuery.getResultList();
        fullTextEntityManager.clear();

        log.info("Search complete ...");

        return results;
    }
}
```

- *Select players with ages in the interval (25,28).* This query (and similar queries) can be treated as range queries. Such a query searches for a value in an interval (boundaries included or not) or for a value below or above the interval boundary (boundaries included or not). You indicate that a range query follows by calling the queryBuilder.range method. The interval is set by calling the from and to methods, and the interval's boundaries can be excluded by calling the excludeLimit method. Wrapping the necessary code into a method named select25To28AgeAction will show this. (See Listing 6-20.)

Listing 6-20. The select25To28AgeAction Method

```
package hogm.jpa.ejb;
...
public class SampleBean {
...
public List<Players> select25To28AgeAction() {

        log.info("Search only Players that have ages between 25 and 28, excluding limits ...");

        FullTextEntityManager fullTextEntityManager =
                                org.hibernate.search.jpa.Search.getFullTextEntityManager(em);

        QueryBuilder queryBuilder = fullTextEntityManager.getSearchFactory()
                                .buildQueryBuilder().forEntity(Players.class).get();

        org.apache.lucene.search.Query query = queryBuilder.range().onField("age")
                                .from(25).to(28).excludeLimit().createQuery();

        FullTextQuery fullTextQuery = fullTextEntityManager.createFullTextQuery(query, Players.class);
        fullTextQuery.initializeObjectsWith(ObjectLookupMethod.SKIP,
                                                DatabaseRetrievalMethod.FIND_BY_ID);

        List<Players> results = fullTextQuery.getResultList();
        fullTextEntityManager.clear();

        log.info("Search complete ...");

        return results;
    }
}
```

There are many other kinds of queries you can write, you just have to delve into the available documentation about Hibernate Search and Apache Lucene. For the queries covered, I developed a complete application that's available in the Apress repository and is named HOGM_MONGODB_JPA_HS. It comes as a NetBeans project and was tested under GlassFish 3 AS. Figure 6-12 shows this application.

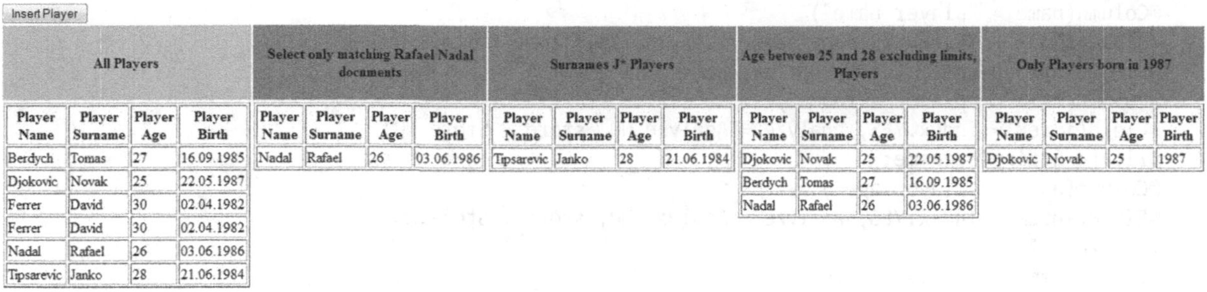
Insert Player

All Players

Player Name	Player Surname	Player Age	Player Birth
Berdych	Tomas	27	16.09.1985
Djokovic	Novak	25	22.05.1987
Ferrer	David	30	02.04.1982
Ferrer	David	30	02.04.1982
Nadal	Rafael	26	03.06.1986
Tipsarevic	Janko	28	21.06.1984

Select only matching Rafael Nadal documents

Player Name	Player Surname	Player Age	Player Birth
Nadal	Rafael	26	03.06.1986

Surnames J* Players

Player Name	Player Surname	Player Age	Player Birth
Tipsarevic	Janko	28	21.06.1984

Age between 25 and 28 excluding limits, Players

Player Name	Player Surname	Player Age	Player Birth
Djokovic	Novak	25	22.05.1987
Berdych	Tomas	27	16.09.1985
Nadal	Rafael	26	03.06.1986

Only Players born in 1987

Player Name	Player Surname	Player Age	Player Birth
Djokovic	Novak	25	1987

Figure 6-12. *The HOGM_MONGODB_JPA_HS application*

■ **Note** You can rebuild the index (deleting it and then reloading all entities from the database) by calling the `startAndWait` method: `fullTextEntityManager.createIndexer().startAndWait();`

When you have associations (or embedded objects), you need to provide a few more annotations. Associated objects (and embedded objects) can be indexed as part of the root entity index. For this, the association is marked with `@IndexedEmbedded`. When the association is bidirectional, the other side must be annotated with `@ContainedIn`. This helps Hibernate Search keep the associations indexing process up to date.

For example, let's suppose that the `Players` entity is in a many-to-many association with the `Tournaments` entity (each player participates in multiple tournaments and each tournament contains multiple players). The annotated `Players` entity listing is shown in Listing 6-21.

Listing 6-21. The Annotated Players Entity

```
package hogm.jpa.entity;

import org.hibernate.search.annotations.Analyze;
import org.hibernate.search.annotations.DateBridge;
import org.hibernate.search.annotations.DocumentId;
import org.hibernate.search.annotations.Field;
import org.hibernate.search.annotations.Index;
import org.hibernate.search.annotations.Indexed;
import org.hibernate.search.annotations.IndexedEmbedded;
import org.hibernate.search.annotations.Resolution;
import org.hibernate.search.annotations.Store;

@Entity
@Indexed
@Table(name = "atp_players")
@GenericGenerator(name = "mongodb_uuidgg", strategy = "uuid2")
public class Players implements Serializable {

    @DocumentId
    @Id
    @GeneratedValue(generator = "mongodb_uuidgg")
    private String id;
```

```
@Column(name = "player_name")
@Field(index = Index.YES, analyze = Analyze.YES, store = Store.NO)
private String name;
@Column(name = "player_surname")
@Field(index = Index.YES, analyze = Analyze.NO, store = Store.NO)
private String surname;
@Column(name = "player_age")
@Field(index = Index.YES, analyze = Analyze.NO, store = Store.NO)
private int age;
@Column(name = "player_birth")
@Field
@DateBridge(resolution = Resolution.YEAR)
@Temporal(javax.persistence.TemporalType.DATE)
private Date birth;
@ManyToMany(cascade = CascadeType.PERSIST,fetch=FetchType.EAGER)
@IndexedEmbedded
private Collection<Tournaments> tournaments= new ArrayList<Tournaments>(0);

    //getters and setters
...
}
```

And the Tournaments entity is shown in Listing 6-22.

Listing 6-22. The Annotated Tournaments Entity

```
package hogm.jpa.entity;

import org.hibernate.search.annotations.Analyze;
import org.hibernate.search.annotations.ContainedIn;
import org.hibernate.search.annotations.DocumentId;
import org.hibernate.search.annotations.Field;
import org.hibernate.search.annotations.Index;
import org.hibernate.search.annotations.Indexed;
import org.hibernate.search.annotations.Store;

@Entity
@Indexed
@Table(name = "atp_tournaments")
@GenericGenerator(name = "mongodb_uuidgg", strategy = "uuid2")
public class Tournaments implements Serializable {

    @DocumentId
    @Id
    @GeneratedValue(generator = "mongodb_uuidgg")
    private String id;
    @Field(index = Index.YES, analyze = Analyze.YES, store = Store.NO)
    private String tournament;
    @ManyToMany(mappedBy = "tournaments", fetch = FetchType.EAGER)
```

```
@ContainedIn
private Collection<Players> players = new ArrayList<Players>(0);

//getters and setters
...
}
```

Now you can write Hibernate Search/Apache Lucene queries. (The official documentation can be a good place to start testing queries for associations.) For testing purposes, I've integrated the preceding entities into an application named HOGM_MONGODB_JPA_ASOCIATIONS_HS that can be downloaded from the Apress repository (there are two queries involved). It comes as a NetBeans project and was tested under GlassFish 3 AS. Figure 6-13 shows this application.

Insert A Set Of Players (before each press drop MongoDB database from shell)										
Players -> Tournaments					**Tournaments -> Players**					
Player Name	**Player Surname**	**Player Age**	**Player Birth**	**Tournament Name**	**Tournament Name**	**Player**				
Tsonga	Jo-Wilfried	27	16.04.1985	China Open BMW Open Aegon Championships	Sony Open Tennis	Federer	Roger	31	08.08.1981	
						Del Potro	Juan Martin	24	23.09.1988	
						Nadal	Rafael	26	03.06.1986	
						Ferrer	David	30	02.04.1982	
Berdych	Tomas	27	16.09.1985	BNP Paribas Open If Stockholm Open BMW Open Brisbane International	Gerry Weber Open	Del Potro	Juan Martin	24	23.09.1988	
						Nadal	Rafael	26	03.06.1986	
						Djokovic	Novak	25	22.05.1987	
Djokovic	Novak	25	22.05.1987	Open Sud de France Gerry Weber Open Coupe Rogers Aegon Championships If Stockholm Open China Open Barclays ATP World Tour Finals BMW Open	If Stockholm Open	Federer	Roger	31	08.08.1981	
						Del Potro	Juan Martin	24	23.09.1988	
						Berdych	Tomas	27	16.09.1985	
						Djokovic	Novak	25	22.05.1987	
						Ferrer	David	30	02.04.1982	
						Murray	Andy	25	15.05.1987	

Figure 6-13. *The HOGM_MONGODB_JPA_ASSOCIATIONS_HS application*

We stop here, but this may be just the beginning of your exploration of the amazing power of Hibernate Search and Apache Lucene combined. I've given you a starting point for querying MongoDB collections via OGM and Hibernate Search/Apache Lucene. From this point forward, it's up to you how much you go in the Hibernate Search/Apache Lucene territory.

Hibernate OGM JP-QL Parser

According to the Hibernate OGM documentation, version 4.0.0Beta1 includes a JP-QL basic parser capable of converting simple queries using Hibernate Search. Currently, there are several limitations in using it, iincluding:

- No join, aggregation, or other relational operations are implied.

- The Hibernate Session API is used (JPA integration is coming).

- The target entities and properties are indexed by Hibernate Search (currently there's no validation).

I tried to work around these limitations, but have not been able to develop a functional application to exploit the JP-QL parser for simple queries. I tried, for the `Players` entity annotated with `@Indexed`, `@Field,` and so on, a simple query, like this:

```
Query query = HibernateUtil.getSessionFactory().getCurrentSession().createQuery("from Players p");
```

Unfortunately, my multiple approaches failed with one single and annoying error: `java.lang.`
`NullPointerException`. The indexing process seems to work fine, but the query results list is always null.

Anyway, this is not such a big issue, since the JP-QL parser is very young and, by the time you read this section, this information may well be obsolete. The JP-QL parser may be more generous with its query support by then. For now, you can use the MongoDB Java driver and, of course, Hibernate Search and Apache Lucene.

Summary

After all the hard work of the previous chapters, in this chapter we gathered the fruits. We were able to work with the stored data by writing queries against MongoDB databases. In particular, in this chapter, you learned how to write queries using Hibernate Search/Apache Lucene and the MongoDB Java driver. My aim was to provide the basic information about writing a pure MongoDB Java driver application and an OGM via Native API and/or via JPA application ready to query a MongoDB database.

CHAPTER 7

■ ■ ■

MongoDB e-Commerce Database Model

The market for open source e-commerce software keeps on growing every year. For proof, just look at the many popular platforms that are used today as starting points for a variety of e-commerce applications. For example, Magento, Zen Cart, and Spree all provide database schemas ready for storing and querying categories, products, orders, inventories, and so on. Despite the differences among these platforms, they all have something in common: they provide a SQL database.

For NoSQL stores, the e-commerce software market is a challenge, with most NoSQL stores considered inappropriate for e-commerce. MongoDB, however, is robust and flexible, with features like support for rich data models, indexed queries, atomic operations, and replicated writes that prompt us to ask: is MongoDB suitable for e-commerce applications? Well, this question waits for an authoritative answer, which will probably emerge after both the enthusiasm and misconceptions regarding MongoDB's suitability for e-commerce application begin to wane, and things start to calm down.

It's generally agreed that MongoDB is fast, reduces the number of tables and associations by using documents (which are conceptually simpler than tables), and provides flexible schemas. But it has some drawbacks that center around transactions, consistency, and durability. SQL databases, in contrast, provide safety, but they're not that fast, have rigid schemas, need dozens of tables (associations), and can slow development progress (sometimes we need to write complex queries). Nevertheless, it seems that "safety" is the operative word, since no e-seller (e-retailer) wants to lose an order or money because of database inconsistency.

Still, "*a full-featured, developer-centric e-commerce platform that makes custom code easy, with powerful templates & expressive syntax*", named Forward (http://getfwd.com/) is ready to show everybody that MongoDB is more than suitable for e-commerce applications. And so, on a smaller scale, I'll try to sustain this affirmation by developing an e-commerce data model using MongoDB, and using it in an enterprise application based on Hibernate OGM via JPA and Hibernate Search/Apache Lucene.

In this chapter, I'll look at converting (or adapting) a specific SQL schema for e-commerce applications to a MongoDB schema. In Figure 7-1, you can see a database schema for a medium-complexity e-commerce application; most of the tables are self-explanatory in an e-commerce context. The main tables are categories, products, orders, and users.

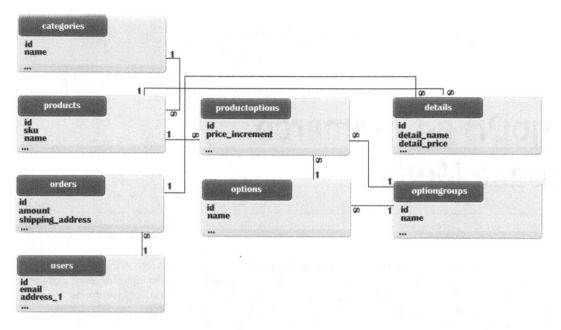

Figure 7-1. *SQL e-commerce database schema*

The main goal is to develop a MongoDB database schema similar to the one in Figure 7-1. By similar, I mean that we want to reproduce the main functionality (the same query capabilities), not the same tables, associations and fields. Moreover, we will write the corresponding JPA entities for it. We're going to use Hibernate OGM via JPA, so we'll need JPA annotations. And we'll be using Hibernate Search and Apache Lucene for querying, so we'll need Hibernate Search-specific annotations for indexing data in Lucene.

Even if you're not an e-retailer, you're probably very familiar with many e-commerce terms from the client perspective, especially categories, products, promotions, orders, shopping carts, purchase orders, payment, shipping addresses and so on. Such terms are well-known to every Internet user, so I won't try to explain them here.

MongoDB E-commerce Database Architecture

In Figure 7-2, you can see the MongoDB e-commerce database architecture I propose, which I named eshop_db. The diagram contains the MongoDB collections, their associations, and the corresponding JPA entities (but not the fields).

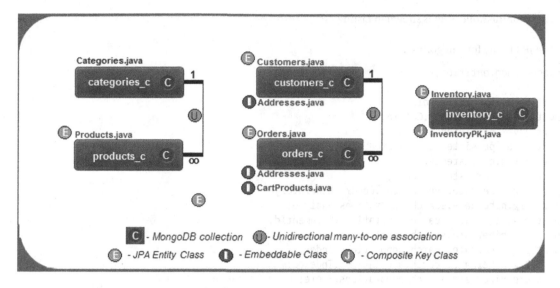

Figure 7-2. *MongoDB E-commerce database schema*

Model the Categories Collection (categories_c)

The `categories_c` collection corresponds to the `categories` table.

Sorting the products by categories is a common capability on most e-commerce sites. Very likely, the SQL table specific to categories stores the name of each category and a one-to-many (or, sometimes, a many-to-many) lazy association to the table responsible for storing products. The idea is to load category names very quickly (without their products), since they appear on the first page of the e-commerce web site. The products can be loaded later, after the user chooses a category. But though this works in the case of SQL, in MongoDB you need to be very careful with associations, since they may start transactions. Our aim is to avoid transactions as much as possible, so I didn't define any association in the `categories_c` collection.

I created the categories collection (`categories_c`) with the structure shown in Figure 7-3. As you can see, each document stores an identifier and the category name:

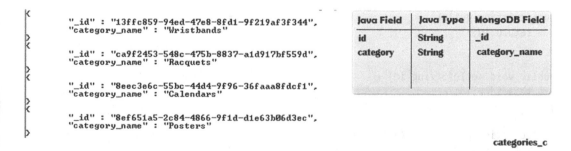

Figure 7-3. *Document sample from the categories_c collection*

The JPA entity for this collection is shown in Listing 7-1.

Listing 7-1. The JPA Entity for categories_c

```
1       package eshop.entities;
2
3       import java.io.Serializable;
4       import javax.persistence.Column;
5       import javax.persistence.Entity;
6       import javax.persistence.GeneratedValue;
7       import javax.persistence.Id;
8       import javax.persistence.Table;
9       import org.hibernate.annotations.GenericGenerator;
10      import org.hibernate.search.annotations.Analyze;
11      import org.hibernate.search.annotations.DocumentId;
12      import org.hibernate.search.annotations.Field;
13      import org.hibernate.search.annotations.Index;
14      import org.hibernate.search.annotations.Indexed;
15      import org.hibernate.search.annotations.Store;
16
17      @Entity
18      @Indexed
19      @Table(name = "categories_c")
20      public class Categories implements Serializable {
21
22          private static final long serialVersionUID = 1L;
23          @DocumentId
24          @Id
25          @GeneratedValue(generator = "uuid")
26          @GenericGenerator(name = "uuid", strategy = "uuid2")
27          private String id;
28          @Column(name = "category_name")
29          @Field(index = Index.YES, analyze = Analyze.NO, store = Store.YES)
30          private String category;
31
32          public String getId() {
33              return id;
34          }
35
36          public void setId(String id) {
37              this.id = id;
38          }
39
40          public String getCategory() {
41              return category;
42          }
43
44          public void setCategory(String category) {
45              this.category = category;
46          }
47
48          @Override
```

```
49          public int hashCode() {
50              int hash = 0;
51              hash += (id != null ? id.hashCode() : 0);
52              return hash;
53          }
54
55          @Override
56          public boolean equals(Object object) {
57              if (!(object instanceof Categories)) {
58                  return false;
59              }
60              Categories other = (Categories) object;
61              if ((this.id == null && other.id != null) || (this.id != null &&
                    !this.id.equals(other.id))) {
62                  return false;
63              }
64              return true;
65          }
66
67          @Override
68          public String toString() {
69              return "eshop.entities.Categories[ id=" + id + " ]";
70          }
71      }
72
```

Notice that line 29 specifies that the category id (id field) and category name (category_name field) should be searchable with Lucene and disables analyzers. We don't need analyzers because we search the category as is (not by the words it contains), and we'll sort the categories by name (Lucene doesn't let you analyze fields used for sorting operations). Moreover, category names are stored in the Lucene index. This consumes space in the index, but not a considerable amount, since you won't want so many categories as to cause concern. This allows us to take advantage of projection (notice that the ids are automatically stored). Using projection allows us, in the future, to add more searchable, non-lazy fields to this collection, such as category code, category description, and so on, but still extract only the categories names. Of course, this is just an approach (not a rule) specific to Lucene. If you choose to use JP-QL queries (when Hibernate OGM provides support for such queries), things will be different.

Model The Products Collection (products_c)

The products_c collection corresponds to the products and productoptions tables.

In the collection dedicated to products (products_c), the document for each product stores two kinds of information: general data, such as SKU, name, price, description and so on; and the kind of data that in a relational model usually needs additional tables, such as a product's gallery and a product's options (for example, colors, sizes, types, and so on). Instead of using additional tables and associations, I'm going to store each product's gallery and options in embedded collections. This makes sense, because these physical details are unique features of the product. Moreover, the products_c collection is the owner side of the unidirectional many-to-one association with the categories_c collection, so it stores the foreign keys of the corresponding categories.

In Figure 7-4, you can see such a document sample.

```
{
        "_id" : "5eb859c8-e01c-4136-a4fb-244bf13211e9",
        "category_id" : "82706202-d7e9-4733-a038-d536eac9fc8c",
        "colors" : [
                {
                        "product_colors" : "Red"
                },
                {
                        "product_colors" : "Khaki"
                },
                {
                        "product_colors" : "Black"
                }
        ],
        "gallery" : [
                {
                        "product_gallery" : "tops_0001_4.png"
                },
                {
                        "product_gallery" : "tops_0001_1.png"
                },
                {
                        "product_gallery" : "tops_0001_3.png"
                },
                {
                        "product_gallery" : "tops_0001_2.png"
                }
        ],
        "product_description" : "This T-Shirt is only for real fans ...",
        "product_name" : "Bull Logo T-Shirt",
        "product_old_price" : 0,
        "product_price" : 26.9,
        "product_sku" : "TOPS_0001",
        "sizes" : [
                {
                        "product_sizes" : "M"
                },
                {
                        "product_sizes" : "L"
                },
                {
                        "product_sizes" : "XXL"
                },
                {
                        "product_sizes" : "XL"
                }
        ]
}
                                                                    products_c
```

Java Field	Java Type	MongoDB Field
id	String	_id
sku	String	product_sku
product	String	product_name
price	double	product_price
old_price	double	product_old_price
description	String	product_description
gallery	List<String>	product_gallery
colors	List<String>	product_colors
sizes	List<String>	product_sizes
@ManyToOne category	Categories	category_id

Figure 7-4. *Sample document from products_c collection*

Each product will be represented by such a document. The colors and sizes embedded collections will be visible only for products that have these options.

The JPA entity for this collection is shown in Listing 7-2.

Listing 7-2. The JPA entity for products_c

```
1     package eshop.entities;
2
3     import java.io.Serializable;
4     import java.util.ArrayList;
5     import java.util.List;
6     import javax.persistence.Column;
7     import javax.persistence.ElementCollection;
8     import javax.persistence.Entity;
9     import javax.persistence.FetchType;
10    import javax.persistence.GeneratedValue;
11    import javax.persistence.Id;
12    import javax.persistence.ManyToOne;
13    import javax.persistence.Table;
14    import org.hibernate.annotations.GenericGenerator;
15    import org.hibernate.search.annotations.Analyze;
16    import org.hibernate.search.annotations.DocumentId;
17    import org.hibernate.search.annotations.Field;
18    import org.hibernate.search.annotations.Index;
19    import org.hibernate.search.annotations.Indexed;
20    import org.hibernate.search.annotations.IndexedEmbedded;
```

```
21      import org.hibernate.search.annotations.NumericField;
22      import org.hibernate.search.annotations.Store;
23
24      @Entity
25      @Indexed
26      @Table(name = "products_c")
27      public class Products implements Serializable {
28
29          private static final long serialVersionUID = 1L;
30          @DocumentId
31          @Id
32          @GeneratedValue(generator = "uuid")
33          @GenericGenerator(name = "uuid", strategy = "uuid2")
34          private String id;
35          @Column(name = "product_sku")
36          @Field(index = Index.YES, analyze = Analyze.NO, store = Store.NO)
37          private String sku;
38          @Column(name = "product_name")
39          @Field(index = Index.YES, analyze = Analyze.YES, store = Store.NO)
40          private String product;
41          @Column(name = "product_price")
42          @NumericField
43          @Field(index = Index.YES, analyze = Analyze.NO, store = Store.NO)
44          private double  price;
45          @Column(name = "product_old_price")
46          @NumericField
47          @Field(index = Index.YES, analyze = Analyze.NO, store = Store.NO)
48          private double old_price;
49          @Column(name = "product_description")
50          @Field(index = Index.YES, analyze = Analyze.NO, store = Store.NO)
51          private String description;
52          @IndexedEmbedded
53          @ManyToOne(fetch = FetchType.LAZY)
54          private Categories category;
55          @IndexedEmbedded
56          @ElementCollection(targetClass = java.lang.String.class,
                                fetch = FetchType.EAGER)
57          @Column(name = "product_gallery")
58          private List<String> gallery = new ArrayList<String>();
59          @IndexedEmbedded
60          @ElementCollection(targetClass = java.lang.String.class,
                                fetch = FetchType.EAGER)
61          @Column(name = "product_colors")
62          private List<String> colors = new ArrayList<String>();
63          @IndexedEmbedded
64          @ElementCollection(targetClass = java.lang.String.class,
                                fetch = FetchType.EAGER)
65          @Column(name = "product_sizes")
66          private List<String> sizes = new ArrayList<String>();
67
```

```java
68          public String getId() {
69              return id;
70          }
71
72          public void setId(String id) {
73              this.id = id;
74          }
75
76          public List<String> getGallery() {
77              return gallery;
78          }
79
80          public void setGallery(List<String> gallery) {
81              this.gallery = gallery;
82          }
83
84          public double getPrice() {
85              return price;
86          }
87
88          public void setPrice(double price) {
89              this.price = price;
90          }
91
92          public double getOld_price() {
93              return old_price;
94          }
95
96          public void setOld_price(double old_price) {
97              this.old_price = old_price;
98          }
99
100         public String getProduct() {
101             return product;
102         }
103
104         public void setProduct(String product) {
105             this.product = product;
106         }
107
108         public String getSku() {
109             return sku;
110         }
111
112         public void setSku(String sku) {
113             this.sku = sku;
114         }
115
```

```
116        public String getDescription() {
117            return description;
118        }
119
120        public List<String> getColors() {
121            return colors;
122        }
123
124        public void setColors(List<String> colors) {
125            this.colors = colors;
126        }
127
128        public List<String> getSizes() {
129            return sizes;
130        }
131
132        public void setSizes(List<String> sizes) {
133            this.sizes = sizes;
134        }
135
136        public void setDescription(String description) {
137            this.description = description;
138        }
139
140        public Categories getCategory() {
141            return category;
142        }
143
144        public void setCategory(Categories category) {
145            this.category = category;
146        }
147
148        @Override
149        public int hashCode() {
150            int hash = 0;
151            hash += (id != null ? id.hashCode() : 0);
152            return hash;
153        }
154
155        @Override
156        public boolean equals(Object object) {
157            if (!(object instanceof Products)) {
158                return false;
159            }
160            Products other = (Products) object;
161            if ((this.id == null && other.id != null) || (this.id != null &&
                   !this.id.equals(other.id))) {
162                return false;
163            }
164            return true;
165        }
166
```

```
167          @Override
168          public String toString() {
169              return "eshop.entities.Products[ id=" + id + " ]";
170          }
171      }
```

Let's take a closer look at some of the main lines of code.

In line 39, the field that corresponds to the product name (product_name) is prepared for Lucene. The part we want to note is analyze = Analyze.YES, which tells Lucene to use the default analyzer for this field. Instead of searching for a product by name (which is usually composed of several words), we can search for it by any of the words its name contains. This helps us easily implement a *search by product name* facility.

As you can see, in lines 42 and 48 the product prices (product_price and product_old_price) are numerical values (doubles). It makes sense to store them as numbers instead of strings so you can perform range queries and calculations, like subtotals, totals, currency conversions and so on. You can tell Lucene that a field represents numerical values by annotating it with @NumericField. When a property is indexed as a numeric field, it enables efficient range querying, and sorting is faster than doing the same query on standard @Field properties.

Lines 52-54 define a unidirectional, many-to-one association between the categories_c and products_c collections. For Lucene, this association should be marked as @IndexedEmbedded, which is used to index associated entities as part of the owning entity. Probably I've said this before, but it's a good moment to point out again that Lucene is not aware of associations, which is why it needs the @IndexedEmbedded and @ContainedIn annotations. Without these annotations, associations like @ManyToMany, @*ToOne, @Embedded, and @ElementCollection will not be indexed and, therefore, will not be searchable. Associations let you easily write Lucene queries similar to SQL queries that contain the WHERE clause, of the type: *select all products from a category where the category field equals something* (which in JP-QL is usually a join).

Lines 55-66 define the product's options and gallery of images. For this example, we used the most common options, color and size, but you can add more. Instead of placing them into another table and creating another association, I prefer to store them using @ElementCollection. When a product doesn't have color or size, it's just skipped. MongoDB documents allow a flexible structure, so when an option isn't specified, the corresponding collection will not be present in document. As a final observation, we're loading the options and gallery using the eager mechanism, because we want to load and display each product with its gallery and options. If you want to load the products in two phases: first a brief overview of the products and then, by user request, the options, use the lazy mechanism instead.

Model the Customers Collection (customers_c)

The customers_c collection corresponds to the users table.

For users (potential customers), we need a separate collection for storing personal data; we name this collection customers_c. Personal data includes information such as name, surname, e-mail address, password, addresses and so on (obviously, you can add more fields). When a user logs into the system, you can easily indentify him by e-mail address and password and load his profile. His orders are not loaded in the same query as his profile. They are loaded lazily only when an explicit request is performed; this allows us to load only the requested orders, not all. Usually, a customer checks just his most recent order status and rarely wants to view an obsolete order. Many e-commerce sites don't provide access to obsolete orders, only to the most recent one.

Each document (entry) in the customers_c collection looks like what's shown in Figure 7-5.

```
"_id" : "7b54b632-c5af-44e5-9370-447e246350f6",
"customer_address_1" : {
        "city" : "Campina",
        "country" : "Romania",
        "fax" : "+44 137 538 1222",
        "number" : "101",
        "phone" : "(0727) 249423",
        "state" : "Prahova",
        "street" : "N. Iorga",
        "zip" : "106044"
},
"customer_address_2" : {
        "city" : "Banesti",
        "country" : "Romania",
        "fax" : "+44 137 538 1222",
        "number" : "118",
        "phone" : "(0727) 249423",
        "state" : "Prahova",
        "street" : "Nationala",
        "zip" : "107050"
},
"customer_email" : "marian@yahoo.com",
"customer_name" : "Marian",
"customer_password" : "marianandrafa",
"customer_registration" : ISODate("2013-05-04T05:27:50.497Z"),
"customer_surname" : "Iordache"
```

Java Field	Java Type	MongoDB Field
id	String	_id
email	String	customer_email
password	String	customer_password
name	String	customer_name
surname	String	customer_surname
registration	Date	customer_registration
customer_address_1 (city, country, fax, number, phone, state, street, zip)	Addresses	customer_address_1 (city, country, fax, number, phone, state, street, zip)
customer_address_2 (city, country, fax, number, phone, state, street, zip)	Addresses	customer_address_2 (city, country, fax, number, phone, state, street, zip)

customers_c

Figure 7-5. *Sample document from the customers_c collection*

Notice that the customer's addresses are stored as embedded documents; this lets us provide multiple addresses without additional tables, using fast queries and lazy loading.

The JPA entity for this collection is shown in Listing 7-3.

Listing 7-3. The JPA Entity for customers_c

```
1    package eshop.entities;
2
3    import eshop.embedded.Addresses;
4    import java.io.Serializable;
5    import java.util.Date;
6    import javax.persistence.Basic;
7    import javax.persistence.Column;
8    import javax.persistence.Embedded;
9    import javax.persistence.Entity;
10   import javax.persistence.FetchType;
11   import javax.persistence.GeneratedValue;
12   import javax.persistence.Id;
13   import javax.persistence.Table;
14   import javax.persistence.Temporal;
15   import org.hibernate.annotations.GenericGenerator;
16   import org.hibernate.search.annotations.Analyze;
17   import org.hibernate.search.annotations.DateBridge;
18   import org.hibernate.search.annotations.DocumentId;
19   import org.hibernate.search.annotations.Field;
20   import org.hibernate.search.annotations.Index;
21   import org.hibernate.search.annotations.Indexed;
22   import org.hibernate.search.annotations.IndexedEmbedded;
23   import org.hibernate.search.annotations.Resolution;
24   import org.hibernate.search.annotations.Store;
25
26   @Entity
27   @Indexed
28   @Table(name = "customers_c")
29   public class Customers implements Serializable {
30
```

```
31          private static final long serialVersionUID = 1L;
32          @DocumentId
33          @Id
34          @GeneratedValue(generator = "uuid")
35          @GenericGenerator(name = "uuid", strategy = "uuid2")
36          private String id;
37          @Column(name = "customer_email")
38          @Field(index = Index.YES, analyze = Analyze.NO, store = Store.NO)
39          private String email;
40          @Column(name = "customer_password")
41          @Field(index = Index.YES, analyze = Analyze.NO, store = Store.NO)
42          private String password;
43          @Column(name = "customer_name")
44          @Field(index = Index.YES, analyze = Analyze.NO, store = Store.NO)
45          private String name;
46          @Column(name = "customer_surname")
47          @Field(index = Index.YES, analyze = Analyze.NO, store = Store.NO)
48          private String surname;
49          @DateBridge(resolution = Resolution.DAY)
50          @Temporal(javax.persistence.TemporalType.DATE)
51          @Column(name = "customer_registration")
52          private Date registration;
53          @Embedded
54          @IndexedEmbedded
55          @Basic(fetch = FetchType.LAZY)
56          private Addresses customer_address_1;
57          @Embedded
58          @IndexedEmbedded
59          @Basic(fetch = FetchType.LAZY)
60          private Addresses customer_address_2;
61
62          public String getId() {
63              return id;
64          }
65
66          public void setId(String id) {
67              this.id = id;
68          }
69
70          public String getEmail() {
71              return email;
72          }
73
74          public void setEmail(String email) {
75              this.email = email;
76          }
77
78          public String getPassword() {
79              return password;
80          }
81
```

```
82          public void setPassword(String password) {
83              this.password = password;
84          }
85
86          public String getName() {
87              return name;
88          }
89
90          public void setName(String name) {
91              this.name = name;
92          }
93
94          public String getSurname() {
95              return surname;
96          }
97
98          public void setSurname(String surname) {
99              this.surname = surname;
100         }
101
102         public Date getRegistration() {
103             return registration;
104         }
105
106         public void setRegistration(Date registration) {
107             this.registration = registration;
108         }
109
110         public Addresses getCustomer_address_1() {
111             return customer_address_1;
112         }
113
114         public void setCustomer_address_1(Addresses customer_address_1) {
115             this.customer_address_1 = customer_address_1;
116         }
117
118         public Addresses getCustomer_address_2() {
119             return customer_address_2;
120         }
121
122         public void setCustomer_address_2(Addresses customer_address_2) {
123             this.customer_address_2 = customer_address_2;
124         }
125
126         @Override
127         public int hashCode() {
128             int hash = 0;
129             hash += (id != null ? id.hashCode() : 0);
130             return hash;
131         }
132
```

```
133         @Override
134         public boolean equals(Object object) {
135             if (!(object instanceof Customers)) {
136                 return false;
137             }
138             Customers other = (Customers) object;
139             if ((this.id == null && other.id != null) || (this.id != null &&
                    !this.id.equals(other.id))) {
140                 return false;
141             }
142             return true;
143         }
144
145         @Override
146         public String toString() {
147             return "eshop.entities.Customers[ id=" + id + " ]";
148         }
149     }
150
```

There are important aspects of this code that deserve explanation.

The code in lines 53-60 is pretty interesting. As you can see, the same embeddable object type appears twice in the same entity (the embeddable object maps the address coordinates, city, zip, street and so on in a class named Addresses). If you've used this technique with SQL and JPA providers such as EclipseLink or Hibernate, you know you had to set at least one of the columns explicitly, because the column name default will not work. In this case, generic JPA fixes the issue with the @AttributeOverride annotation (see www.docs.oracle.com/javaee/6/api/javax/persistence/AttributeOverride.html). In NoSQL and Hibernate OGM, however, you don't need to use this adjustment to column names.

The embeddable class representing an address is shown in Listing 7-4.

Listing 7-4. The Embeddable Addresses Class

```
1       package eshop.embedded;
2
3       import java.io.Serializable;
4       import javax.persistence.Embeddable;
5       import org.hibernate.search.annotations.Analyze;
6       import org.hibernate.search.annotations.Field;
7       import org.hibernate.search.annotations.Index;
8       import org.hibernate.search.annotations.Store;
9
10      @Embeddable
11      public class Addresses implements Serializable {
12
13          @Field(index = Index.YES, analyze = Analyze.NO, store = Store.NO)
14          private String city;
15          @Field(index = Index.YES, analyze = Analyze.NO, store = Store.NO)
16          private String state;
17          @Field(index = Index.YES, analyze = Analyze.NO, store = Store.NO)
18          private String street;
19          @Field(index = Index.YES, analyze = Analyze.NO, store = Store.NO)
20          private String number;
```

```
21          @Field(index = Index.YES, analyze = Analyze.NO, store = Store.NO)
22          private String zip;
23          @Field(index = Index.YES, analyze = Analyze.NO, store = Store.NO)
24          private String country;
25          @Field(index = Index.YES, analyze = Analyze.NO, store = Store.NO)
26          private String phone;
27          @Field(index = Index.YES, analyze = Analyze.NO, store = Store.NO)
28          private String fax;
29
30          public String getCity() {
31              return city;
32          }
33
34          public void setCity(String city) {
35              this.city = city;
36          }
37
38          public String getNumber() {
39              return number;
40          }
41
42          public void setNumber(String number) {
43              this.number = number;
44          }
45
46          public String getState() {
47              return state;
48          }
49
50          public void setState(String state) {
51              this.state = state;
52          }
53
54          public String getStreet() {
55              return street;
56          }
57
58          public void setStreet(String street) {
59              this.street = street;
60          }
61
62          public String getZip() {
63              return zip;
64          }
65
66          public void setZip(String zip) {
67              this.zip = zip;
68          }
69
```

```
70          public String getCountry() {
71              return country;
72          }
73
74          public void setCountry(String country) {
75              this.country = country;
76          }
77
78          public String getPhone() {
79              return phone;
80          }
81
82          public void setPhone(String phone) {
83              this.phone = phone;
84          }
85
86          public String getFax() {
87              return fax;
88          }
89
90          public void setFax(String fax) {
91              this.fax = fax;
92          }
93      }
```

Model The Orders Collection (orders_c)

The orders_c collection corresponds to the orders and details tables.

The orders are stored in a separate collection, named orders_c. For each order, we store status (an order can pass through multiple statuses, such as *PURCHASED, SHIPPED, CANCELED* and so on); subtotal (this represents the order value in money); order creation date; shipping address; and the order's products. You can add more fields, such as an order identifier (*#nnnn,* for example), an order friendly name, an order expiration date, and so on.

The shipping address is represented by an embedded document and the order's products are stored as an embedded collection. Therefore, we don't need supplementary collections or associations, the queries are very easy to perform, and we can load the shipping address and the order's products either lazily or eagerly, depending on how we implement the web site GUI.

In this collection, we need to store the foreign keys that indicate the customers who purchased the orders. For this I defined a unidirectional many-to-one association between orders and customers.

I haven't yet said anything about the current shopping cart—the order hasn't been submitted yet. The shopping cart can support multiple content modifications in a single (or multiple) session(s) of a customer, adding new products, deleting others, clearing the cart, modifying a product's quantity, and so forth. It's not useful to reflect all of these modifications in the database, since each requires at least one query for updating the "conversation" between customer and shopping cart. For this, you can take a programmatic approach, storing the shopping cart in a customer session, or in a view scope or conversational scope. You can also use cookies, or any specific design pattern that can help implement this task. The idea is to modify the database only when an order is actually placed.

Of course, if your data is highly critical or you need to persist over multiple sessions (for example, if the user might come back after a week), then it's a good idea to persist the shopping cart to the database using a separate collection or as a document inside the orders_c collection. After all, a shopping cart is just an order that has not been placed, so it can be stored like a normal order with a status of, perhaps, *unpurchased.* If you decide to persist the shopping cart, be careful to correctly synchronize it with the inventory. This is mandatory for preventing "overselling;" the application must move items from inventory to the cart and back to again in some cases, for instance if the user drops one or more products or even abandons the whole purchase. Taking a product from inventory and moving it to the cart (or the reverse) is an operation specific to transactions, so you have to deal with rollback issues. Obviously, if you don't have an inventory, things are much simpler.

In Figure 7-6, you can see a document sample for an order.

```
"_id" : "3b99defd-46cc-4fb5-babf-9c690fa8324c",
"cart" : [
        {
                "product_price" : 2.95,
                "product_size" : "Unavailable",
                "product_sku" : "CALENDAR_0004",
                "unique_identification_number" : "1996502",
                "product_color" : "Unavailable",
                "product_name" : "Rafael Nadal 2010 Calendar",
                "product_quantity" : "3"
        },
        {
                "product_price" : 89.9,
                "product_size" : "L",
                "product_sku" : "TOPS_0003",
                "unique_identification_number" : "1244535",
                "product_color" : "Khaki",
                "product_name" : "Power Court N98 Jacket",
                "product_quantity" : "1"
        },
        {
                "product_price" : 15.95,
                "product_size" : "Unavailable",
                "product_sku" : "POSTER_0001",
                "unique_identification_number" : "1676705",
                "product_color" : "Unavailable",
                "product_name" : "HIS?ORY Poster",
                "product_quantity" : "2"
        }
],
"customer_id" : "a8461a37-0c46-4676-8300-e4d0c10a2669",
"order_status" : "PURCHASED",
"order_subtotal" : 130.64,
"orderdate" : ISODate("2013-05-04T08:45:39.571Z"),
"shipping_address" : {
        "city" : "Bucuresti",
        "country" : "Romania ",
        "fax" : "02332247433",
        "number" : "2324",
        "phone" : "07275655422",
        "state" : "Bucuresti",
        "street" : "Yoni",
        "zip" : "107050"
}
```

Java Field	Java Type	MongoDB Field
id	String	_id
status	String	order_status
subtotal	double	order_subtotal
orderdate	Date	orderdate
cart (sku, name, price, color, size, quantity, uin)	List<CartProducts>	cart (product_sku, product_name, product_price, product_color, product_size, product_quantity, unique_identification_number)
shipping_address (city, country, fax, number, phone, state, street, zip)	Addresses	shipping_address (city, country, fax, number, phone, state, street, zip)
@ManyToOne customer	Customers	customer_id

orders_c

Figure 7-6. *Sample document from the orders_c collection*

By convention, when a product does not have color or size, we store a flag like "Unavailable".

The JPA entity for this collection is shown in Listing 7-5:

Listing 7-5. The JPA Entity for orders_c

```
1       package eshop.entities;
2
3       import eshop.embedded.Addresses;
4       import eshop.embedded.CartProducts;
5       import java.io.Serializable;
6       import java.util.ArrayList;
7       import java.util.Date;
8       import java.util.List;
9       import javax.persistence.AttributeOverride;
10      import javax.persistence.AttributeOverrides;
11      import javax.persistence.Basic;
12      import javax.persistence.Column;
13      import javax.persistence.ElementCollection;
14      import javax.persistence.Embedded;
15      import javax.persistence.Entity;
16      import javax.persistence.FetchType;
17      import javax.persistence.GeneratedValue;
18      import javax.persistence.Id;
```

```
19        import javax.persistence.ManyToOne;
20        import javax.persistence.Table;
21        import javax.persistence.Temporal;
22        import org.hibernate.annotations.GenericGenerator;
23        import org.hibernate.search.annotations.Analyze;
24        import org.hibernate.search.annotations.DateBridge;
25        import org.hibernate.search.annotations.DocumentId;
26        import org.hibernate.search.annotations.Field;
27        import org.hibernate.search.annotations.Index;
28        import org.hibernate.search.annotations.Indexed;
29        import org.hibernate.search.annotations.IndexedEmbedded;
30        import org.hibernate.search.annotations.NumericField;
31        import org.hibernate.search.annotations.Resolution;
32        import org.hibernate.search.annotations.Store;
33
34        @Entity
35        @Indexed
36        @Table(name = "orders_c")
37        public class Orders implements Serializable {
38
39            private static final long serialVersionUID = 1L;
40            @DocumentId
41            @Id
42            @GeneratedValue(generator = "uuid")
43            @GenericGenerator(name = "uuid", strategy = "uuid2")
44            private String id;
45            @Column(name = "order_status")
46            @Field(index = Index.YES, analyze = Analyze.NO, store = Store.NO)
47            private String status;
48            @Column(name = "order_subtotal")
49            @NumericField
50            @Field(index = Index.YES, analyze = Analyze.NO, store = Store.NO)
51            private double subtotal;
52            @DateBridge(resolution = Resolution.HOUR)
53            @Temporal(javax.persistence.TemporalType.DATE)
54            private Date orderdate;
55            @Embedded
56            @IndexedEmbedded
57            @Basic(fetch = FetchType.EAGER)
58            private Addresses shipping_address;
59            @IndexedEmbedded
60            @ElementCollection(targetClass = eshop.embedded.CartProducts.class,
61            fetch = FetchType.EAGER)
62            @AttributeOverrides({
63                @AttributeOverride(name = "sku",
64                column =
65                @Column(name = "product_sku")),
66                @AttributeOverride(name = "name",
67                column =
68                @Column(name = "product_name")),
69                @AttributeOverride(name = "price",
```

```
70              column =
71              @Column(name = "product_price")),
72              @AttributeOverride(name = "color",
73              column =
74              @Column(name = "product_color")),
75              @AttributeOverride(name = "size",
76              column =
77              @Column(name = "product_size")),
78              @AttributeOverride(name = "quantity",
79              column =
80              @Column(name = "product_quantity")),
81              @AttributeOverride(name = "uin",
82              column =
83              @Column(name = "unique_identification_number")),})
84      private List<CartProducts> cart = new ArrayList<CartProducts>(0);
85      @IndexedEmbedded
86      @ManyToOne(fetch = FetchType.LAZY)
87      private Customers customer;
88
89      public String getId() {
90          return id;
91      }
92
93      public void setId(String id) {
94          this.id = id;
95      }
96
97      public String getStatus() {
98          return status;
99      }
100
101     public void setStatus(String status) {
102         this.status = status;
103     }
104
105     public Addresses getShipping_address() {
106         return shipping_address;
107     }
108
109     public void setShipping_address(Addresses shipping_address) {
110         this.shipping_address = shipping_address;
111     }
112
113     public List<CartProducts> getCart() {
114         return cart;
115     }
116
117     public void setCart(List<CartProducts> cart) {
118         this.cart = cart;
119     }
120
```

```
121         public Customers getCustomer() {
122             return customer;
123         }
124
125         public void setCustomer(Customers customer) {
126             this.customer = customer;
127         }
128
129         @Override
130         public int hashCode() {
131             int hash = 0;
132             hash += (id != null ? id.hashCode() : 0);
133             return hash;
134         }
135
136         public double getSubtotal() {
137             return subtotal;
138         }
139
140         public void setSubtotal(double subtotal) {
141             this.subtotal = subtotal;
142         }
143
144         public Date getOrderdate() {
145             return orderdate;
146         }
147
148         public void setOrderdate(Date orderdate) {
149             this.orderdate = orderdate;
150         }
151
152         @Override
153         public boolean equals(Object object) {
154             if (!(object instanceof Orders)) {
155                 return false;
156             }
157             Orders other = (Orders) object;
158             if ((this.id == null && other.id != null) || (this.id != null &&
                     !this.id.equals(other.id))) {
159                 return false;
160             }
161             return true;
162         }
163
164         @Override
165         public String toString() {
166             return "eshop.entities.Orders[ id=" + id + " ]";
167         }
168     }
```

Let's discuss the main lines of code for this entity.

Lines 55-58 represent the mapping of the shipping address. As you can see, I prefer to use an embedded document for each order. I loaded it eagerly, but lazy loading is also an option, depending on what you want to display when you load an order.

From the Lucene perspective, I need the @IndexedEmbedded annotation, because I want to index this embeddable class as part of the owning entity. The Addresses embeddable class (annotated with @Embeddable) is shown above in Listing 7-4.

In lines 59-84, an element-collection (mapped in MongoDB as an embedded collection) stores an order's products. The type of the element-collection is an embeddable class. The main thing to notice here is that I've used the @AttributeOverrides annotation; if we don't override the columns names of the embeddable collection, they default to something like *cart.collection&&element.price*. This is not very friendly, so @AttributeOverrides can be very useful in such cases.

This embeddable class is named CartProducts and is shown in Listing 7-6.

Listing 7-6. The Embeddable CartProducts Class

```
1       package eshop.embedded;
2
3       import java.io.Serializable;
4       import javax.persistence.Embeddable;
5       import org.hibernate.search.annotations.Analyze;
6       import org.hibernate.search.annotations.Field;
7       import org.hibernate.search.annotations.Index;
8       import org.hibernate.search.annotations.NumericField;
9       import org.hibernate.search.annotations.Store;
10
11      @Embeddable
12      public class CartProducts implements Serializable {
13
14          @Field(index = Index.YES, analyze = Analyze.NO, store = Store.NO)
15          private String sku;
16          @Field(index = Index.YES, analyze = Analyze.NO, store = Store.NO)
17          private String name;
18          @NumericField
19          @Field(index = Index.YES, analyze = Analyze.NO, store = Store.NO)
20          private double price;
21          @Field(index = Index.YES, analyze = Analyze.NO, store = Store.NO)
22          private String color;
23          @Field(index = Index.YES, analyze = Analyze.NO, store = Store.NO)
24          private String size;
25          @Field(index = Index.YES, analyze = Analyze.NO, store = Store.NO)
26          private String quantity;
27          @Field(index = Index.YES, analyze = Analyze.NO, store = Store.NO)
28          private String uin;
29
30          public String getSku() {
31              return sku;
32          }
33
34          public void setSku(String sku) {
35              this.sku = sku;
36          }
37
```

```
38          public String getName() {
39              return name;
40          }
41
42          public void setName(String name) {
43              this.name = name;
44          }
45
46          public double getPrice() {
47              return price;
48          }
49
50          public void setPrice(double price) {
51              this.price = price;
52          }
53
54          public String getColor() {
55              return color;
56          }
57
58          public void setColor(String color) {
59              this.color = color;
60          }
61
62          public String getSize() {
63              return size;
64          }
65
66          public void setSize(String size) {
67              this.size = size;
68          }
69
70          public String getQuantity() {
71              return quantity;
72          }
73
74          public void setQuantity(String quantity) {
75              this.quantity = quantity;
76          }
77
78          public String getUin() {
79              return uin;
80          }
81
82          public void setUin(String uin) {
83              this.uin = uin;
84          }
85      }
86
```

From the Lucene perspective, we need the @IndexedEmbedded annotation because we want to index this embeddable collection in the entity owner index.

Lines 85-87 define the unidirectional association between the orders_c and customers_c collections. For Lucene, this association should be marked as @IndexedEmbedded, which is used to index associated entities as part of the owning entity. This association allows us to easily write Lucene queries similar to SQL queries that contain the WHERE clause, of the type: *select all orders from an order where the customer field equals something* (which, in JP-QL, is usually a join).

Model The Inventory Collection (inventory_c)

This collection doesn't have a corresponding table in Figure 7-1. Not all e-commerce sites need inventory management. But, for those that do, MongoDB provides a few solutions. One solution is to store a separate document for each physical product in the warehouse. This will prevent concurrent access to data, since every document will have a unique lock on that product. In this approach, we rely on the fact that MongoDB supports atomic operations on individual documents. For cases where the warehouse doesn't contain too many products (and this depends on your definition of "too many"), this approach will work quite well.

Another approach is to store a document for a group of identical products and use a field in this document to represent the number of products. In this case, you need to deal with the situation of multiple users updating this field, by extracting or returning a product from the same group (there's also an administrator who occasionally repopulates the inventory). I choose this approach and deal with concurrent updates by using optimistic locking. If you need to lock a document for your exclusive use until you've finished with it, use pessimistic locking, but be carefully to avoid (or deal with) deadlocks. In general, optimistic locking is good when you don't expect imminent collisions but, since the transaction is aborted (not rolled back), you need to pay the price and deal with it somehow. On the other hand, pessimistic locking is used when a collision is anticipated, and it's used when collisions are imminent. It can be pretty tricky to decide which locking option to choose, but here's a rule of thumb: use pessimistic locking if you have to guarantee the integrity of important data, like banking data, and use optimistic locking for everything else.

The MongoDB collection for storing inventory is named inventory_c. For each group of identical products, I've created a composite key from the product SKU and the color and size. Besides the id, each document contains a numeric field for storing the number of available products, named inventory. The version field is used for optimistic locking. See Figure 7-7.

```
"_id" : {
        "sku" : "TOPS_0002",
        "sku_color" : "Khaki",
        "sku_size" : "M"
},
"inventory" : 8,
"version" : NumberLong(0)


"_id" : {
        "sku" : "TOPS_0002",
        "sku_color" : "Khaki",
        "sku_size" : "XXL"
},
"inventory" : 8,
"version" : NumberLong(0)


"_id" : {
        "sku" : "TOPS_0003",
        "sku_color" : "Red",
        "sku_size" : "S"
},
"inventory" : 14,
"version" : NumberLong(0)
```

Java Field	Java Type	MongoDB Field
composite id	InventoryPK	_id
inventory	int	inventory
version	Long	version

inventory_c

Figure 7-7. Sample document from the customers_c collection showing the inventory field

The JPA entity for inventory_c is shown in Listing 7-7.

Listing 7-7. The JPA Entity for inventory_c

```
1        package eshop.entities;
2
3        import java.io.Serializable;
4        import javax.persistence.Column;
5        import javax.persistence.Entity;
6        import javax.persistence.Id;
7        import javax.persistence.IdClass;
8        import javax.persistence.Table;
9        import javax.persistence.Version;
10
11       @Entity
12       @IdClass(eshop.embedded.InventoryPK.class)
13       @Table(name = "inventory_c")
14       public class Inventory implements Serializable {
15
16           private static final long serialVersionUID = 1L;
17           @Id
18           private String sku;
19           @Id
20           private String sku_color;
21           @Id
22           private String sku_size;
23           @Version
24           private Long version;
25           @Column(name = "inventory")
26           private int inventory;
27
28           public int getInventory() {
29               return inventory;
30           }
31
32           public void setInventory(int inventory) {
33               this.inventory = inventory;
34           }
35
36           public String getSku() {
37               return sku;
38           }
39
40           public void setSku(String sku) {
41               this.sku = sku;
42           }
43
44           public String getSku_color() {
45               return sku_color;
46           }
47
```

```
48          public void setSku_color(String sku_color) {
49              this.sku_color = sku_color;
50          }
51
52          public String getSku_size() {
53              return sku_size;
54          }
55
56          public void setSku_size(String sku_size) {
57              this.sku_size = sku_size;
58          }
59
60          public Long getVersion() {
61              return version;
62          }
63
64          protected void setVersion(Long version) {
65              this.version = version;
66          }
67
68          @Override
69          public int hashCode() {
70              int hash = 7;
71              hash = 13 * hash + (this.sku != null ? this.sku.hashCode() : 0);
72              return hash;
73          }
74
75          @Override
76          public boolean equals(Object obj) {
77              if (obj == null) {
78                  return false;
79              }
80              if (getClass() != obj.getClass()) {
81                  return false;
82              }
83              final Inventory other = (Inventory) obj;
84              if ((this.sku == null) ? (other.sku != null) :
                    !this.sku.equals(other.sku)) {
85                  return false;
86              }
87              return true;
88          }
89      }
```

And the composite key class is:

```
1       package eshop.embedded;
2
3       import java.io.Serializable;
4
5       public class InventoryPK implements Serializable{
6
7           private String sku;
8           private String sku_color;
9           private String sku_size;
10
11          public InventoryPK(){
12          }
13
14          public InventoryPK(String sku, String sku_color, String sku_size) {
15              this.sku = sku;
16              this.sku_color = sku_color;
17              this.sku_size = sku_size;
18          }
19
20          @Override
21          public int hashCode() {
22              int hash = 7;
23              hash = 83 * hash + (this.sku != null ? this.sku.hashCode() : 0);
24              hash = 83 * hash + (this.sku_color != null ?
                this.sku_color.hashCode() : 0);
25              hash = 83 * hash + (this.sku_size != null ?
                this.sku_size.hashCode() : 0);
26              return hash;
27          }
28
29          @Override
30          public boolean equals(Object obj) {
31              if (obj == null) {
32                  return false;
33              }
34              if (getClass() != obj.getClass()) {
35                  return false;
36              }
37              final InventoryPK other = (InventoryPK) obj;
38              if ((this.sku == null) ? (other.sku != null) :
                  !this.sku.equals(other.sku)) {
39                  return false;
40              }
41              if ((this.sku_color == null) ? (other.sku_color != null) :
                  !this.sku_color.equals(other.sku_color)) {
42                  return false;
43              }
44              if ((this.sku_size == null) ? (other.sku_size != null) :
```

```
                    !this.sku_size.equals(other.sku_size)) {
45                      return false;
46                  }
47              return true;
48          }
49      }
```

Summary

In this chapter, you saw my proposal for a MongoDB e-commerce database. Of course, this is just a sketch that, obviously, is open for improvement. I presented the proposed architecture and the database collections, and we've created the necessary entities and embeddable classes. In the next chapter, we'll continue to develop an enterprise application based on this database architecture.

CHAPTER 8

■ ■ ■

MongoDB e-Commerce Database Querying

In Chapter 7 we developed a MongoDB database model for an e-commerce application. Now we'll write the necessary queries for using the database and see how to perform common tasks for an e-commerce platform, including:

- Display categories of products.

- Display promotional products.

- Display products from a category (with pagination).

- Search for a product by name (or by the words in the name).

- Find a customer (for login, editing the profile, saving orders, and so on).

- Save an order for synchronizing the shopping cart with the database.

- Check the inventory for a certain product and quantity.

- Restore the quantity when products are removed from shopping cart.

Each of these tasks will be accomplished in a Hibernate Search/Apache Lucene query (since JP-QL is insufficiently developed, we need to use the full-text search engine provided by Apache). The Hibernate Search queries will be written in JPA style.

For testing the database, I developed an e-commerce web site inspired by the official e-shop of the tennis player Rafael Nadal (`www.rafaelnadal-shop.com/en`). The web site is based on:

- Java EE 6 (EJB 3.0, JSF 2.0)

- Hibernate OGM 4.0.0 Beta2

- MongoDB 2.2.2

- MongoDB Java Driver 2.8.0

- Hibernate Search 4.2.0 Beta 1

- Apache Lucene 3.6.0

- PrimeFaces 3.4.2

Don't worry if you're not familiar with JSF or PrimeFaces. You can implement the same functionality without them, using other approaches such as JSP and servlets. Moreover, you can drop EJB and implement the business layer as you wish. You can also use the Hibernate Native API instead of JPA. These technologies are not essential and, as long as you understand the e-commerce database model and the queries we'll discuss, you can glue everything into an e-commerce application using the technologies you prefer.

You'll find the complete source code for the application, named RafaEShop, in the Apress repository. The application was developed as a NetBeans 7.2.1 project and was tested under GlassFish v3 AS. Figure 8-1 shows the interaction of the classes.

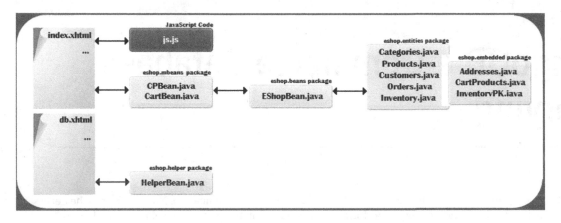

Figure 8-1. *The interaction of the classes in the RafaEShop application*

For localhost testing purposes, follow these steps (assuming the application is deployed and the MongoDB server is running):

1. Ensure you don't have a database named eshop_db in MongoDB.

2. Access the page http://localhost:8080/RafaEShop/faces/db.xhtml, as shown in Figure 8-2. (Obviously, you need to adjust the address and port to reflect your application server).

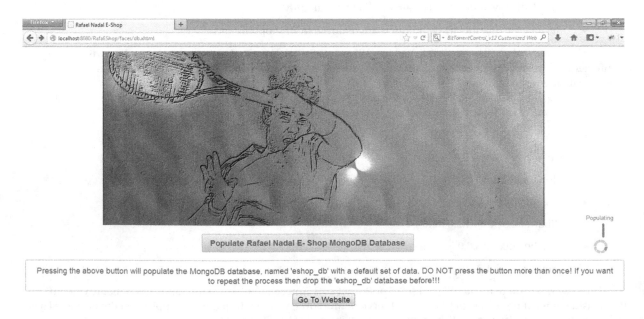

Figure 8-2. *The user interface for populating the eshop_db database*

3. Press, ONLY ONCE, the button labeled *"Populate Rafael Nadal E-Shop MongoDB Database;"* pressing the button more than once will cause errors.

4. Navigate to the web site by pressing the button labeled, *"Go To Website."* This button navigates to the web site start page.

Now you should see something like what's shown in Figure 8-3.

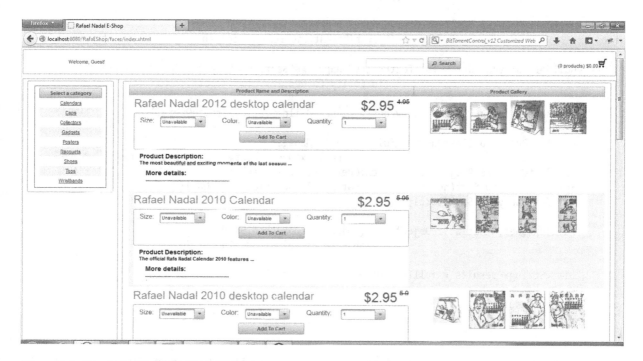

Figure 8-3. *The Rafael Nadal E-Shop GUI*

If you need to restore the database (for whatever reason), follow these steps:

1. Drop the eshop_db database. You can do this from the MongoDB shell, like this:

```
mongo eshop_db
db.dropDatabase()
```

2. Navigate to the D root folder and delete the eshop folder (this is where Lucene indexes data).

3. Repeat the steps 1-4, from above.

Now let's "dissect" Figure 8-2 in terms of Lucene queries.

Display the Categories of Products

The first query will extract the category names and ids from the categories_c collection (the Categories entity). The names are visible to users and the ids help identify a category in order to retrieve its products; we display the categories sorted by name. You can find this code in EshopBean.java, shown in Listing 8-1.

Listing 8-1. EshopBean.java

```java
package eshop.beans;
...
public class EShopBean {
...
public List<String> extractCategories() {

    FullTextEntityManager fullTextEntityManager =
                                    org.hibernate.search.jpa.Search.getFullTextEntityManager(em);

    QueryBuilder queryBuilder = fullTextEntityManager.getSearchFactory().buildQueryBuilder().
                                    forEntity(Categories.class).get();

        org.apache.lucene.search.Query query = queryBuilder.all().createQuery();

        FullTextQuery fullTextQuery = fullTextEntityManager
                                    .createFullTextQuery(query, Categories.class);
        fullTextQuery.setProjection(FullTextQuery.ID, "category");
        Sort sort = new Sort(new SortField("category", SortField.STRING));
        fullTextQuery.setSort(sort);

        fullTextQuery.initializeObjectsWith(ObjectLookupMethod.SKIP,
                                    DatabaseRetrievalMethod.FIND_BY_ID);

        List<String> results = fullTextQuery.getResultList();

        return results;
    }
}
```

The query is pretty simple. We extract all `Categories` instances (sorted by category names) by projecting the category names and ids. In Figure 8-4, you can see how categories are listed in the browser.

Figure 8-4. *Displaying product categories*

Display the Promotional Products

In addition to the category names, the first page of our web site contains a list of the promotional products; these products can belong to different categories. This is a common approach on many e-commerce web sites, but you can also display the newest products or the bestsellers. In this case, it's easy to recognize the promotional products by checking the MongoDB field product_old_price (old_price in Products entity) of the documents in the products_c collection (the Products entity). All products with an old price bigger than 0 are assumed to be promotional products. Therefore, the query looks like the code in Listing 8-2.

Listing 8-2. Query for Displaying Promotional Products

```
package eshop.beans;
...
public class EShopBean {
...
public List<Products> extractPromotionalProducts() {

        FullTextEntityManager fullTextEntityManager =
org.hibernate.search.jpa.Search.getFullTextEntityManager(em);

        org.apache.lucene.search.Query query = NumericRangeQuery
                                    .newDoubleRange("old_price", 0.0d, 1000d, false, true);
        FullTextQuery fullTextQuery = fullTextEntityManager
                                    .createFullTextQuery(query, Products.class);
        Sort sort = new Sort(new SortField("price", SortField.DOUBLE));
        fullTextQuery.setSort(sort);
```

```
fullTextQuery.initializeObjectsWith(ObjectLookupMethod.SKIP,
                              DatabaseRetrievalMethod.FIND_BY_ID);

List results = fullTextQuery.getResultList();

return results;
    }
}
```

Notice that the promotional products are displayed in ascending order by price. Obviously, you can present the products in a web browser in a number of different ways. In Figure 8-5, you can see our custom design. Notice that promotional products have the old price to the right of the current price.

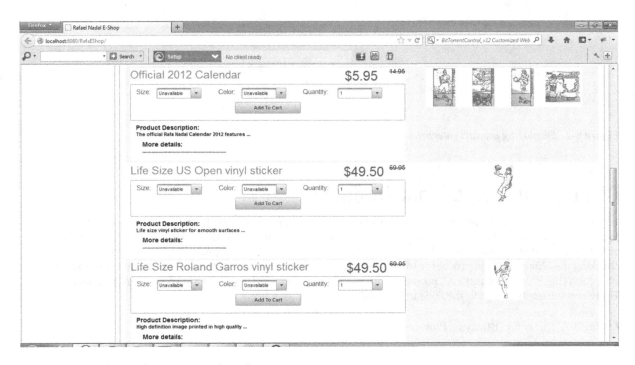

Figure 8-5. *Displaying the promotional products*

As you can see, we haven't yet provided pagination for the promotional products. Next we'll look at how to provide pagination when displaying the products from a selected category, and you can adapt the same mechansim here.

Display the Products From a Category

When a user selects a category, we need to provide a list of the products grouped under that category. Since we have the category id, it's very easy to extract the products, as shown in Listing 8-3.

Listing 8-3. Extracting the Products

```
package eshop.beans;
...
public class EShopBean {
...
public Map<Integer, List<Products>> extractProducts(String id, int page) {

        FullTextEntityManager fullTextEntityManager =
                                org.hibernate.search.jpa.Search.getFullTextEntityManager(em);

        QueryBuilder queryBuilder = fullTextEntityManager.getSearchFactory().
                                        buildQueryBuilder().forEntity(Products.class).get();
        org.apache.lucene.search.Query query = queryBuilder.keyword().
                                        onField("category.id").matching(id).createQuery();

        FullTextQuery fullTextQuery = fullTextEntityManager
                                        .createFullTextQuery(query, Products.class);
        Sort sort = new Sort(new SortField("price", SortField.DOUBLE));
        fullTextQuery.setSort(sort);

        fullTextQuery.initializeObjectsWith(ObjectLookupMethod.SKIP,
                                        DatabaseRetrievalMethod.FIND_BY_ID);

        fullTextQuery.setFirstResult(page * 3);
        fullTextQuery.setMaxResults(3);
        List<Products> results = fullTextQuery.getResultList();

        Map<Integer, List<Products>> results_and_total = new HashMap<Integer, List<Products>>();
        results_and_total.put(fullTextQuery.getResultSize(), results);

        return results_and_total;
    }
}
```

Returning type Map<Integer, List<Products>> may look strange, but it's actually very simple to understand. Since a category may contain many products, we need to implement the pagination mechanism and load from the database only one page per query (the page size is set to three products). For calculating the number of pages, we need to know the number of products in the selected category, even if we extract only some of them. Lucene is able to return the total number of products even if you query only for some. The total number of products is stored as the key of the returned map, while the products list is the value of this map. Here's what the code for this looks like:

- `fullTextQuery.setFirstResult(int n);` Sets the position of the first result of retrieving the data or, in other words, it skips the first "n" elements from the result set.

- `fullTextQuery.setMaxResults(int n);`, which is used to set the number of results to retrieve starting from the first result.

- `fullTextQuery.getResultSize();` Returns the number of all results that match the query, even if we retrieve only a subset of results.

In Figure 8-6, for example, you can see the last product from the Racquets category. Under the products list, you can see the navigation link to the previous page and the pagination status of type current_page of total_pages:

Figure 8-6. *Displaying the products of a category using pagination*

Search for a Product by Name

One task an e-commerce web site has to perform is providing an easy way to search for a specific product or a number of products without navigating through categories and pages of products. Usually, a user knows the product name or has an idea of what he's looking for. For example, he may know that the product is named "*Babolat AeroPro Drive GT Racquet*," or he may know only that he's looking a "*racquet.*" The hard part is when the user knows only keywords that should appear in the name of the products(s).

Many query engines handle such problems with custom queries, but Lucene was especially designed to search in text, so searching for keywords in text is a piece of cake. The easiest way to accomplish this kind of search is to activate the default analyzer for the product field in the Products entity (set analyze = Analyze.YES). For complex searching, you can write your own analyzers, or mix analyzers, and so on. And you can use wildcards if you need more fine-grained control of keywords.

The code in Listing 8-4 locates a product (or group of products) that contains a keyword (or a list of keywords separated by spaces) within the name. (I arbitrarily chose not to sort the results.)

Listing 8-4. Locating a Product by Keyword

```
package eshop.beans;
...
public class EShopBean {
...
public List<Products> searchProducts(String search) {

        FullTextEntityManager fullTextEntityManager =
                            org.hibernate.search.jpa.Search.getFullTextEntityManager(em);

        QueryBuilder queryBuilder = fullTextEntityManager.getSearchFactory().
                            buildQueryBuilder().forEntity(Products.class).get();
        org.apache.lucene.search.Query query = queryBuilder.keyword().
                            onField("product").matching(search).createQuery();
```

```
FullTextQuery fullTextQuery = fullTextEntityManager
                            .createFullTextQuery(query, Products.class);

fullTextQuery.initializeObjectsWith(ObjectLookupMethod.SKIP,
                            DatabaseRetrievalMethod.FIND_BY_ID);
fullTextQuery.setMaxResults(3);

List results = fullTextQuery.getResultList();

return results;
    }
}
```

A limitation of our search is that it returns at most three results (the first three). If you want to return more, or even all, you will need to implement the pagination mechanism to not return too much data in a single query.

For example, I tested the search for the keyword "*t-shirts*" and obtained the results shown in Figure 8-7.

Figure 8-7. *Searching for a product by keyword*

Find a Customer By E-mail And Password

Each customer must have a unique account that contains his name, surname, e-mail address, password, and so on in the Customers entity (the customers_c collection). When the customer logs in to the web site, views or modifies his profile, places an order, or takes other actions, we need to be able to extract the customer details from the database. The query in Listing 8-5 locates a customer in the customers_c collection by the e-mail address and password.

Listing 8-5. Locating a Customer

```
package eshop.beans;
...
public class EShopBean {
...
public Customers extractCustomer(String email, String password) {
```

```
FullTextEntityManager fullTextEntityManager =
                          org.hibernate.search.jpa.Search.getFullTextEntityManager(em);

QueryBuilder queryBuilder = fullTextEntityManager.getSearchFactory().buildQueryBuilder().
                            forEntity(Customers.class).get();
org.apache.lucene.search.Query query = queryBuilder.bool().must(queryBuilder.keyword()
                          .onField("email").matching(email).createQuery()).
                          must(queryBuilder.keyword()
                          .onField("password").matching(password).createQuery()).
                          createQuery();

FullTextQuery fullTextQuery = fullTextEntityManager
                          .createFullTextQuery(query, Customers.class);

fullTextQuery.initializeObjectsWith(ObjectLookupMethod.SKIP,
                          DatabaseRetrievalMethod.FIND_BY_ID);

List results = fullTextQuery.getResultList();

if (results.isEmpty()) {
    return null;
}

return (Customers) results.get(0);
    }
}
```

Place an Order

This query does not need Lucene. When a customer places an order, the application should have the customer (because he or she is logged in); the shipping address (it's provided by the customer); and the shopping cart (stored in the customer's session). With these, it's very easy to persist an order, like this:

```
package eshop.beans;
...
public class EShopBean {
...
private EntityManager em;
...
Orders new_order = new Orders();
...
//for each product
new_order.getCart().add(cart_product);
...
new_order.setShipping_address(shipping_address);
new_order.setCustomer(customer);

new_order.setOrderdate(Calendar.getInstance().getTime());
new_order.setSubtotal(payment);
new_order.setStatus("PURCHASED");
```

```
...
em.persist(new_order);
...
}
```

This query affects only a single document, providing atomicity.

Check the Inventory

A customer can add a product to his shopping cart only if the product is available in the warehouse inventory. Programmatically speaking, this means we need to know the product details and the required quantity; check if it's available in the inventory; and, if it is, remove the quantity from the inventory.

However, removing from inventory can lead to inconsistent data, which is clearly undesirable. This can be avoided by using optimistic locking (or even pessimistic locking), but there's a price to pay when an optimistic locking exception is thrown. A simple solution is to provide a message such as, *"The product was not added to your cart. Sorry for the inconvenience, please try again . . .",* or to wait a few seconds and repeat the query for a certain number of times or until the product is not available in the inventory anymore. The first solution gives the customer a quick response, while the second solution puts him in a waiting queue. I chose to return a message that urges the user to try again. The code is shown in Listing 8-6.

Listing 8-6. Checking Inventory

```
package eshop.beans;
...
public class EShopBean {
...
public int checkInventory(String sku, String color, String size, int quantity) {

        InventoryPK pk = new InventoryPK(sku, color, size);

        Inventory inventory = em.find(Inventory.class, pk, LockModeType.OPTIMISTIC);
        int amount = inventory.getInventory();
        if (amount > 0) {
            if (amount >= quantity) {
                amount = amount - quantity;
                inventory.setInventory(amount);
                try {
                    em.merge(inventory);
                } catch (OptimisticLockException e) {
                    return -9999;
                }

                return quantity;
            } else {
                inventory.setInventory(0);
                try {
                    em.merge(inventory);
                } catch (OptimisticLockException e) {
                    return -9999;
                }
```

```
                    return amount;
            }
        } else {
            return amount;
        }
    }
}
```

When the inventory contains fewer products than the required quantity, we add to the shopping cart only the quantity available and inform the user with a message. Figure 8-8 shows the messages that might appear when the user tries to add a product to his shopping cart.

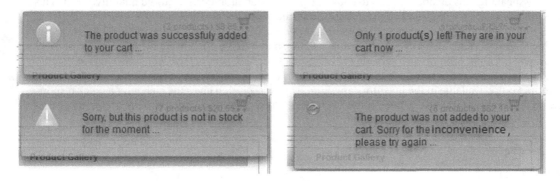

Figure 8-8. *Possible messages when adding a product to the shopping cart*

Of course, there are many ways to improve this, such as displaying a message next to each product that says either "*In Stock*" or "*Not in Stock,*" and deactivating the Add to Cart button for the latter.

Restore the Inventory

Customers can drop products from their shopping carts before placing the order, or the session might expire if the user get distracted and doesn't complete the order in a timely fashion (our application doesn't implement this case). When this happens, we need to restore the stock by adding the dropped product back to inventory. Practically, the process is the reverse of removing products from inventory, so the same problem of inconsistent data may arise. Optimistic locking (or pessimistic locking) can solve this, but, again, we have to deal with a possible optimistic locking exception. Obviously, you can't return a message to the customer that says, "*Sorry, we can't remove the product from your cart...*" because that would be very annoying. In our case, we just remove the product from the shopping cart (since it's stored in the session) and try only once to restore the inventory. But you could repeat the query, storing the quantity somewhere else and try to restore it later; or you could use an in-memory secondary inventory; or find any other approach that fits your needs.

Here's the code for restoring the inventory:

```
package eshop.beans;
...
public class EShopBean {
...
public int refreshInventory(String sku, String color, String size, int quantity) {
```

```
    InventoryPK pk = new InventoryPK(sku, color, size);

    Inventory inventory = em.find(Inventory.class, pk, LockModeType.OPTIMISTIC);
    int amount = inventory.getInventory();

    amount = amount + quantity;

    inventory.setInventory(amount);

    try {
        em.merge(inventory);
    } catch (OptimisticLockException e) {
        return -9999;
    }

    return quantity;
    }
}
```

When a product is removed from the shopping cart (even if the inventory could not actually be restored), the user should see a message like the one in Figure 8-9.

Figure 8-9. *Message indicating that removing a product from the shopping cart was successful*

At this point, we have a set of queries that compare well with many e-commerce web sites. Obviously, there are many others that could be added, either using this database model or by modifying the model itself.

Considerations for Developing the Admin GUI

So far, we've talked about the e-commerce platform only from the perspective of a customer (user). But the administrative aspects are also important for e-commerce platforms. You can develop a powerful admin GUI based on our database model just by writing the proper queries. For example, our database model facilitates the most common tasks that an administrator must accomplish:

- You can easily create a new category, rename or delete existing ones, and so on.

- You can insert new products into a category, delete existing products, or modify products characteristics.

- You can view or modify customer profiles and orders.

- You can easily populate the inventory and tracking status.

- You can create several statistics regarding selling, bestsellers, and more.

All these tasks can be accomplished atomically (affecting only one document per query).

Summary

In this chapter, you learned how to query the MongoDB e-commerce database modeled in Chapter 7. You saw how easy it is to write Lucene queries to achieve the main features of an e-commerce platform and avoid transactions. Using MongoDB atomicity per document, embedded collections, nested documents, and some tricky queries, we were able to create an e-commerce site that provides most of the common facilities of a real e-commerce platform. At this point, you can easily write an admin side, add a powerful login mechanism, modify certain parameters such as the products page size, and much more.

CHAPTER 9

■ ■ ■

Migrate MongoDB Database to Cloud

In this chapter, you'll see how to migrate a MongoDB database from your local computer to two cloud platforms, MongoHQ and MongoLab. Cloud computing typically means that hardware and software resources are available as services over a network (usually, the Internet).

I'll show you how to migrate the MongoDB eshop_db database developed in Chapter 7 to the cloud, but you can use any other database as long as you follow the steps in order. It's extremely easy to adapt the process to any other MongoDB database.

Migrating the MongoDB Database to the MongoHQ Cloud

The first cloud computing platform I'll present is MongoHQ (www.mongohq.com/home). When you access this link, you should see something like what's shown in Figure 9-1.

Figure 9-1. MongoHQ cloud platform—the home page

Suppose you have a MongoDB database on a local computer (for example, the eshop_db database) and you want it to run on the MongoHQ cloud platform. Here are the steps you need to follow:

1. To create a free account, first press the Sign Up button. You'll see a simple form like the one in Figure 9-2. Fill out the form and create the account (for this exercise, you can skip the credit card information).

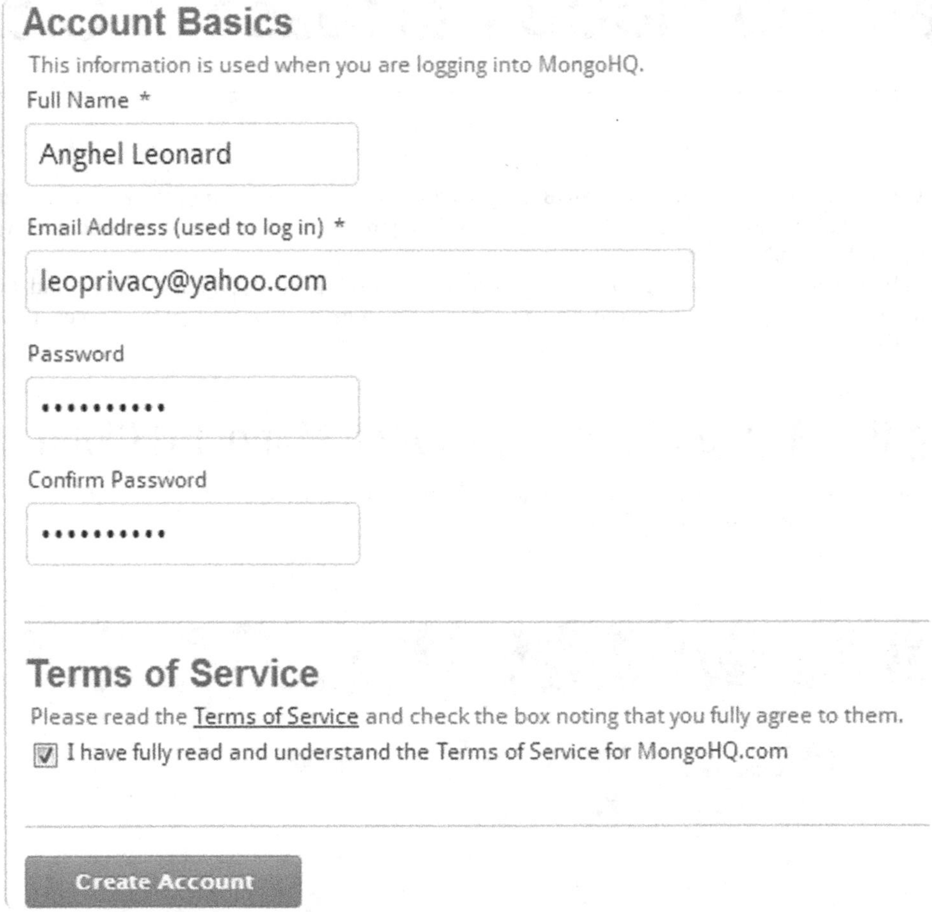

Account Basics

This information is used when you are logging into MongoHQ.

Full Name *

Anghel Leonard

Email Address (used to log in) *

leoprivacy@yahoo.com

Password

•••••••••

Confirm Password

•••••••••

Terms of Service

Please read the Terms of Service and check the box noting that you fully agree to them.

☑ I have fully read and understand the Terms of Service for MongoHQ.com

    Create Account

Figure 9-2. MongoHQ cloud platform—creating a new account

2. Use these credentials to authenticate yourself in the MongoHQ system. Enter your e-mail address and password and press the Sign In button, as shown in Figure 9-3.

Figure 9-3. MongoHQ cloud platform—logging in

3.   After you log in, you'll see the New Database panel, where you can choose a database type. For testing purposes, you can choose a free database, such as Sandbox or Azure Sandbox. Once you select a database type, additional information will be provided below it. As you can see in Figure 9-4, I chose Sandbox.

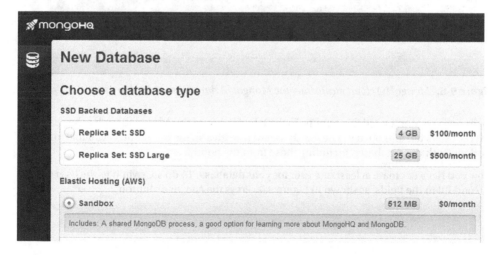

Figure 9-4. MongoHQ cloud platform—choosing the Sandbox database type

4.   After selecting the database type, scroll down and locate the *Name your database* input text field. Type the name of the MongoDB database exactly as you want it to appear in the cloud (see Figure 9-5). Then press the Create Database button and wait until the empty database is prepared for you.

Figure 9-5. *MongoHQ cloud platform—naming your MongoDB database*

5. After a few seconds, the database should be ready. A popup will inform you that the database is empty, but you can copy an external database or a MongoHQ database or start creating collections. In addition, the popup displays the information you need to connect to the database either from the MongoDB shell or by using a MongoDB URI (see Figure 9-6). The MongoDB URI is specific to each user, which means you have to adjust each command to your own URI.

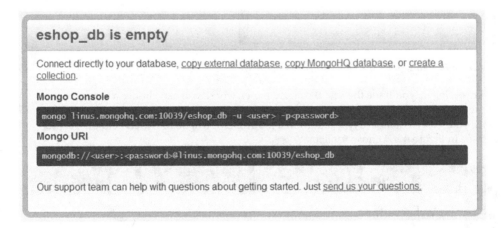

Figure 9-6. *MongoHQ cloud platform—the MongoDB database is ready to use*

6. Right now, we don't need this popup. To the left of it, locate the Admin tab under the Collections tab and open it. The Admin wizard provides all the operations available for working with the databases, including those from the popup.

7. Now you have to create at least one user for your database. To do so, switch to the Users tab and fill in the fields, as shown in Figure 9-7. Press the Add user button.

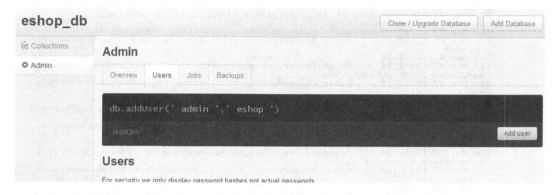

Figure 9-7. *MongoHQ cloud platform—create a new user for the MongoDB database*

8. If the user is successfully created, you'll see the entry, as shown in Figure 9-8.

Figure 9-8. *MongoHQ cloud platform—the new user document*

9. So far, so good! Now you can export the eshop_db collections from your local computer to the brand-new eshop_db database created in the MongoHQ cloud. You can accomplish this task by using two MongoDB utilities: mongodump and mongorestore. Both are available as executables in the {MongoDB_HOME}/bin folder. Start the MongoDB server, open a shell command, and navigate to the /bin folder.

■ **Note** You can find more information about the mongodump and mongorestore utilities in the MongoDB Manual at http://docs.mongodb.org/manual/reference/mongodump/ and http://docs.mongodb.org/manual/reference/mongorestore/.

---

10. Use the mongodump utility to export the eshop_db database content in binary format (you can get either JSON or CSV as the output format using the mongoexport command). The output of this utility should be stored in a separate folder. I specified a folder named eshop_tmp within the {MongoDB_HOME} folder (it will be automatically created). Here's the complete command (shown also in Figure 9-9):

```
mongodump -h localhost:27017 -d eshop_db -o ../eshop_tmp
```

```
D:\mongodb\bin>mongodump -h localhost:27017 -d eshop_db -o ../eshop_tmp
connected to: localhost:27017
Thu Mar 07 13:32:34 DATABASE: eshop_db    to      ../eshop_tmp/eshop_db
Thu Mar 07 13:32:34       eshop_db.categories_c to ../eshop_tmp/eshop_db/categorie
s_c.bson
Thu Mar 07 13:32:34            9 objects
Thu Mar 07 13:32:34       Metadata for eshop_db.categories_c to ../eshop_tmp/eshop
_db/categories_c.metadata.json
Thu Mar 07 13:32:34       eshop_db.products_c to ../eshop_tmp/eshop_db/products_c.
bson
Thu Mar 07 13:32:34            25 objects
Thu Mar 07 13:32:34       Metadata for eshop_db.products_c to ../eshop_tmp/eshop_d
b/products_c.metadata.json
Thu Mar 07 13:32:34       eshop_db.inventory_c to ../eshop_tmp/eshop_db/inventory_
c.bson
Thu Mar 07 13:32:34            59 objects
Thu Mar 07 13:32:34       Metadata for eshop_db.inventory_c to ../eshop_tmp/eshop_
db/inventory_c.metadata.json
Thu Mar 07 13:32:34       eshop_db.customers_c to ../eshop_tmp/eshop_db/customers_
c.bson
Thu Mar 07 13:32:34            3 objects
Thu Mar 07 13:32:34       Metadata for eshop_db.customers_c to ../eshop_tmp/eshop_
db/customers_c.metadata.json
```

Figure 9-9. *Exporting the eshop_db database in binary format (still on the local computer)*

11. The database, in binary format, can now be imported to the cloud using the mongorestore utility. Basically, mongorestore is used to import the content from a binary database dump into a specific database. Here's the command (also shown in Figure 9-10):

```
mongorestore -h linus.mongohq.com:10039 -d eshop_db -u admin -p eshop ../eshop_tmp/eshop_db
```

```
D:\mongodb\bin>mongorestore -h linus.mongohq.com:10039 -d eshop_db -u admin -p e
shop ../eshop_tmp/eshop_db
connected to: linus.mongohq.com:10039
Sun Mar 10 07:19:24 ../eshop_tmp/eshop_db/categories_c.bson
Sun Mar 10 07:19:24       going into namespace [eshop_db.categories_c]
9 objects found
Sun Mar 10 07:19:24       Creating index: { key: { _id: 1 }, ns: "eshop_db.categor
ies_c", name: "_id_" }
Sun Mar 10 07:19:24 ../eshop_tmp/eshop_db/customers_c.bson
Sun Mar 10 07:19:24       going into namespace [eshop_db.customers_c]
3 objects found
Sun Mar 10 07:19:24       Creating index: { key: { _id: 1 }, ns: "eshop_db.custome
rs_c", name: "_id_" }
Sun Mar 10 07:19:24 ../eshop_tmp/eshop_db/inventory_c.bson
Sun Mar 10 07:19:24       going into namespace [eshop_db.inventory_c]
59 objects found
Sun Mar 10 07:19:25       Creating index: { key: { _id: 1 }, ns: "eshop_db.invento
ry_c", name: "_id_" }
Sun Mar 10 07:19:25 ../eshop_tmp/eshop_db/products_c.bson
Sun Mar 10 07:19:25       going into namespace [eshop_db.products_c]
25 objects found
Sun Mar 10 07:19:25       Creating index: { key: { _id: 1 }, ns: "eshop_db.product
s_c", name: "_id_" }
```

Figure 9-10. *Importing eshop_db database in the MongoHQ cloud*

Each collection was successfully imported. You can see the names of the collections by navigating to the Collections tab, as shown in Figure 9-11.

eshop_db

Clone / Upgra

Collections

Admin

Collections

collection name	documents	size
categories_c	9	8 KB
customers_c	3	28 KB
inventory_c	59	8 KB
orders_c	0	8 KB
products_c	25	28 KB

Figure 9-11. The collections of eshop_db database listed in MongoHQ

Mission accomplished! The eshop_db database is in the MongoHQ cloud.

Notice that there are many other tasks you can accomplish in the Admin wizard: delete a database, clone a database, create a collection, and so on. Each task is pretty intuitive and assisted by friendly MongoHQ interfaces.

Migrating the MongoDB Database to the MongoLab Cloud

MongoLab (https://mongolab.com/welcome/) is the second cloud computing platform I'll present in this chapter. When you access the link, you should see something like what's shown in Figure 9-12.

Figure 9-12. MongoLab cloud platform - start page

We'll start again from a MongoDB database, such as the eshop_db database, on a local computer. Again, you want to make it run on the cloud. Here are the steps to do this using MongoLab:

1. To create a free account, first press the Sign Up button. You'll see a simple form, such as the one in Figure 9-13. Fill out the form and create the account.

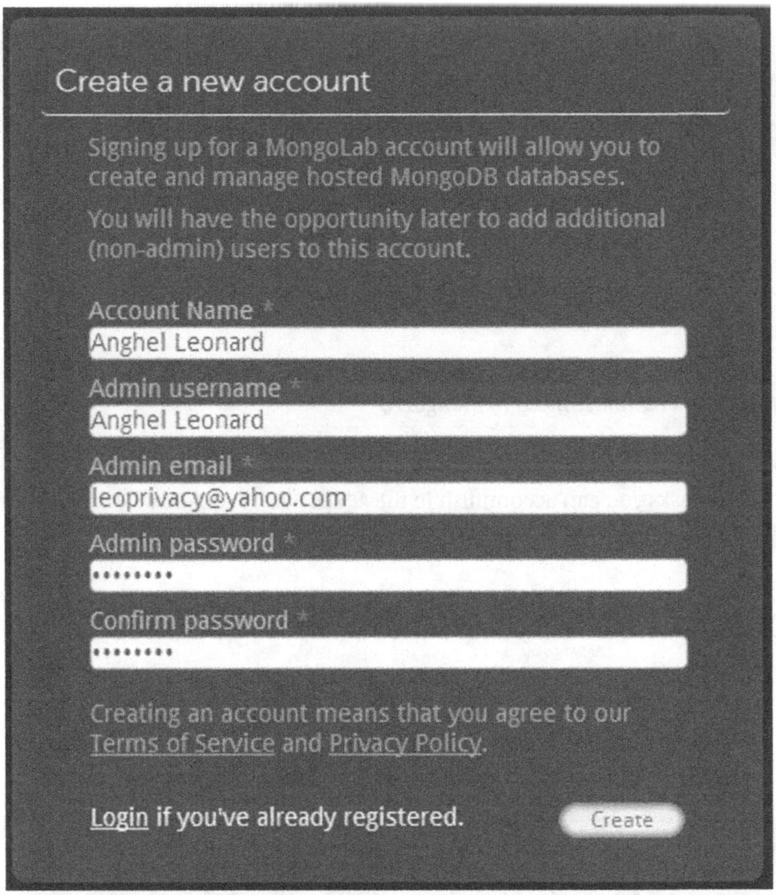

Figure 9-13. *MongoLab cloud platform—creating a new account*

2. Use these credentials to authenticate yourself in the MongoLab system. Fill in the username and password and press the Log In button, as shown in Figure 9-14.

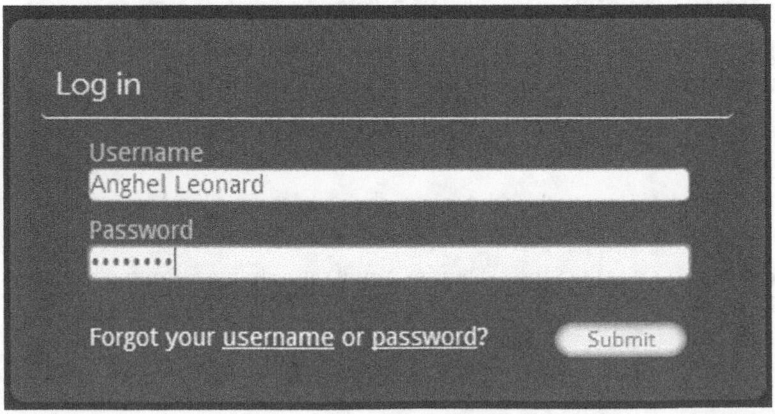

Figure 9-14. *MongoLab cloud platform—log-in form*

3. After logging in, you'll see the Databases administration panel where you can create new databases, remote connections, and dedicated clusters. For testing purposes, you can create a new MongoDB database by pressing the Create new button in the Databases section (see Figure 9-15).

Figure 9-15. *MongoLab cloud platform—Databases section*

4. Next, you need to fill in some fields and make some selections in the Create Shared Plan database wizard. Start by typing the database name as eshop_db, then select the cloud provider. I just accepted the default. Select the free, shared plan because it's perfect for testing purposes. Finally, create at least one user for this database by filling in the fields in the New database user section. I used *admin* for the username and *eshop* for the password. Press the Create database button (see Figure 9-16).

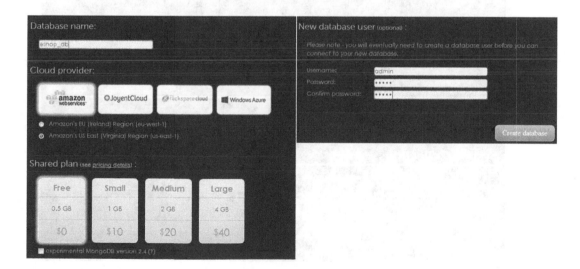

Figure 9-16. *MongoLab cloud platform—creating a new MongoDB database*

5. After a few seconds the database is created and listed in the Databases section, as shown in Figure 9-17:

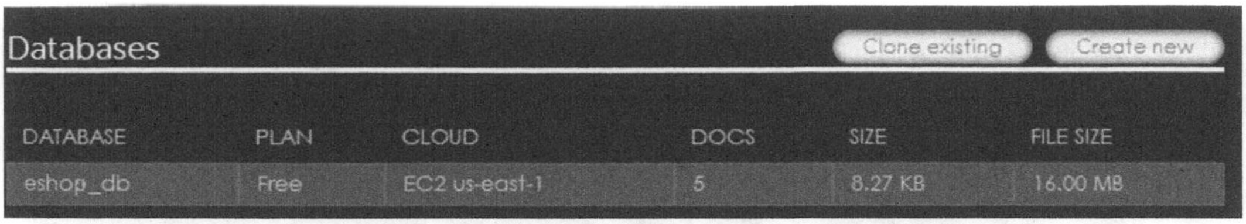

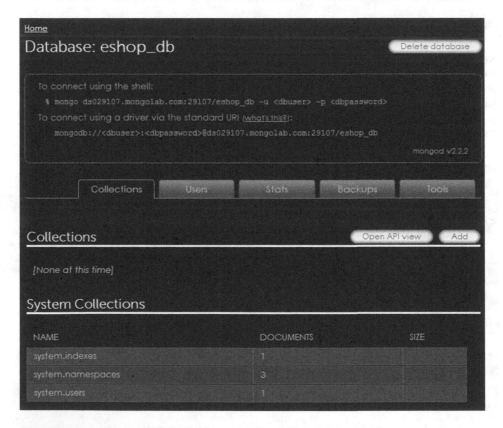

Figure 9-17. *MongoLab cloud platform—the eshop_db database listed in MongoLab*

6. Select this database to see further details, such as the connection information, collections, system collections, users, stats, and so on (see Figure 9-18). This information is specific to your account.

Figure 9-18. *MongoLab cloud platform—the eshop_db database details*

You're ready to import the eshop_db database content to the MongoLab cloud. Just as you did earlier, you can use the mongodump and mongorestore utilities. Assuming you've already used mongodump to export the database content to binary format, all you need to do is call mongorestore based on the connection information listed under the database name, as shown in Figure 9-18. Here's the mongostore command (also shown in Figure 9-19):

```
mongorestore -h ds029107.mongolab.com:29107 -d eshop_db -u admin -p eshop ../eshop_tmp/eshop_db
```

```
D:\mongodb\bin>mongorestore -h ds029107.mongolab.com:29107 -d eshop_db -u admin
 -p eshop ../eshop_tmp/eshop_db
connected to: ds029107.mongolab.com:29107
Sun Mar 10 09:30:09 ../eshop_tmp/eshop_db/categories_c.bson
Sun Mar 10 09:30:09      going into namespace [eshop_db.categories_c]
9 objects found
Sun Mar 10 09:30:10      Creating index: { key: { _id: 1 }, ns: "eshop_db.categor
ies_c", name: "_id_" }
Sun Mar 10 09:30:10 ../eshop_tmp/eshop_db/customers_c.bson
Sun Mar 10 09:30:10      going into namespace [eshop_db.customers_c]
3 objects found
Sun Mar 10 09:30:10      Creating index: { key: { _id: 1 }, ns: "eshop_db.custome
rs_c", name: "_id_" }
Sun Mar 10 09:30:10 ../eshop_tmp/eshop_db/inventory_c.bson
Sun Mar 10 09:30:10      going into namespace [eshop_db.inventory_c]
59 objects found
Sun Mar 10 09:30:10      Creating index: { key: { _id: 1 }, ns: "eshop_db.invento
ry_c", name: "_id_" }
Sun Mar 10 09:30:10 ../eshop_tmp/eshop_db/products_c.bson
Sun Mar 10 09:30:10      going into namespace [eshop_db.products_c]
25 objects found
Sun Mar 10 09:30:11      Creating index: { key: { _id: 1 }, ns: "eshop_db.product
s_c", name: "_id_" }
```

Figure 9-19. *Importing the eshop_db database content in MongoLab cloud*

A quick page refresh will reveal the imported collection under eshop_db, as in Figure 9-20.

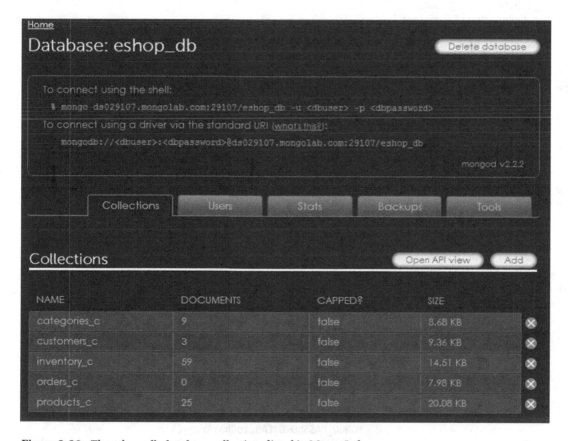

Figure 9-20. *The eshop_db database collections listed in MongoLab*

Mission accomplished! The eshop_db database is now in the MongoLab cloud.

Notice that the Tools wizard provides detailed information about importing and exporting data in MongoLab. And in addition to mongodump and mongorestore, you can also access the mongoimport and mongoexport utilities.

Connecting to the MongoHQ or MongoLab Cloud Database

You can easily test the connection to the eshop_db database deployed to the MongoHQ or MongoLab cloud as long as you correctly integrate the connection data (host, port, user, and password) into the application context. The application in Listing 9-1 is based on the MongoDB Java driver. It connects to the eshop_db database and displays the collection sizes (the number of documents). Adjust the MONGO_* constants to correspond to yours if the provided values don't work.

Listing 9-1. Testing the Connection to the eshop_db Database

```
package testcloudauth;

import com.mongodb.DB;
import com.mongodb.DBCollection;
import com.mongodb.Mongo;
import com.mongodb.MongoException;
import java.net.UnknownHostException;

public class TestCloudAuth {

    //for MongoHQ
    private static final String MONGO_HOST_HQ = "linus.mongohq.com";
    private static final int MONGO_PORT_HQ = 10039;
    private static final String MONGO_USER_HQ = "admin";
    private static final String MONGO_PASSWORD_HQ = "eshop";
    private static final String MONGO_DATABASE_HQ = "eshop_db";

    //for MongoLab
    private static final String MONGO_HOST_LAB = "ds029107.mongolab.com";
    private static final int MONGO_PORT_LAB = 29107;
    private static final String MONGO_USER_LAB = "admin";
    private static final String MONGO_PASSWORD_LAB = "eshop";
    private static final String MONGO_DATABASE_LAB = "eshop_db";

    public static void main(String[] args) {
        try {

            Mongo mongo_hq = new Mongo(MONGO_HOST_HQ, MONGO_PORT_HQ);
            DB db_hq = mongo_hq.getDB(MONGO_DATABASE_HQ);
            Mongo mongo_lab = new Mongo(MONGO_HOST_LAB, MONGO_PORT_LAB);
            DB db_lab = mongo_lab.getDB(MONGO_DATABASE_LAB);

            boolean auth_hq = db_hq.authenticate(MONGO_USER_HQ,
                                    MONGO_PASSWORD_HQ.toCharArray());
            boolean auth_lab = db_lab.authenticate(MONGO_USER_LAB,
                                    MONGO_PASSWORD_LAB.toCharArray());
```

```
        if (auth_hq) {

            System.out.println("Connected at MongoHQ:");
            DBCollection collection_categories_c_hq = db_hq.getCollection("categories_c");
            DBCollection collection_customers_c_hq = db_hq.getCollection("customers_c");
            DBCollection collection_inventory_c_hq = db_hq.getCollection("inventory_c");
            DBCollection collection_products_c_hq = db_hq.getCollection("products_c");
            DBCollection collection_orders_c_hq = db_hq.getCollection("orders_c");
            System.out.println("TOTAL DOCUMENTS IN categories_c (MongoHQ):" +
                                    collection_categories_c_hq.count());
            System.out.println("TOTAL DOCUMENTS IN customers_c (MongoHQ):" +
                                    collection_customers_c_hq.count());
            System.out.println("TOTAL DOCUMENTS IN inventory_c (MongoHQ):" +
                                    collection_inventory_c_hq.count());
            System.out.println("TOTAL DOCUMENTS IN products_c (MongoHQ):" +
                                    collection_products_c_hq.count());
            System.out.println("TOTAL DOCUMENTS IN orders_c (MongoHQ):" +
                                    collection_orders_c_hq.count());
        } else {
            System.out.println("Sorry, connection to MongoHQ (eshop_db database) failed ...");
        }

        if (auth_lab) {
            System.out.println("Connected at Mongolab:");
            DBCollection collection_categories_c_lab = db_lab.getCollection("categories_c");
            DBCollection collection_customers_c_lab = db_lab.getCollection("customers_c");
            DBCollection collection_inventory_c_lab = db_lab.getCollection("inventory_c");
            DBCollection collection_products_c_lab = db_lab.getCollection("products_c");
            DBCollection collection_orders_c_lab = db_lab.getCollection("orders_c");
            System.out.println("TOTAL DOCUMENTS IN categories_c (Mongolab):" +
                                    collection_categories_c_lab.count());
            System.out.println("TOTAL DOCUMENTS IN customers_c (Mongolab):" +
                                    collection_customers_c_lab.count());
            System.out.println("TOTAL DOCUMENTS IN inventory_c (Mongolab):" +
                                    collection_inventory_c_lab.count());
            System.out.println("TOTAL DOCUMENTS IN products_c (Mongolab):" +
                                    collection_products_c_lab.count());
            System.out.println("TOTAL DOCUMENTS IN orders_c (Mongolab):" +
                                    collection_orders_c_lab.count());
        } else {
            System.out.println("Sorry, connection to Mongolab (eshop_db database) failed ...");
        }
    } catch (UnknownHostException | MongoException e) {
        System.err.println(e.getMessage());
    }
  }
}
```

If the connection is successfully established, the output will be similar to what you see in Figure 9-21.

```
Output ✖  TestCloudAuth.java

▷▷  Java DB Database Process ✖   GlassFish Server 3.1.2 ✖   TestMongoHQAuth (run) ✖

▷▷  run:
    Connected at MongoHQ:
    TOTAL DOCUMENTS IN categories_c (MongoHQ):9
    TOTAL DOCUMENTS IN customers_c (MongoHQ):3
    TOTAL DOCUMENTS IN inventory_c (MongoHQ):59
    TOTAL DOCUMENTS IN products_c (MongoHQ):25
    TOTAL DOCUMENTS IN orders_c (MongoHQ):0
    Connected at Mongolab:
    TOTAL DOCUMENTS IN categories_c (Mongolab):9
    TOTAL DOCUMENTS IN customers_c (Mongolab):3
    TOTAL DOCUMENTS IN inventory_c (Mongolab):59
    TOTAL DOCUMENTS IN products_c (Mongolab):25
    TOTAL DOCUMENTS IN orders_c (Mongolab):0
    BUILD SUCCESSFUL (total time: 3 seconds)
```

Figure 9-21. *Output of the TestCloudAuth application*

The complete source code for this application, called TestMongoHQAuth, is available in the Apress repository. It comes as a NetBeans project and was tested for the presented cases.

The same connection can be configured in Hibernate OGM via JPA or Hibernate Native API. For example, the persistence.xml file can be modified to connect to the eshop_db database under MongoHQ, like this:

```
...
<property name="hibernate.ogm.mongodb.database" value="eshop_db"/>
<property name="hibernate.ogm.mongodb.host" value="linus.mongohq.com"/>
<property name="hibernate.ogm.mongodb.port" value="10039"/>
<property name="hibernate.ogm.mongodb.username" value="admin"/>
<property name="hibernate.ogm.mongodb.password" value="eshop"/>
...
```

Summary

In this chapter, you saw how to migrate a MongoDB database from your local computer to the MongoHQ and MongoLab cloud platforms. In both cases, I used free accounts, and I exported the binary version of the eshop_db database modeled in Chapter 7 to the cloud. I used the MongoDB mongodump utility to obtain the binary version of this database, and the export was achieved using the MongoDB mongorestore utility. Moreover, you saw how to test the connection and do some queries against each cloud provider from a Java application. The application uses the Java MongoDB driver, but I also showed you how to configure the same connection using the JPA persistence.xml file.

CHAPTER 10

■ ■ ■

Migrating RafaEShop Application on OpenShift

In Chapter 9 you saw how to migrate MongoDB databases to two cloud platforms—MongoHQ and MongoLab. As their names suggest, these platforms are cloud-based, hosted database solutions dedicated to MongoDB, which means that the applications that use these databases must be hosted in another place. But if you don't have such a place, or you want to have the entire application (not just the database) in the cloud, you have to focus more on cloud computing platforms, like OpenShift from Red Hat. As quoted on the www.openshift.com web site, "*OpenShift is Red Hat's free, auto-scaling Platform as a Service (PaaS) for applications. As an application platform in the cloud, OpenShift manages the stack so you can focus on your code.*"

OpenShift allows you to use almost any programming language, framework, and middleware, supports many kinds of architectures and servers, provides out-of-the-box templates for various types of applications, maintains dedicated tools for developing and migrating applications, and is always focused on assistance and documentation for developers.

OpenShift uses the notion of a *cartridge* to refer to all the supported servers, frameworks, database management systems, and so on. For example, GlassFish AS, MongoDB, MySQL, SwitchYard, Cron, RockMongo, and JBoss AS are all cartridges, and applications are built on one or more cartridges. As you'll see, OpenShift provides a user interface for adding, removing, and configuring cartridges of applications, but its real power comes from the OpenShift Client tools, known as *rhc*. For simple applications (like some web applications), it's very convenient to use the OpenShift GUI, while for more complex applications (web applications with databases, web services, and the like) a mix of both GUI and rhc provides full control.

In this chapter, you'll see how to migrate the RafaEShop application to the OpenShift cloud. The application was hosted and tested on GlassFish AS 3 running on localhost, but now we're going to migrate it to GlassFish AS 3 and JBoss AS 7 running in the cloud. The aim is to apply the necessary modifications to the source code (the MongoDB connection credentials, configuration files, and so on) and migrate this code to the cloud, first on GlassFish AS 3 as a Web Archive (WAR), and, second, on JBoss AS 7 as a WAR and a Maven project. At the end, you'll have three applications in the cloud: one deployed on GlassFish AS 3 and two deployed on JBoss AS 7.

Creating a Free Account on OpenShift

Before getting started with OpenShift, you need to create a free account at www.openshift.com/. This can be accomplished quickly and easily by pressing the SIGN UP link, which opens a form like the one shown in Figure 10-1.

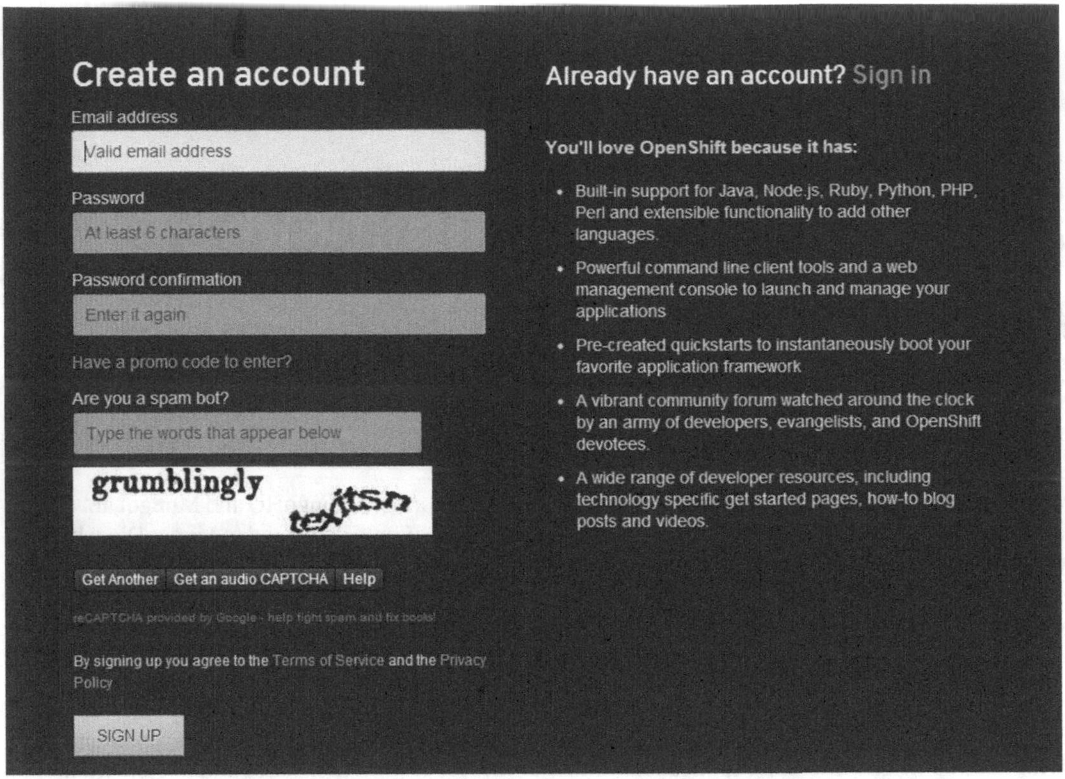

Figure 10-1. *Creating a free OpenShift account*

Notice that you have to provide a valid e-mail address because you'll receive an e-mail from OpenShift containing a link for activating the account (Figure 10-2).

Figure 10-2. *Activating your account from e-mail*

After creating and activating your account, you have to accept the legal terms and conditions. Read them and then press the I Accept button (Figure 10-3).

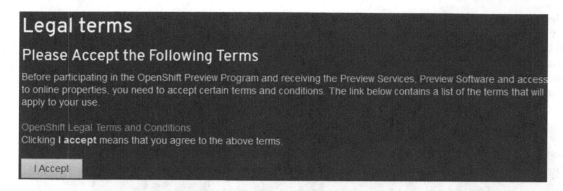

Legal terms
Please Accept the Following Terms
Before participating in the OpenShift Preview Program and receiving the Preview Services, Preview Software and access to online properties, you need to accept certain terms and conditions. The link below contains a list of the terms that will apply to your use.
OpenShift Legal Terms and Conditions
Clicking I accept means that you agree to the above terms.
I Accept

Figure 10-3. *OpenShift legal terms*

Once you accept the legal terms, you'll be redirected to your personal management console where you can see and create applications, get help, and modify account settings (see Figure 10-4). By default, the `Create Application` wizard will be active.

My Applications
Create Application
Help
My Account

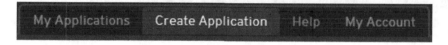

Figure 10-4. *User management console tabs*

From now on, the management console page can be accessed by clicking the `MY APPS` link on the OpenShift start page and signing in using your e-mail address and password, as shown in Figure 10-5.

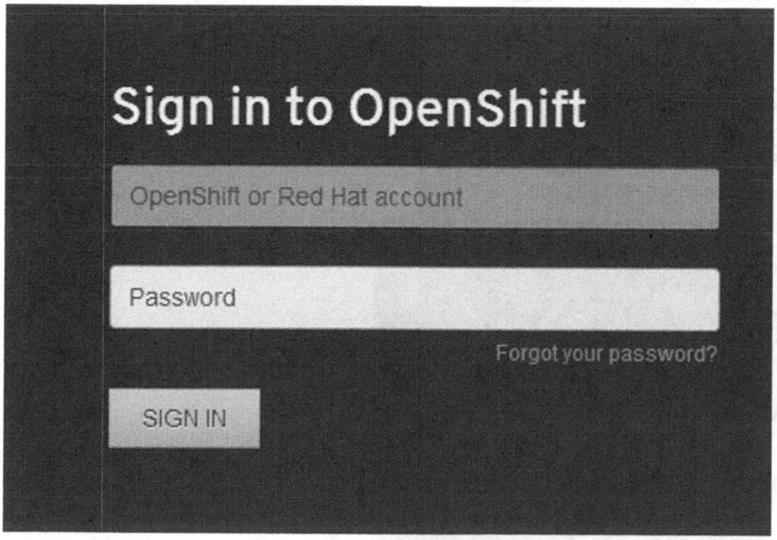

Sign in to OpenShift
OpenShift or Red Hat account
Password
Forgot your password?
SIGN IN

Figure 10-5. *Signing in to OpenShift*

If you sign in successfully, you should see the Create Application wizard (Figure 10-6). This wizard starts automatically because you don't yet have any application available. Once you do, the default wizard will be My Applications. Note that a free OpenShift account allows you to have at most three applications in the cloud. When you reach three applications, you can't create a new one until you delete or scale down an existing one. (The message you'll get is: "*Currently you do not have enough free gears available to create a new application. You can either scale down or delete existing applications to free up resources.*")

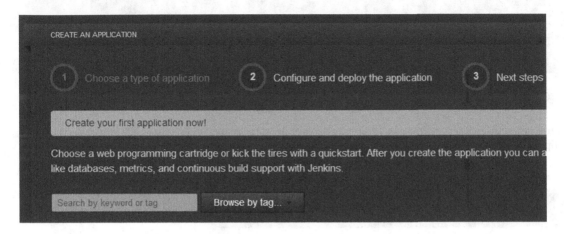

Figure 10-6. *OpenShift Create Application wizard*

Before creating your first application, you must create a *namespace* that's unique to your account and is the suffix of the public URLs OpenShift will assign to your applications. (If you don't create the namespace now, you'll be prompted for it later.) First, in your personal management console, switch to the My Account wizard, shown in Figure 10-7. (If you don't see this image, click on the Create a domain for your application link, in the Domain section).

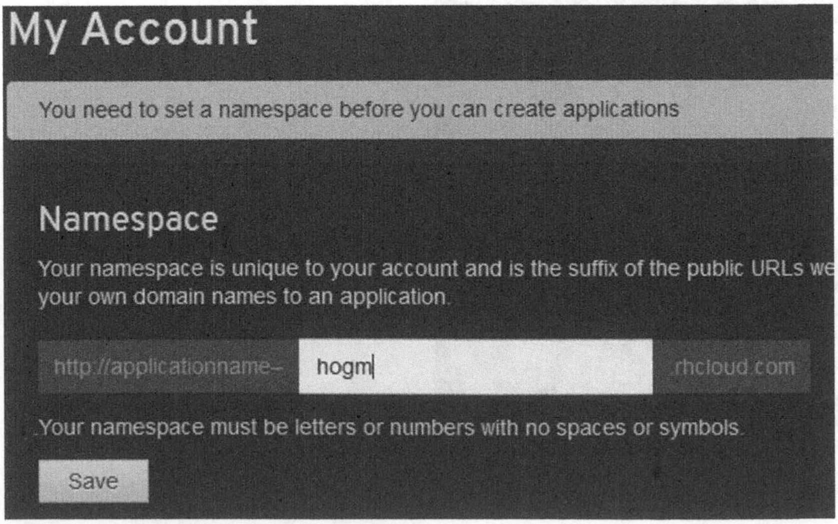

Figure 10-7. *OpenShift My Account wizard*

Type a valid namespace and save it. As you can see in Figure 10-7, I typed *hogm*. After the namespace is successfully created, you'll see a message like the one in Figure 10-8. (Note that in place of the Public Keys message, you might see an SSH Keys section, with a link indicating to upload your public key to access the code.)

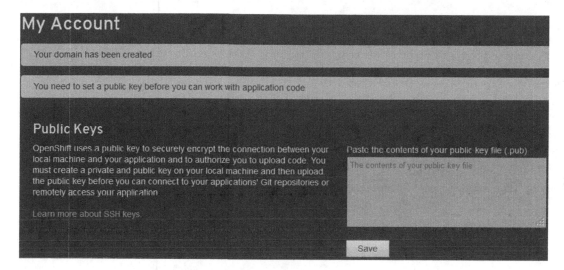

Figure 10-8. *Domain was successfully created*

There are two important messages in Figure 10-8. The first confirms that the domain was created successfully, and the second tells you need an SSH public key to securely encrypt the connection between your local machine and your applications. I'll show you later how to do this from the shell so you can sign out.

At this point, you have an account and a domain, but there are a few more steps before you can start migrating the RafaEShop application. To communicate with the OpenShift platform from the local shell, you need to install and configure the OpenShift RHC Client Tools (rhc) on your machine. These tools, which were built and packaged using the Ruby programming language, will help you with many tasks, such as uploading or removing applications to or from the cloud; monitoring server status and logs; controlling available services (start/stop/restart); adding and removing security permissions; forwarding ports, and so on. Some of the capabilities provided by these tools are also available through OpenShift wizards, but the power of these tools goes beyond OpenShift web GUIs.

Installing the OpenShift RHC Client Tools on Windows

In this section, you'll see how to install the OpenShift RHC Client Tools on Windows. You'll also install the Git version control system, which is used by rhc to provide powerful command-line support for controlling your application.

Installing Ruby

Because rhc is built and packaged using Ruby, you need to install Ruby on your computer. The recommended version is Ruby 1.9.x; I installed Ruby 1.9.3-p392, available at http://rubyinstaller.org/downloads/. For Windows, Ruby comes as an executable file, so the installation process is monitored and guided by an intuitive wizard. During installation, many settings have default values that fit most cases, but you must select the "*Add Ruby executables to your PATH*" check box to run Ruby from the shell (Figure 10-9).

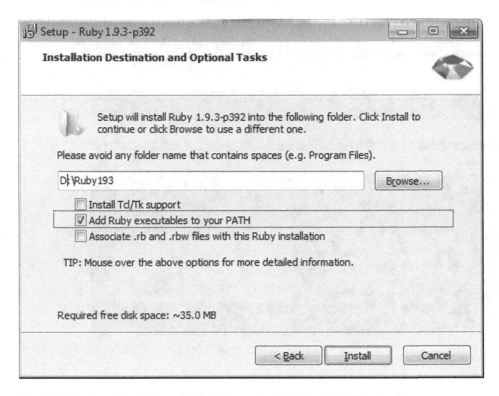

Figure 10-9. Installing Ruby; adding Ruby executables to your PATH

■ **Note** If you decide to install Ruby versions later than 1.9.x (Ruby 2.0.0, for example), you might get a warning of type "*DL is deprecated, please use Fiddle*" in the shell. Everything else should work as expected.

Installing Git

As quoted on the www.git-scm.com web site, "*Git is a free and open source distributed version control system designed to handle everything from small to very large projects with speed and efficiency.*" OpenShift rhc needs Git to provide version control for your source code, so you need to download and install it from www.git-scm.com/downloads.

   I downloaded Git 1.8.1.2 and installed it using the installation wizard. During installation, ensure that Git is added to your PATH so you can run it from the shell (Figure 10-10).

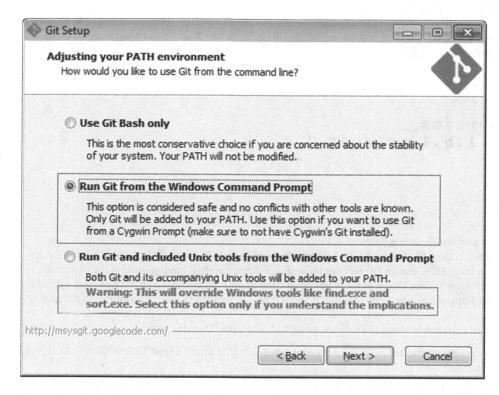

Figure 10-10. *Installing Git; adding Git executables to your PATH*

If you don't want to alter your PATH, you can use the Git Bash shell (the first radio button in Figure 10-10), which will put a shortcut on your desktop.

Testing Ruby and Git from the Shell

Before going further, it's a good idea to do a quick test of Ruby and Git by executing some simple commands. To test Ruby, open a shell and type the following command, which is also shown in Figure 10-11:

```
ruby -e 'puts "Hello from Ruby"'
```

```
D:\>ruby -e 'puts "Hello from Ruby"'
Hello from Ruby

D:\>_
```

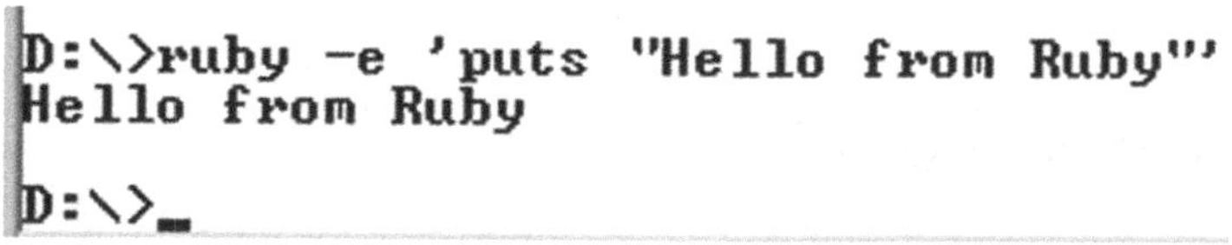

Figure 10-11. *Testing Ruby*

The output of this command is also visible in this figure.

Now type the following command, which is also shown in Figure 10-12, to test that Git was successfully installed and is available from the shell:

```
git -version
```

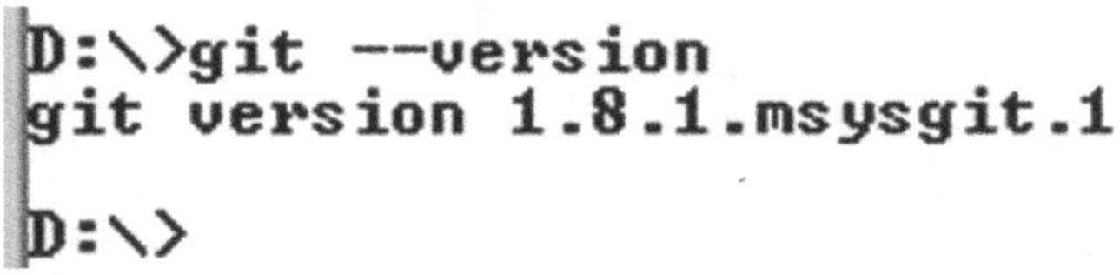

```
D:\>git --version
git version 1.8.1.msysgit.1

D:\>
```

Figure 10-12. *Testing Git*

The expected output is also visible in this figure.

There are situations when adding the Ruby and Git paths to the Windows PATH during installation doesn't have the expected result. In such cases, Ruby and/or Git will not be available from the shell, and instead of the expected results, you'll get an error message stating "*'ruby or git' is not recognized as an internal or external command, operable program or batch file.*" If this happens to you, keep reading. If you did get the expected results, just jump to the next section.

This issue can be fixed in at least two ways. I like to use a batch (`*.bat`) file. The idea is simple:

- Create a file named `autoexec.bat` anywhere on your computer (the name doesn't actually have to be *autoexec*).

- In this file, add a line like the SET PATH entry in Figure 10-13, adjusting the Ruby and Git paths to correspond to yours.

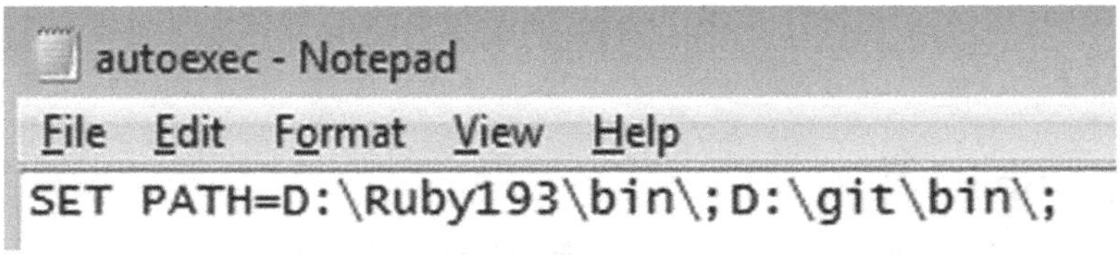

```
autoexec - Notepad
File   Edit   Format   View   Help
SET PATH=D:\Ruby193\bin\;D:\git\bin\;
```

Figure 10-13. *Creating a Windows .bat file*

- Open a shell, navigate to the location of the `.bat` file, and type the file name (see Figure 10-14).

```
C:\bat>autoexec

C:\bat>SET PATH=D:\Ruby193\bin\;D:\git\bin\;

C:\bat>
```

Figure 10-14. *Running the batch file*

Now, Ruby should be accessible from the shell. Keep in mind that each time you open a new shell, you need to run this command to be able to access Ruby and Git. This can be a pain, but it works. If you already have such a `.bat` file, then just add these entries in the SET PATH section. For example, my `autoexec.bat` looks like what's shown in Figure 10-15.

```
SET JAVA_HOME=C:\Program Files\Java\jdk1.7.0_09\
SET PATH=C:\WINDOWS\system32;D:\apache-maven-3.0.4\bin\;D:\apache-ant-1.8.4\bin\;D:\Forge_1.1.3\bin;D:\git\bin\;D:\Ruby193\bin\
```

Figure 10-15. *Windows batch file sample for settings paths*

Another approach is to use Windows wizards:

1. From the Desktop, right-click My Computer and click Properties.

2. Click the Advanced System Settings link in the left column (Figure 10-16).

Figure 10-16. *Windows 7 Control Panel*

3. In the System Properties window, click the Environment Variables button.

4. Locate the Path variable (Figure 10-17) and add to it the Ruby and Git paths.

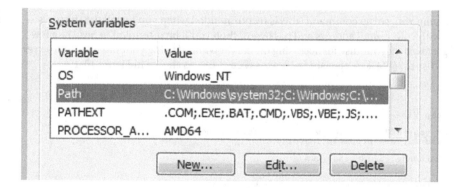

Figure 10-17. *Adding Ruby and Git paths in Windows 7*

5. Restart your machine and test Ruby and Git from the shell.

Installing the OpenShift Gem

Finally, we'll install the OpenShift gem. After Ruby and Git are correctly installed, we'll use the RubyGems package manager (included in Ruby) to install the OpenShift client tools. This is straightforward and consists of a simple command, gem install rhc, as shown in Figure 10-18. This command downloads and installs the rhc gem from www.rubygems.org/gems/rhc.

```
D:\>gem install rhc
Fetching: net-ssh-2.6.6.gem (100%)
Fetching: archive-tar-minitar-0.5.2.gem (100%)
Fetching: highline-1.6.16.gem (100%)
Fetching: commander-4.1.3.gem (100%)
Fetching: httpclient-2.3.3.gem (100%)
Fetching: open4-1.3.0.gem (100%)
Fetching: rhc-1.5.13.gem (100%)
========================================================================

If this is your first time installing the RHC tools, please run 'rhc setup'

========================================================================
Successfully installed net-ssh-2.6.6
Successfully installed archive-tar-minitar-0.5.2
Successfully installed highline-1.6.16
Successfully installed commander-4.1.3
Successfully installed httpclient-2.3.3
Successfully installed open4-1.3.0
Successfully installed rhc-1.5.13
7 gems installed
Installing ri documentation for net-ssh-2.6.6...
Installing ri documentation for archive-tar-minitar-0.5.2...
Installing ri documentation for highline-1.6.16...
Installing ri documentation for commander-4.1.3...
Installing ri documentation for httpclient-2.3.3...
Installing ri documentation for open4-1.3.0...
Installing ri documentation for rhc-1.5.13...
Installing RDoc documentation for net-ssh-2.6.6...
Installing RDoc documentation for archive-tar-minitar-0.5.2...
Installing RDoc documentation for highline-1.6.16...
Installing RDoc documentation for commander-4.1.3...
Installing RDoc documentation for httpclient-2.3.3...
Installing RDoc documentation for open4-1.3.0...
Installing RDoc documentation for rhc-1.5.13...

D:\>
```

Figure 10-18. *Downloading and installing the OpenShift gem*

After installation completes, run the rhc setup command (this is recommended when you install the rhc tools for the first time). To do this, sign in with your e-mail address and password, then you'll be prompted to answer a few questions. The first is about creating a *token* on your disk for accessing the server without using your password. Type *yes* and the token will be saved in the C:/Users/{USER}/.openshift/express.conf file, as shown in Figure 10-19.

```
D:\>rhc setup
OpenShift Client Tools (RHC) Setup Wizard

This wizard will help you upload your SSH keys, set your application namespace,
and check that other programs like Git are properly installed.

Login to openshift.redhat.com: rafanadalworld@yahoo.com
Password: **********

OpenShift can create and store a token on disk which allows to you to access
the server without using your password. The key is stored in your home
directory and should be kept secret. You can delete the key at any time by
running 'rhc logout'.
Generate a token now? (yes|no) yes
Generating an authorization token for this client ... lasts about 1 day

Saving configuration to C:\Users\Anghel Leonard\.openshift\express.conf ... done
```

Figure 10-19. *The rhc setup shell wizard; generating a token*

Remember the SSH public key needed to securely encrypt communication between your local machine and your applications? Well, you should now be informed that you don't have such a key and that OpenShift can create and upload to the server an SSH key for you. Type *yes;* the SSH key will be saved locally in the C:/Users/{USER}/.ssh/id_rsa.pub file and uploaded to the server, as shown in Figure 10-20.

```
No SSH keys were found. We will generate a pair of keys for you.
   Created: C:/Users/Anghel Leonard/.ssh/id_rsa.pub
Your public SSH key must be uploaded to the OpenShift server to access code.
Upload now? (yes!no) yes

Since you do not have any keys associated with your OpenShift account, your new
key will be uploaded as the 'default' key.

  Type:        ssh-rsa
  Fingerprint: 83:72:28:9d:a6:23:63:17:bb:91:f6:f6:04:b9:d1:6b

Uploading key 'default' from C:\Users\Anghel Leonard\.ssh\id_rsa.pub ... done
```

Figure 10-20. *The rhc setup shell wizard; creating and uploading the SSH key*

After a few informational messages and a list of applications that can be created on OpenShift, you should see a message like "*Your client tools are now configured*" (see Figure 10-21).

```
You are using 0 of 3 total gears
The following gear sizes are available to you: small

Your client tools are now configured.
```

Figure 10-21. *The rhc setup shell wizard; the configuration was successful*

This message confirms that rch was successfully created and everything is set to start developing applications.
The SSH key was successfully generated and uploaded. You can check this in your personal management console, in the My Account wizard, as shown in Figure 10-22.

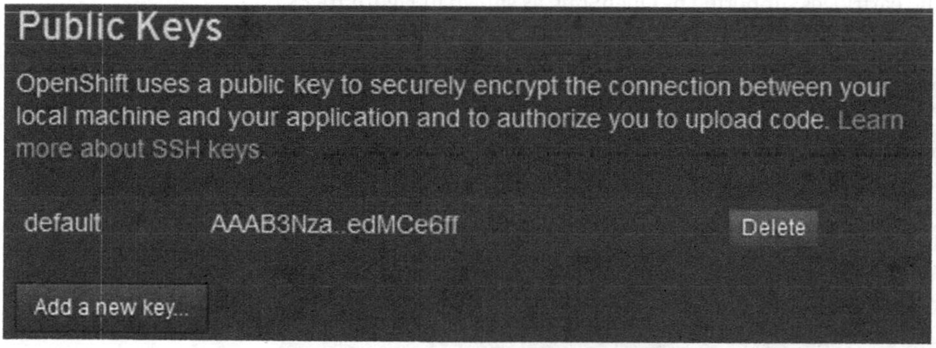

Figure 10-22. *Accessing your SSH key using the My Account wizard*

■ **Note** This section describes installing the rhc tools only on Windows. But rhc can also run on other operating systems, such as Mac OS X, Fedora 16, 17, and 18, Red Hat Enterprise Linux 6.4, Ubuntu, and more. To see how to install rhc on these operating systems, please see the instructions at www.openshift.com/developers/rhc-client-tools-install.

Fixing a Known Issue

In Windows 7 it's very possible to get the error *"Permission denied (publickey, gssapi-keyex, gssapi-with-mic)"* when you try to execute Git commands. The easiest way to fix this is to copy the two files named id_rsa from the C:/Users/{USER}/.ssh folder to the {GIT_HOME}/.ssh folder. This should fix the issue!

Migrating the RafaEShop Application to OpenShift with JBoss AS 7

Now let's see how to migrate the RafaEShop application from your computer to OpenShift cloud on JBoss AS 7. We're going to look at two scenarios: one for migrating this application as a WAR (Web Archive) and one as a Maven project.

■ **Note**   Of course, if you are interested in only one of the scenarios, only read about that one and ignore all references to the other.

To start, though, there are several steps to complete that are common to both.

Step 1: Create a base folder. Create a folder named JBossAS on one of your local disks (such as D:/JBossAS). We will use this as the base folder for our two scenarios.

Step 2: Create two scenario folders. In the D:/JBossAS folder, create two subfolders, one named war, and the other named mvn.

Step 3: Create a default project based on the JBoss Application Server 7.1 cartridge.

Before deploying an application such as RafaEShop, you need to create a default JBoss Application Server 7.1 application. This is one of the cartridges supported by OpenShift, as shown in Figure 10-23.

JBoss Application Server 7.1

The leading open source Java EE6 application server for enterprise Java applications. Popular development frameworks include Seam, CDI, Weld, and Spring.

http://www.jboss.org

JAVA   JBOSS

Figure 10-23. JBoss Application Server 7.1 cartridge

This step can be accomplished from the OpenShift GUI or from the shell. I prefer the latter, so open a shell and navigate to the D:/JBossAS/war folder. Use the rhc tools to create the new project by using the following command, which is also shown in Figure 10-24:

```
rhc app create -a RafaEShopW -t jbossas-7
```

```
D:\JBossAS\war>rhc app create -a RafaEShopW -t jbossas-7
Application Options
--------------------
   Namespace:  hogm
   Cartridges: jbossas-7
   Gear Size:  default
   Scaling:    no

Creating application 'RafaEShopW' ... done

Waiting for your DNS name to be available ... done

Downloading the application Git repository ...
Cloning into 'RafaEShopW'...
Warning: Permanently added the RSA host key for IP address '107.20.46.229' to th
e list of known hosts.
remote: Counting objects: 39, done.
remote: Compressing objects: 100% (31/31), done.
rRemote: Total 39 (delta 1), reused 0 (delta 0)eceiving objects:  43% (17/39)
Receiving objects:  69% (27/39)
Receiving objects: 100% (39/39), 19.99 KiB, done.
Resolving deltas: 100% (1/1), done.

Your application code is now in 'RafaEShopW'

RafaEShopW @ http://RafaEShopW-hogm.rhcloud.com/ (uuid:
514ffd57500446021e000087)
----------------------------------------------------------------------------
-
   Created: 7:31 AM
   Gears:   1 (defaults to small)
   Git URL:
ssh://514ffd57500446021e000087@RafaEShopW-hogm.rhcloud.com/~/git/RafaEShopW.git/

   SSH:     514ffd57500446021e000087@RafaEShopW-hogm.rhcloud.com

   jbossas-7 (JBoss Application Server 7.1)
   ---------------------------------------------
     Gears: 1 small

RESULT:
Application RafaEShopW was created.
```

Figure 10-24. Creating the JBoss Application Server 7.1 default application

---

■ **Note**   During this step, you may receive the question "*Are you sure you want to continue connecting (yes/no)?*" The answer is yes. OpenShift needs to add this host to the list of trusted hosts.

Switch to the D:/JBossAS/mvn folder and repeat this step, this time typing the following:

```
rhc app create -a RafaEShopM -t jbossas-7
```

Now you have two identical default applications. We'll deploy the RafaEShop application as a WAR file under RafaEShopW and as a Maven project under RafaEShopM.

At this point, if you check the D:/JBossAS/war and D:/JBossAS/mvn folders, you'll see that the applications were created in the RafaEShopW and RafaEShopM subfolders. Here you'll find several folders and files, described in the D:/JBossAS/war/RafaEShopW/README.txt and the D:/JBossAS/war/RafaEShopM/README.txt) files, from which I've copied the following fragment:

deployments/ - location for built wars

src/ - Maven src structure

pom.xml - Maven build file

.openshift/ - location for openshift specific files

.openshift/config/ - location for configuration files such as standalone.xml (used to modify jboss config such as datasources)

.openshift/action_hooks/pre_build - Script that gets run every git push before the build (on the CI system if available)

.openshift/action_hooks/build - Script that gets run every git push as part of the build process (on the CI system if available)

.openshift/action_hooks/deploy - Script that gets run every git push after build but before the app is restarted

.openshift/action_hooks/post_deploy - Script that gets run every git push after the app is restarted

.openshift/action_hooks/pre_start_jbossas-7 - Script that gets run prior to starting AS7

.openshift/action_hooks/post_start_jbossas-7 - Script that gets run after AS7 is started

.openshift/action_hooks/pre_stop_jbossas-7 - Script that gets run prior to stopping AS7

.openshift/action_hooks/post_stop_jbossas-7 - Script that gets run after AS7 is stopped

.openshift/markers - directory for files used to control application behavior. See README in markers directory

Read the entire file for complete details. The application links are available in your personal management console, as shown in Figure 10-25. The links are functional, and they open the default welcome page of the applications.

Figure 10-25. *Two JBoss Application Server 7.1 application links*

If you click on an application's link, you'll see the application details, such as the Git repository associated with the application, and you'll be able to manage cartridges (see Figure 10-26).

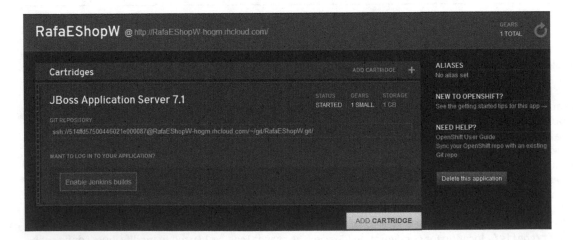

Figure 10-26. *RafaEShopW application details*

Now that you've seen the structure of a default JBoss Application Server 7.1 application, it's time to go further. Step 4: Add a MongoDB NoSQL Database 2.2 cartridge (see Figure 10-27).

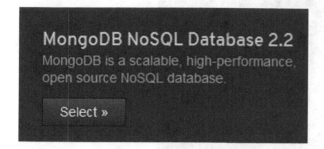

Figure 10-27. MongoDB NoSQL Database 2.2 cartridge

This will add a MongoDB server instance ready to be populated with data. By default, OpenShift will create a MongoDB database with the same name as the application. As you can see in Figure 10-27, there's a Select button that lets you add this cartridge using a dedicated wizard. I'll let you explore that approach on your own, while I show you how to do this from the shell using rhc. Use the following rhc command, which is also shown in Figure 10-28, to add the MongoDB to the RafaEShopW application:

```
rhc cartridge add -a RafaEShopW -c mongodb-2.2
```

```
D:\JBossAS\war>rhc cartridge add -a RafaEShopW -c mongodb-2.2
Adding mongodb-2.2 to application 'RafaEShopW' ... Success

mongodb-2.2 (MongoDB NoSQL Database 2.2)
----------------------------------------
  Gears:          Located with jbossas-7
  Connection URL:
mongodb://$OPENSHIFT_MONGODB_DB_HOST:$OPENSHIFT_MONGODB_DB_PORT/
  Database Name:  RafaEShopW
  Password:       hi_qnUdFqEBg
  Username:       admin

RESULT:
Added mongodb-2.2 to application RafaEShopW

MongoDB 2.2 database added.  Please make note of these credentials:

      Root User: admin
  Root Password: hi_qnUdFqEBg
  Database Name: RafaEShopW

Connection URL:
mongodb://$OPENSHIFT_MONGODB_DB_HOST:$OPENSHIFT_MONGODB_DB_PORT/

You can manage your new MongoDB by also embedding rockmongo-1.1
The rockmongo username and password will be the same as the MongoDB credentials
above.
```

Figure 10-28. Adding the MongoDB NoSQL Database 2.2 cartridge using rhc tools

Repeat this step to obtain a MongoDB instance for the RafaEShopM application by switching to the D:/JBossAS/mvn folder and typing the following command:

```
rhc cartridge add -a RafaEShopM -c mongodb-2.2
```

Notice that the MongoDB database was added and you have access to it through the listed credentials. The MongoDB cartridge is now available in your personal management console, as shown in Figure 10-29.

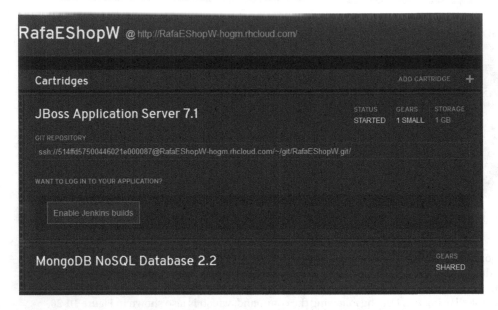

Figure 10-29. *MongoDB cartridge is listed in the RafaEShopW application*

Step 5: Add the RockMongo 1.1 cartridge, as shown in Figure 10-30. (This step is optional.)

Figure 10-30. *RockMongo 1.1 cartridge*

Adding the RockMongo administration tool is not mandatory, but it can be very useful to have access to the MongoDB database through a friendly web GUI that makes it easy to manage database content (add and delete collections, query data, manage users, import and export data, and so on). You can add this cartridge from the shell (for the RafaEShopW application) by using the following command, which is also shown in Figure 10-31:

```
rhc cartridge add -a RafaEShopW -c rockmongo-1.1
```

```
D:\JBossAS\war>rhc cartridge add -a RafaEShopW -c rockmongo-1.1
Adding rockmongo-1.1 to application 'RafaEShopW' ... Success

rockmongo-1.1 <RockMongo 1.1>
-------------------------------
   Gears:          Located with jbossas-7, mongodb-2.2
   Connection URL: https://RafaEShopW-hogm.rhcloud.com/rockmongo/

RESULT:
Added rockmongo-1.1 to application RafaEShopW

rockmongo-1.1 added.  Please make note of these MongoDB credentials
again:

   RockMongo User    : admin
   RockMongo Password: hi_qnUdFqEBg

URL: https://RafaEShopW-hogm.rhcloud.com/rockmongo/
```

Figure 10-31. *Adding the RockMongo 1.1 cartridge using rhc tools*

Of course, you can also try the visual approach by pressing the Select button.

After you add the RockMongo cartridge, you can access it from the listed URL https://RafaEShopW-hogm.rhcloud.com/rockmongo/. (The credentials are the same as for the MongoDB managed instance: user: *admin*, password: *hi_qnUdFqEBg*). In Figure 10-32, I accessed the RockMongo interface for the MongoDB instance belonging to the *RafaEShopW* application.

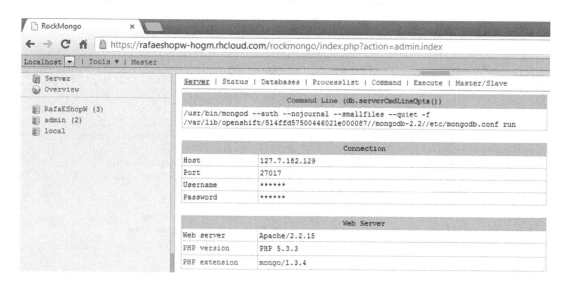

Figure 10-32. *RockMongo interface for the RafaEShopW database*

Repeat this step to add the RockMongo cartridge to the *RafaEShopM* application. Switch to D:/JBossAS/mvn and type the following:

```
rhc cartridge add -a RafaEShopM -c rockmongo-1.1
```

Sign in to OpenShift to see the RockMongo cartridge, as shown in Figure 10-33.

Figure 10-33. *RockMongo cartridge is listed in the RafaEShopW application*

Step 6: Add the `org.hibernate:ogm` module to JBoss AS 7.

In Chapter 4, in the section "*Hibernate OGM in a built-in JTA environment (EJB 3, JBoss AS 7),*" you saw how to add in JBoss AS 7 the module for Hibernate OGM. The same module must be added to the `D:/JBossAS/war/RafaEShopW/.openshift/config/modules` folder (and to the equivalent folder for `RafaESHopM`). Simply copy the `{JBOSS_HOME}/modules/org/hibernate/main` and `{JBOSS_HOME}/modules/org/hibernate/ogm` folders, as shown in Figure 10-34.

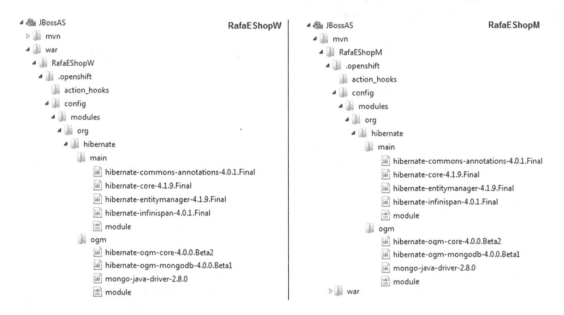

Figure 10-34. *Adding the Hibernate OGM-specific module to JBoss AS 7*

Step 7: Adjust the `persistence.xml` settings. You need to modify the `persistence.xml` file according to your cloud application. I recommend you work on a copy of this file. The original is located in the `{RafaEShop_HOME}/src/conf` folder and currently contains the settings shown in Listing 10-1.

Listing 10-1. Original `persistence.xml` File

```xml
<?xml version="1.0" encoding="UTF-8"?>
<persistence version="2.0" xmlns="http://java.sun.com/xml/ns/persistence"
xmlns:xsi="http://www.w3.org/2001/XMLSchema-instance"
xsi:schemaLocation="http://java.sun.com/xml/ns/persistence
http://java.sun.com/xml/ns/persistence/persistence_2_0.xsd">
    <persistence-unit name="HOGM_eSHOP-ejbPU" transaction-type="JTA">
        <provider>org.hibernate.ogm.jpa.HibernateOgmPersistence</provider>
        <class>eshop.entities.Categories</class>
        <class>eshop.entities.Customers</class>
        <class>eshop.entities.Inventory</class>
        <class>eshop.entities.Orders</class>
        <class>eshop.entities.Products</class>
    <properties>
        <property name="hibernate.search.default.directory_provider" value="filesystem"/>
        <property name="hibernate.search.default.indexBase" value="D:/eshop"/>
        <property name="hibernate.search.default.locking_strategy" value="single"/>
        <property name="hibernate.transaction.jta.platform"
                   value="org.hibernate.service.jta.platform.internal.SunOneJtaPlatform"/>
        <property name="hibernate.ogm.datastore.provider" value="mongodb"/>
        <property name="hibernate.ogm.datastore.grid_dialect"
                   value="org.hibernate.ogm.dialect.mongodb.MongoDBDialect"/>
        <property name="hibernate.ogm.mongodb.database" value="eshop_db"/>
        <property name="hibernate.ogm.mongodb.host" value="127.0.0.1"/>
        <property name="hibernate.ogm.mongodb.port" value="27017"/>
    </properties>
</persistence-unit>
</persistence>
```

You have to adjust several settings, as shown in the following set of instructions (this is specific to the RafaEShopW application).

Apache Lucene indexes are stored in the file system, in the D:/eshop folder. You need to modify this folder path (base folder) with a valid cloud folder path. Or, to make it much simpler, you can use a memory-based directory by replacing the following code:

```xml
<property name="hibernate.search.default.directory_provider" value="filesystem"/>
<property name="hibernate.search.default.indexBase" value="D:/eshop"/>
<property name="hibernate.search.default.locking_strategy" value="single"/>
```

with this code:

```xml
<property name="hibernate.search.default.directory_provider" value="ram"/>
<property name="hibernate.search.default.locking_strategy" value="single"/>
```

Because the application is being deployed on JBoss AS, you need to adjust the JTA platform by replacing the following setting:

```xml
<property name="hibernate.transaction.jta.platform"
        value="org.hibernate.service.jta.platform.internal.SunOneJtaPlatform"/>
```

315

with this setting:

```
<property name="hibernate.transaction.jta.platform"
        value="org.hibernate.service.jta.platform.internal.JBossAppServerJtaPlatform"/>
```

Also, you need to add a few properties that help JBoss AS locate and use the org.hibernate:ogm module, as described in Chapter 4, in the section *Hibernate OGM in a built-in JTA environment (EJB 3, JBoss AS 7):*

```
<property name="jboss.as.jpa.adapterModule" value="org.jboss.as.jpa.hibernate:4"/>
<property name="jboss.as.jpa.providerModule" value="org.hibernate:ogm"/>
<property name="jboss.as.jpa.classtransformer" value="false"/>
<property name="hibernate.listeners.envers.autoRegister" value="false"/>
```

Finally, you need to set the MongoDB database name, host, port, user, and password. To do this, replace the following code:

```
<property name="hibernate.ogm.mongodb.database" value="eshop_db"/>
<property name="hibernate.ogm.mongodb.host" value="127.0.0.1"/>
<property name="hibernate.ogm.mongodb.port" value="27017"/>
```

with this code:

```
<property name="hibernate.ogm.mongodb.database" value="RafaEShopW"/>
<property name="hibernate.ogm.mongodb.host" value="127.7.182.129"/>
<property name="hibernate.ogm.mongodb.port" value="27017"/>
<property name="hibernate.ogm.mongodb.username" value="admin"/>
<property name="hibernate.ogm.mongodb.password" value="hi_qnUdFqEBg"/>
```

■ **Note** The MongoDB remote server IP address can be easily obtained if you connect to the MongoDB server using RockMongo. In Figure 10-32, you can see the IP address 127.7.182.129 listed in the Host field. The port is always 27017, while the user and password are those used for the connection with RockMongo and provided by OpenShift when you added the MongoDB cartridge.

The "new" persistence.xml is shown in Listing 10-2.

Listing 10-2. New persistence.xml File

```xml
<?xml version="1.0" encoding="UTF-8"?>
<persistence version="2.0" xmlns="http://java.sun.com/xml/ns/persistence"
xmlns:xsi="http://www.w3.org/2001/XMLSchema-instance"
xsi:schemaLocation="http://java.sun.com/xml/ns/persistence
http://java.sun.com/xml/ns/persistence/persistence_2_0.xsd">
    <persistence-unit name="HOGM_eSHOP-ejbPU" transaction-type="JTA">
        <provider>org.hibernate.ogm.jpa.HibernateOgmPersistence</provider>
        <class>eshop.entities.Categories</class>
        <class>eshop.entities.Customers</class>
        <class>eshop.entities.Inventory</class>
        <class>eshop.entities.Orders</class>
        <class>eshop.entities.Products</class>
```

```
<properties>
    <property name="hibernate.search.default.directory_provider" value="ram"/>
    <property name="hibernate.search.default.locking_strategy" value="single"/>
    <property name="jboss.as.jpa.adapterModule" value="org.jboss.as.jpa.hibernate:4"/>
    <property name="jboss.as.jpa.providerModule" value="org.hibernate:ogm"/>
    <property name="jboss.as.jpa.classtransformer" value="false"/>
    <property name="hibernate.listeners.envers.autoRegister" value="false"/>
    <property name="hibernate.transaction.jta.platform"
              value="org.hibernate.service.jta.platform.internal.JBossAppServerJtaPlatform"/>
    <property name="hibernate.ogm.datastore.provider" value="mongodb"/>
    <property name="hibernate.ogm.datastore.grid_dialect"
              value="org.hibernate.ogm.dialect.mongodb.MongoDBDialect"/>
    <property name="hibernate.ogm.mongodb.database" value="RafaEShopW"/>
    <property name="hibernate.ogm.mongodb.host" value="127.7.182.129"/>
    <property name="hibernate.ogm.mongodb.port" value="27017"/>
    <property name="hibernate.ogm.mongodb.username" value="admin"/>
    <property name="hibernate.ogm.mongodb.password" value="hi_qnUdFqEBg"/>
</properties>
</persistence-unit>
</persistence>
```

Repeat Step 7 for the RafaEShopM application. All you need to modify is the MongoDB database name and credentials. Now, you have two persistence.xml files, one for the RafaEShopW application and one for the RafaEShopM application. Just keep them handy.

Now we're done with the steps that are common to both the WAR and Maven projects.

Monitoring the JBoss AS 7 Log

OpenShift will restart the JBoss AS instance for every Git commit session. More specifically, when you commit changes, OpenShift stops the JBoss AS instance, uploads and processes the changes, and starts JBoss AS instance again. If something goes wrong during the restart (for example, if there's an error in the code or a missing JAR), then the JBoss AS instance starts with errors, which means that the application will not be available online. In such cases, it's very helpful to be able to look at the JBoss AS log for debugging purposes; otherwise, it's very difficult to know what's happening.

You can monitor (in real-time) the server log by opening a Secure Shell (SSH) session to your application.

■ **Note**　The easiest way to find the specific SSH command you need for connecting to your application is to access the application page and copy from there (as shown in Figure 10-35 for the RafaEShopW application). More details about remote access using SSH are available at www.openshift.com/developers/remote-access.

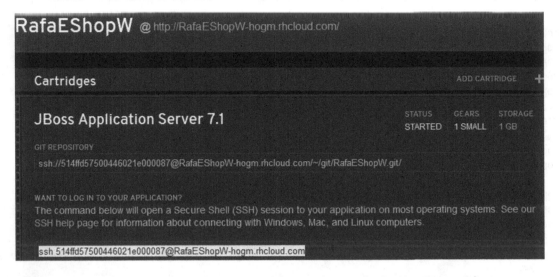

Figure 10-35. *Finding the specific SSH command for an application (RafaEShopW sample)*

This can be done from the shell using the following ssh command, which is also shown in Figure 10-36:

ssh 514ffd57500446021e000087@RafaEShopW-hogm.rhcloud.com

```
D:\JBossAS\war>ssh 514ffd57500446021e000087@RafaEShopW-hogm.rhcloud.com
*************************************************************************
You are accessing a service that is for use only by authorized users.
If you do not have authorization, discontinue use at once.
Any use of the services is subject to the applicable terms of the
agreement which can be found at:
https://openshift.redhat.com/app/legal

*************************************************************************

Welcome to OpenShift shell

This shell will assist you in managing OpenShift applications.

!!! IMPORTANT !!! IMPORTANT !!! IMPORTANT !!!
Shell access is quite powerful and it is possible for you to
accidentally damage your application.  Proceed with care!
If worse comes to worst, destroy your application with 'rhc app delete'
and recreate it
!!! IMPORTANT !!! IMPORTANT !!! IMPORTANT !!!

Type "help" for more info.

[RafaEShopW-hogm.rhcloud.com 514ffd57500446021e000087]\> _
```

Figure 10-36. *Executing the ssh command from the shell*

This is for opening a Secure Shell session to the RafaEShopW application; it's very intuitive to do the same thing for the RafaEShopM application.

Next, type the tail_all command, as shown in Figure 10-37. Notice that this command will tail all available logs for the current application. (The logs specific to JBoss AS are jbossas-7/logs/boot.log and jbossas-7/logs/server.log.)

```
[RafaEShopW-hogm.rhcloud.com 514ffd57500446021e000087]\> tail_all
==> jbossas-7/logs/server.log <==
2013/03/26 00:12:58,120 INFO  [org.jboss.as.messaging] <MSC service thread 1-3>
JBAS011605: Unbound messaging object to jndi name java:/RemoteConnectionFactory
2013/03/26 00:12:58,109 INFO  [org.jboss.as.osgi] <MSC service thread 1-1> JBAS0
11942: Stopping OSGi Framework
2013/03/26 00:12:58,124 INFO  [org.jboss.as.messaging] <MSC service thread 1-4>
JBAS011605: Unbound messaging object to jndi name java:/ConnectionFactory
2013/03/26 00:12:58,307 INFO  [org.jboss.as.messaging] <MSC service thread 1-3>
JBAS011605: Unbound messaging object to jndi name java:/topic/test
2013/03/26 00:12:58,322 INFO  [org.jboss.as.messaging] <MSC service thread 1-3>
JBAS011605: Unbound messaging object to jndi name java:jboss/exported/jms/topic/
test
2013/03/26 00:12:58,324 INFO  [org.jboss.as.messaging] <MSC service thread 1-3>
JBAS011605: Unbound messaging object to jndi name java:/queue/test
2013/03/26 00:12:58,328 INFO  [org.jboss.as.messaging] <MSC service thread 1-3>
JBAS011605: Unbound messaging object to jndi name java:jboss/exported/jms/queue/
test
2013/03/26 00:12:58,414 INFO  [org.apache.coyote.http11.Http11Protocol] <MSC ser
vice thread 1-1> Pausing Coyote HTTP/1.1 on http-127.7.182.129-127.7.182.129-808
0
2013/03/26 00:12:58,416 INFO  [org.apache.coyote.http11.Http11Protocol] <MSC ser
vice thread 1-1> Stopping Coyote HTTP/1.1 on http-127.7.182.129-127.7.182.129-80
80
2013/03/26 00:12:58,523 INFO  [org.jboss.as.deployment.connector] <MSC service t
hread 1-3> JBAS010410: Unbound JCA ConnectionFactory [java:/JmsXA]

==> jbossas-7/logs/server.log.2013-03-25 <==
2013/03/25 03:31:58,754 INFO  [org.jboss.as.deployment.connector] <MSC service t
hread 1-4> JBAS010406: Registered connection factory java:/JmsXA
2013/03/25 03:31:58,784 INFO  [org.jboss.as.messaging] <MSC service thread 1-2>
JBAS011601: Bound messaging object to jndi name java:/topic/test
2013/03/25 03:31:58,790 INFO  [org.jboss.as.messaging] <MSC service thread 1-2>
JBAS011601: Bound messaging object to jndi name java:jboss/exported/jms/topic/te
st
2013/03/25 03:31:58,777 INFO  [org.hornetq.ra.HornetQResourceAdapter] <MSC servi
ce thread 1-4> HornetQ resource adaptor started
2013/03/25 03:31:58,799 INFO  [org.jboss.as.connector.services.ResourceAdapterAc
tivatorService$ResourceAdapterActivator] <MSC service thread 1-4> IJ020002: Depl
oyed: file://RaActivatorhornetq-ra
2013/03/25 03:31:58,812 INFO  [org.jboss.as.deployment.connector] <MSC service t
hread 1-1> JBAS010401: Bound JCA ConnectionFactory [java:/JmsXA]
2013/03/25 03:31:58,941 INFO  [org.jboss.as.server.deployment] <MSC service thre
ad 1-3> JBAS015876: Starting deployment of "ROOT.war"
2013/03/25 03:32:03,011 INFO  [org.jboss.web] <MSC service thread 1-2> JBAS01821
4: Registering web context:
2013/03/25 03:32:03,206 INFO  [org.jboss.as] <MSC service thread 1-2> JBAS015874
: JBoss AS 7.1.0.Final "Thunder" started in 13896ms - Started 211 of 326 service
s (112 services are passive or on-demand)
2013/03/25 03:32:03,509 INFO  [org.jboss.as.server] <DeploymentScanner-threads -
```

Figure 10-37. *Tail JBoss AS logs*

Now you can monitor the logs in real-time. Don't close the monitor during commits because this process is "connected" to the logs files; just open another shell for other commands.

■ **Note**   Besides `tail_all`, the Secure Shell session allows you to execute other commands. To see the list of these commands with a description, type the `help` command after the SSH session is established.

Commit Changes

Every change made in the local application folder should be committed on OpenShift (you have to synchronize the content of this folder with the application on OpenShift). For this, you can use Git commands (open a shell for monitoring server logs, if you haven't already done so).

Open a new shell and navigate to the D:/JBossAS/war/RafaEShopW folder (this is also valid for the RafaEShopM application). Type the command git add ., as shown in Figure 10-38, to prepare the content staged for the next commit. Don't worry about LF-CRLF warnings.

```
D:\JBossAS\war\RafaEShopW>git add .
warning: LF will be replaced by CRLF in .openshift/config/modules/org/hibernate/
main/module.xml.
The file will have its original line endings in your working directory.
warning: LF will be replaced by CRLF in .openshift/config/modules/org/hibernate/
ogm/module.xml.
The file will have its original line endings in your working directory.
```

Figure 10-38. Executing the git add . command

Good to know (details at *www.kernel.org/pub/software/scm/git/docs/git-add.html*):

git add -A Stages All

git add . Stages new and modified, without deleted

git add -u Stages modified and deleted, without new

Type the command git commit -m "first commit" (the text *first commit* can be any text, as long as it's different for every execution of this command). The changes are stored and listed, in this case, in the new JBoss AS module files, as shown in Figure 10-39.

```
D:\JBossAS\war\RafaEShopW>git commit -m "first commit"
[master 3471457] first commit
warning: LF will be replaced by CRLF in .openshift/config/modules/org/hibernate/
main/module.xml.
The file will have its original line endings in your working directory.
warning: LF will be replaced by CRLF in .openshift/config/modules/org/hibernate/
ogm/module.xml.
The file will have its original line endings in your working directory.
 9 files changed, 70 insertions(+)
 create mode 100644 .openshift/config/modules/org/hibernate/main/hibernate-commo
ns-annotations-4.0.1.Final.jar
 create mode 100644 .openshift/config/modules/org/hibernate/main/hibernate-core-
4.1.9.Final.jar
 create mode 100644 .openshift/config/modules/org/hibernate/main/hibernate-entit
ymanager-4.1.9.Final.jar
 create mode 100644 .openshift/config/modules/org/hibernate/main/hibernate-infin
ispan-4.0.1.Final.jar
 create mode 100644 .openshift/config/modules/org/hibernate/main/module.xml
 create mode 100644 .openshift/config/modules/org/hibernate/ogm/hibernate-ogm-co
re-4.0.0.Beta2.jar
 create mode 100644 .openshift/config/modules/org/hibernate/ogm/hibernate-ogm-mo
ngodb-4.0.0.Beta1.jar
 create mode 100644 .openshift/config/modules/org/hibernate/ogm/module.xml
 create mode 100644 .openshift/config/modules/org/hibernate/ogm/mongo-java-drive
r-2.8.0.jar
```

Figure 10-39. Executing the git commit -m "first commit" command

Good to know (details at www.kernel.org/pub/software/scm/git/docs/git-commit.html):

If you make a commit and then find a mistake immediately afterwards, you can recover from it using the git reset command.

Use the git push command to propagate changes to OpenShift (see Figure 10-40). During execution of this command, which can take from a few seconds to several minutes, you can check the server log, which is updated in real-time. Notice how the server is stopped and started during push. When no changes are detected, you'll see a message that informs you that everything is up to date.

```
D:\JBossAS\war\RafaEShopW>git push

...
0087/app-root/runtime/repo/src/main/webapp]
remote: [INFO] Webapp assembled in [199 msecs]
remote: [INFO] Building war: /var/lib/openshift/514ffd57500446021e000087/app-roo
t/runtime/repo/deployments/ROOT.war
remote: [INFO] WEB-INF/web.xml already added, skipping
remote: [INFO] ------------------------------------------------------------
------
remote: [INFO] BUILD SUCCESS
remote: [INFO] ------------------------------------------------------------
------
remote: [INFO] Total time: 22.117s
remote: [INFO] Finished at: Tue Mar 26 04:25:08 EDT 2013
remote: [INFO] Final Memory: 8M/165M
remote: [INFO] ------------------------------------------------------------
------
remote: Running .openshift/action_hooks/build
remote: Running .openshift/action_hooks/deploy
remote: hot_deploy_added=false
remote: MongoDB already running
remote: Found 127.7.182.129:8080 listening port
remote: Done
remote: Running .openshift/action_hooks/post_deploy
To ssh://514ffd57500446021e000087@RafaEShopW-hogm.rhcloud.com/~/git/RafaEShopW.g
it/
   8b4e3ab..3471457  master -> master
```

Figure 10-40. *Executing the git push command*

Good to know (details at *www.kernel.org/pub/software/scm/git/docs/git-push.html*):
git push --delete All listed changes are deleted from the remote repository.

Migrating the RafaEShop Application as a WAR

After all this hard work, it's time to prepare the RafaEShop WAR for deployment under JBoss AS 7 in the cloud. First, locate the WAR in your local project RafaEShop/dist folder or in the Apress repository in the RafaEShop/dist folder. Copy this WAR to the D:/JBossAS/war/RafaEShopW/deployments folder. Finally, override the persistence.xml file in the RafaEShop WAR archive (you can use any archive tool, like WinRAR).

Before committing the WAR in the cloud, there's one more step to complete. You need to add to the /lib folder two more JARs, named jackson-core-asl-1.9.12.jar (http://mvnrepository.com/artifact/org.codehaus.jackson/jackson-core-asl) and jackson-mapper-asl-1.9.12.jar (http://mvnrepository.com/artifact/org.codehaus.jackson/jackson-mapper-asl).

Finally, commit the changes, as shown in Figure 10-41.

```
D:\JBossAS\war\RafaEShopW>git add .

D:\JBossAS\war\RafaEShopW>git commit -m "second commit"
[master 7f98b5a] second commit
 1 file changed, 0 insertions(+), 0 deletions(-)
 create mode 100644 deployments/RafaEShop.war

D:\JBossAS\war\RafaEShopW>git push
Counting objects: 6, done.
Delta compression using up to 8 threads.
Compressing objects: 100% (4/4), done.
Writing objects:  75% (3/4), 15.98 MiB | 1.12 MiB/s

...
```

Figure 10-41. *Committing the RafaEShop WAR*

The application was successfully deployed and started. The JBoss server log should look like what's shown in Figure 10-42.

```
2013/03/26 04:46:10,813 INFO  [org.jboss.as.server] (DeploymentScanner-t
 2) JBAS018559: Deployed "RafaEShop.war"
```

Figure 10-42. *JBoss AS log*

If you're interested only in this application, you can jump to the "Test It!" section.

Migrating the RafaEShop Application as a Maven Project

Now I'll focus on the RafaEShopM application. A quick look at the /mvn/RafaEShopM folder reveals a pom.xml file and a /src folder with three subfolders: /main/java, /main/resources, and /main/webapp. This is actually the default application created by OpenShift; it's a simple demo that runs on JBoss AS 7 and serves as a starting point for developers.

As you can see, this demo has a Maven project structure, which means that we should be able to replace it with the RafaEShop application. To do this, we have to add the RafaEShop components in the right places and adjust the pom.xml accordingly.

Following are the steps for deploying the RafaEShop application as a Maven project:

Step 1: Locate the RafaEShop NetBeans project. You can download the RafaEShop NetBeans project from the Apress repository.

Step 2: Empty the contents of /webapp folder. Just delete the current contents of the D:/JBossAS/mvn/RafaEShopM/src/main/webapp folder.

Step 3: Copy the RafaEShop sources. Copy the folder {RafaEShop_HOME}/src/java/eshop folder to the D:/JBossAS/mvn/RafaEShopM/src/main/java folder, as shown in Figure 10-43.

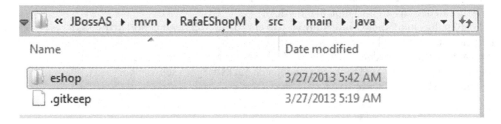

Figure 10-43. *Copying the /eshop folder from the RafaEShop application to the RafaEShopM application*

Step 4: Copy the RafaEShop /web folder contents. Copy the contents of the {RafaEShop_HOME}/web folder to the D:/JBossAS/mvn/RafaEShopM/src/main/webapp folder, as shown in Figure 10-44.

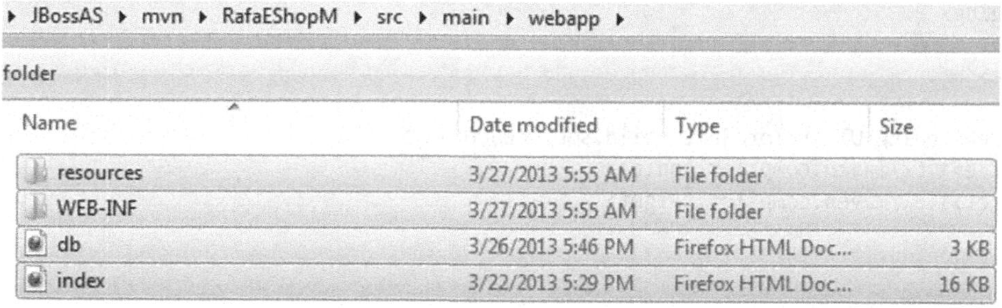

Figure 10-44. Copying the /web folder contents from the RafaEShop application to the RafaEShopM application

Step 5: Create the /META-INF folder. Create an empty folder named META-INF in
D:/JBossAS/mvn/RafaEShopM/src/main/resources (see Figure 10-45).

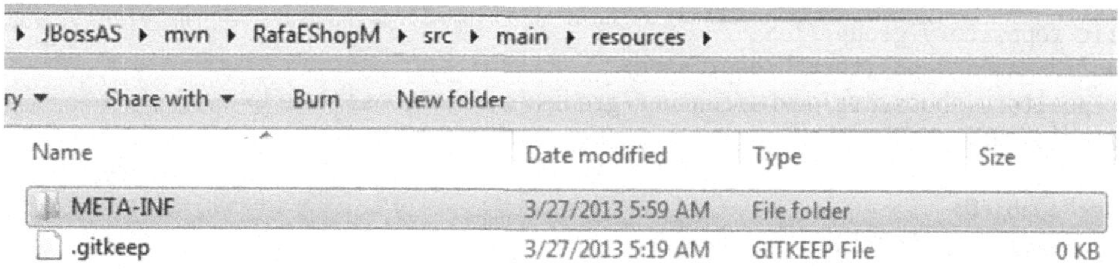

Figure 10-45. Creating the empty META-INF folder

Step 6: Copy persistence.xml. Earlier, in the section, "*Migrating the RafaEShop Application to OpenShift
with JBoss AS 7,*" you created a persistence.xml file for the RafaEShopM application. Now, copy it to the
D:/JBossAS/mvn/RafaEShopM/src/main/resources/META-INF folder (see Figure 10-46).

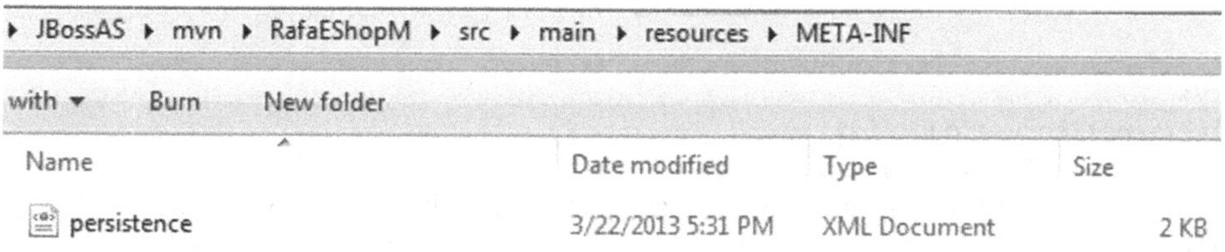

Figure 10-46. Copying the persistence.xml file

Step 7: Adjust pom.xml. Edit the default pom.xml file, as shown in Listing 10-3. You have to add the necessary
dependencies (Hibernate OGM, Hibernate Search, and PrimeFaces).

Listing 10-3. Editing the pom.xml File

```
<project xmlns="http://maven.apache.org/POM/4.0.0" xmlns:xsi="http://www.w3.org/2001/XMLSchema-instance"
  xsi:schemaLocation="http://maven.apache.org/POM/4.0.0 http://maven.apache.org/maven-v4_0_0.xsd">
  <modelVersion>4.0.0</modelVersion>
  <groupId>RafaEShopM</groupId>
  <artifactId>RafaEShopM</artifactId>
```

```xml
<packaging>war</packaging>
<version>1.0</version>
<name>RafaEShopM</name>
<properties>
  <project.build.sourceEncoding>UTF-8</project.build.sourceEncoding>
  <maven.compiler.source>1.6</maven.compiler.source>
  <maven.compiler.target>1.6</maven.compiler.target>
</properties>

<repositories>
    <repository>
        <id>prime-repo</id>
        <name>PrimeFaces Maven Repository</name>
        <url>http://repository.primefaces.org</url>
        <layout>default</layout>
    </repository>
    <repository>
        <id>jboss-public-repository-group</id>
        <name>JBoss Public Maven Repository Group</name>
        <url>https://repository.jboss.org/nexus/content/groups/public-jboss/</url>
        <layout>default</layout>
        <releases>
          <enabled>true</enabled>
          <updatePolicy>never</updatePolicy>
        </releases>
        <snapshots>
          <enabled>true</enabled>
          <updatePolicy>never</updatePolicy>
        </snapshots>
    </repository>
</repositories>

<!--
<pluginRepositories>
    <pluginRepository>
      <id>jboss-public-repository-group</id>
      <name>JBoss Public Maven Repository Group</name>
      <url>https://repository.jboss.org/nexus/content/groups/public-jboss/</url>
      <layout>default</layout>
      <releases>
        <enabled>true</enabled>
        <updatePolicy>never</updatePolicy>
      </releases>
      <snapshots>
        <enabled>true</enabled>
        <updatePolicy>never</updatePolicy>
      </snapshots>
    </pluginRepository>
  </pluginRepositories>
  -->
```

```xml
<dependencyManagement>
        <dependencies>
            <dependency>
                <groupId>org.primefaces</groupId>
                <artifactId>primefaces</artifactId>
                <version>3.4.2</version>
            </dependency>
            <dependency>
            <groupId>org.hibernate</groupId>
            <artifactId>hibernate-search</artifactId>
            <version>4.2.0.Beta1</version>
            </dependency>
            <dependency>
                <groupId>org.hibernate.ogm</groupId>
                <artifactId>hibernate-ogm-core</artifactId>
                <version>4.0.0.Beta2</version>
            </dependency>
            <dependency>
                <groupId>org.hibernate.ogm</groupId>
                <artifactId>hibernate-ogm-mongodb</artifactId>
                <version>4.0.0.Beta1</version>
            </dependency>
        </dependencies>
</dependencyManagement>

<dependencies>
  <dependency>
    <groupId>org.primefaces</groupId>
    <artifactId>primefaces</artifactId>
    <version>3.4.2</version>
  </dependency>
        <dependency>
            <groupId>org.hibernate</groupId>
            <artifactId>hibernate-search</artifactId>
            <version>4.2.0.Beta1</version>
    </dependency>
        <dependency>
        <groupId>org.hibernate.ogm</groupId>
        <artifactId>hibernate-ogm-core</artifactId>
        <version>4.0.0.Beta2</version>
    </dependency>
    <dependency>
        <groupId>org.hibernate.ogm</groupId>
        <artifactId>hibernate-ogm-mongodb</artifactId>
        <version>4.0.0.Beta1</version>
    </dependency>
  <dependency>
```

```
    <groupId>org.jboss.spec</groupId>
    <artifactId>jboss-javaee-6.0</artifactId>
    <version>1.0.0.Final</version>
    <type>pom</type>
    <scope>provided</scope>
  </dependency>
</dependencies>
<profiles>
  <profile>
    <!-- When built in OpenShift the 'openshift' profile will be used when invoking mvn. -->
    <!-- Use this profile for any OpenShift specific customization your app will need. -->
    <!-- By default that is to put the resulting archive into the 'deployments' folder. -->
    <!-- http://maven.apache.org/guides/mini/guide-building-for-different-environments.html -->
    <id>openshift</id>
    <build>
        <finalName>RafaEShopM</finalName>
        <plugins>
          <plugin>
            <artifactId>maven-war-plugin</artifactId>
            <version>2.1.1</version>
            <configuration>
              <outputDirectory>deployments</outputDirectory>
              <warName>RafaEShop</warName>
            </configuration>
          </plugin>
        </plugins>
    </build>
  </profile>
</profiles>
</project>
```

Finally, commit the changes, as shown in Figure 10-47.

```
D:\JBossAS\mvn\RafaEShopM>git add .

D:\JBossAS\mvn\RafaEShopM>git commit -m "first commit"
[master a098afc] first commit
 1 file changed, 14 insertions(+), 15 deletions(-)

D:\JBossAS\mvn\RafaEShopM>git push
Counting objects: 5, done.
Delta compression using up to 8 threads.
Compressing objects: 100% (3/3), done.
Writing objects: 100% (3/3), 394 bytes, done.
Total 3 (delta 2), reused 0 (delta 0)
remote: restart_on_add=false

...
```

Figure 10-47. *Commit RafaEShop as an Apache Maven project*

The application was successfully deployed and started. The JBoss server log should look like what's shown in Figure 10-48.

```
2013/03/27 03:47:21,297 INFO  [org.jboss.as.server] (DeploymentScanner-threads -
2) JBAS018559: Deployed "RafaEShop.war"
```

Figure 10-48. *RafaEShop was successfully deployed*

If you are interested only in this application, you can now jump to the "Test It!" section.

Migrating the RafaEShop Application to OpenShift with GlassFish 3 AS

In the first part of this chapter you saw that OpenShift offers excellent support for JBoss AS. In just a few minutes you can obtain a default application running on JBoss AS, and with several clicks and commands you can build and deploy your own applications as WARs or even as Apache Maven projects.

In the second part of this chapter, we're going to see how to migrate the RafaEShop application from your computer to the OpenShift cloud on GlassFish 3 AS. At the time of this writing, OpenShift does not provide a default GlassFish cartridge, but it does allow you to extend OpenShift to support GlassFish (or other unsupported languages, frameworks, and middleware) using the Do-It-Yourself application type, as shown in Figure 10-49.

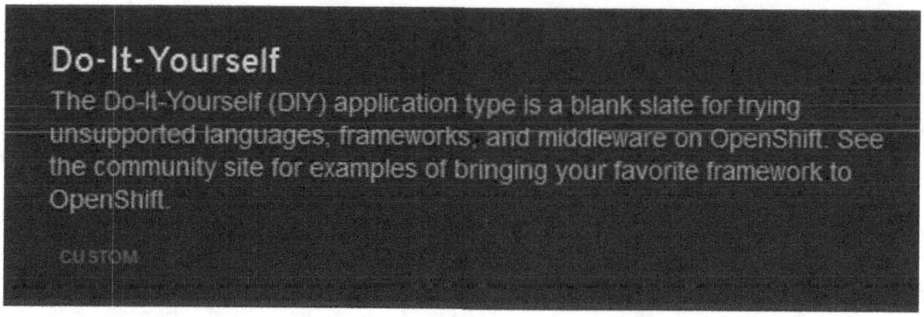

Figure 10-49. *Do-It-Yourself cartridge*

Following are the steps for creating such applications:

Step 1: Prepare GlassFish AS for OpenShift. Before creating a DIY application, you need to prepare GlassFish for working with OpenShift. There are several modifications that affect GlassFish domain configuration, so it's not recommended you perform these modifications on your local GlassFish distribution. It's much better to download a new GlassFish distribution from `download.java.net/glassfish/3.1.2.2/release/glassfish-3.1.2.2.zip` (version 3.1.2.2 was used in this example) and extract the ZIP archive content in a convenient place on your computer.

Here are the modifications you'll need to make:

- Bind the HTTP listener to the application IP (represented by the environment variable $OPENSHIFT_INTERNAL_IP).

- Disable the administrator console.

- Disable other listeners.

- Update some ports to permitted ones.

327

These modifications will affect a single GlassFish file, {GlassFish_HOME}/glassfish/domains/domain1/config/
domain.xml. The modified version of this document will be shown completely after I present the list
of modifications. You'll find more details about the contents and format of this file at
http://docs.oracle.com/cd/E19798-01/821-1753/abhar/index.html.

You should make the following modifications. These modifications are indicated by the OpenShift Blog at
https://www.openshift.com/blogs and are presented in order from the top of the document to the bottom:

Modification 1: Replace "*localhost*" with "*OPENSHIFT_INTERNAL_IP*," as shown in Figure 10-50.

```
54          <property value="1527" name="PortNumber" />
55          <property value="APP" name="Password" />
56          <property value="APP" name="User" />
57          <!-- REPLACE 'localhost' WITH OPENSHIFT_INTERNAL_IP -->
58          <!-- <property value="localhost" name="serverName" /> -->
59          <property value="OPENSHIFT_INTERNAL_IP" name="serverName" />
60          <property value="sun-appserv-samples" name="DatabaseName" />
61          <property value=";create=true" name="connectionAttributes" />
```

Figure 10-50. Modification 1

Modification 2: Replace "*localhost*" with "*OPENSHIFT_INTERNAL_IP*," as shown in Figure 10-51.

```
68        </server>
69      </servers>
70      <nodes>
71          <!-- REPLACE 'localhost' WITH OPENSHIFT_INTERNAL_IP -->
72          <!-- <node name="localhost-domain1" type="CONFIG" node-host="localhost" install-dir="${com.sun.aas.productRoot}"/> -->
73          <node name="localhost-domain1" type="CONFIG" node-host="OPENSHIFT_INTERNAL_IP" install-dir="${com.sun.aas.productRoot}"/>
74      </nodes>
75      <configs>
```

Figure 10-51. Modification 2

Modification 3: Remove "*http-listener-2*," as shown in Figure 10-52.

```
76      <config name="server-config">
77        <http-service>
78          <access-log/>
79          <!-- REMOVE 'http-listener-2' -->
80          <!-- <virtual-server id="server" network-listeners="http-listener-1,http-listener-2"/> -->
81          <virtual-server id="server" network-listeners="http-listener-1"/>
82          <virtual-server id="__asadmin" network-listeners="admin-listener"/>
83        </http-service>
```

Figure 10-52. Modification 3

Modification 4: Comment the lines <*iiop-service*></*iiop-service*>, as shown in Figure 10-53.

```
82      <virtual-server id="__asadmin" network-listeners="admin-listener"/>
83    </http-service>
84    <!-- COMMENT <iiop-service> -->
85    <!--
86    <iiop-service>
87      <orb use-thread-pool-ids="thread-pool-1" />
88      <iiop-listener address="0.0.0.0" port="3700" id="orb-listener-1" lazy-init="true"/>
89      <iiop-listener security-enabled="true" address="0.0.0.0" port="3820" id="SSL">
90        <ssl classname="com.sun.enterprise.security.ssl.GlassfishSSLImpl" cert-nickname="s1as" />
91      </iiop-listener>
92      <iiop-listener security-enabled="true" address="0.0.0.0" port="3920" id="SSL_MUTUALAUTH">
93        <ssl classname="com.sun.enterprise.security.ssl.GlassfishSSLImpl" cert-nickname="s1as" client-auth-enabled="true" />
94      </iiop-listener>
95    </iiop-service>
96    -->
97    <admin-service auth-realm-name="admin-realm" type="das-and-server" system-jmx-connector-name="system">
```

Figure 10-53. *Modification 4*

Modification 5: Replace "*0.0.0.0*" with "*OPENSHIFT_INTERNAL_IP*" and "*8686*" with "*7600*," as shown in Figure 10-54.

```
94      </iiop-listener>
95    </iiop-service>
96    -->
97    <admin-service auth-realm-name="admin-realm" type="das-and-server" system-jmx-connector-name="system">
98      <!-- REPLACE '0.0.0.0' WITH OPENSHIFT_INTERNAL_IP AND '8686' WITH 7600 -->
99      <!-- <jmx-connector auth-realm-name="admin-realm" security-enabled="false" address="0.0.0.0" port="8686" name="system" /> -->
100     <jmx-connector auth-realm-name="admin-realm" security-enabled="false" address="OPENSHIFT_INTERNAL_IP" port="7600" name="system" />
101       <property value="/admin" name="adminConsoleContextRoot" />
```

Figure 10-54. *Modification 5*

Modification 6: Replace "*localhost*" with "*OPENSHIFT_INTERNAL_IP*" and "*7676*" with "*5445*," as shown in Figure 10-55.

```
119   <mdb-container steady-pool-size="0" max-pool-size="32" pool-resize-quantity="8" >
120   </mdb-container>
121   <jms-service type="EMBEDDED" default-jms-host="default_JMS_host">
122     <!-- REPLACE 'localhost' WITH OPENSHIFT_INTERNAL_IP AND '7676' WITH 5445 -->
123     <!-- <jms-host name="default_JMS_host" host="localhost" port="7676" admin-user-name="admin" admin-password="admin" lazy-init="true"/> -->
124     <jms-host name="default_JMS_host" host="OPENSHIFT_INTERNAL_IP" port="5445" admin-user-name="admin" admin-password="admin" lazy-init="true"/>
125   </jms-service>
126   <security-service>
```

Figure 10-55. *Modification 6*

Modification 7: Replace "*127.0.0.1*" with "*OPENSHIFT_INTERNAL_IP*," as shown in Figure 10-56.

```
213         <jvm-options>-Dosgi.shell.telnet.maxconn=1</jvm-options>
214         <!-- From which hosts users can connect -->
215         <!-- REPLACE '127.0.0.1' WITH OPENSHIFT_INTERNAL_IP -->
216         <!-- <jvm-options>-Dosgi.shell.telnet.ip=127.0.0.1</jvm-options> -->
217         <jvm-options>-Dosgi.shell.telnet.ip=OPENSHIFT_INTERNAL_IP</jvm-options>
218         <!-- Gogo shell configuration -->
219         <jvm-options>-Dgosh.args=--nointeractive</jvm-options>
```

Figure 10-56. *Modification 7*

Modification 8: Comment the lines <protocol></protocol>, as shown in Figure 10-57.

```
243              <file-cache enabled="false"></file-cache>
244          </http>
245        </protocol>
246        <!-- COMMENT <protocol> -->
247        <!--
248        <protocol security-enabled="true" name="http-listener-2">
249          <http default-virtual-server="server" max-connections="250">
250            <file-cache enabled="false"></file-cache>
251          </http>
252          <ssl classname="com.sun.enterprise.security.ssl.GlassfishSSLImpl" cert-nickname="s1as"></ssl>
253        </protocol>
254        -->
255        <protocol name="admin-listener">
256          <http default-virtual-server="__asadmin" max-connections="250" encoded-slash-enabled="true" >
```

Figure 10-57. Modification 8

Modification 9: Add *address="OPENSHIFT_INTERNAL_IP,"* as shown in Figure 10-58.

```
261        <network-listeners>
262          <!-- ADD address="OPENSHIFT_INTERNAL_IP" -->
263          <!-- <network-listener port="8080" protocol="http-listener-1" transport="tcp" name="http-listener-1" thread-pool="http-thread-pool"></network
264          <network-listener address="OPENSHIFT_INTERNAL_IP" port="8080" protocol="http-listener-1" transport="tcp" name="http-listener-1" thread-pool="
```

Figure 10-58. Modification 9

Modification 10: Comment the lines *<network-listener></network-listener>*, as shown in Figure 10-59.

```
264          <network-listener address="OPENSHIFT_INTERNAL_IP" port="8080" protocol="http-listener-1" transport="tcp" name="http-listener-1" thread-po
265          <!-- COMMENT <network-listener> -->
266          <!-- <network-listener port="8181" protocol="http-listener-2" transport="tcp" name="http-listener-2" thread-pool="http-thread-pool"></net
267          <!-- <network-listener port="4848" protocol="admin-listener" transport="tcp" name="admin-listener" thread-pool="admin-thread-pool"></netw
268        </network-listeners>
269        <transports>
```

Figure 10-59. Modification 10

Modification 11: Delete *http-listener-2,* as shown in Figure 10-60.

```
280        <http-service>
281          <access-log/>
282          <!-- DELETE http-listener-2 -->
283          <!-- <virtual-server id="server" network-listeners="http-listener-1, http-listener-2" > -->
284          <virtual-server id="server" network-listeners="http-listener-1" >
285            <property name="default-web-xml" value="${com.sun.aas.instanceRoot}/config/default-web.xml"/>
```

Figure 10-60. Modification 11

Modification 12: Comment the lines *<iiop-service></iiop-service>*, as shown in Figure 10-61.

```
287        <virtual-server id="__asadmin" network-listeners="admin-listener" />
288      </http-service>
289      <!-- COMMENT <iiop-service> -->
290      <!--
291      <iiop-service>
292        <orb use-thread-pool-ids="thread-pool-1" />
293        <iiop-listener port="${IIOP_LISTENER_PORT}" id="orb-listener-1" address="0.0.0.0" />
294        <iiop-listener port="${IIOP_SSL_LISTENER_PORT}" id="SSL" address="0.0.0.0" security-enabled="true">
295          <ssl classname="com.sun.enterprise.security.ssl.GlassfishSSLImpl" cert-nickname="s1as" />
296        </iiop-listener>
297        <iiop-listener port="${IIOP_SSL_MUTUALAUTH_PORT}" id="SSL_MUTUALAUTH" address="0.0.0.0" security-enabled="true">
298          <ssl classname="com.sun.enterprise.security.ssl.GlassfishSSLImpl" cert-nickname="s1as" client-auth-enabled="true" />
299        </iiop-listener>
300      </iiop-service>
301      -->
302      <admin-service system-jmx-connector-name="system" type="server">
303        <!-- JSR 160  "system-jmx-connector" -->
```

Figure 10-61. *Modification 12*

Modification 13: Replace "*127.0.0.1*" with "*OPENSHIFT_INTERNAL_IP*," as shown in Figure 10-62.

```
401        <!-- How many concurrent users can connect to this remote shell -->
402        <jvm-options>-Dosgi.shell.telnet.maxconn=1</jvm-options>
403        <!-- From which hosts users can connect -->
404        <!-- REPLACE '127.0.0.1' WITH OPENSHIFT_INTERNAL_IP -->
405        <!-- <jvm-options>-Dosgi.shell.telnet.ip=127.0.0.1</jvm-options> -->
406        <jvm-options>-Dosgi.shell.telnet.ip=OPENSHIFT_INTERNAL_IP</jvm-options>
407        <!-- Gogo shell configuration -->
408        <jvm-options>-Dgosh.args=--noshutdown -c noop=true</jvm-options>
```

Figure 10-62. *Modification 13*

Modification 14: Comment the lines *<protocol></protocol>*, as shown in Figure 10-63.

```
436          <file-cache />
437        </http>
438      </protocol>
439      <!-- COMMENT <protocol> -->
440      <!--
441      <protocol security-enabled="true" name="http-listener-2">
442        <http default-virtual-server="server">
443          <file-cache />
444        </http>
445        <ssl classname="com.sun.enterprise.security.ssl.GlassfishSSLImpl" cert-nickname="s1as" />
446      </protocol>
447      -->
448      <protocol name="admin-listener">
449        <http default-virtual-server="__asadmin" max-connections="250">
```

Figure 10-63. *Modification 14*

Modification 15: Replace "*0.0.0.0*" with "*OPENSHIFT_INTERNAL_IP*" and "*${HTTP_LISTENER_PORT}*" with "*9999*," as shown in Figure 10-64.

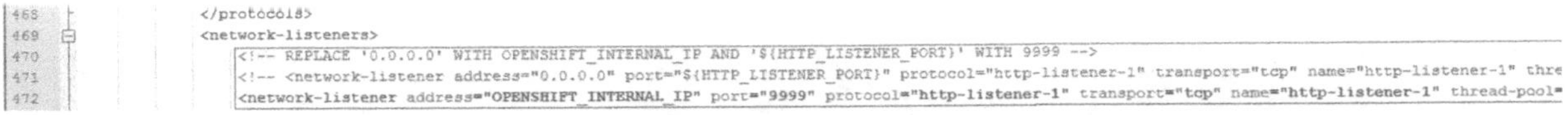

Figure 10-64. *Modification 15*

Modification 16: Comment the lines *<network-listener></network-listener>,* as shown in Figure 10-65.

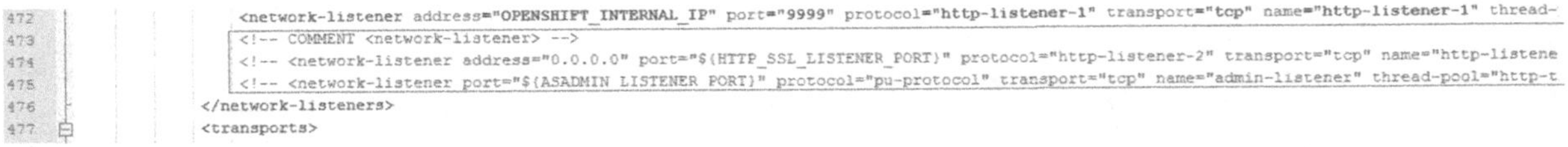

Figure 10-65. *Modification 16*

■ **Note**　The real environment variable is $OPENSHIFT_INTERNAL_IP. The string OPENSHIFT_INTERNAL_IP is just a placeholder, so you can use any other text.

After all the modifications are performed, the domain.xml becomes what you see in Listing 10-4.

Listing 10-4. Modified domain.xml File

```
<!--

DO NOT ALTER OR REMOVE COPYRIGHT NOTICES OR THIS HEADER.

Copyright (c) 2010-2012 Oracle and/or its affiliates. All rights reserved.

The contents of this file are subject to the terms of either the GNU
General Public License Version 2 only ("GPL") or the Common Development
and Distribution License("CDDL") (collectively, the "License").  You
may not use this file except in compliance with the License.  You can
obtain a copy of the License at
https://glassfish.dev.java.net/public/CDDL+GPL_1_1.html
or packager/legal/LICENSE.txt.  See the License for the specific
language governing permissions and limitations under the License.

When distributing the software, include this License Header Notice in each
file and include the License file at packager/legal/LICENSE.txt.

GPL Classpath Exception:
Oracle designates this particular file as subject to the "Classpath"
exception as provided by Oracle in the GPL Version 2 section of the License
file that accompanied this code.

Modifications:
If applicable, add the following below the License Header, with the fields
enclosed by brackets [] replaced by your own identifying information:
"Portions Copyright [year] [name of copyright owner]"
```

```
Contributor(s):
If you wish your version of this file to be governed by only the CDDL or
only the GPL Version 2, indicate your decision by adding "[Contributor]
elects to include this software in this distribution under the [CDDL or GPL
Version 2] license."  If you don't indicate a single choice of license, a
recipient has the option to distribute your version of this file under
either the CDDL, the GPL Version 2 or to extend the choice of license to
its licensees as provided above.  However, if you add GPL Version 2 code
and therefore, elected the GPL Version 2 license, then the option applies
only if the new code is made subject to such option by the copyright
holder.

-->

<?xml version="1.0" encoding="UTF-8"?>
<domain log-root="${com.sun.aas.instanceRoot}/logs" application-root="${com.sun.aas.instanceRoot}/
applications" version="10.0">
  <system-applications />
  <applications />
  <resources>
    <jdbc-resource pool-name="__TimerPool" jndi-name="jdbc/__TimerPool" object-type="system-admin" />
    <jdbc-resource pool-name="DerbyPool" jndi-name="jdbc/__default" />
    <jdbc-connection-pool name="__TimerPool" datasource-classname="org.apache.derby.jdbc.
                                            EmbeddedXADataSource" res-type="javax.sql.XADataSource">
      <property value="${com.sun.aas.instanceRoot}/lib/databases/ejbtimer" name="databaseName" />
      <property value=";create=true" name="connectionAttributes" />
    </jdbc-connection-pool>
    <jdbc-connection-pool is-isolation-level-guaranteed="false" name="DerbyPool"
     datasource-classname="org.apache.derby.jdbc.ClientDataSource" res-type="javax.sql.DataSource">
      <property value="1527" name="PortNumber" />
      <property value="APP" name="Password" />
      <property value="APP" name="User" />
      <property value="OPENSHIFT_INTERNAL_IP" name="serverName" />
      <property value="sun-appserv-samples" name="DatabaseName" />
      <property value=";create=true" name="connectionAttributes" />
    </jdbc-connection-pool>
  </resources>
  <servers>
    <server name="server" config-ref="server-config">
      <resource-ref ref="jdbc/__TimerPool" />
      <resource-ref ref="jdbc/__default" />
    </server>
  </servers>
  <nodes>
    <node name="localhost-domain1" type="CONFIG" node-host="OPENSHIFT_INTERNAL_IP"
                                            install-dir="${com.sun.aas.productRoot}" />
  </nodes>
  <configs>
    <config name="server-config">
      <http-service>
        <access-log />
```

```
      <virtual-server id="server" network-listeners="http-listener-1" />
      <virtual-server id="__asadmin" network-listeners="admin-listener" />
  </http-service>
  <admin-service auth-realm-name="admin-realm" type="das-and-server"
                                              system-jmx-connector-name="system">
      <jmx-connector auth-realm-name="admin-realm" security-enabled="false"
                              address="OPENSHIFT_INTERNAL_IP" port="7600" name="system" />
      <property value="/admin" name="adminConsoleContextRoot" />
      <property value="${com.sun.aas.installRoot}/lib/install/applications/admingui.war"
                                              name="adminConsoleDownloadLocation" />
      <property value="${com.sun.aas.installRoot}/.." name="ipsRoot" />
  </admin-service>
  <connector-service shutdown-timeout-in-seconds="30" />
  <web-container>
    <session-config>
      <session-manager>
        <manager-properties />
        <store-properties />
      </session-manager>
      <session-properties />
    </session-config>
  </web-container>
  <ejb-container steady-pool-size="0" max-pool-size="32"
            session-store="${com.sun.aas.instanceRoot}/session-store" pool-resize-quantity="8">
    <ejb-timer-service />
  </ejb-container>
  <mdb-container steady-pool-size="0" max-pool-size="32" pool-resize-quantity="8" />
  <jms-service type="EMBEDDED" default-jms-host="default_JMS_host">
    <jms-host name="default_JMS_host" host="OPENSHIFT_INTERNAL_IP"
                  port="5445" admin-user-name="admin" admin-password="admin" lazy-init="true" />
  </jms-service>
  <security-service>
    <auth-realm classname="com.sun.enterprise.security.auth.realm.file.FileRealm"
                                                            name="admin-realm">
      <property value="${com.sun.aas.instanceRoot}/config/admin-keyfile" name="file" />
      <property value="fileRealm" name="jaas-context" />
    </auth-realm>
    <auth-realm classname="com.sun.enterprise.security.auth.realm.file.FileRealm" name="file">
      <property value="${com.sun.aas.instanceRoot}/config/keyfile" name="file" />
      <property value="fileRealm" name="jaas-context" />
    </auth-realm>
    <auth-realm classname="com.sun.enterprise.security.auth.realm.certificate.CertificateRealm"
                                                            name="certificate" />
    <jacc-provider policy-configuration-factory-provider="com.sun.enterprise.security.provider.
PolicyConfigurationFactoryImpl" policy-provider="com.sun.enterprise.security.provider.PolicyWrapper"
name="default">
        <property value="${com.sun.aas.instanceRoot}/generated/policy" name="repository" />
    </jacc-provider>
    <jacc-provider policy-configuration-factory-provider="com.sun.enterprise.security.jacc.
provider.SimplePolicyConfigurationFactory" policy-provider="com.sun.enterprise.security.jacc.
provider.SimplePolicyProvider" name="simple" />
```

```
<audit-module classname="com.sun.enterprise.security.Audit" name="default">
  <property value="false" name="auditOn" />
</audit-module>
<message-security-config auth-layer="SOAP">
  <provider-config provider-id="XWS_ClientProvider"
      class-name="com.sun.xml.wss.provider.ClientSecurityAuthModule" provider-type="client">
    <request-policy auth-source="content" />
    <response-policy auth-source="content" />
    <property value="s1as" name="encryption.key.alias" />
    <property value="s1as" name="signature.key.alias" />
    <property value="false" name="dynamic.username.password" />
    <property value="false" name="debug" />
  </provider-config>
  <provider-config provider-id="ClientProvider"
      class-name="com.sun.xml.wss.provider.ClientSecurityAuthModule" provider-type="client">
    <request-policy auth-source="content" />
    <response-policy auth-source="content" />
    <property value="s1as" name="encryption.key.alias" />
    <property value="s1as" name="signature.key.alias" />
    <property value="false" name="dynamic.username.password" />
    <property value="false" name="debug" />
    <property value="${com.sun.aas.instanceRoot}/config/wss-server-config-1.0.xml"
                                                    name="security.config" />
  </provider-config>
  <provider-config provider-id="XWS_ServerProvider"
      class-name="com.sun.xml.wss.provider.ServerSecurityAuthModule" provider-type="server">
    <request-policy auth-source="content" />
    <response-policy auth-source="content" />
    <property value="s1as" name="encryption.key.alias" />
    <property value="s1as" name="signature.key.alias" />
    <property value="false" name="debug" />
  </provider-config>
  <provider-config provider-id="ServerProvider"
      class-name="com.sun.xml.wss.provider.ServerSecurityAuthModule" provider-type="server">
    <request-policy auth-source="content" />
    <response-policy auth-source="content" />
    <property value="s1as" name="encryption.key.alias" />
    <property value="s1as" name="signature.key.alias" />
    <property value="false" name="debug" />
    <property value="${com.sun.aas.instanceRoot}/config/wss-server-config-1.0.xml"
                                                    name="security.config" />
  </provider-config>
</message-security-config>
<message-security-config auth-layer="HttpServlet">
  <provider-config provider-type="server" provider-id="GFConsoleAuthModule"
              class-name="org.glassfish.admingui.common.security.AdminConsoleAuthModule">
    <request-policy auth-source="sender" />
    <response-policy />
    <property name="restAuthURL"
              value="http://localhost:${ADMIN_LISTENER_PORT}/management/sessions" />
    <property name="loginPage" value="/login.jsf" />
```

```
            <property name="loginErrorPage" value="/loginError.jst" />
        </provider-config>
    </message-security-config>
    <property value="SHA-256" name="default-digest-algorithm" />
</security-service>
<transaction-service tx-log-dir="${com.sun.aas.instanceRoot}/logs" />
<java-config classpath-suffix="" system-classpath="" debug-options="-Xdebug
                            -Xrunjdwp:transport=dt_socket,server=y,suspend=n,address=9009">
    <jvm-options>-XX:MaxPermSize=192m</jvm-options>
    <jvm-options>-XX:PermSize=64m</jvm-options>
    <jvm-options>-client</jvm-options>
    <jvm-options>-Djava.awt.headless=true</jvm-options>
    <jvm-options>-Djavax.management.builder.initial=com.sun.enterprise.v3.admin.
                                                AppServerMBeanServerBuilder</jvm-options>
    <jvm-options>-XX:+UnlockDiagnosticVMOptions</jvm-options>
    <jvm-options>-Djava.endorsed.dirs=${com.sun.aas.installRoot}/modules/endorsed${path.
                            separator}${com.sun.aas.installRoot}/lib/endorsed</jvm-options>
    <jvm-options>-Djava.security.policy=${com.sun.aas.instanceRoot}/config/server.policy</jvm-options>
    <jvm-options>-Djava.security.auth.login.config=${com.sun.aas.instanceRoot}/config/login.
                                                        conf</jvm-options>
    <jvm-options>-Dcom.sun.enterprise.security.httpsOutboundKeyAlias=s1as</jvm-options>
    <jvm-options>-Xmx512m</jvm-options>
    <jvm-options>-Djavax.net.ssl.keyStore=${com.sun.aas.instanceRoot}/config/
                                                        keystore.jks</jvm-options>
    <jvm-options>-Djavax.net.ssl.trustStore=${com.sun.aas.instanceRoot}/config/
                                                        cacerts.jks</jvm-options>
    <jvm-options>-Djava.ext.dirs=${com.sun.aas.javaRoot}/lib/ext${path.separator}${com.sun.aas.
        javaRoot}/jre/lib/ext${path.separator}${com.sun.aas.instanceRoot}/lib/ext</jvm-options>
    <jvm-options>-Djdbc.drivers=org.apache.derby.jdbc.ClientDriver</jvm-options>
    <jvm-options>-DANTLR_USE_DIRECT_CLASS_LOADING=true</jvm-options>
    <jvm-options>-Dcom.sun.enterprise.config.config_environment_factory_class=com.sun.
                    enterprise.config.serverbeans.AppserverConfigEnvironmentFactory</jvm-options>
    <!-- Configuration of various third-party OSGi bundles like
        Felix Remote Shell, FileInstall, etc. -->
    <!-- Port on which remote shell listens for connections.-->
    <jvm-options>-Dosgi.shell.telnet.port=6666</jvm-options>
    <!-- How many concurrent users can connect to this remote shell -->
    <jvm-options>-Dosgi.shell.telnet.maxconn=1</jvm-options>
    <!-- From which hosts users can connect -->
    <jvm-options>-Dosgi.shell.telnet.ip=OPENSHIFT_INTERNAL_IP</jvm-options>
    <!-- Gogo shell configuration -->
    <jvm-options>-Dgosh.args=--nointeractive</jvm-options>
    <!-- Directory being watched by fileinstall. -->
    <jvm-options>-Dfelix.fileinstall.dir=${com.sun.aas.installRoot}/modules/autostart/</jvm-options>
    <!-- Time period fileinstaller thread in ms. -->
    <jvm-options>-Dfelix.fileinstall.poll=5000</jvm-options>
    <!-- log level: 1 for error, 2 for warning, 3 for info and 4 for debug. -->
    <jvm-options>-Dfelix.fileinstall.log.level=2</jvm-options>
    <!-- should new bundles be started or installed only?
        true => start, false => only install
    -->
    <jvm-options>-Dfelix.fileinstall.bundles.new.start=true</jvm-options>
```

```xml
      <!-- should watched bundles be started transiently or persistently -->
      <jvm-options>-Dfelix.fileinstall.bundles.startTransient=true</jvm-options>
      <!-- Should changes to configuration be saved in corresponding cfg file? false: no, true: yes
          If we don't set false, everytime server starts from clean osgi cache, the file gets rewritten.
      -->
      <jvm-options>-Dfelix.fileinstall.disableConfigSave=false</jvm-options>
      <!-- End of OSGi bundle configurations -->
      <jvm-options>-XX:NewRatio=2</jvm-options>
    </java-config>
    <network-config>
      <protocols>
        <protocol name="http-listener-1">
          <http default-virtual-server="server" max-connections="250">
            <file-cache enabled="false" />
          </http>
        </protocol>
        <protocol name="admin-listener">
          <http default-virtual-server="__asadmin" max-connections="250"
                                                    encoded-slash-enabled="true">
            <file-cache enabled="false" />
          </http>
        </protocol>
      </protocols>
      <network-listeners>
        <network-listener address="OPENSHIFT_INTERNAL_IP" port="8080" protocol="http-listener-1"
                          transport="tcp" name="http-listener-1" thread-pool="http-thread-pool" />
      </network-listeners>
      <transports>
        <transport name="tcp" />
      </transports>
    </network-config>
    <thread-pools>
      <thread-pool name="admin-thread-pool" max-thread-pool-size="50" max-queue-size="256" />
      <thread-pool name="http-thread-pool" max-queue-size="4096" />
      <thread-pool name="thread-pool-1" max-thread-pool-size="200" />
    </thread-pools>
  </config>
  <config name="default-config" dynamic-reconfiguration-enabled="true">
    <http-service>
      <access-log />
      <virtual-server id="server" network-listeners="http-listener-1">
        <property name="default-web-xml" value="${com.sun.aas.instanceRoot}/config/default-web.xml" />
      </virtual-server>
      <virtual-server id="__asadmin" network-listeners="admin-listener" />
    </http-service>
    <admin-service system-jmx-connector-name="system" type="server">
      <!-- JSR 160 "system-jmx-connector" -->
      <jmx-connector address="0.0.0.0" auth-realm-name="admin-realm" name="system"
              port="${JMX_SYSTEM_CONNECTOR_PORT}" protocol="rmi_jrmp" security-enabled="false" />
```

```
    <!-- JSR 160  "system-jmx-connector"  >
    <property value="${com.sun.aas.installRoot}/lib/install/applications/admingui.war"
                                          name="adminConsoleDownloadLocation" />
  </admin-service>
  <web-container>
    <session-config>
      <session-manager>
        <manager-properties />
        <store-properties />
      </session-manager>
      <session-properties />
    </session-config>
  </web-container>
  <ejb-container session-store="${com.sun.aas.instanceRoot}/session-store">
    <ejb-timer-service />
  </ejb-container>
  <mdb-container />
  <jms-service type="EMBEDDED" default-jms-host="default_JMS_host"
                                          addresslist-behavior="priority">
    <jms-host name="default_JMS_host" host="localhost" port="${JMS_PROVIDER_PORT}"
                          admin-user-name="admin" admin-password="admin" lazy-init="true" />
  </jms-service>
  <log-service log-rotation-limit-in-bytes="2000000"
                                    file="${com.sun.aas.instanceRoot}/logs/server.log">
    <module-log-levels />
  </log-service>
  <security-service>
    <auth-realm classname="com.sun.enterprise.security.auth.realm.file.FileRealm"
                                                    name="admin-realm">
      <property name="file" value="${com.sun.aas.instanceRoot}/config/admin-keyfile" />
      <property name="jaas-context" value="fileRealm" />
    </auth-realm>
    <auth-realm classname="com.sun.enterprise.security.auth.realm.file.FileRealm" name="file">
      <property name="file" value="${com.sun.aas.instanceRoot}/config/keyfile" />
      <property name="jaas-context" value="fileRealm" />
    </auth-realm>
    <auth-realm classname="com.sun.enterprise.security.auth.realm.certificate.CertificateRealm"
                                                    name="cetificate" />
    <jacc-provider policy-provider="com.sun.enterprise.security.provider.PolicyWrapper"
name="default" policy-configuration-factory-provider="com.sun.enterprise.security.provider.
PolicyConfigurationFactoryImpl">
      <property name="repository" value="${com.sun.aas.instanceRoot}/generated/policy" />
    </jacc-provider>
    <jacc-provider policy-provider="com.sun.enterprise.security.jacc.provider.SimplePolicyProvider"
name="simple" policy-configuration-factory-provider="com.sun.enterprise.security.jacc.provider.
SimplePolicyConfigurationFactory" />
    <audit-module classname="com.sun.enterprise.security.Audit" name="default">
      <property name="auditOn" value="false" />
    </audit-module>
```

```xml
<message-security-config auth-layer="SOAP">
    <provider-config provider-type="client" provider-id="XWS_ClientProvider"
                        class-name="com.sun.xml.wss.provider.ClientSecurityAuthModule">
        <request-policy auth-source="content" />
        <response-policy auth-source="content" />
        <property name="encryption.key.alias" value="s1as" />
        <property name="signature.key.alias" value="s1as" />
        <property name="dynamic.username.password" value="false" />
        <property name="debug" value="false" />
    </provider-config>
    <provider-config provider-type="client" provider-id="ClientProvider"
                        class-name="com.sun.xml.wss.provider.ClientSecurityAuthModule">
        <request-policy auth-source="content" />
        <response-policy auth-source="content" />
        <property name="encryption.key.alias" value="s1as" />
        <property name="signature.key.alias" value="s1as" />
        <property name="dynamic.username.password" value="false" />
        <property name="debug" value="false" />
        <property name="security.config"
                    value="${com.sun.aas.instanceRoot}/config/wss-server-config-1.0.xml" />
    </provider-config>
    <provider-config provider-type="server" provider-id="XWS_ServerProvider"
                        class-name="com.sun.xml.wss.provider.ServerSecurityAuthModule">
        <request-policy auth-source="content" />
        <response-policy auth-source="content" />
        <property name="encryption.key.alias" value="s1as" />
        <property name="signature.key.alias" value="s1as" />
        <property name="debug" value="false" />
    </provider-config>
    <provider-config provider-type="server" provider-id="ServerProvider"
                        class-name="com.sun.xml.wss.provider.ServerSecurityAuthModule">
        <request-policy auth-source="content" />
        <response-policy auth-source="content" />
        <property name="encryption.key.alias" value="s1as" />
        <property name="signature.key.alias" value="s1as" />
        <property name="debug" value="false" />
        <property name="security.config"
                    value="${com.sun.aas.instanceRoot}/config/wss-server-config-1.0.xml" />
    </provider-config>
</message-security-config>
</security-service>
<transaction-service tx-log-dir="${com.sun.aas.instanceRoot}/logs" automatic-recovery="true" />
<diagnostic-service />
<java-config debug-options="-Xdebug -Xrunjdwp:transport=dt_socket,server=y,suspend=n,
                    address=${JAVA_DEBUGGER_PORT}" system-classpath="" classpath-suffix="">
    <jvm-options>-XX:MaxPermSize=192m</jvm-options>
    <jvm-options>-XX:PermSize=64m</jvm-options>
    <jvm-options>-server</jvm-options>
    <jvm-options>-Djava.awt.headless=true</jvm-options>
    <jvm-options>-XX:+UnlockDiagnosticVMOptions</jvm-options>
    <jvm-options>-Djava.endorsed.dirs=${com.sun.aas.installRoot}/modules/endorsed${path.separator}
                            ${com.sun.aas.installRoot}/lib/endorsed</jvm-options>
```

```
<jvm-options>-
        Djava.security.policy=${com.sun.aas.instanceRoot}/config/server.policy</jvm-options>
<jvm-options>-Djava.security.auth.login.config=${com.sun.aas.instanceRoot}/config/
                                                login.conf</jvm-options>
<jvm-options>-Dcom.sun.enterprise.security.httpsOutboundKeyAlias=s1as</jvm-options>
<jvm-options>-
        Djavax.net.ssl.keyStore=${com.sun.aas.instanceRoot}/config/keystore.jks</jvm-options>
<jvm-options>-
        Djavax.net.ssl.trustStore=${com.sun.aas.instanceRoot}/config/cacerts.jks</jvm-options>
<jvm-options>-Djava.ext.dirs=${com.sun.aas.javaRoot}/lib/ext${path.separator}${com.sun.aas.
        javaRoot}/jre/lib/ext${path.separator}${com.sun.aas.instanceRoot}/lib/ext</jvm-options>
<jvm-options>-Djdbc.drivers=org.apache.derby.jdbc.ClientDriver</jvm-options>
<jvm-options>-DANTLR_USE_DIRECT_CLASS_LOADING=true</jvm-options>
<jvm-options>-Dcom.sun.enterprise.config.config_environment_factory_class=com.sun.
                enterprise.config.serverbeans.AppserverConfigEnvironmentFactory</jvm-options>
<jvm-options>-XX:NewRatio=2</jvm-options>
<jvm-options>-Xmx512m</jvm-options>
<!-- Port on which remote shell listens for connections.-->
<jvm-options>-Dosgi.shell.telnet.port=${OSGI_SHELL_TELNET_PORT}</jvm-options>
<!-- How many concurrent users can connect to this remote shell -->
<jvm-options>-Dosgi.shell.telnet.maxconn=1</jvm-options>
<!-- From which hosts users can connect -->
<jvm-options>-Dosgi.shell.telnet.ip=OPENSHIFT_INTERNAL_IP</jvm-options>
<!-- Gogo shell configuration -->
<jvm-options>-Dgosh.args=--noshutdown -c noop=true</jvm-options>
<!-- Directory being watched by fileinstall. -->
<jvm-options>-Dfelix.fileinstall.dir=${com.sun.aas.installRoot}/modules/autostart/</jvm-options>
<!-- Time period fileinstaller thread in ms. -->
<jvm-options>-Dfelix.fileinstall.poll=5000</jvm-options>
<!-- log level: 1 for error, 2 for warning, 3 for info and 4 for debug. -->
<jvm-options>-Dfelix.fileinstall.log.level=3</jvm-options>
<!-- should new bundles be started or installed only?
        true => start, false => only install
    -->
<jvm-options>-Dfelix.fileinstall.bundles.new.start=true</jvm-options>
<!-- should watched bundles be started transiently or persistently -->
<jvm-options>-Dfelix.fileinstall.bundles.startTransient=true</jvm-options>
<!-- Should changes to configuration be saved in corresponding cfg file? false: no, true: yes
        If we don't set false, everytime server starts from clean osgi cache, the file
                                                gets rewritten.
    -->
<jvm-options>-Dfelix.fileinstall.disableConfigSave=false</jvm-options>
<!-- End of OSGi bundle configurations -->
</java-config>
<availability-service>
  <web-container-availability />
  <ejb-container-availability sfsb-store-pool-name="jdbc/hastore" />
  <jms-availability />
</availability-service>
<network-config>
  <protocols>
```

```
    <protocol name="http-listener-1">
      <http default-virtual-server="server">
        <file-cache />
      </http>
    </protocol>
    <protocol name="admin-listener">
      <http default-virtual-server="__asadmin" max-connections="250">
        <file-cache enabled="false" />
      </http>
    </protocol>
    <protocol security-enabled="true" name="sec-admin-listener">
      <http default-virtual-server="__asadmin" encoded-slash-enabled="true">
        <file-cache />
      </http>
      <ssl client-auth="want" classname="com.sun.enterprise.security.ssl.GlassfishSSLImpl"
                                              cert-nickname="glassfish-instance" />
    </protocol>
    <protocol name="admin-http-redirect">
      <http-redirect secure="true" />
    </protocol>
    <protocol name="pu-protocol">
      <port-unification>
        <protocol-finder protocol="sec-admin-listener" name="http-finder"
                                   classname="com.sun.grizzly.config.HttpProtocolFinder" />
        <protocol-finder protocol="admin-http-redirect" name="admin-http-redirect"
                                   classname="com.sun.grizzly.config.HttpProtocolFinder" />
      </port-unification>
    </protocol>
  </protocols>
  <network-listeners>
    <network-listener address="OPENSHIFT_INTERNAL_IP" port="9999" protocol="http-listener-1"
                    transport="tcp" name="http-listener-1" thread-pool="http-thread-pool" />
  </network-listeners>
  <transports>
    <transport name="tcp" />
  </transports>
</network-config>
<thread-pools>
  <thread-pool name="http-thread-pool" />
  <thread-pool max-thread-pool-size="200" idle-thread-timeout-in-seconds="120"
                                                            name="thread-pool-1" />
</thread-pools>
<group-management-service />
<management-rules />
<system-property name="ASADMIN_LISTENER_PORT" value="24848" />
<system-property name="HTTP_LISTENER_PORT" value="28080" />
<system-property name="HTTP_SSL_LISTENER_PORT" value="28181" />
<system-property name="JMS_PROVIDER_PORT" value="27676" />
<system-property name="IIOP_LISTENER_PORT" value="23700" />
<system-property name="IIOP_SSL_LISTENER_PORT" value="23820" />
<system-property name="IIOP_SSL_MUTUALAUTH_PORT" value="23920" />
<system-property name="JMX_SYSTEM_CONNECTOR_PORT" value="28686" />
```

```
        <system-property name="OSGI_SHELL_TELNET_PORT" value="26666" />
        <system-property name="JAVA_DEBUGGER_PORT" value="29009" />
    </config>
  </configs>
  <property name="administrative.domain.name" value="domain1" />
  <secure-admin special-admin-indicator="3047aff3-3214-4ac9-aa5e-a5dad78b2eea">
    <secure-admin-principal dn="CN=localhost,OU=GlassFish,O=Oracle Corporation,
L=Santa Clara,ST=California,C=US" />
    <secure-admin-principal dn="CN=localhost-instance,OU=GlassFish,O=Oracle Corporation,
L=Santa Clara,ST=California,C=US" />
  </secure-admin>
</domain>
```

Done! GlassFish is prepared and you can go on to the next step.

Step 2: Create the DIY application stub. It's time to create the OpenShift default DIY application:

- Create an empty folder on local disk D: and name it GlassFishAS.

- Open a shell and navigate to the GlassFishAS folder.

- Type the command rhc app create -a RafaEShop -t diy-0.1, as shown in Figure 10-66.

```
D:\GlassFishAS>rhc app create -a RafaEShop -t diy-0.1
Application Options
-----------------------
  Namespace:  hogm
  Cartridges: diy-0.1
  Gear Size:  default
  Scaling:    no

Creating application 'RafaEShop' ... done

Waiting for your DNS name to be available ... done

Downloading the application Git repository ...
Cloning into 'RafaEShop'...
Warning: Permanently added the RSA host key for IP address '107.22.157.93' to th
e list of known hosts.
remote: Counting objects: 25, done.
Receiving objects: 100% (25/25), 7.48 KiB, done.
Resolving deltas: 100% (1/1), done.
remote: Compressing objects: 100% (21/21), done.
remote: Total 25 (delta 1), reused 25 (delta 1)

Your application code is now in 'RafaEShop'

RafaEShop @ http://RafaEShop-hogm.rhcloud.com/ (uuid: 515466444382ece1bb0001c2)
-------------------------------------------------------------------------------
  Created: 3:48 PM
  Gears:   1 (defaults to small)
  Git URL:
ssh://515466444382ece1bb0001c2@RafaEShop-hogm.rhcloud.com/~/git/RafaEShop.git/
  SSH:     515466444382ece1bb0001c2@RafaEShop-hogm.rhcloud.com

  diy-0.1 (Do-It-Yourself)
  ------------------------
    Gears: 1 small

RESULT:
Application RafaEShop was created.
Disclaimer: This is an experimental cartridge that provides a way to try
unsupported languages, frameworks, and middleware on Openshift.
```

Figure 10-66. Creating the default DIY application

Just for a quick check, sign in to the OpenShift web site and locate the application link in your management console (Figure 10-67).

Figure 10-67. Application links listed in the management console

---

■ **Note**   Before going further, take your time and read the D:/GlassFishAS/RafaEShop/README.txt file. This file describes the application folders and some environment variables.

Step 3: Copy the GlassFish files. Now copy the GlassFish files into the D:/GlassFishAS/RafaEShop/diy folder, as shown in Figure 10-68.

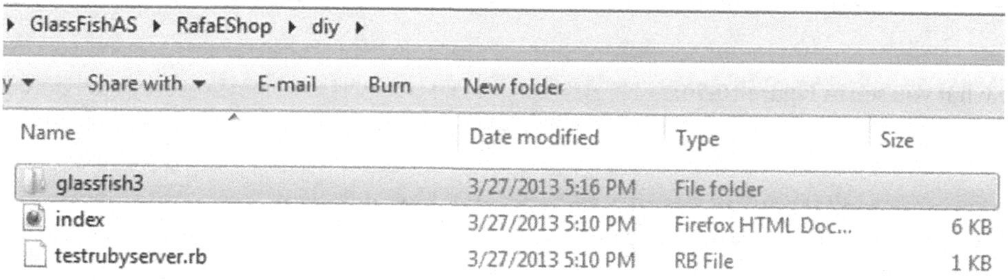

Name	Date modified	Type	Size
glassfish3	3/27/2013 5:16 PM	File folder	
index	3/27/2013 5:10 PM	Firefox HTML Doc...	6 KB
testrubyserver.rb	3/27/2013 5:10 PM	RB File	1 KB

Figure 10-68. Copying GlassFish files

Step 4: Modify the start and stop action hooks (you should be familiar with these files from the README.txt file).

You need to adjust the start file before starting the GlassFish server. Locate the file D:/GlassFishAS/RafaEShop/.openshift/action_hooks/start and append to its code the following lines. These modifications are indicated by the OpenShift Blog at https://www.openshift.com/blogs:

```
cd $OPENSHIFT_REPO_DIR/diy/glassfish3/glassfish/domains/domain1/config/
mv domain.xml domain.xml_2
sed 's/'$( grep serverName domain.xml_2 | cut -d\" -f 2 )'/'$OPENSHIFT_INTERNAL_IP'/g'
domain.xml_2 > domain.xml
../../../bin/asadmin start-domain &> $OPENSHIFT_DIY_LOG_DIR/server.log
```

The start file should look like what you see in Figure 10-69.

```
1  #!/bin/bash
2  # The logic to start up your application should be put in this
3  # script. The application will work only if it binds to
4  # $OPENSHIFT_INTERNAL_IP:8080
5  nohup $OPENSHIFT_REPO_DIR/diy/testrubyserver.rb $OPENSHIFT_INTERNAL_IP $OPENSHIFT_REPO_DIR/diy > $OPENSHIFT_HOMEDIR/
6  cd $OPENSHIFT_REPO_DIR/diy/glassfish3/glassfish/domains/domain1/config/
7  mv domain.xml domain.xml_2
8  sed 's/'$( grep serverName domain.xml_2 | cut -d\" -f 2 )'/'$OPENSHIFT_INTERNAL_IP'/g' domain.xml_2 > domain.xml
9  ../../../bin/asadmin start-domain &> $OPENSHIFT_DIY_LOG_DIR/server.log
```

Figure 10-69. *Modifying the start file*

GlassFish is stopped according to the D:/GlassFishAS/RafaEShop/.openshift/action_hooks/stop file. The default contents of this file should be replaced with the following lines. These modifications are indicated by the OpenShift Blog at https://www.openshift.com/blogs:

```
#!/bin/bash
# The logic to stop your application should be put in this script.
kill `ps -ef | grep glassfish3 | grep -v grep | awk '{ print $2 }'` > /dev/null 2>&1
exit 0
```

Now it should look like what you see in Figure 10-70.

```
1  #!/bin/bash
2  # The logic to stop your application should be put in this script.
3  kill `ps -ef | grep glassfish3 | grep -v grep | awk '{ print $2 }'` > /dev/null 2>&1
4  exit 0
```

Figure 10-70. *Modifying the stop file*

Step 5: Add the MongoDB NoSQL Database 2.2 cartridge, as you saw earlier in Figure 10-27. In the first part of this chapter, you saw how to add the MongoDB cartridge. The process is exactly the same, so type the command rhc cartridge add -a RafaEShop -c mongodb-2.2 in the shell, as shown in Figure 10-71.

```
D:\GlassFishAS>rhc cartridge add -a RafaEShop -c mongodb-2.2
Adding mongodb-2.2 to application 'RafaEShop' ... Success

mongodb-2.2 <MongoDB NoSQL Database 2.2>
------------------------------------------
  Gears:             Located with diy-0.1
  Connection URL:
mongodb://$OPENSHIFT_MONGODB_DB_HOST:$OPENSHIFT_MONGODB_DB_PORT/
  Database Name:     RafaEShop
  Password:          YhH7s7eLYrR4
  Username:          admin

RESULT:
Added mongodb-2.2 to application RafaEShop

MongoDB 2.2 database added.  Please make note of these credentials:

        Root User: admin
    Root Password: YhH7s7eLYrR4
    Database Name: RafaEShop

Connection URL:
mongodb://$OPENSHIFT_MONGODB_DB_HOST:$OPENSHIFT_MONGODB_DB_PORT/

You can manage your new MongoDB by also embedding rockmongo-1.1
The rockmongo username and password will be the same as the MongoDB credentials
above.
```

Figure 10-71. *Adding the MongoDB cartridge*

Step 6: Add the RockMongo 1.1 cartridge, as you saw earlier in Figure 10-30.

It can be useful to add the RockMongo administration tool for managing MongoDB databases using a visual approach. Use the following command to add RockMongo, as shown in Figure 10-72:

```
rhc cartridge add -a RafaEShop -c rockmongo-1.1
```

```
D:\GlassFishAS>rhc cartridge add -a RafaEShop -c rockmongo-1.1
Adding rockmongo-1.1 to application 'RafaEShop' ... Success

rockmongo-1.1 <RockMongo 1.1>
------------------------------------------
  Gears:            Located with diy-0.1, mongodb-2.2
  Connection URL: https://RafaEShop-hogm.rhcloud.com/rockmongo/

RESULT:
Added rockmongo-1.1 to application RafaEShop

rockmongo-1.1 added.  Please make note of these MongoDB credentials again:

  RockMongo User    : admin
  RockMongo Password: YhH7s7eLYrR4

URL: https://RafaEShop-hogm.rhcloud.com/rockmongo/
```

Figure 10-72. *Adding the RockMongo cartridge*

Step 7: Adjust the persistence.xml settings. Locate the persistence.xml file in the RafaEShop application. You need to modify these file settings to work with the new MongoDB database; I recommend you make a copy of it before modifying it. At this point, the persistence.xml file should have the contents shown in Listing 10-5.

Listing 10-3. Modified persistence.xml File

```xml
<?xml version="1.0" encoding="UTF-8"?>
<persistence version="2.0" xmlns="http://java.sun.com/xml/ns/persistence"
xmlns:xsi="http://www.w3.org/2001/XMLSchema-instance"
xsi:schemaLocation="http://java.sun.com/xml/ns/persistence
http://java.sun.com/xml/ns/persistence/persistence_2_0.xsd">
    <persistence-unit name="HOGM_eSHOP-ejbPU" transaction-type="JTA">
        <provider>org.hibernate.ogm.jpa.HibernateOgmPersistence</provider>
        <class>eshop.entities.Categories</class>
        <class>eshop.entities.Customers</class>
        <class>eshop.entities.Inventory</class>
        <class>eshop.entities.Orders</class>
        <class>eshop.entities.Products</class>
    <properties>
        <property name="hibernate.search.default.directory_provider"
                value="filesystem"/>
        <property name="hibernate.search.default.indexBase" value="D:/eshop"/>
        <property name="hibernate.search.default.locking_strategy"
                value="single"/>
        <property name="hibernate.transaction.jta.platform"
                value="org.hibernate.service.jta.platform.
                                        internal.SunOneJtaPlatform"/>
        <property name="hibernate.ogm.datastore.provider" value="mongodb"/>
        <property name="hibernate.ogm.datastore.grid_dialect"
                value="org.hibernate.ogm.dialect.mongodb.MongoDBDialect"/>
        <property name="hibernate.ogm.mongodb.database" value="eshop_db"/>
        <property name="hibernate.ogm.mongodb.host" value="127.0.0.1"/>
        <property name="hibernate.ogm.mongodb.port" value="27017"/>
    </properties>
</persistence-unit>
</persistence>
```

You have to adjust several settings, as shown in the following set of instructions.

Apache Lucene indexes are stored in the file system (in the D:/eshop folder). You need to modify this folder path (base folder) with a valid cloud folder path. As a simpler option, you can use a memory-based directory by replacing the following code:

```xml
<property name="hibernate.search.default.directory_provider"
        value="filesystem"/>
<property name="hibernate.search.default.indexBase" value="D:/eshop"/>
<property name="hibernate.search.default.locking_strategy"
        value="single"/>
```

with this code:

```xml
<property name="hibernate.search.default.directory_provider"
        value="ram"/>
<property name="hibernate.search.default.locking_strategy"
        value="single"/>
```

Set the MongoDB database name, host, port, user, and password. To do so, replace the following snippet of code:

```
<property name="hibernate.ogm.mongodb.database" value="eshop_db"/>
<property name="hibernate.ogm.mongodb.host" value="127.0.0.1"/>
<property name="hibernate.ogm.mongodb.port" value="27017"/>
```

with this code:

```
<property name="hibernate.ogm.mongodb.database" value="RafaEShop"/>
<property name="hibernate.ogm.mongodb.host" value="127.9.57.129"/>
<property name="hibernate.ogm.mongodb.port" value="27017"/>
<property name="hibernate.ogm.mongodb.username" value="admin"/>
<property name="hibernate.ogm.mongodb.password" value="YhH7s7eLYrR4"/>
```

The "new" persistence.xml should be the following:

```
<?xml version="1.0" encoding="UTF-8"?>
<persistence version="2.0" xmlns="http://java.sun.com/xml/ns/persistence"
xmlns:xsi="http://www.w3.org/2001/XMLSchema-instance" xsi:schemaLocation=
"http://java.sun.com/xml/ns/persistence http://java.sun.com/xml/ns/persistence/persistence_2_0.xsd">
    <persistence-unit name="HOGM_eSHOP-ejbPU" transaction-type="JTA">
        <provider>org.hibernate.ogm.jpa.HibernateOgmPersistence</provider>
        <class>eshop.entities.Categories</class>
        <class>eshop.entities.Customers</class>
        <class>eshop.entities.Inventory</class>
        <class>eshop.entities.Orders</class>
        <class>eshop.entities.Products</class>
    <properties>
        <property name="hibernate.search.default.directory_provider"
                value="ram"/>
        <property name="hibernate.search.default.locking_strategy"
                value="single"/>
        <property name="hibernate.transaction.jta.platform"
                value="org.hibernate.service.jta.platform.
                                        internal.SunOneJtaPlatform"/>
        <property name="hibernate.ogm.datastore.provider" value="mongodb"/>
        <property name="hibernate.ogm.datastore.grid_dialect"
                value="org.hibernate.ogm.dialect.mongodb.MongoDBDialect"/>
        <property name="hibernate.ogm.mongodb.database" value="RafaEShop"/>
        <property name="hibernate.ogm.mongodb.host" value="127.9.57.129"/>
        <property name="hibernate.ogm.mongodb.port" value="27017"/>
        <property name="hibernate.ogm.mongodb.username" value="admin"/>
        <property name="hibernate.ogm.mongodb.password" value="YhH7s7eLYrR4"/>
    </properties>
</persistence-unit>
</persistence>
```

Step 8: Add the RafaEShop WAR in GlassFish. Locate the RafaEShop application WAR in your local project RafaEShop/dist folder or in the Apress repository in the RafaEShop/dist folder.

Copy this WAR to the D:/GlassFishAS/RafaEShop/diy/glassfish3/glassfish/domains/domain1/autodeploy folder (see Figure 10-73). Finally, override the persistence.xml file in the RafaEShop WAR archive. You can use any archive tool, such as WinRAR.

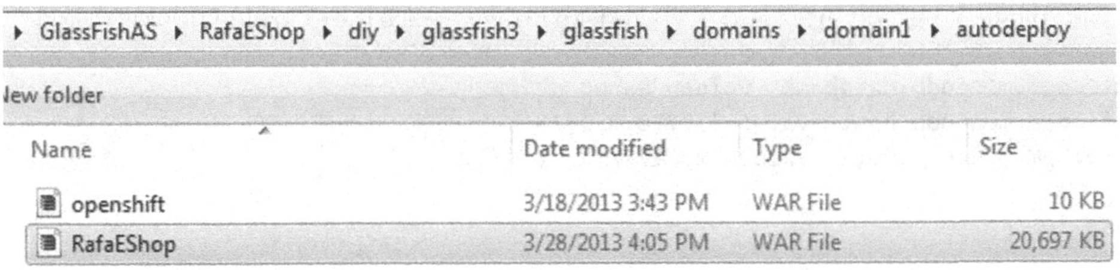

| ▶ GlassFishAS ▶ RafaEShop ▶ diy ▶ glassfish3 ▶ glassfish ▶ domains ▶ domain1 ▶ autodeploy |

New folder

Name	Date modified	Type	Size
📄 openshift	3/18/2013 3:43 PM	WAR File	10 KB
📄 RafaEShop	3/28/2013 4:05 PM	WAR File	20,697 KB

Figure 10-73. *Copying the RafaEShop WAR*

Notice that in this folder, besides your WAR, there's another WAR named openshift. This is the default application generated by OpenShift when you used the DIY cartridge.

You have completed the final step. You can now upload the application to the OpenShift platform. However, before committing the changes it's a good idea to open a separate process for monitoring the GlassFish AS start/stop status.

Monitoring GlassFish Start/Stop

If you read the first part of this chapter, you are already familiar with connections made using a secure shell session and how to open such a connection from your computer. You can now open an SSH session to monitor the GlassFish AS start/stop status in real-time using the following command, as shown in Figure 10-74:

ssh 515466444382ece1bb0001c2@RafaEShop-hogm.rhcloud.com.

```
D:\GlassFishAS\RafaEShop>ssh 515466444382ece1bb0001c2@RafaEShop-hogm.rhcloud.com

*******************************************************************************
    You are accessing a service that is for use only by authorized users.
    If you do not have authorization, discontinue use at once.
    Any use of the services is subject to the applicable terms of the
    agreement which can be found at:
    https://openshift.redhat.com/app/legal

*******************************************************************************
    Welcome to OpenShift shell

    This shell will assist you in managing OpenShift applications.

    !!! IMPORTANT !!! IMPORTANT !!! IMPORTANT !!!
    Shell access is quite powerful and it is possible for you to
    accidentally damage your application.  Proceed with care!
    If worse comes to worst, destroy your application with 'rhc app delete'
    and recreate it
    !!! IMPORTANT !!! IMPORTANT !!! IMPORTANT !!!

    Type "help" for more info.
```

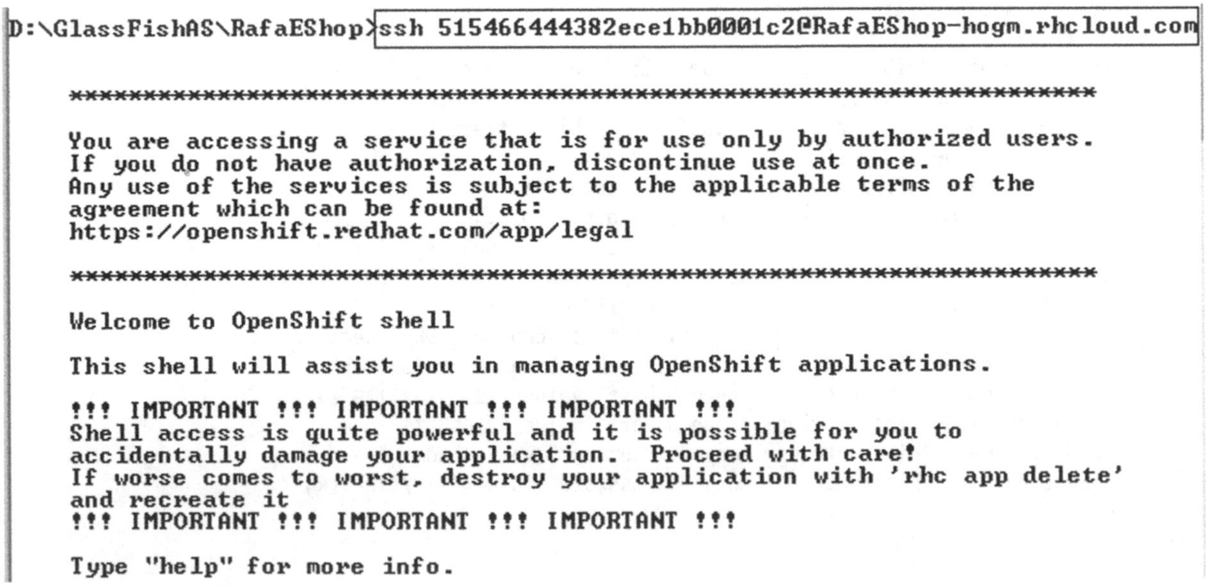

Figure 10-74. *Monitoring the GlassFish start/stop status*

Next, type the `tail_all` command. This command will tail all available logs for the current application, including the server start/stop status. Most probably, at this point you'll see some errors or notices from the RockoMongo log. Ignore them for now and leave this process open.

Commit Changes

Each time you commit changes to your application, OpenShift will automatically stop GlassFish AS, commit the changes, and start GlassFish AS again. Open a new shell, navigate to the `D:/GlassFishAS/RafaEShop` folder, and type the following three commands:

```
git add .
git commit -m "first commit"
git push
```

Because this is the first commit, it will take some time until everything is pushed to the application.

At the end of the commit, GlassFish is started and, in the shell that's monitoring this action, you should see something like what's shown in Figure 10-75.

```
/usr/bin/tail: diy-0.1/logs/server.log: file truncated
Warning: asadmin extension directory is missing: /var/lib/openshift/515466444382
ece1bb0001c2/app-root/runtime/repo/diy/glassfish3/glassfish/lib/asadmin
Waiting for domain1 to start ...................
Successfully started the domain : domain1
domain  Location: /var/lib/openshift/515466444382ece1bb0001c2/app-root/runtime/r
epo/diy/glassfish3/glassfish/domains/domain1
Log File: /var/lib/openshift/515466444382ece1bb0001c2/app-root/runtime/repo/diy/
glassfish3/glassfish/domains/domain1/logs/server.log
Admin Port: -1
Command start-domain executed successfully.
```

Figure 10-75. GlassFish domain was successfully started

Obviously, this is exactly the message we expected. If you see this message, jump directly to the section *"Monitoring the GlassFish Log."* If not, you have a problem, perhaps the one described next.

Fixing Known Issues

Sometimes, instead of success you'll get a message stating *"Permission denied!"* (see Figure 10-76).

```
remote: MongoDB already running              /usr/bin/tail: diy-0.1/logs/server.log: file truncated
remote: Failed to start diy-0.1              /var/lib/openshift/515466444382ece1bb0001c2/app-root/runtime/repo/
remote: Running .openshift/action_hooks/post_deploy  tion_hooks/start: line 9: ../../../bin/asadmin: Permission denied
To ssh://515466444382ece1bb0001c2@RafaEShop-hogm.rhc
   4db2eaa..bffc566  master -> master
```

Figure 10-76. Permission denied

To fix this problem, you need to grant yourself certain permissions to application files and directories. Open a new SSH session (don't close the one monitoring the GlassFish start/stop status) and type the following chmod commands (also shown in Figure 10-77).

```
chmod +x app-root/runtime/repo/diy/glassfish3/bin/*
chmod +x diy-0.1/repo/diy/glassfish3/glassfish/bin/*
chmod +x diy-0.1/runtime/repo/.openshift/action_hooks/*
```

```
[RafaEShop-hogm.rhcloud.com 515466444382ece1bb0001c2]\> chmod +x app-root/runti
me/repo/diy/glassfish3/bin/*
[RafaEShop-hogm.rhcloud.com 515466444382ece1bb0001c2]\> chmod +x diy-0.1/repo/d
iy/glassfish3/glassfish/bin/*
[RafaEShop-hogm.rhcloud.com 515466444382ece1bb0001c2]\> chmod +x diy-0.1/runtim
e/repo/.openshift/action_hooks/*
```

Figure 10-77. *Grant permission to application files*

Start the application again by typing the command ctl_app start (see Figure 10-78).

```
[RafaEShop-hogm.rhcloud.com 515466444382ece1bb0001c2]\> ctl_app start
```

Figure 10-78. *Starting the application from the shell*

■ **Note** To stop the application, type ctl_app stop. To restart the application, type ctl_app restart. More details about these commands (and others) can be obtained by typing the help command.

This time, in the shell that monitors the GlassFish domain start/stop status, you should see a success message like the one in Figure 10-75.

Monitoring the GlassFish Log

When the GlassFish domain successfully starts, you can see the location and name of the GlassFish log file, as in Figure 10-79 (this was extracted from Figure 10-75).

```
Log File: /var/lib/openshift/515466444382ece1bb0001c2/app-root/runtime/repo/diy/
glassfish3/glassfish/domains/domain1/logs/server.log
```

Figure 10-79. *Locating the GlassFish AS log file*

The contents of server.log can be listed in a shell (you need to be patient until the application is deployed). Open a new SSH session and type the following command, which is also shown in Figure 10-80:

```
tail app-root/rutime/repo/diy/glassfish3/glassfish/domains/domain1/logs/server.log
```

```
[RafaEShop-hogm.rhcloud.com 515466444382ece1bb0001c2]\> tail app-root/runtime/r
epo/diy/glassfish3/glassfish/domains/domain1/logs/server.log

...
[#|2013-03-29T01:59:01.878-0400|INFO|glassfish3.1.2|javax.enterprise.system.tool
s.deployment.org.glassfish.deployment.common|_ThreadID=28;_ThreadName=Thread-2;|
[AutoDeploy] Successfully autodeployed : /var/lib/openshift/515466444382ece1bb00
01c2/app-root/runtime/repo/diy/glassfish3/glassfish/domains/domain1/autodeploy/R
afaEShop.war.|#]
```

Figure 10-80. *Listing the contents of the GlassFish AS log file*

Based on this log content, you can easily debug your application.

In Figure 10-80, the log message indicates that the application RafaEShop was successfully deployed. Now you can close all the shells and enjoy the application.

Test It!

Since you've gotten this far, you've probably successfully deployed the application in at least one of the three presented approaches. No matter which approach you selected, the test can be performed is the same manner. If you tried all three approaches, your OpenShift management console should look like the one in Figure 10-81.

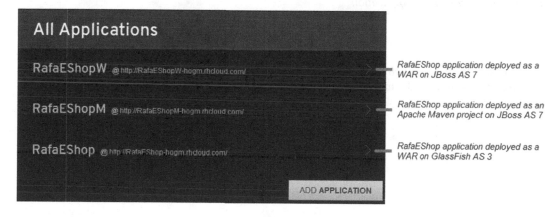

Figure 10-81. *All the application links listed in the management console*

■ **Note**   I'm going to present the steps for testing the RafaEShopW application deployed as a WAR on GlassFish AS 3. You can easily adapt these steps for the other two approaches.

Because this is the first time you're running the application, you need to populate the MongoDB e-commerce database. As you know, this can be done from the db.xhml administration page. The link to this is http://rafaeshopw-hogm.rhcloud.com/RafaEShop/faces/db.xhtml.

After populating the database, you can access the e-shop at
http://rafaeshopw-hogm.rhcloud.com/RafaEShop/faces/index.xhtml (see Figure 10-82).

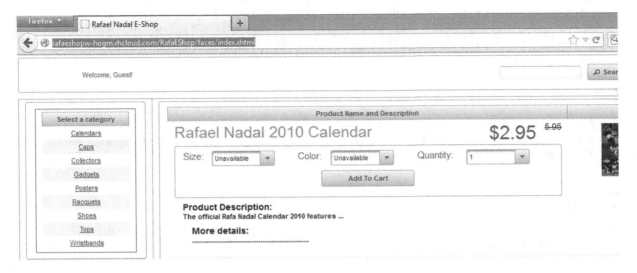

Figure 10-82. *Running the RafaEShopW application*

Cautions

In case you need to repopulate the MongoDB database (from the db.xhtml administration page), DO NOT FORGET
to drop the existing collections. You can do this easily from the RockMongo interface by pressing the Drop All button,
as shown in Figure 10-83.

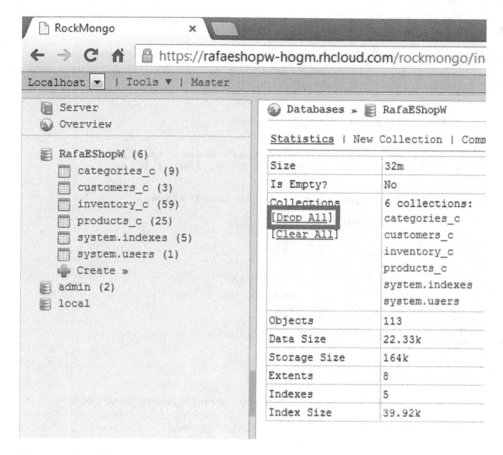

Figure 10-83. *Dropping database collections from the RockMongo interface*

Then restart the server. You can use either the `ctl_app restart` command or the management console, as shown in Figure 10-84.

Figure 10-84. *Restarting the application*

Restarting the server will reset the Lucene indexes (since they are stored in RAM), which means that you also need to drop the database collections and repopulate the database from the `db.xhml` administration page.

Trying to populate the MongoDB database without using the `db.xhml` administration page will cause errors. Because the application isn't capable of indexing an existing database, the Lucene indexes will not be updated.

Don't worry that initially the `orders_c` collection is missing. This will be created when the first purchase order is submitted.

Good To Know

OpenShift allows you to remotely connect to available services using port forwarding (generally speaking, this technique lets you connect remote computers to services within a private local area network). This can be done using the rhc command rhc port-forward -a RafaEShopW, as shown in Figure 10-85.

```
D:\JBossAS\war>rhc port-forward -a RafaEShopW
Checking available ports...
Forwarding ports
Only one usage of each socket address (protocol/network address/port) is
normally permitted. - bind(2) while forwarding port 8080. Trying local
port 8081

To connect to a service running on OpenShift, use the Local address

    Service Local                     OpenShift
    ======  ================  ====    ==================
    httpd   127.0.0.1:8080    =>      127.7.182.130:8080
    java    127.0.0.1:3528    =>      127.7.182.129:3528
    java    127.0.0.1:4447    =>      127.7.182.129:4447
    java    127.0.0.1:5445    =>      127.7.182.129:5445
    java    127.0.0.1:5455    =>      127.7.182.129:5455
    java    127.0.0.1:8081    =>      127.7.182.129:8080
    java    127.0.0.1:9990    =>      127.7.182.129:9990
    java    127.0.0.1:9999    =>      127.7.182.129:9999
    mongod  127.0.0.1:27017   =>      127.7.182.129:27017
Press CTRL-C to terminate port forwarding
```

Figure 10-85. *Port forwarding*

In Figure 10-85, you can see the available ports for the RafaEShopW application. Notice that the mongod server is also listed.

Disclaimer

When this book was written, the applications I discussed were available online. I can't guarantee that when you read this book, OpenShift will make these applications available (if the applications don't have much traffic, OpenShift might shut down the servers).

Summary

In this final chapter, you saw how to migrate the RafaEShop application to the OpenShift PaaS. The chapter began with several introductory tasks, such as creating an account on OpenShift, activating and signing into this account, and becoming familiar with OpenShift web interface. Further, you saw how to deploy RafaEShop as a WAR and as an Apache Maven project on JBoss AS 7 running in the cloud. In the second part of this chapter, you configured a GlassFish AS 3 domain for running in OpenShift, and you deployed the RafaEShop application on this domain.

Index